Studies in Russian and East European History and Society

Series Editors: **R. W. Davies, E. A. Rees, M. J. Ilič** and **J. R. Smith** at the Centre for Russian and East European Studies, University of Birmingham

Recent titles include:

Lynne Attwood
CREATING THE NEW SOVIET WOMAN

John Barber and Mark Harrison (*editors*)
THE SOVIET DEFENCE-INDUSTRY COMPLEX FROM STALIN TO KHRUSHCHEV

Vincent Barnett
KONDRATIEV AND THE DYNAMICS OF ECONOMIC DEVELOPMENT

R. W. Davies
SOVIET HISTORY IN THE YELTSIN ERA

Linda Edmondson (*editor*)
GENDER IN RUSSIAN HISTORY AND CULTURE

James Hughes
STALINISM IN A RUSSIAN PROVINCE

Melanie Ilič
WOMEN WORKERS IN THE SOVIET INTERWAR ECONOMY
WOMEN IN THE STALIN ERA (*editor*)

Peter Kirkow
RUSSIA'S PROVINCES

Maureen Perrie
THE CULT OF IVAN THE TERRIBLE IN STALIN'S RUSSIA

E. A. Rees (*editor*)
DECISION-MAKING IN THE STALINIST COMMAND ECONOMY
CENTRE–LOCAL RELATIONS IN THE STALINIST STATE, 1928–1941

Lennart Samuelson
PLANS FOR STALIN'S WAR MACHINE
Tukhachevskii and Military-Economic Planning, 1925–1941

Vera Tolz
RUSSIAN ACADEMICIANS AND THE REVOLUTION

J. N. Westwood
SOVIET RAILWAYS TO RUSSIAN RAILWAYS

Stephen G. Wheatcroft (*editor*)
CHALLENGING TRADITIONAL VIEWS OF RUSSIAN HISTORY

Galina M. Yemelianova
RUSSIA AND ISLAM
A Historical Survey

Studies in Russian and East European History and Society
Series Standing Order ISBN 0–333–71239–0
(*outside North America only*)

You can receive future titles in this series as they are published by placing a standing order. Please contact your bookseller or, in case of difficulty, write to us at the address below with your name and address, the title of the series and the ISBN quoted above.

Customer Services Department, Macmillan Distribution Ltd, Houndmills, Basingstoke, Hampshire RG21 6XS, England

Centre–Local Relations in the Stalinist State, 1928–1941

Edited by

E. A. Rees

Editorial matter selection and Introduction © E. A. Rees 2002
Chapters 1–8 © Palgrave Macmillan Ltd 2002

First published 2002 by
PALGRAVE MACMILLAN
Houndmills, Basingstoke, Hampshire RG21 6XS and
175 Fifth Avenue, New York, N.Y. 10010
Companies and representatives throughout the world

PALGRAVE MACMILLAN is the global academic imprint of the Palgrave
Macmillan division of St. Martin's Press, LLC and of Palgrave Macmillan Ltd.
Macmillan® is a registered trademark in the United States, United Kingdom
and other countries. Palgrave is a registered trademark in the European
Union and other countries.

ISBN 1–4039–0118–X

This book is printed on paper suitable for recycling and made from fully
managed and sustained forest sources.

A catalogue record for this book is available from the British Library.

Library of Congress Cataloging-in-Publication Data
Centre–local relations in the Stalinist state 1928–1941 / edited by E. A. Rees.
      p.   cm. — (Studies in Russian and East European history and society)
   Includes bibliographical references and indices.
   ISBN 1–4039–0118–X
   1. Central–local government relations—Soviet Union. 2. Soviet Union—
   Politics and government—1971–1936. 3. Soviet Union—Politics and
   government—1936–1953. I. Rees, E. A. II. Series.

   JN6520.S8 C46 2002
   320.8′0947′09043—dc21
                                                                2002072326

10   9   8   7   6   5   4   3   2   1
11   10   09   08   07   06   05   04   03   02

Printed and bound in Great Britain by
Antony Rowe Ltd, Chippenham and Eastbourne

Contents

List of Tables	vi
Preface	vii
Notes on the Contributors	viii
Glossary of Russian Terms and Acronyms	ix
Introduction	1
1 The Changing Nature of Centre–Local Relations in the USSR, 1928–36 *E. A. Rees*	9
2 The First Generation of Stalinist 'Party Generals' *Oleg Khlevnyuk*	37
3 Republican and Regional Leaders at the XVII Party Congress in 1934 *E. A. Rees*	65
4 Moscow City and Oblast *E. A. Rees*	92
5 The Karelian ASSR *Nick Baron*	116
6 The Donbass *Hiroaki Kuromiya*	149
7 Vinnitsa Oblast *Valery Vasil'iev*	167
8 The Great Purges and the XVIII Party Congress of 1939 *E. A. Rees*	191
Bibliography	212
Name Index	219
Subject Index	223

List of Tables

1.1 Second Five-Year Plan: planned capital investment
in the republics and regions   28
2.1 Length of party membership (*stazh*) of party secretaries,
January 1933   42
2.2 Length of party membership (*stazh*) of party secretaries,
February 1937   57
2.3 Level of education of party secretaries, February 1937 59
5.1 Top three Karelian industrial sectors, 1928–9 to 1937 121
5.2 Top three Karelian industrial sectors, 1932 and 1937   121
5.3 Planned BBK capital investment in Central Karelia, 1934–7 127
5.4 Projected timber-felling targets for Karelia, 1937   132
5.5 Major capital investment in the Karelian Second Five-Year Plan 133
5.6 Timber-felling output in Karelia, 1932–7   140
5.7 Actual distribution of output in Karelian industry, 1932–7 143

Preface

This work examines the process of decision-making in the USSR during the 1930s, focusing primarily on the formulation and implementation of the Second Five Year-Plan from 1932 to 1937. It summarises the findings of the research project funded by the British Economic and Social Research Council (ESRC) on 'Centre–Local Relations in the Stalinist Command Economy' carried out at the Centre for Russian and East European Studies, The University of Birmingham from 1994 to 1998. ESRC finance provided money for travel to Moscow, library purchases, funds for secretarial support, the salary of one research fellow and financial support for a Russian and a Ukrainian collaborator.

The project drew on newly available archival materials from the Russian State Archives of the Economy (RGAE), the State Archives of the Russian Federation (GARF, formerly TsGAOR) and from the Russian State Archives of Social–Political History (RGASPI, formerly RTsKhIDNI). It draws also on materials from several regional archives: the Central State Archives of Moscow Oblast (TsGAMO); the Central State Archive of the Republic of Karelia (TsGA RK); the Archives of the Federal Security Agency of the Russian Federation in the Republic of Karelia (Arkhiv FSB RF po RK); the State Archive of Social–Political Movements and Formations of the Republic of Karelia (GAOPDF RK); the Central State Archives of Social Organisations of Ukraine (TsDAGO); the State Archives of Donet'sk oblast (DADO); and the State Archives of Vinnitsa oblast (GAVO).

The Glossary (pp. ix–xiv) lists the key terms and acronyms used in the book.

E. A. Rees

Notes on the Contributors

Nick Baron completed his PhD on the role of the Gulag in the development of Karelia ASSR in the 1930s at the Centre for Russian and East European Studies, University of Birmingham. He is currently employed as a Researcher in the Department of History, University of Manchester, on a project studying the refugee crisis in Russia and Eastern Europe at the end of the First World War.

Oleg Khlevnyuk is a full-time employee of the State Archives of the Russian Federation (GARF). He specialises on the history of the Stalin era, and has published widely. His main publications are *1937 god: protivostoyanie* (Moscow, 1991), *1937-i: Stalin, NKVD i sovetskoe obshchestvo* (Moscow, 1992), *Stalin i Ordzhonikidze: Konflikty v Politbyuro v 30-e gody* (Moscow, 1993) and *Politbyuro: Mekhanizmy politicheskoi vlasti v 1930-e gody* (Moscow, 1996). His works in English include *In Stalin's Shadow: The Career of 'Sergo' Ordzhonikidze* (New York, London, 1995).

Hiroaki Kuromiya was educated at Tokyo and Princeton Universities and was formerly a Mellon postdoctoral fellow at Harvard University's Russian Research Centre and a Research Fellow at King's College, Cambridge. He is Professor of History at Indiana University, Bloomington. He is the author of *Stalinist Industrial Revolution: Politics and Workers 1928–1932* (Cambridge, 1988) and *Freedom and Terror in the Donbas: A Ukrainian–Russian Borderland, 1870s–1990s* (Cambridge University Press, 1999).

E. A. Rees is Professor of Eastern European History at the European University Institute, Florence, Italy. He is the author of two monographs: *State Control in Soviet Russia: The Rise and the Fall of the Workers' and Peasants' Inspectorate* (London, New York, 1984) and *Stalinism and Soviet Rail Transport, 1928–1941* (Basingstoke, New York, 1995). He is the editor and main author of *Decision-Making in the Stalinist Command Economy, 1932–1937* (London, New York, 1997) and *The Soviet Communist Party in Disarray* (Basingstoke, 1992).

Valery Vasil'iev, formerly of the Vinnitsa Pedagogical Institute, is employed as a full-time Researcher attached to the Ukrainian Academy of Science, and is based in Kiev. He specialises on the history of Ukraine in the Soviet period. He is joint editor and author with Professor Lynne Viola of a major study of collectivisation and peasant resistance in Ukraine: *Kollektivizatsiya i krest'yanskoe soprotivlenie na Ukraine (noyabr' 1929–mart 1930gg)* (Vinnitsa, 1997).

Glossary of Russian Terms and Acronyms

akitv	Communist party activist
artel	form of collective farm, involving collective ownership of livestock
ASSR	Autonomous Soviet Socialist Republic
batrak	rural labourer, landless peasant
BBK	Belomorsko-Baltiskii Kombinat (White Sea–Baltic Industrial Combine)
BBVP	Belomorsko-Baltiskii Vodnyi Put (White Sea–Baltic Water Way)
bednyak	poor peasant
Borot'bist	Ukrainian nationalist and socialist party
bunt	spontaneous peasant uprising
buro	bureau
CBE	Central Black Earth
CC	Tsentral'nyi komitet (Central Committee of the Communist Party)
CCC	see TsKK
Cheka	Chrezvychainaya Komissiya (Extraordinary Commission, political police), later GPU or OGPU, NKVD
Chekist	official of the Cheka, OGPU, NKVD
CPSU	Communist Party of the Soviet Union
CPUk	Communist Party of the Ukraine
dekulakisation	expropriation of kulaks
Donbass	Donetskii ugol'nyi bassein (Donets coal basin)
Donnarpit	Donbass Public Catering
edinolichniki	individual peasant proprietors
edinonachaliya	one-man management in industry
fond	archival file
GARF	State Archives of the Russian Federation
GES	hydro-electric power station
Gidroelektropoekt	Hydro-electricity Planning Administration
Glavenergo	Chief Administration of Energy (NKTyazhProm)
Glavidroenergo	Chief Administration of Hydro-Electric Energy
glavk	glavnoe upravlenie (Chief Administration)
Glavsevles	Administration for Northern Timber Industry

Glavzapbumprom	Administration of Western Timber Industry
Goelro	Gosudarstvennaya komissiya po elektrifikatsii Rossii (State Commission for the Electrification of Russia)
gorispolkom	city soviet executive committee
gorkom	city party committee
Gosbank	Gosudarastvennyi Bank (State Bank)
Gosplan	Gosudarstvennaya Planovaya Komissiya (State Planning Commission)
GPU	see OGPU
guberniya	province
gubkom	provincial party committee
gubrevkom	provincial revolutionary committee
Gulag	Glavnoe upravlenie lagerei (Main Administration of Labour Camps)
ispolkom	ispolnitel'nyi komitet (executive committee of the soviet)
Karplan	Karelian Gosplan
khozraschet	commercial profit-and-loss accounting
KK	Control Commission, local body of TsKK
KMA	Kursk Magnetic Anomaly
kolkhoz	kollektivnoe khozyaistvo (collective farm)
kolkhoznik	collective farm worker
Kolkhoztsentr	Vserossiiskii Sel'skokhozyaistvennykh Kollektivov (All-Russian Union of Agricultural Collectives)
komandirovki	business trips or assignments
kombinat	industrial combine
Komsomol	Kommunisticheskii Soyuz Molodezhi (Communist League of Youth)
KomZag	Komitet po zagotovkam sel'sko-khozyaistvennykh produktov (Committee for Agricultural Procurements)
KPK	Komissiya Partinnoi Kontrol (Commission of Party Control)
krai	territory
kraikom	territorial party committee
krugovaya poruka	official networks of self-protection
KSK	Komissiya Sovetskoi Kontrol (Commission of Soviet Control)
KTK	Karelian Labour Commune
kulak	rich peasant
lespromkhoz(y)	administrative unit(s) for management of the timber industry
Magnitostroi	construction project for building Magnitogorsk
Metrostroi	construction project for building the Moscow metro

Moskanalstroi	construction project for building the Moscow–Volga canal
Mossoviet	Moscow Soviet
MK	Moscow party committee
MTS	Mashino-traktornaya stantsiya (Machine tractor station)
narkom	narodnyi komissar (people's commissar)
NEP	Novaya ekonomicheskaya politika (New Economic Policy)
nezamozhniki	committees of poor peasants in Ukraine
NKFin	Narodnyi Komissariat Finansov (People's Commissariat of Finance)
NKInDel	Narodnyi Komissariat po Inostrannym Delam (People's Commissariat for Foreign Affairs)
NKLegProm	Narodnyi Komissariat Legkoi Promyshlennosti (People's Commissariat of Light Industry)
NKLes	Narodnyi Komissariat Lesnoi Promyshlennosti (People's Commissariat of Timber Industry)
NKPishProm	Narodnyi Komissariat Pishchevoi Promyshlennosti (People's Commissariat of Food Industry)
NKPros	Narodnyi Komissariat Prosveshcheniya (People's Commissariat of Education)
NKPS	Narodnyi Komissariat Putei Soobshcheniya (People's Commissariat of Ways of Communication, i.e. Transport)
NKPT	Narodnyi Komissariat Pocht i Telegrafov (People's Commissariat of Posts and Telegraphs)
NKRKI	Narodnyi Komissariat Raboche-Krest'yanskoi Inspektsii (People's Commissariat of Workers' and Peasants' Inspection or Rabkrin)
NKSnab	Narodnyi Komissariat Snabzheniya (People's Commissariat of Supply)
NKSovkhoz	Narodnyi Komissariat Zernovykh i Zhivotnovodcheskikh Sovkhozov (People's Commissariat of Grain and Lifestock rearing State Farms)
NKSvyaz	Narodnyi Komissariat Svyazi (People's Commissariat of Communications)
NKTorg	Narodnyi Komissariat Vneshnei i Vnutrennoi Torgovli (People's Commissariat of External and Internal Trade)
NKTrud	Narodnyi Komissariat Truda (People's Commissariat of Labour)
NKTyazhProm	Narodnyi Komissariat Tyazheloi Promyshlennosti (People's Commissariat of Heavy Industry)
NKVD	Narodnyi Komissariat Vnutrennykh Del (People's Commissariat of Internal Affairs)
NKVMDel	Narodnyi Komissariat Voenno-Morskoi Del (People's Commissariat of Military and Naval Affairs)

NKVodTrans	Narodnyi Komissariat Vodnogo Transporta (People's Commissariat of Water Transport)
NKYust	Narodnyi Komissariat Yustitsii (People's Commissariat of Justice)
NKZagatovok	Narodnyi Komissariat Zagatovka (People's Commissariat of Procurements)
NKZem	Narodnyi Komissariat Zemledeliya (People's Commissariat of Agriculture)
nomenklatura	appointment lists controlled directly or indirectly by the party, officials included on such lists
obispolkom	province soviet executive committee
obkom	province party committee
oblast	province
OGPU (GPU)	Ob"edinennoe Gosudarstvennoe Politicheskoe Upravlenie (Unified State Political Administration, Soviet Political Police); see also NKVD
okrug	administrative unit, between region and district
okrugkom	party committee of the okrug
oprosom	decisions taken by consultation (of Politburo members)
Orgburo	Organisational Bureau of the Central Committee
Orgraspred	Central Committee's Department for Assignment of leading party officials
ORPO	Central Committee's Department of Leading Party Organs
Osoaviakhim	Soviet civil defence organisation
partorg	party organisers
podkulachnik	'sub-kulak'
politotdel(y)	politicheskie otdel(y) (political department(s))
politruky	political workers
prodnalog	tax in kind, levied on the peasantry after 1921
prodrazverstka	state system of compulsory requistioning
pud	measure of weight, equalling 36.1 British pounds
pyatiletka	period of the Five-Year Plan
Rabkrin	see NKRKI
raiispolkom	district soviet executive committee
raikom	district party committee
raion	district, administrative unit
RSFSR	Rossiiskaya Sovetskaya Federativnaya Sotsialisticheskaya Respublika (Russian Soviet Federative Socialist Republic)
ruble	unit of currency
Sel'khozsnab	agricultural supply agency
serednyak	middle peasant
sovkhoz	sovetskoe khozyaistvo (state farm)

Sovnarkom	Sovet Narodnykh Komissarov (Council of People's Commissars)
SSR	Soviet socialist republic, union republic of the USSR
stazh	length of party membership
STO	Sovet Truda i Oborony (Council of Labour and Defence)
Sunastroi	construction project for daming the Suna river in Karelia
SVU	Spilka Vyzvolenia Ukrainy (Association for the Liberation of Ukraine)
svodki	official reports
terakty	terrorist acts
tolkachi	'pushers', officials entrusted with procuring supplies
toz	tovarishchestvo po sovmestnoi (association for the joint cultivation of land [the simplest form of kolkhoz])
Traktortsentr	Vsesoyuznyi tsentr mashinno-traktornykh statsii (All-Union Centre of Machine-Tractor Stations)
troika	commission or group of three persons with extra judicial powers
trudoden'	labour day, measure of work
tsentner	100 kilograms
Tsentrosoyuz	Vsesoyuznyi tsentral'nyi soyuz potrebitel'skikh obshchestv (All-Union Central Union of Consumer Cooperative Societies)
TsIK	Tsentral'nyi Ispolnitel'nyi Komitet (Central Executive Committee of the Soviets of the USSR)
TsKK	Tsentral'naya kontrol'naya komissiya (Central Control Commission of the party)
TsSU	Tsentral'noe Statisticheskoe Upravlenie (Central Statistical Administration)
TsUNKhU	Tsentral'noe upravlenie narodno-khozyaistvennogo ucheta (Central Administration of National Economic Records)
uezd	district
UKK	Urals-Kusnetsk Combine
UkSSR	Ukrainian Soviet Socialist Republic
UNKhU	Karelian Statistical Administration
UNKVD	Leningrad Administration of the NKVD
USLON	Solovetskii Camp of Special Designation (OGPU)
USSR	Union of Soviet Socialist Republics
Vesenkha	Vysshii Sovet Narodnogo Khozyaistva (Supreme Council of the National Economy)
VKP(b)	All Union Communist Party (Bolshevik), see CPSU
volost	district
vozhd'	leader

VTsIK	Vserossiiskii Tsentral'nyi Ispolnitel'nyi Komitet (All-Russian Central Executive Committee of Soviets)
VTsSPS	Vsesoyuznyi Tsentral'nyi Soviet Professional'nykh soyuzo (All-Union Central Council of the Trade Unions)
VUkTsIK	All-Ukrainian Central Executive Committee (of Soviets)
vydvizhentsy	individuals promoted into official positions
zapiski	official notes or correspondence
Zhelles	Timber felling trust of the railways (NKPS)
ZIS	Moscow Stalin Motor Works
ZSFSR	Transcaucasian Soviet Federated Socialist Republic

Introduction

E. A. Rees

The Russian Empire and its successor, the USSR, in the twentieth century experienced acutely the conflicting centripetal and centrifugal pressures of centre–local relations. The centrifugal forces were those forces pulling power away from the centre, the pressure from different national and ethnic groups seeking to break away from the grip of the capital, the pressures from provincial centres and regions seeking greater autonomy, the pressure of peasant communities and organised workers to assert themselves. The centripetal forces were those pulling power back into the centre, extending the reach of the central authorities, imposing its control over those national groups, provincial and regional centres and communities which sought to move outside the centre's ambit of control.

With the weakening of the centre, the centrifugal forces in three critical periods assumed a dominating influence: the revolutionary crisis of 1905–6; the revolution and civil war period 1917–21; the period of Gorbachev's reforms and the collapse of the communist state 1985–91. By contrast, the country also experienced acute centripetal trends towards extreme centralisation of power. The most extreme manifestation of this trend was witnessed during the Stalin era, but elements of this trend also existed during the tsarist era with its prolonged periods of emergency rule. Aspects of this system also outlived Stalin. Between these two polar opposites, of extreme centralisation and disintegration, lay periods of relative moderation: the years of the tsarist constitutional experiment after 1906; the NEP period of the 1920s; the reform era under Khrushchev. These periods of 'balance' were themselves distinguished by all the hallmarks of a highly unitary, centralised state.

The pattern of Russian and Soviet history indicates a profound difficulty in establishing a stable balance between central and local power; periods of relative balance tended to lead either towards disintegration or a turn back towards extreme centralisation and authoritarianism. At the centre of this lies the problem of the nature of the Russian and Soviet state, in terms of the way the state both sought to order the internal regime within the country itself and to define the country's relationship with the outside world.

1

The problem of centre–local relations in the Russian/Soviet case assumed a particular form on account of the country's immense size and lack of natural borders. The uncertainty regarding borders was highlighted by periodic adjustment as a result of war, civil war, secession and conquest. The problem of central control was compounded by the extraordinary diversity of peoples over which the state's power held sway. It was shaped by the nature of the society over which the state ruled, although both state and society were profoundly affected by their mutual interactions. It was highlighted by the underdevelopment of civil society, the weakness of the rule of law and by the state's control over the means of communication. The power of the state was limited by its own rudimentary administrative and policing apparatus, which often was reflected in a problem of undergovernment and underpolicing, and consequent recourse to repressive methods of rule. The weakness of transport and communications networks imposed limits on the centre's control over these territories. The weakness of central control fostered insecurity, which predisposed the centre to extreme measures to enforce its will.

Centre–local relations in the Russian/Soviet case were shaped very much by the problem of internal and external security and the way these two concerns interacted with one another. The internal weakness of the state was seen as an invitation to foreign powers to pursue an aggressive policy, with internal and external enemies working in concert to weaken the state. By the same token, critics saw the system of tight internal control as the concomitant of its potential for pursuing an assertive foreign policy. The military strength of the state was seen to rest on its ability to mobilise the internal resources of a materially poor society, through taxation and conscription as well as by the promotion of economic sectors which directly supported the needs of the military. The pressure that such policies imposed on the civilian population itself exacerbated the internal security situation. The pursuit of 'great power' ambitions of necessity imposed limits on the scope for internal reform and democratisation. In both the tsarist and Soviet eras, the claims of internal and external security were used to justify authoritarian methods of rule.

As a consequence the Russian/Soviet state developed in a unique way. In Russia absolutism survived until 1917, based on the power of the centralised state bureaucracy, the armed forces and the internal security apparatus. This system was replicated in the provinces, based on the figure of the centrally appointed governor. This system was recreated with some important modifications in the Soviet period. The way in which the tsarist and Soviet state addressed the problems of defence and foreign policy, of internal security and of economic development and modernisation, all had a direct bearing on centre–local relations.

The Bolsheviks attempted after 1917 to recast relations between the central authorities and the localities. This was done as part of the critique of the tsarist state, its highly centralised, bureaucratic character, and in terms of the state's relations, particularly with its non-Russian citizens, and the great disparity evident in terms of the economic, social and cultural development of the different parts of the Empire. The redefining of the role of the Soviet state was seen in terms of a broader vision of the Soviet state's relations with the external world.

Following the period of state disintegration of 1917–21, there was a period of stabilisation in the 1920s, which was followed again by a reversion to a system of ultra-centralisation and draconian authoritarian methods of rule. This volume seeks to determine the turning points in that process, whereby the power of the centre over the localities was reasserted; the way in which the relationship between the centre and different local centre of power were redefined; and the changing priorities of the central leadership in this period with regard to the republics and provinces. As such, it seeks to understand the central dynamics driving the development of the Soviet state and the role of economic planning in the transformation of relations between the centre and the localities.

In this study the 'centre' is defined as those party and governmental bodies that exercised power in deciding policy which touched on the most important issues regarding the functioning of the state, in its fullest sense, in terms of the extension of its powers across the whole extent of the territory under its control, and in terms of its relations to other states. It includes the highest bodies of the ruling Communist Party – the Politburo, Secretariat, Orgburo, the Central Committee and the governmental apparatus of Sovnarkom and the Council of Labour and Defence and the commissariats and commissions attached to them. The 'local' is defined as the territorial units of administration, primarily the republican tier, the city (gorod), the province (okrug and oblast) and the district (raion) level.

The study of centre–local relations as a discipline developed strongly from the early 1980s, focusing on the problems of state and nation-building.[1] In the study of western political systems it embraced a wide range of approaches, through the study of regional economic policies, the development of local government institutions, budgetary and taxation policy, etc.[2] On a theoretical level it saw attempts to conceptualise centre–local relations in a variety of ways – the study of 'internal colonialism', frontiers and spatial geographic studies.[3] It was a major focus of literature on devolution and studies on the process of state centralisation and the erosion of local autonomy.[4]

In the academic literature on the USSR the problem of centre–local relations has usually been studied as part of the question of nationalities policy, regionalism, federalism,[5] or as an aspect of location policy in economic decision-making.[6] It was also studied as an aspect of the working of the Soviet 'totalitarian' state. In the 1960s and 1970s a number of studies explored the role of republican and regional political elites on economic and political decision-making at the centre.[7] This involved studying the role of these local leaders in articulating policy demands and their impact on policy-making.[8] It involved studies of the nature of the Soviet ruling elite and of the central role of clientelistic relations extending to the republics and provinces.[9]

The study of centre–local relations brings into play three specific principles of administrative organisation. Firstly, the territorial principle – the extent to which government and administration is devolved to specific administrative tiers based on territory (the *horizontal* axis of administration). A second principle is the branch principle of administration, or the *vertical* axis, whereby administration is carried out on the basis of specific fields or branches of activities (industry, agriculture, trade, transport, education, health, justice), conducted by centralised agencies without regard for any regional, territorial, national or ethnic particularity of the territories being administered. A third principle is the *functional*, based on particular aspects of administration (personnel, organisation, finance and control). Most systems of administration involve a complex interweaving of the three principles at least at some basic level. Yet clear distinctions can be drawn between different administrative systems. Some political systems accord specific rights and powers to subordinate administrative tiers, through the development of strong local government, or through the creation of federal institutions. Unitary states, in contrast, diminish the rights of territorial level and seek uniformity of administration and subordination to the centre.

This volume deals with centre–local relations in the USSR in the 1930s and focuses primarily on the formation of economic policy, although some attention is drawn to wider issues of nationalities policy, security and defence concerns, which inevitably influenced economic policy-making. It examines how the shift from a mixed economy to a predominantly planned economy influenced the distribution of power between these various decision-making centres. It looks at the allocation of resources, and examines how far the local (republican and provincial) authorities in the USSR were able to affect the planning process. It examines also the development of control strategies by the centre over the periphery, and the way in which the role of the local authorities was redefined over time, and the position which they were assigned within the political system and the planned economy.

The question of how far a system of state planning can accommodate a system of devolved decision-making is a vexed question.[10] During the formation of the First and Second Five-Year Plans there was at least a commitment to involving republican and regional planning authorities in the planning process. Their actual power was more questionable. The nature of the planning system, and the very high targets set during these phases of planning, contributed to the process of centralising decision-making.

Economic decision-making in the USSR involved a complex set of relations between six major actors: first, the central party and government authorities; second, the planning agency; third, the control and security agencies; fourth, the economic commissariats; fifth, the republican, regional and local authorities; and sixth, the economic units themselves, whether factories, works or farms. These individual components, their interrelationships, and their relative power all underwent a remarkable degree of variation over time. The relations between these institutions and the wider society constitute another dimension of the policy process.

This raises important questions about the way in which the Soviet political system can be characterised. Merle Fainsod, with access to Soviet archives seized by the German army in 1941 for Smolensk, which formed the basis of his book *Smolensk under Soviet Rule*, published in 1958, significantly modified his understanding of the operation of the Soviet political system. In the first edition of his *How Russia is Ruled* (1953), he presented the Soviet political system unambiguously as a totalitarian regime. In the second edition, published in 1963, he presented the Soviet system as an imperfect totalitarianism, characterised by defective control and riddled with conflict between different agencies and different administrative tiers.

A pioneering study of the role of the provincial party leaders in the Soviet planned economy was Jerry F. Hough, *The Soviet Prefects* (1969).[11] As a study of the workings of the provincial party leadership in the post-Stalin era it remains unsurpassed. Hough noted six basic functions which regional party secretaries performed in industry: (1) The supervision of the local soviets and their executive committees (ispolkoms) and departments to ensure that *party policy* was properly interpreted and put into effect; generally checking on efficiency, monitoring performance, exposing shortcomings, corruption and mismanagement; (2) Overseeing *cadres policy*, monitoring the operation of system of party-controlled appointment (nomenklatura) and filling particular posts; (3) Exercising general *political supervision* of the region, ensuring party discipline, overseeing ideological control, combating slackness in the party, promoting activism, ensuring contact with the population; monitoring the work of the press; developing agitation–propaganda work; monitoring labour discipline and identifying causes of discontent; (4) *Economic supervision* in the oblast, ensuring that enterprises fulfilled their plans; assisting managers in overcoming supply bottlenecks; ensuring greater flexibility and responsiveness in the planning system; (5) Providing an element of *regional coordination* amongst enterprises and ergonomic units, which were subordinated to centralised ministries that were organised on branch principles; crisis management, dealing with unforeseen events; overriding the plan and commandeering resources to deal with emergencies; (6) The *representation of the region in the centre*, promoting schemes for the region's development, lobbying for investment and resources in competition with other regions. Ambitious regional party secretaries, Hough argued, had to demonstrate initiative, show a capacity to innovate and promote growth; they could not simply passively put central decisions into effect.

At what stage the integration of the provincial and republican party leadership into the management of the planned economy occurred, however, remained at this time unclear. Could these leaders have performed such diverse and complex functions within the highly centralised Stalinist state of the 1930s or was it only with the relaxation of the post-Stalin era that these leaders were able to develop these roles?

An important aspect of centre–local relations during the terror of the 1930s has been examined by J. Arch Getty, in *Origins of the Great Purges* (1985) and with Oleg Naumov, in *The Road to Terror* (1999).[12] In these works, Getty challenges the older totalitarian view of the Soviet state. He argues that the Soviet state faced a continuing problem in maintaining control over the localities. There was as constant erosion of central control, with the emergence of powerful political cliques in the republics and localities that frustrated the centre's aspirations for a smooth-running, centralised system of administration that would do its bidding. Getty argues that this conflict between the centre and the localities was one of the key factors behind the unleashing of the terror in 1936–8.

Access to Soviet party and state archives at central, republican and regional level now allows scholars to address these questions and to examine the ways in which centre–local relations evolved in the Soviet state through the 1920s and 1930s. It is now possible to begin to construct political portraits of those anonymous figures that controlled the Stalinist state in the republics and provinces in these crucial decades. This volume explores the nature of centre–local relations in the 1930s, examines the influence of the regional and republican leaders in shaping and implementing the policies of the Second Five-Year Plan, analyses how far centre–local relations were conflict ridden and investigates to what extent the local cliques represented a challenge or threat to the power of the centre and the extent to which these conflicts contributed to the terror. The demise of the traditional Communist structures of power has focused attention anew on the problem of centre–local relations in these states.[13] This allows us to place in a much wider historical context the problems of governance in these countries.

The work presents eight chapters, each of which explores the theme of centre–local relations as they evolved in the USSR from the 1920s to the 1930s. It provides a study of Moscow, the capital, and its relations with the central authorities, and, by contrast, a study of one of the remoter peripheral regions, the Karelian ASSR. It provides a study of a major industrial region, the Donbass, and a major agricultural region, Vinnitsa oblast, both of which were part of the Ukraine SSR, and therefore serve to illustrate the threefold level of relations: oblast, republican and all-union. There are also two case studies of the activities of republican and regional leaders as lobbyists at the XVII (1934) and XVIII (1939) party congresses. We also have a study of the formation of the regional elites in the 1930s and their relations to the central authorities. The chapters complement each another to provide a detailed study of centre–local relations in this period. Each chapter, however, is intended to stand on its own. The five authors who have contributed to this volume are responsible only for the views expressed in their chapters. No final conclusion is offered, although a very high degree of consensus may be discerned amongst the contributors.

This work is intended as a contribution to the study of the decision-making process in the Stalinist era, and to the study of the evolution of the Soviet state. It is intended to complement an earlier volume on decision-making within the central economic commissariats in the 1930s (E. A. Rees, ed., *Decision-Making in the Stalinist Command Economy, 1932–1937*). A third volume (*The Nature of Stalin's Dictatorship: The Politburo, 1928–1953*) will examine the process of decision-making at the highest level of the Soviet political system, Stalin's private office, the Politburo, Sovnakom and the party and state apparatus.

Notes

1. Edward Shils, *Center and Periphery: Essays in Macrosociology* (Chicago and London, 1975); *Center and Periphery: Spatial Variations in Politics* (Beverly Hills, 1980); Stein Rokkan, *Building States and Nations* (Beverly Hills, 1973); Stein Rokkan, *Centre–Periphery Structures in Europe* (Frankfurt an Main, 1987); Stein Rokkan, *Economy, Territory, Identity: Politics of West European Peripheries* (London, 1983); Peter Flora, Stein Kuhnle and Derek Urwin (eds), *State Formation, Nation Building and Mass Politics in Europe* (Oxford, 1995).
2. Yves Mény and V. Wright (eds), *Centre–Periphery relations in Western Europe* (1985); Sidney Tarrow, *Between Center and Periphery* (New Haven, 1977); Douglas Ashford, *British Dogmatism and French Pragmatism: Centre–Local Policy Making in the Welfare State* (London, 1981); J. Becquart-Leclerq, 'Relational Power and Center–Periphery Linkages in French Local Politics', *Sociology and Sociological Research*, 1977, 62, pp. 21–42.
3. M. Hechter, *Internal Colonialism: The Celtic Fringe in British National Development* (London, 1975); David Drakakis-Smith (ed.), *Internal Colonialism: Essays Around a Theme* (Edinburgh, 1983); Vicente Granados-Cabelos, *Internal Colonialism: A Critique* (Birmingham, 1984).
4. G. Ross Stephens, 'State Centralization and the Erosion of Local Autonomy', *Journal of Politics*, 36, 1974, pp. 44–76; Douglas Ashford, 'Territorial Politics and Equality: Decentralization and the Modern State', *Political Studies*, 27(1), 1979, pp. 71–83.
5. V. Aspaturian, 'Theory and Practice of Soviet Federalism', *Journal of Politics*, 12(1), 1950, pp. 20–51.
6. Iwan S. Koropeckyi, 'The Development of Soviet Location Theory Before the Second World War', *Soviet Studies*, 19, 1967, pp. 232–44.
7. Ronald J. Hill, *Soviet Political Elites: The Case of Tiraspol* (London, 1977); Donna Bahry, *Outside Moscow: Power, Politics and Budgetary Policy in the Soviet Republics* (New York, 1987); Philip D. Stewart, *Political Power in the Soviet Union* (Indianapolis, 1968); Joel Moses, *Regional Party Leadership and Policy-Making in the USSR* (New York, 1974); William Taubman, *Governing Soviet Cities: Bureaucratic Politics and Urban Development in the USSR* (New York, 1973); Everett M. Jacobs (ed.), *Soviet Local Politics and Government* (London, 1983); Jan Ake Dellenbrant, *Soviet Regional*

Policy (Stockholm, 1980); Daniel N. Nelson, 'Dilemmas of Local Politics in Communist States', *Journal of Politics*, 41, 1979, pp. 23–54.

8. George W. Breslauer, 'Regional Party Leaders; Demand Articulation and the Nature of Centre–Periphery Relations in the USSR', *Slavic Review*, 4, 1986, pp. 50–72; George W. Breslauer, 'Is There a Generation Gap in the Soviet Political Establishment? Demand Articulation by RSFSR Provincial Party First Secretaries', *Soviet Studies*, 36(1), 1984, pp. 10–25; Howard Biddulph, 'Local Interest Articulation at CPSU Congresses', *World Politics*, 36(1), 1983, pp. 25–52.

9. T. H. Rigby, *Political Elites in the USSR: Central Leaders and Local Cadres from Lenin to Gorbachev* (Aldershot, 1990); T. H. Rigby and Bohdan Harasymiw, *Leadership Selection and Patron–Client relations in the USSR and Yugoslavia* (London, 1983); Evan Mawdsley, and Stephen White, *The Soviet Elite from Lenin to Gorbachev: The Central Committee and its Members* (Oxford, 2000).

10. A. Nove, *The Economics of Feasible Socialism* (London, 1984); F. A. Hayek, *The Road to Serfdom* (London, 1976, first published 1941); Ludwig von Mises, *Socialism* (London, 1936).

11. Jerry F. Hough, *The Soviet Prefects: The Local Party Organs in Industrial Decision-Making* (Harvard University Press, 1969); Jerry F. Hough, 'The Party Apparatchiki', in H. Gordon Skilling and Franklyn Griffiths (eds), *Interest Groups in Soviet Politics* (Princeton, 1971).

12. J. Arch Getty, *Origins of the Great Purges* (Cambridge, 1985) J. Arch Getty and O. V. Naumov, *The Road to Terror* (New Haven, London, 1999).

13. The studies of centre–regional relations in post-Communist Russia are vast. Here we note just one Russian contribution to the debate: O. V. Gritsai, *Tsentr i periferiya v regional'nom razvitii* (Moscow, 1991). On the impact of economic reform on centre–local relations in China, see Linda Chelan Li, *Centre and Provinces: China 1978–1993: Power as Non Zero-Sum* (Oxford, 1998); Shaun Breslin, *China in the 1980s: Centre–Province Relations in Reforming the Socialist State* (Basingstoke, London, 1996).

1
The Changing Nature of Centre–Local Relations in the USSR, 1928–36

E. A. Rees

The relations between the central and regional authorities in the Russian Empire and the USSR were always problematical. This in part reflected the difficulties of governing a vast territory of great geographical and ethnic diversity. It also stemmed from the kinds of objectives that the rulers of this country set themselves. The question of ordering centre–local relations posed acute difficulties, especially against the background of the partial disintegration of the state itself in 1917–20. In the wake of revolution and civil war the Soviet authorities attempted to reorder centre–local relations. This was done within the strong political framework provided by the Communist one-party state, supported by the Cheka and the Red Army. The reconquest of territories held by the Whites and other nationalist forces provided the background to a bold experiment in state-building. The Bolsheviks encountered problems in establishing control over territories where their rule viewed as alien and illegitimate. The Soviet regime itself, based on its experience during the civil war, distinguished between regions that were considered loyal, disloyal or neutral. The New Economic Policy (NEP), introduced in 1921, was a strategy both for reviving the economy, and for reordering the central authorities relations with their local territorial units. With the abandonment of NEP in 1929 centre–local relations were again to be fundamentally transformed.

Centre–local relations in the USSR in the 1920s

At the outset the Soviet authorities introduced a new principle in state-building, the recognition of the national and ethnic principle, which the tsarist regime had for the most part ignored. The old tsarist system of administration, based on the appointment by the centre of provincial governors, who were unaccountable to the local population, was to be dispensed with. The constitution of the USSR of 1922 enshrined this principle into the organisation of the state, by the creation of union republics and autonomous regions based on nationality.

The transformation of Russia from the highly unitary system of the tsarist state to the Soviet state with its commitment to some form of devolved power in the 1920s involved a dramatic change. The Soviet constitution of 1922 embraced the principles of federalism, but this was always a qualified federalism, in which the power of the respective national federal units was extremely uneven. The Communist one-party state was essentially unitary in structure, especially so after 1929. After the crisis of peasant uprisings and famine in 1921–2 the balance between the centre and the localities was shaped by the limited capabilities of the central party–state apparatus, by the revival of the market economy and by the need to integrate this multi-national state, at least in part on the basis of compliance if not of active consent.

The principle of Soviet state organisation was based on a critique of the tsarist state. The tsarist state was viewed as an imperialistic state, constructed partly through military conquest, with the Russian core exploiting its colonial, non-Russian periphery. A policy of Russification and the suppression of local languages and cultures complemented military and economic domination of the periphery. The tsarist state was characterised by great discrepancies between regions in terms of their economic, social and cultural development. Frontier regions provided military bases for the projection of Russian military and imperial ambitions. These regions also provided raw materials and markets for Russian and foreign industry.

The professed objective of Soviet policy was to raise the economic and cultural level of the more backward regions and to bring them up to the same level as the most advanced regions of the USSR. Only Soviet power, it was argued, was able to develop these regions. On this basis the backward republics and regions would be more firmly integrated into the state on the basis of their perceived self-interest. Central to this was the policy not only of toleration, but also of active encouragement for local languages and cultures. Alongside this went the policy of *korenizatsiya*, the promotion of cadres from the titular national groups, and their recruitment into the Communist Party. The resolution of the XII party congress which enshrined the main features of Soviet nationalities policy was based on a report presented by Stalin.[1]

Underlying this policy lay a number of basic principles. First, that the Russian people, the Russian language and culture did not enjoy a position of privilege *vis-à-vis* the other peoples within the USSR. Secondly, it was assumed that concessions on language and cultural questions to the non-Russian peoples would serve to strengthen support for the regime amongst them, and that it was possible to distinguish between cultural nationalism and political nationalism or what was construed as 'bourgeois nationalism', that is the desire for independence and secession from the Soviet state. These concessions, as well as the economic benefits bestowed by official policy, were to provide the cement that would bind the state together.

Lenin famously in 1921, writing on official policy in Turkestan, stressed the need to win over the native populations in the non-Russian regions, and to combat 'Great Russian chauvinism' within the party's own ranks. This, he argued, was vital as part of the Communist party's strategy for revolution in India and the Far East.[2] At the same time Soviet control over large parts of Russia and the non-Russian regions of the former empire, including Ukraine, the Caucasus and Central Asia, was established only by military conquest. In the case of Turkestan the Bolsheviks' struggle with the armed forces of the so-called 'Basmachi' continued until at least 1925.

The development of Soviet nationalities policy in the 1920s paralleled the concessions to the peasantry and NEPmen, and the relaxation on religious policy after 1924. These measures were intended to serve the same end of constructing a more solid base of popular support for the Soviet regime in the country. These concessions were shaped by the political crisis of 1921, and were given further impetus by the rebellion of the Georgian peasants in 1924.

An illustration of this new line was the development of the policy of 'Ukrainisation', which was carried through by Stalin's appointee as General Secretary of Ukraine, Lazar Kaganovich, from 1925. Ukraine, because of its importance economically, strategically and because of its distinct cultural identity represented a major test of the regime's ability to administer this vast multi-national state. 'Ukrainisation' set as its avowed aim the use of the Ukrainian language in the republic's party, soviet, trade union and military organisations, and the promotion of Ukrainian language in education and in the mass media. From 1928 the protocols of the Ukrainian Politburo were recorded not in Russian but in Ukrainian. Efforts were also directed at recruiting Ukrainians into the party.[3]

It was assumed that with the economic development of Ukraine there would be an influx of peasants into industry, and that in time the republic's towns and working class would become overwhelmingly Ukrainian-speaking. Official policy aimed to anticipate and guide this process. This conciliatory policy pursued towards the non-Russian nationalities in no way was intended to diminish the party's control, and the instruments of repression always remained in reserve.[4]

This policy was dictated from the centre, and the local political leadership in the republic was required to carry it out. Within the Ukrainian political leadership those of a more nationalist stamp embraced it enthusiastically, but others were more critical, and in some cases were very hostile to the policy. What is remarkable is that Ukrainisation was implemented in a situation where the overwhelming majority of the working class and of the urban population was Russian-speaking. In 1927–8 the policy came under a hail of criticism both from the Russian-dominated party and trade union bodies in Ukraine and from those on the left of the party at all-union level.

It was condemned by G. E. Zinoviev,[5] by Yu. Larin[6] as well as by V. Vaganyan in his book *O natsional'noi kulture*.[7] On the left of the party there remained a strong current, which has been termed 'national nihilist', which saw the withering away of national differences and national identity as the party's objective.

Ukraine in the 1920s enjoyed a limited but significant degree of autonomy. The republican authorities were bound by the general economic policy of the centre, but were also capable of pushing their own demands within those confines. Ukraine in particular vigorously promoted schemes for the development of the industries of the republic, notably the Dneprostroi hydro-electric project, the reconstruction of the southern metallurgical works and the reconstruction of the Donbass coalfield. It was in part as a result of this pressure that Ukraine was accorded the central place in the First Five-Year Plan's industrialisation project.

The policy of Ukrainisation, Kaganovich argued in 1927, would provide the model for the revolutionary movements in Hungary, Poland, Bulgaria and Czechoslovakia. Similarly, nationalities policy towards the Finns and the Karelians in Karelia would provide a model for the Scandinavian countries, just as Soviet policy in Central Asia was a model for the Far East. Successful revolution in these countries would, it was anticipated, seek to unite their new socialist republics with the USSR. It was therefore imperative that the relations between the constituent republics of the USSR and the centre were organised on the basis of equity and justice.[8]

At the XVI party congress in June 1930 Stalin again stressed that the party was committed to promoting the full flowering of the cultures and languages of the people's of the USSR. He rejected the argument that it was time to abolish the national republics and regions. Instead, he argued, it was necessary to continue the policy of creating a system that was 'national in form but socialist in content'. In this speech he criticised local nationalism, but stressed that Great-Russian chauvinism constituted 'the chief danger in the Party in the sphere of the national question'.[9]

In 1930 the trial of the Association for the Liberation of Ukraine (Spilka Vyzvolenia Ukrainy or SVU) was held. A number of prominent Ukrainian intellectuals were accused of plotting, with Polish and German intelligence agencies, to separate the Ukraine from the USSR. The trial heralded the tightening of control over intellectual life in Ukraine. It also marked in part a retreat on Ukrainisation, particularly the abandonment of moves towards the use of Ukrainian within the main economic organisations. In other areas, Ukrainisation continued.

Stalin and the republican and regional party secretaries

Central to any understanding of the way in which the Soviet political system developed from the 1920s into the 1930s is the question of Stalin's own personal power and his relationship with the powerful republican and regional leaders. Earlier historians, notably I. Deutscher, R. V. Daniels and T. H. Rigby, emphasised Stalin's control over the central party Secretariat as the determining factor in creating a disciplined body of supporters in the power struggle following Lenin's death.[10] This view argues that through control over appointments and promotions at local level Stalin created a regional base of support. He was able also to control the delegations which attended the party congresses and thereby to control the debate and more particularly the process of election of the Central Committee. The position of the republican and regional party leaders was constrained by the discipline imposed by the doctrine of democratic centralism and the increasingly rigid definition of party ideology. Loyalty to the party transcended allegiance to republic or region. The terms 'oblastnik' was a term of contempt for those who adhered too narrowly to a provincial view of political interests.

The Central Committee was expanded from 40 members and 17 candidates at the time of Lenin's death to 71 members and 50 candidates by 1927. The membership of the Central Committee represented a certain diversity of institutional and regional interests, with between 35 and 45 per cent made up of leaders of regional and republican party organisations.[11]

Stalin did not act at the behest of the regional party leaders but he had to construct an alliance with these leaders from 1927, to set the policy agenda and to win them around to his point of view. He did this through a series of campaigns – the anti-kulak campaign of the winter of 1927–8; the Shakhty affair and the campaign against the bourgeois specialists from 1928 onwards; the war scare of 1927; the Smolensk scandal and the attack on corruption in the regional party organisations, the self-criticism campaign and the drive to promote a new generation of specialists. All these separate campaigns were coordinated into one unified campaign against the so-called 'Right' Opposition in 1928–9.

In this abrupt change of course away from NEP and towards forced development of heavy industry Stalin could appeal primarily to those heavy industrial regions that sought new investment (the Urals, Ukraine and Leningrad). Other regions based on light industry (notably Moscow oblast) and the agricultural regions, which had benefited under NEP, might be expected to be more circumspect in their support of the 'left turn'. But Stalin's appeal was not simply based on the material self-interests of particular regions, but on the basis of a broader vision of socialist transformation of the USSR and the building up of its defence base.

In the summer of 1928, after the crisis of grain procurement in the preceding winter, it appeared as though the 'Right' could control the party. In the second half of 1928 their grip was weakened. The defeat of N. A. Uglanov, first secretary of the Moscow party organisation, engineered by Stalin and his supporters, marked a watershed. The return to the rhetoric of class warfare, to the administrative measures of war communism and to the heady idea of a renewed socialist offensive against capitalist remnants provided the unifying ideological and policy basis of the group in the party leadership around Stalin.

The strengthening of the central leadership's position brooked no opposition. Internal party democracy was already severely eroded by 1923. In the attacks on the Joint Opposition in 1927 Stalin had recourse to the party's Central Control Commission and to the GPU; control of the party press and manipulation of party meetings was a central part of the campaign. The enthusiasm with which regional party secretaries embraced the policy of 'revolution from above' needs to take these factors into account. The scope for regional and republican leaders to come together to formulate alternative policies, or to question the official line, was already very limited. Once Stalin's position became unassailable after 1928, almost no republican or regional secretaries were to challenge the 'general' line. The direction and tone of policy was set by the centre.

Notwithstanding its vast size, the USSR was made up of a relatively small number of key economic regions, with a very clear hierarchy reflecting their relative importance. Within the Politburo only the most important regions were represented: the two capitals Moscow (L. B. Kamenev, then N. A. Uglanov) and Leningrad (G. E. Zinoviev, then S. M. Kirov), and Ukraine (L. M. Kaganovich, then S. V. Kosior). The number of key regions (if we look at the proceedings of the XVII party congress, Chapter 3 in this volume) was no more than about a dozen. These regional authorities had far greater resources, carried much greater political weight and were in a much stronger bargaining position than the others. This made the centre's task of controlling the republics and regions more straightforward than might otherwise be thought. What, however, made the task of control difficult was the sheer scale of work undertaken in those years. The problem was to ensure that the party chiefs in these regions were efficient and loyal and that they were able to ensure the same of their subordinates.

The Secretariat and Orgburo and the Department for Assignment (Orgraspred) exercised close control over party appointments. The Central Committees of republican party bodies, obkoms, kraikoms and gorkoms were required periodically to report on their activities to the Orgburo. The Orgburo also carried out periodic inspections of the work of lower party bodies, and dispatched instructors to ensure that policy was properly implemented. The regional party secretaries were increasingly appointed from the centre, although central nominees had to be formally elected by the local party organisations. Those assigned to these posts were usually old revolutionaries with some standing in the party. Many built up their expertise as regional bosses, who were often transferred from post to post around the Union.

Stalin was also able to place his supporters in key positions of power within the regional and republican apparatus. James Hughes, in analysing the 'patrimonial' basis of Stalin's power, identifies a number of key appointments from the summer of 1924 whereby officials close to Stalin, many of them having worked with him in the Secretariat and Orgburo, were placed in key positions. In 1924 Orgburo member N. A. Uglanov replaced I. A. Zelenskii, a Kamenev supporter, as Moscow regional party secretary. In 1925 L. M. Kaganovich was transferred from Orgraspred to become General Secretary of the Ukrainian Communist Party. S. I. Syrtsov in January 1926 was made first secretary of the Siberian kraikom, filling a vacancy left by the promotion of the existing secretary S. V. Kosior to the party Secretariat. At the same time S. M. Kirov, who had played a role in suppressing the Astrakhan workers in 1920 and led the Baku party organisation, was made Leningrad regional party secretary in place of Zinoviev.

Hughes adds:

> the network-building process is evident in the latter 1920s from the movements between Secretariat and Orgburo posts and regional leadership positions of A. A. Andreev (Orgburo to North Caucasus), D. E. Sulimov (Orgburo to Urals), S. V. Kosior exchanging posts with Kaganovich (Secretariat and Orgburo to Ukraine), N. M. Shevernik (secretariat and Orgburo to Urals), K. Ya. Bauman (Orgburo to Moscow), I. M. Vareikis (Secretariat to Central Black Earth region). By 1927–28 such an exchange between centre and region was an established method of continual supervision of the system.[12]

This pattern continued into the 1930s: P. P. Postyshev was transferred from the Secretariat to the post of second secretary of the Ukrainian Communist party in 1933, and A. A. Zhdanov was brought in from Gorky into the party Secretariat, and then appointed first secretary of Leningrad gorkom, following Kirov's assassination in 1934.

The centre's control over appointments greatly increased its power over the republics and regions. This power was by no means absolute. Stalin in 1928 tactfully withdrew Kaganovich from Ukraine because of opposition from other senior party figures in the republic to his authoritarian methods of rule. Uglanov, head of the Moscow party organisation, in 1928 threw his lot in with the 'Rightists'. S. I. Syrtsov, promoted by Stalin as chairman of Sovnarkom RSFSR, became one of his bitterest critics. Bauman, first secretary of the Moscow party organisation and a candidate member of the Politburo, was removed in 1930 because of excesses in carrying out collectivisation. Even the dependable A. A. Andreev, first secretary of the North Caucasus kraikom, in 1929 expressed reservations with regard to aspects of collectivisation policy and the issue of whether the kulaks could or could not be admitted into the kolkhozy.

The interaction between the central and regional authorities was often complex, and the flow of influences was often two-way. This is reflected in the development of the Urals–Siberian method of grain procurement at the end of 1928. The strategy emerged out of a complex interaction between the Moscow authorities and the regional authorities of the Urals and West Siberia.[13]

The outlook of republican and regional leadership had been shaped in the struggle with the Right, for the First Five-Year Plan and in the struggle for collectivisation and 'dekulakisation'. Leading party secretaries from the main grain-growing regions participated in formulating the policy. Competition between these leaders helped to force the pace of collectivisation in 1929–30. They had been distinguished by their commitment to carrying through the 'revolution from above' and by their apparent loyalty to Stalin. Particular leaders, notably B. P. Sheboldaev of North Caucasus, M. M. Khataevich of Central Volga, R. I. Eikhe of West Siberia, K. Ya. Bauman in Moscow oblast and then in Central Asia distinguished themselves by their resolute commitment to fighting the 'war' against the 'kulaks'.[14]

Stalin's article 'Dizzy with Success' in March 1930, which called a halt to forced collectivisation and placed the blame for excesses on local party workers, created a crisis in centre–local relations. Local party workers were reluctant to accept responsibility for the crisis. This did not mean that they rejected the policy of collectivisation and dekulakisation. On the contrary they considered the policy had failed because of the lack of resolve of the central leadership to carry it through.[15]

The First Five-Year Plan

The XV party congress in December 1927, in its resolution on the drafting of the Five-Year Plan, noted the need for special attention to be devoted to 'the raising of the economic and cultural positions of the borderland and backward regions' whilst 'not losing sight, however, of the connection between the needs and wants of the regions and those of the Soviet Union as a whole'.[16]

G. F. Grin'ko, who in 1930 took over as commissar of finance, in his book on the First Five-Year Plan, argued that the country was divided for economic administrative purposes on the basis of three principles, first, economic rationale; secondly, nationalities policy; and thirdly, defence considerations. From the time of the Goelro electrification project of 1920 the USSR was organised into distinct economic regions, the so-called 'Gosplan regions': the Urals, Siberia, North Caucasus, the Central Industrial region, Lower and Central Volga, etc., based on scientific and economic considerations.[17] This principle had, however, to be reconciled with the rights of different nationalities in the USSR, in accordance with the party's nationalities policy. According to Grin'ko, himself an ardent Ukrainian patriot, Ukraine, on the basis of purely economic considerations, should have been split into three regions: the southern coal and iron ore extracting regions of the Donetsk Basin and Krivoi Rog; the Black Sea steppe agricultural region; and the north-western region of intensive agriculture based on Kiev. However, because of the overriding importance of the principle of nationality in this case, the Ukraine had to be organised as a single entity.[18]

From the standpoint of the USSR as a whole, however, this concession to Ukrainian national sensibilities created a potential problem, of lopsided development with an overly powerful Ukrainian lobby being able to influence overall economic policy.

The importance of political considerations was reflected in the treatment accorded to the key Donetsk coal basin in Ukraine. The eastern section of the basin, including Shakhty, was attached to the North Caucasus region, with its capital at Rostov. This was based on the perceived need to attach a strong proletarian centre to the North Caucasus, considered as a Russian Vendeé, the base for the White Armies during the civil war, and a Cossack region with strong kulak farmers.[19]

Central Asia and the Transcaucasus, Grin'ko argued, had been 'typical semi-colonial dependencies of Russian tsarism'. In the Transcaucasus, with its heterogeneity and intermixture of nationalities and its history of racial conflict, a federation of national republics and regions had been created, with authority to carry out all plans of economic development in the region.[20] In direct contrast in 1924 Central Asia was organised into three autonomous national republics of Turkmenistan, Uzbekistan and Tadzhikistan. But major economic projects, such as irrigation schemes, which affected the interests of the entire region, were to be entrusted to the Central Asian Economic Council, which embraced all the national republics. This was based partly on considerations of administrative convenience. But it may have also been intended as a means of impeding the growth of pan-Islamic ideas and movements amongst the Moslem population.

Grin'ko claimed that the very structure of the First Five-Year Plan was in part 'a result of the rivalry and conflicting claims among the individual economic regions with the central authorities of the Soviet Union'. However, he stressed the positive aspect of this process, arguing that it did not constitute a 'centrifugal' tendency. Separatist tendencies, reflecting the bourgeois and petty bourgeois aspirations of part of society, were kept in check by the Soviet regime's socialist character (i.e. the one-party state).[21] The system of economic planning, Grin'ko argued, involved a combination of the branch principle of administration, of vertical administration, based on different sectors of industry, agriculture and transportation, with the territorial or horizontal principle of planning based on the economic regions and national republics.

The development of regional specialisation, Grin'ko argued, was an integral part of the general plan of socialist development of the USSR. The well-established Moscow and Leningrad industrial districts would decline in relative terms,[22] but the privileged position of Ukraine would be enhanced.

The share of these regions in the total capital of the country during the plan was to be reduced from 65 per cent to about 55 per cent, but distributed as follows: the share of Leningrad reduced from 10 to 7.3 per cent; that of the Central Industrial Region from 31 to 21 per cent and that of Ukraine increased from 24.5 to 26.2 per cent, making it the major industrial region in the USSR.[23] Grin'ko's projection regarding the future relative importance of Ukraine and Moscow was to be confounded by developments in the 1930s.

The shifting balance of centre–local relations, 1929–33

After 1929 centre–local relations were fundamentally reordered. Industriali-sation and collectivisation were carried out as part of the centrally initiated and directed 'revolution from above'. Associated with this was the unleash-ing of the 'cultural revolution', which was directed not only at entrenched bureaucratic power but was increasingly focused on what were considered cultural survivals, particularly in the non-Russian republics, that were deemed incompatible with the emergent socialist system.

An initial hypothesis associated with the planning experiments connected with Goelro was that it was possible to achieve a harmonious combination of central and regional planning.[24] In practice the First Five-Year Plan saw the relentless imposition of central directives and, because of the exaggerated nature of the targets set, the recourse by the centre to the commandeering of resources and their allocation to priority projects. The location policy for industry assumed growing importance with various considerations being balanced: the need to raise the economic level of the more backward regions and attain a greater dispersion of industrial activities; the need to locate industry closer to the main reserves of raw materials; the need to avoid overburdening the transport system with expensive hauls; and finally and of critical importance the question of defence and the location of industry away from vulnerable frontier zones and the creation of a new industrial base in the East.[25]

The industrialisation and collectivisation drives greatly increased the economic functions of the regional and republican party secretaries. Their role was to ensure administrative flexibility, to identify problems and to advance their own schemes for the development of their regions. The centre delegated to them responsibility and expected them to exercise initiative and independent judgement within the parameters set by central policy. They were subject to close scrutiny by the centre, but they developed also their own vested interests, cultivating their own networks and their own cliques of officials. Republican and regional party secretaries were not just the passive creatures of the centre. They were caught also between the pressures from the centre and those from lower down the hierarchy, the secretaries of the raikoms. A complex series of strategies were developed to evade or subvert central control.

While the Soviet authorities remained committed to the development of all the major republics and regions of the USSR, they also recognised a distinct division of labour, on the basis of which these areas would be integrated into the economic system as a whole. In the course of the First Five-Year Plan the balance shifted towards regional specialisation: Moscow and Leningrad were recognised as specialist industrial regions, based on advanced technology; the Ukraine specialised on ferrous metallurgy, coal, engineering and grain production; Central Asia was given over to cotton; Karelia was given over to timber and energy production. This process of specialisation made regions even more dependent on the centre for essential investment and supplies (grain to the timber regions of the north and to the cotton-growing regions of Central Asia). At the same time stress was placed on the self-reliance of regions in ensuring their own supply of food.

Changing priorities

Stalin in his speech to the XVI party congress on 27 June 1930 highlighted the problem of 'the proper distribution of industry throughout the USSR'. He noted that the country's reliance on 'the coal and metallurgical base in the Ukraine' was an obstacle to the development of the major industrial centres of the Urals and West Siberia. It was essential, he declared, to immediately begin building a second industrial base, namely the Urals–Kuznetsk Combine (UKK), utilising Kuznetsk coking coal and Urals iron ore.[26]

D. E. Sulimov and I. D. Kabakov, as first secretaries of the Urals obkom, vigorously promoted the scheme for a major investment drive to revitalise the Urals metallurgical industry. The first secretary of Urals kraikom, N. M. Shvernik, was ousted in 1929 by the obkom for failing to defend the interests of the Urals metallurgical industry with sufficient determination. The Urals Planning Commission and the representatives of the enterprises of the region promoted the scheme. It was strongly backed by Russian interests and particularly by Sovnarkom RSFSR. Through the 1920s the Urals metallurgical industry was in bitter competition with the Ukrainian metallurgical industry, which sought to establish for itself the dominant position as the country's principal metallurgical base.[27]

The Central Committee on 15 May 1930 approved the scheme for the Urals–Kuznetsk Combine, but the investment for the development of the Greater Urals was significantly less than what the Urals kraikom had sought. Debate on the project had begun in earnest at the end of 1929. It was vigorously supported in the centre by G. M. Krzhizhanovskii, head of Gosplan, and by V. V. Kuibyshev, head of Vesenkha. It was promoted for both economic and defence reasons. The Ukraine, Krzhizhanovskii argued, had to be considered a frontier zone, and thus vulnerable in the event of war. The project was opposed by Ukrainian interests. With the approval of the project, investment in the metallurgical industry of Ukraine was sharply curtailed.[28] Support for the project was no doubt shaped also in part by the idea that it corrected or balanced the Ukrainian bias in the industrialisation plans of 1928 by building up the RSFSR.

The dramatic shift in centre–local relations at the end of the 1920s is illustrated by the change in relations between Moscow and Ukraine. In July 1928 Kaganovich was withdrawn from Ukraine and replaced as General Secretary there by Stanislav Kosior. Kosior had earlier worked in the central party Secretariat; he remained as head of the Ukrainian party until 1938. Vlas Chubar' remained as head of Sovnarkom Ukraine until 1934. Within the Ukrainian Politburo other figures remained of note, such as G. I. Petrovskii, a long-standing member of the Ukrainian Politburo, and from 1926 a member of the all-union Politburo.

In 1929 the approval of the First Five-Year Plan and the launch of agricultural collectivisation and dekulakisation delivered a major blow to the limited autonomy enjoyed by Ukraine and other republics. In December 1929 the People's Commissariat of Agriculture (NKZem) of the USSR was created, headed by Ya. A. Yakovlev, and was entrusted with responsibility for implementing collectivisation and creating the new collective farm system. This involved a major step towards strengthening central control. The creation of NKZem USSR was criticised by M. Skrypnik, one of the leading politicians in Ukraine and a strong advocate of Soviet federalism, as a step towards weakening the authority of the republican organisation, and as a precedent which would be followed in other fields.[29]

Skrypnik's forebodings were amply borne out. With the initiation of the First Five-Year Plan Vesenkha USSR extended its authority over the republican Vesenkhas. In 1929 virtually all of the large industrial enterprises of Ukraine were transferred to the union commissariat. Vesenkha Ukraine, having the ground cut from under its feet was transformed virtually into the People's Commissariat of Light Industry Ukraine.[30] The authority of the republican tier of government was severely weakened. Vesenkha USSR dealt directly with the enterprises under its control in the regions, and where it needed consultation with the territorial authorities was inclined to deal with the oblast as much as the republican tier.

The powers of republican and regional authorities were significantly curbed by the budgetary reform of 1930, whereby the Commissariat of Finance of the USSR collected turnover tax centrally. Thereafter the republics were granted allocations from the centre as a form of subsidy. The budgets of most of the republican and regional authorities were very small, and went mainly on financing local social and cultural services. The economic development of the republics and regions was largely financed from the centre. The central authorities maintained control over the republican authorities through regulating their revenues and by establishing norms of expenditure.[31]

By the early 1930s certain policy areas were already outside the purview of the Ukrainian Politburo: economic planning, heavy industry; rail transport;

internal security; defence–foreign policy. This left other areas where it continued to exercise some influence: light industry and trade; the urban economy, housing and public services; water transport; agriculture; cultural, educational, social and health questions. The Ukrainian Politburo, unlike the all-union Politburo in Moscow, continued to meet on a regular weekly basis throughout the 1930s. Much of its work was given over to supervising the operation of the economy, carrying out investigations at Moscow's behest into those sectors of the economy which were deemed to be failing, and monitoring the state of the tractor and combine harvester parks. A constant stream of telegrams flowed between the all-union Politburo and the Ukrainian Politburo, with the Ukrainian Politburo seeking clearance for even relatively minor matters from Moscow.

It is notable that the all-union organs of administration, already at the beginning of the 1930s regarded as their structural sub-departments not only the republican commissariats but also even the Ukrainian government. For example the head of NKZem USSR, Ya. A. Yakovlev, and the chairman of Tsentrosoyuz, Ivanov, on 1 March 1931 sent a telegram to the head of the Ukrainian government Chubar', chairman of Sovnarkom Ukraine, in which they demanded by 2 o'clock that day an answer concerning the release of land from around the city suburbs under market gardening to the consumer cooperatives. If this demand was not fulfilled they threatened Chubar' with taking the matter to the Procuracy.

Chubar' telegrammed a reply that he would not sign the order requested and protested that the threat to take the matter to the Procuracy was unwarranted and politically mischievous. Moreover, he raised the matter at a session of the Ukrainian Politburo. There it was noted that cases of threats from the side of the all-union organs in relation to Sovnarkom Ukraine had become more frequent and it was decided to bring it to the attention of all-union Central Committee.[32]

The famine, 1932–3

The relations between the republics and the centre were illustrated by the response to the famine crisis in 1932–3. Centrally appointed plenipotentiaries were sent to Ukraine to impose grain procurement targets on an unwilling Ukrainian party leadership. By 1931 there was already concern about the situation in many of the grain-producing regions. Moscow kept a close eye on developments. Secretariat plenipotentiaries and Central Committee members were sent to the regions which were experiencing difficulties. Kaganovich, former General Secretary of the Ukrainian Communist Party, was dispatched on numerous occasions to the republic to sort out problems.

In the spring of 1932, faced by serious food supply problems, market controls were relaxed in order to provide incentives to the collective farms and individual peasants to release more food. In the summer of 1932 concern over the harvest and procurement targets created a new strain in centre–local relations. In 1932–3 party leaders from Central Black Earth, Central Volga, West Siberia and Kazakhstan informed Moscow of the dire situation in their areas with regard to food supply and the associated cuts in rations.[33] In the course of 1932 a limited market reform was introduced. While some regional leaders, such as B. P. Sheboldaev of North Caucasus, voiced opposition to free market prices, others, such as R. I. Eikhe, of West Siberia, and M. M. Khataevich, of Central Volga, argued for still more flexibility.[34]

In June 1932 Kaganovich wrote to Stalin: 'The regions are pushing hard on the problem of grain, and we are refusing the overwhelming majority'.[35] Stalin summoned a conference of party secretaries and chairmen of soviet executive committees from the main grain-producing regions and republics for the end of June. Stalin insisted that the first secretaries should be held 'personally responsible' for fulfilling the grain procurement campaign. The conference adopted a draft resolution based on Stalin's instructions that was strongly critical of the work of local organisations in Ukraine and the Urals. It demanded action to curb kulak influence and to 'smash opposition' to official policy.[36]

On 2 July 1932 Stalin wrote to Kaganovich concerning the situation in Ukraine. He railed at Kosior and Chubar' for their opportunism, their irresponsibility, and proposed that they should be dismissed.[37] At a meeting with Kosior on 23 June, Kaganovich warned him that they would have to make an example of him of how not to lead party organisations.

V. M. Molotov and Kaganovich attended the III All-Ukrainian Party Conference on 6–9 July 1932 as representatives of the centre. At the conference Kosior, Chubar' and Skrypnik, reflecting a mood strongly voiced in the Ukrainian Central Committee and by the raikom secretaries, called for greater realism in procurement policy.[38] Molotov and Kaganovich insisted that there could be no let-up in collectivisation and in pressure on the kolkhozy to supply more grain. Stalin had ordered a delivery of 7.7 million tons of grain from the Ukraine; after considerable argument the Ukrainians finally managed to get the figure reduced to 6.6 million tons, but this was still far beyond a realistic target. In his address Kaganovich severely criticised the party's work in the countryside. A central difficulty, he noted, was the mechanical way in which grain delivery quotas were allocation to the 400 raions, regardless of local circumstances. The Central Committee had sent its plenipotentiaries to the republic to overcome this problem. He dismissed the claim by many raion workers that the plenipotentiaries had only made matters worse.

On 11 August 1932 Stalin, in a letter to Kaganovich, expressed alarm at the situation in Ukraine. He openly voiced his contempt for the republican leadership: Kosior vacillated between the demands of the Central Committee and those of the raikoms; Chubar' was no leader, and S. F. Redens, as head of OGPU, was failing to fight counter-revolution. The Ukrainian party with 500,000 members was infested with conscious and unconscious Ukrainian nationalists or Petluraists (followers of the Ukrainian partisan Simon Petlura). He proposed that Kaganovich take over as General Secretary of the Ukrainian party in place of Kosior, whilst retaining his post as party Secretary. V. A. Balitskii should take over as head of the Ukrainian OGPU, and Redens demoted to deputy. Chubar' should be sacked as head of Sovnarkom Ukraine, possibly replaced by Grin'ko. The republic had to be strengthened: 'We must not spare any money on this.' If this was not done, Stalin warned 'we may lose Ukraine'.[39]

In a few days Stalin changed his mind. In a note to Kaganovich and Molotov, he confided that besides Kaganovich there was no other obvious candidate to replace Kosior in the Ukraine, but it was impossible to transfer him there as this would weaken the Secretariat of the Central Committee at a critical time.[40]

In August Stalin, on vacation, drafted the law on the theft of cooperative and collective farm property, and the theft of goods from transport.[41] Kaganovich, writing to Stalin, welcomed the proposal on the grounds that regional leaders were seeking greater powers, as they feared the kulaks would walk all over them.[42]

In the autumn of 1932 a high-powered commission, headed by Kaganovich, was sent to the Northern Caucasus to investigate the difficulties in grain procurement.[43] It met with the North Caucasus kraikom in Rostov on Don on 2 November and appointed plenipotentiaries for each district. Other special commissions were sent to Kharkov and Saratov, areas where disorder and resistance was intense. On 4 November the Central Committee–Central Control Commission plenum appointed a special commission, headed by M. F. Shkiryatov, to purge the North Caucasus, some Ukrainian and Lower Volga raions of 'people hostile to Communism conducting a kulak policy' and who were reluctant to implement the grain collections and sowing campaigns.[44]

In November the North Caucasus kraikom buro, with Kaganovich in attendance, resolved to smash all the saboteurs and counter-revolutionaries responsible for the failure of grain collection and the autumn sowing. As a result the inhabitants of sixteen villages of the North Caucasus were deported to the far north. Mass repression was applied under the directives of Molotov and Kaganovich, in North Caucasus, the Ukraine and Belorussia.[45] As the first secretary of North Caucasus krai, Sheboldaev, was to put it 'the kulaks again in 1932, this time from the base of the collective farm, tried to fight us about grain... But we did not understand it', so that the Central Committee had to send in 'a group of Central Committee members under Comrade Kaganovich to us, to help us correct the situation'.[46]

At the joint plenum of the Politburo and the presidium TsKK on 27 November Stalin accused local communist officials of idealising the kolkhozy, which had been infiltrated by kulaks and other anti-Soviet elements.[47] At the joint Central Committee–Central Control Commission plenum in January 1933 Stalin said that the 'causes of the difficulties connected with the grain collections' must be sought in the Party itself. The Kharkov first secretary R. Ya. Terekhov told him flatly that famine raged in the Ukraine. Stalin sneered at him as a romancer and all attempts to discuss the matter were simply dismissed out of hand.[48] Kaganovich stressed Stalin's role in directing policy, citing his speech to the Politburo–Presidium TsKK on 27 November 1932.[49] Kaganovich condemned the failure of leadership of the obkoms and raikoms, accusing them of turning a blind eye to the activities of 'kulaks' and adopting a 'tender-hearted' approach to the work of counter-revolutionaries.

On January 11 the Central Committee plenum decided to establish an agricultural department (Sel'khozotdel), headed by Kaganovich. On his recommendation new political departments (*politotdely*) were set up in the sovkhozy and the MTS.[50] The plenum approved a new purge of the party ranks and passed a resolution condemning the Eismont–Tolmachev–Smirnov group.[51] A special resolution of the Central Committee sought to define the responsibilities of the MTS, the *politotdely* and the raikom so as to avoid conflicts between them.[52] The purge, conducted under the direction of Kaganovich, fell disproportionately on the rural party organisations.

The famine of 1932–3 wrought devastation across great parts of the Soviet Union. Its worst impact was felt in Ukraine, North Caucasus, the Lower Volga and Kazakhstan. The crisis exacerbated relations between the republican and regional (obkoms and raikoms) authorities, and between these bodies and the central authorities in Moscow.

The tightening of central controls, 1932–34

With the defeat of the internal party opposition, the developing famine crisis and the mounting concern about internal security political control within the Soviet leadership was dramatically centralised. This was encouraged by a growing preoccupation with external security, prompted by the Japanese seizure of Manchuria in 1931 and Hitler's advent to power in Germany in 1933.

The demise of the formal meetings of the Politburo, Orgburo and Secretariat, especially evident from the start of 1933, following the earlier demise of the Central Committee plenum, drastically reduced the opportunities which local leaders had to speak before party fora.[53] Some opportunities for lobbying and advancing local interests remained, through the party and government bodies and through the commissariats, and even through direct contact with Stalin and other leaders. In 1934, in what appears to be a determined effort to improve centre–local relations and to mollify local party bosses, certain days were set aside in Stalin's appointment diary for meetings with republican and regional leaders, coinciding with Central Committee plena. This practice, however, was soon abandoned.[54]

These changes point to a drastic tightening of central controls over the whole political system in 1932–3. At the same time sharp contradictions and acute tensions marked the political situation. Stalin and his colleagues, as in 1930, attempted to unload the blame for the crisis in agriculture onto the shoulders of republican, provincial and district party officials. At the same time as Stalin's powers were strengthened his authority was being called into question as never before. Even within the tightly regulated Stalinist state catastrophic policy failure could produce political rumblings that had unknowable consequences. This is reflected most clearly in the emergence of the various underground groups with their own manifestos: the Syrtsov–Lominadze group; the Ryutin Platform; and the Eismont–Smirnov–Tolmachev group.[55]

The Ryutin Platform of 1932 depicted Stalin as someone who had been intent on personal dictatorship since 1924–5, 'selecting people personally loyal to him for posts on the Central Committee and on the secretariats of the gubkom and obkom committees'. Ryutin offered the following judgement: 'The entire top leadership of the Party, beginning with Stalin and ending with the secretaries of the oblast committees are, on the whole, fully aware that they are breaking with Leninism, that they are perpetrating violence against both the Party and non-party masses, they are killing the cause of socialism.'[56]

The acute tensions in centre–local relations in 1932–3 resulted in the removal of a number of prominent republican and regional party secretaries (see Chapters 2 and 3). In the case of Ukraine Stalin, having failed to find suitable replacements for Kosior and Chubar', instead decided to put in a counterweight in the person of P. P. Postyshev. Postyshev was a Kaganovich protégé, and from 1930 onwards worked in the Secretariat and Orgburo in Moscow. In 1933 he was sent to Ukraine to take over the leadership of the Kharkov party organisation and as second secretary of the Ukrainian party. In 1934 he was elected a candidate member of the Politburo CPSU.[57]

The shake-up in the leadership of the republican party organisation in 1932–3 was associated with moves to further limit its autonomy, regarding both economic and nationalities policy. The centre launched a major campaign against 'bourgeois nationalism' in Ukraine, Belorussia, Transcaucasus and Central Asia. The policy of concessions with regard to the non-Russian language and culture was increasingly curtailed. The influence of organisations representing the interests of the republics within the central governmental apparatus was diminished.

During collectivisation, 'dekulakisation' and the famine the Soviet state demonstrated its enormous power over the countryside. The regime's strong points were the main urban–industrial centres. The disturbances in Ivanovo in 1932 thus acquired great significance, demonstrating the potential vulnerability of the regime in its own heartland.[58] This provided the background to the new purge of the party ranks begun in 1933. It was also the background to the reintroduction of the internal passport system from 1933 onwards, which was aimed at 'cleansing' the main urban centres of unreliable elements. A crucial new dimension in centre–local relations was introduced, the distinction between 'regime' and 'non-regime' areas of the country.[59]

The Second Five-Year Plan

At the end of 1930 determined efforts were made to strengthen Sovnarkom and Gosplan, and to tie them more closely to the Politburo, with the aim of imposing greater authority and discipline in the field of economic planning. This was intended to check the power of the all-union commissariats and the strong regional lobbies who were seen as having contributed to the relentless raising of targets in 1929–30, which destroyed the coherence of the First Five-Year Plan. Kuibyshev was appointed head of Gosplan in November 1930, occupying simultaneously the post of vice chairman of Sovnarkom and STO. Molotov took over as chairman of Sovnarkom and STO in December 1930. Gosplan was further strengthened by the creation of the Central Administration of National Economic Records (TsUNKhU) in December 1931, as a commission of Gosplan in place of the Central Statistical Administration (TsSU). The task of TsUNKhU was to compile data on the state of the economy, and to compile assessments of the state of the harvest on the basis of which procurement targets could be set.

Sovnarkom USSR on 25 March 1932 set a timetable for the compilation of the Second Five-Year Plan. Gosplan USSR was to give its schema to Union commissariats and republican and local planning organisations by 1 April. Union commissariats were to present their preliminary control figures to Gosplan by 10 July, republican commissariats theirs by 20 July. By 20 August, Gosplan USSR should present a draft plan to the Sovnarkom USSR. Then, on the basis of control figures ratified by the government, Gosplan would issue directives and limits to the commissariats, republics and oblasts, who should each return their plans – broken down both by branch and territory – by the end of November. Finally the Second Five-Year Plan was to be presented to the Sovnarkom USSR by January 1933.[60] The basic instruction concerning the drawing up of the plan by Gosplan in 1932 assigned a key place to the regional location of the country's productive forces, and to defining the role of the regions within a Union-wide division of labour.[61]

The draft of the Second Five-Year Plan, compiled by Gosplan USSR at the beginning of 1934, comprised two volumes, the second of which dealt with the Plan of Development of the Regions. In his foreword to the volume Kuibyshev, chairman of Gosplan, claimed that extensive consultation with the republics and regions, their planning departments and research institutes had been undertaken in drafting the plan. Gosplan USSR organised seven conferences for examining the perspective development of various groups of regions, culminating in the All-Union Conference on the Location of the Productive Forces, convened with the participation of the Academy of Sciences USSR, the main people's commissariats and representatives of the republics, krais and oblasts.[62]

The reality was rather different. There was in fact little consultation between Gosplan USSR and the republican, krai and oblast authorities. Many of these regional authorities were so disrupted by the famine in 1932–3 and their authority so shaken, that their input was very small. The declining influence of Ukraine over economic policy was reflected in the fact that no draft Second Five-Year Plan for the republic was drawn up. A similar situation existed in other key regions, such as the Urals.[63]

Molotov and Kuibyshev submitted the plan to the XVII party congress in January–February 1934. The congress discussed and approved the plan's basic outlines. Consultation continued after the congress and the Second Five-Year Plan was finally approved in November 1934.

Molotov and Kuibyshev in their reports to the XVII party congress emphasised the new shift of investment eastwards, closer to raw materials' supplies. The reality was more complex. The pattern of investment during the Second Five-Year Plan reflected clearly a new set of priorities. The total planned investment in the USSR during the Second Five-Year Plan was 133.4 milliard rubles, of which 98.8 milliard rubles were assigned according to territory. The remaining partly 34.5 milliard rubles were accounted for by military–defence and internal security expenditure.

Of the figure assigned to territories 70.5 per cent went to the RSFSR and just 16.8 per cent to Ukraine, 1.8 per cent to Belorussia, 5.25 per cent to the Transcaucasus and 5.62 per cent to Central Asia.[64] Ukraine was accorded a much less privileged position than in the First Five-Year Plan. Capital investment in Ukraine was very close to the relative proportion of the Ukrainian population in the USSR–17.8 per cent (30 million out of 168 million). By contrast Moscow oblast with a population of 10 million (5.9 per cent of the total) received 10.7 milliard rubles (10.8 per cent of the total).

Heavy industry remained the main beneficiary of the plan, with 46.7 milliard rubles assigned to NKTyazhProm. Of this sum the RSFSR was assigned 27 milliard rubles (70 per cent) and Ukraine 8.2 milliard rubles (20.9 per cent). Three regions received particularly favourable treatment: the Urals region, Moscow oblast and Ukraine. Together the Urals oblast and West Siberia krai took 24.16 per cent of the total, significantly outmatching Ukraine. For agriculture (NKZem and NKSovkhoz) a total capital investment of 14.7 milliard rubles was proposed; the RSFSR was granted 9.8 milliard rubles (69 per cent) and Ukraine was to receive 2.1 milliard rubles (14.7 per cent) (Table 1.1).

There was a significant shift in industrial and agricultural investment away from the Ukraine. But this was something more complex than a shift to the East. The two major winners were the Moscow oblast and the Urals oblast. Other regions who did well were Leningrad oblast, the West Siberia

Table 1.1   Second Five-Year Plan: planned capital investment in the republics and regions

	Investment in NKTyazhProm (milliard rubles)	(%)	Investment in NKZem/ NKSovkhoz (milliard rubles)	(%)	All capital investment (milliard rubles)	(%)
USSR	46.76		14.75		133.4	
Assigned by territory	39.05		14.25		98.8	
RSFSR	27.21	69.7	9.8	68.9	69.69	70.5
Ukraine SSR	8.2	20.9	2.1	14.7	16.6	16.8
ZSFSR	2.29	5.8	0.6	4.5	5.1	5.2
Bel. SSR	0.1	0.2	0.4	3.0	1.7	1.7
C. Asia	1.2	3.2	1.2	8.7	5.5	5.6
Moscow oblast	3.5	9.0	0.56	3.9	10.76	10.9
Urals oblast	7.1	18.3	0.75	5.3	10.49	10.6
Leningrad oblast	1.9	4.9	0.30	2.1	5.62	5.7
West Siberia krai	2.3	5.9	0.96	6.7	5.33	5.4
North Caucasus	1.8	4.7	1.11	7.8	4.67	4.7
Far Eastern krai	0.35	2.5	1.0	2.6	4.07	4.1
Kazakhstan ASSR	1.5	4.0	0.89	6.2	4.0	4.1
Gorky krai	1.7	4.4	0.44	3.1	3.9	4.0
Ivanovo	1.2	3.2	0.2	1.9	3.1	3.1
Lower Volga	0.7	1.9	0.9	6.5	3.0	3.0
Central Volga	1.1	2.8	0.9	6.5	2.9	2.9
CBE	0.6	1.7	0.7	5.4	2.5	2.5
E. Siberia	0.5	1.3	0.3	2.1	2.2	2.2

Source: Proekt vtorogo pyatiletnego plana razitiviya narodnogo khozyaisva SSSR (1933–1937). Tom 2 Plan razvitiya raionov (Moscow, 1934), pp. 240–1.

krai, the North Caucasus krai, the Far Eastern krai, Kazakhstan ASSR and Gorky krai. The high investment in the North Caucasus, Kazakhstan ASSR and the Central and Lower Volga, was partly intended to undo the damage caused by the famine. In the case of the Lower Volga krai it was linked to the ambitious project for irrigating the Trans-Volga region. The high investment in the Far Eastern krai reflected defence considerations.

In the RSFSR in addition to the 13 regions noted above there were another seven regions whose total capital investment varied from a high of 1.7 milliard rubles to a low of 0.2 milliard rubles (in descending order of importance they were Bashkir ASSR, Western oblast, Northern krai, Tartar ASSR, the Crimean ASSR, the Karelian ASSR and Yakutia ASSR.) The total capital investment in these seven regions amounted to 6.4 milliard rubles.

The Ukraine was to remain the country's premier coal and metal base, although with the development of the UKK and other regions its contribution to the country's production as a proportion would decline. Out of 16.6 milliard rubles assigned to Ukraine, some 8.2 milliard rubles (49 per cent) was assigned to heavy industry (NKTyazhProm), representing 17.5 per cent of the investment for the whole of the USSR. The coal industry was to receive 1.3 milliard rubles (38.8 per cent), non-ferrous metallurgical industry 3.8 milliard rubles (42.9 per cent); machine-building 810 million rubles (11.1 per cent); chemical and coke chemicals 1.1 milliard rubles (26.7 per cent). Light industry received a mere 954 million rubles (11.4 per cent). Investment in NKZem and NKSovkhoz was 2.12 milliard rubles (14.2 per cent).

The figures of the plan indicate that, whereas Ukraine was to remain a major heavy industrial region, the dominant position which it had occupied during the First Five-Year Plan was past. Within Ukraine itself the dominance of the Donbass coalfield and the southern metallurgical works was underlined. At the same time investment in heavy industry in Ukraine was assigned to NKTyazhProm, largely by-passing the republican authorities.

Centre–local relations, 1934–6

The Soviet economy in the 1920s like the tsarist economy, was characterised by a diversity of economic forms (*mnogoukladnost*). Much of that diversity disappeared with the introduction of the First Five-Year Plan and the collectivisation of agriculture. This was reflected also in a fundamental change in the balance of institutional power. In 1921–8 economic policy was largely shaped by those agencies concerned with the operation of the market economy – fundamentally the integration of the economy through the mechanism of the market, price regulation and taxation – NKFin, NKTorg. After 1928 economic power moved to those commissariats concerned with planning and state ownership and regulation of the economy – principally Gosplan, Vesenkha – supported by the key agency of party–state control TsKK–NKRKI. In agriculture the creation of NKZem USSR, Kolkhoztsentr and Traktortsentr involved a move from the administration of the rural economy to its administrative reorganisation, subordination and regulation. The Committee for Agricultural Procurements (KomZag), headed by Kuibyshev, was established in February 1932, attached to Sovnarkom-STO. Its regional plenipotentiaries became an indispensable part of the mechanism of central control over agriculture.

Local party authorities were themselves accountable for how policy was implemented in their region. A system of control by party plenipotentiaries and investigating commissions was evolved. To deal with particular problems in agriculture and on rail transport the system of (*politotdely*) was instituted in 1933. At the Central Committee plenum of 22–28 November 1934, largely as a result of pressure from regional party secretaries, the *politotdely* in the MTS were abolished.[65] The *politotdely* in the sovkhozy remained in existence through the 1930s.

The establishment of the Commission of Party Control and the Commission of Soviet Control, replacing TsKK–NKRKI, in 1934 was intended to create a stronger system of control from the centre, which was not beholdien to local party authorities, and whose prime responsibility was to ensure that policy was implemented. The creation of the Central Committee's Department for Leading Party Organs (ORPO) by the XVII party congress further strengthened the oversight of republican and provincial party committees.

The purge of the party ranks, authorised in January 1933, was carried out by a special Central Purge Commission, operating with own purge commissions in the localities, not under control of the local leadership. About 18 per cent of party members were expelled. The creation of the all-union Procuracy in July 1933, the NKVD USSR in February 1934, and the People's Commissariat of Justice USSR in July 1936 were important steps in strengthening central control over judicial policy. These moves, J. Arch Getty argues, were partly motivated by the desire to control the arbitrary and excessive resort to repressive means by provincial and republican organs of justice.[66]

The role of the republican and regional party authorities was increasingly defined by the needs of the planned economy as coordinators, problem-solvers and trouble-shooters. They were required to carry out investigations and to enforce policy at the behest of the centre. In 1933 the Ukrainian party leaders were required by the centre to investigate defects in the coal and metallurgical industries, on the railways and in agriculture. In agriculture, where the control by the branch commissariats NKZem and NKSovkhoz were necessarily weaker, the republican and regional authorities retained some vestige of authority, with much of their work being organised around the autumn and spring sowing campaign, the harvest campaign and the grain procurement campaign.

Agricultural policy, 1933–6

Stalin, as is clear from his correspondence with Kaganovich in the years 1931–6, showed great personal interest in the figures for grain procurement from the republics and regions. Pleas for adjustments in procurement targets almost invariably went to him for arbitration. Stalin clearly considered himself an authority in this field. It may also be the case that it was easier for him to exercise authority over these targets, which involved the degree of pressure to be applied to the peasants and collective farms, than over targets for industrial production, which involved much more complex problems in reconciling the figures for different enterprises and institutions. For industrial targets it was safer to leave the technical details to Gosplan and Sovnarkom.

In September 1933, with the poor harvests in the Central Volga, Lower Volga, southern part of Urals and Western Kazakhstan, M. A. Chernov, the head of the Committee for Agricultural Procurements, proposed reductions in procurement targets. To oversee the procurement campaign M. A. Chernov was sent to the Lower Volga, A. I. Mikoyan was sent to the North Caucasus. Close scrutiny was also kept on the progress of the autumn sowing campaign.[67] In response to high procurement targets local authorities attempted to evade controls by organising their own grain, seed and fodder funds; in response to attempts to impose tight financial and credit controls local authorities resorted to creating money substitutes.

In 1934, despite indications of a good harvest, Stalin feared that complacency in the republics and regions would undermine the procurement campaign. In August Khataevich, of Dnepropetrovsk obkom, requested that the procurement target for his oblast be reduced by 6 million puds. The Ukrainian leadership scaled this down to 4 million puds, a target which the Politburo in Moscow then approved. From August to October the central authorities maintained relentless pressure on the republics and provinces to realise the plan targets. Stalin was kept informed at every stage and played a major role in guiding policy, displaying a clear understanding of the provinces, which were failing, and those who were doing well.[68]

In August 1934 leading party officials were dispatched to oversee the procurement campaign in the various regions. Stalin in his communications with Kaganovich stressed the need to maintain pressure on the regions to meet their targets. K. V. Ryndin, 'a petty demagogue', first secretary of Chelyabinsk obkom, he instructed, should be told that if he failed to meet his target he would be ousted.[69] In October Kaganovich wrote to Stalin about the difficulties of getting the procurement target fulfilled: 'On the scene in Siberia and the Chelyabinsk oblast I had to lash out, of course, as harshly as I could against the opportunists and blind leaders. The results don't seem to be too bad, Siberia will finish by the 1st [November] and Chelyabinsk by the latest by 25th'.[70]

In 1935, with a record harvest, Stalin insisted on pushing up the grain procurement targets as a reserve against future uncertainties. He demanded that pressure be maintained on the republics, especially Ukraine, and the regions, to meet these targets.[71]

In 1936 there was a very poor harvest caused by drought, but the centre's response was more temperate than in 1933 or 1934. In September and October Kaganovich dispatched a number of telegrams to Stalin, at his holiday retreat in Sochi, relaying the demands from the Azov–Black Sea krai, Stalingrad, Voronezh, Kursk, Sverdlovsk, Saratov, Gorky obkoms and Bashkir ASSR for their procurement targets to be reduced–with recommendations for somewhat lower cuts than those proposed. By 1936 the Soviet government had built up a substantial grain reserve to cope with such emergencies. In all cases Stalin agreed to a reduction in the procurement targets, although in some instances he proposed smaller reductions than those suggested by Kaganovich.[72]

In the field of industrial policy the regional administration was concerned with ensuring plan fulfilment. The Stakhanov movement, which developed from August 1935, reflects the roles that the regional administration performed within the economy. The Stakhanov movement in the coal industry, and the analogous movement on the railways, was pioneered in the Donbass, with the Donetsk obkom, headed by S. A. Sarkis, playing a leading role in developing this initiative. There may also have been some input in developing this movement from NKTyazhProm and NKPS. Only subsequently did the central party and state authorities take up and promote this idea on a national scale, extending it to all sectors of the economy and all regions of the country.[73]

The regional authorities were required to develop the Stakhanov movement in all branches of the economy. Not all regional leaders were enthusiastic about this campaign. Early in 1936 the Politburo instituted a major investigation, carried out by KPK, headed by N. I. Ezhov, into industry in the Sverdlovsk region. Ezhov in his report to the Politburo severely censured party secretary I. D. Kabakov for systematically neglecting the Stakhanovite movement.[74]

Conclusions

The main shift in centre–local relations occurred in the period 1929–34, and it occurred in two phases. The first phase, in 1929–30, was associated with the collectivisation of agriculture and the development of the First Five-Year Plan. In this period the autonomy of the republican', and to a lesser extent the regional, tier of administration was weakened by their loss of economic powers: through the transfer of powers over agriculture to NKZem USSR and NKSovkhoz USSR and the Committee for Agricultural Procurements (KomZag); through the takeover of republican and regional industries by Vesenkha USSR: through the weakening of the budgetary powers of the republics and regions. In the second phase, 1932–4, the weakening of the localities was directly related to the famine and its repercussions. This led to a fundamental change in the way in which the political system was structured with the development of a plethora of administrative agencies of central control (politotdely, purge commission, KPK–KSK, ORPO). After 1933 the attack on bourgeois nationalism also circumscribed the autonomy of the republican organisations.

These developments fundamentally changed relations between the centre, the republics and the province level of administration. They reflected a change from a system of horizontal integration based largely on the market to one based mainly on vertical integration, and branch administration of the planned economy. These changes taken together were associated with a dramatic strengthening of Stalin's personal power and the decline of the instruments of collective decision-making. In the process the role of the republican and provincial tiers of administration was considerably weakened. The political–administrative system, however, still required considerable delegation of power to lower-level officials in policy implementation. The elaborate system of central controls developed in this period imposed severe limits on local initiative but such controls could not, and did not, seek to extinguish that initiative

From 1934–36 a certain stability re-entered the system in terms of central and local relations. But it was a period marked by attempts by the centre to achieve more discipline amongst lower administrative tiers (through the checking and exchange of party cards) and the development of strategies to promote greater economic efficiency (Stakhanovism). It was a period characterised by growing alarm at the international situation, and by a growing trend towards economic autarchy and isolationism. This obsessive preoccupation with control was bound to create confusion in responsibility and to undermine initiative. The terror in 1936–8 again fundamentally restructured centre–local relations.

Notes

1. *Kommunisticheskaya partiya Sovetskogo Soyuza v rezolyutsiyakh i resheniyakh s"ezdov, konferentsii i plenumov TsK* (Moscow, 1976), Vol. X, p. 234.
2. V. L. Lenin, *Polnoe sobranie sochinenii* (Moscow, 1965), Vol. 53, pp. 189–90.
3. James E. Mace, *Communism and the Dilemmas of National Liberation: National Communism in Soviet Ukraine, 1918–1933* (Cambridge, Mass., 1983).
4. Terry Martin, 'Nationalities Policy and the Nature of the Soviet Bureaucracy', *Cahiers du Monde russe*, 40(1–2), January–June 1999, pp. 113–24. Martin argues that the development of Soviet nationalities policy in the 1920s and specifically the policy of Ukrainisation can be correctly understood only by relating the policy to specific institutions. He distinguishes between 'soft-line' institutions, which dealt directly with the public, whose task was to present official policy in the most attractive light, to win popular consent and foster participation within official institutions and the 'hard line' institutions which were concerned with control, surveillance and where necessary repression, intimidation and terror.
5. L. M. Kaganovich, *Dva goda ot IX do X s"ezda KP(b)U* (Moscow, Kharkov, 1927).
6. Yu. Larin, 'Ob izvrashcheniyakh pri proveidenii natsional'noi politiki', *Bol'shevik*, No. 23–24, 1926, pp. 50–8; No. 1, 1927, pp. 59–69.
7. V. Vaganyan, *O natsional'noi kulture* (Moscow, 1927), pp. 120–7, 175.
8. Mace, *Communism*, p. 107.
9. J. V. Stalin, *Works* (Moscow, 1955), Vol. 12, p. 382.
10. I. Deutscher, *Stalin: A Political Biography* (Penguin edn, 1966), Chapter 7. R. V. Daniels, 'The Secretariat and the Local Organisations of the Russian Communist Party, 1921–23', *American Slavic and East European Review*, 3 (1957), p. 36; T. H. Rigby, 'Early Provincial Cliques and the Rise of Stalin', *Soviet Studies*, I, 1981, pp. 3–28.
11. James R. Harris, *The Great Urals: Regionalism and the Evolution of the Soviet System* (Ithaca, London, 1999), pp. 43–4.
12. James Hughes, 'Patrimonialism and the Stalinist System: The Case of S. I. Syrtsov', *Europe–Asia Studies*, 48(4), 1996, pp. 551–68.

13. On the development of the 'Urals–Siberian' method of grain collection from 1928 onwards, involving meetings of the village elders (the skhod) to levy a higher proportion of the burden on the richer households, scholars have expressed conflicting views. Yuzuru Tanuichi argues that the policy emanated from the centre, while James Hughes has argued that the central authorities took up proposals which originated in West Siberia, Yuzuru Taniuchi, 'Decision-making on the Urals–Siberian Method', in Julian Cooper, Mauren Perrie and E. A. Rees (eds), *Soviet History 1917–53* (London, 1995); James Hughes, *Stalinism in a Russian Province* (London, 1996).

14. R. W. Davies, *The Socialist Offensive: The Collectivisation of Soviet Agriculture, 1929–1930* (London, 1980) on Eikhe, pp. 158, 217, 234, 236, 249, 408; on Vareikis, pp. 158, 171, 185, 194; on Sheboldaev, pp. 152n., 154, 155, 161, 162–3, 164, 185, 190n., 191, 240); Robert Conquest, *The Harvest of Sorrow* (London, 1986), pp. 120, 121, 147, 161, 261, 275.

15. Davies, *The Socialist Offensive*, pp. 319–23.

16. G. T. Grin'ko, *The Five-Year Plan of the Soviet Union: A Political Interpretation* (London, 1930), pp. 328–9.

17. G. M. Krzhizhanovskii (ed.), *Voprosy ekonomicheskogo raionirovaniya SSSR: Sbornik materialov i statei* (Moscow, 1957).

18. Grin'ko, *The Five-Year Plan*, pp. 313–14.

19. Grin'ko, *The Five-Year Plan*, p. 321.

20. Grin'ko, *The Five-Year Plan*, p. 314.

21. Grin'ko, *The Five-Year Plan*, p. 315.

22. Grin'ko, *The Five-Year Plan*, p. 316.

23. Grin'ko, *The Five-Year Plan*, p. 326.

24. R. W. Davies, 'The Decentralization of Industry: Some Notes on the Background', *Soviet Studies*, IX(4), 1958, pp. 353–67.

25. H. Schwartz, *Russia's Soviet Economy*, 2nd edn (New York, 1954), pp. 217–19, 222–4, 645–8.

26. *Works*, Vol. 12, pp. 334–5.

27. Harris, *The Great Urals*, esp. Chapter 2.

28. R. W. Davies, *The Soviet Economy in Turmoil, 1929–1930* (London, 1989), pp. 206–8; R. W. Davies, 'A Note on Defence Aspects of the Ural–Kuznetsk Combine', *Soviet Studies*, XXVI, 1974, pp. 255–80.

29. *XVII s"ezd Vsesoyuznoi Kommunisticheskoi Party (b), 26 yanvarya–10 fevralya 1934g. Stenograficheskii otchet* (Moscow, 1934), p. 69.

30. TsGAOO Ukrainy, 1/5/138 8. V. I. Kuz'min, *V bor'be za sotsialisticheskuyu rekonstruktsiyu 1926–1937. Ekonomicheskaya politika Sovetskogo gosudarstva* (Moscow, 1976), p. 140.

31. R. W. Davies, *The Development of the Soviet Budgetary System* (Cambridge, 1958), pp. 304–13.

32. TsGAOO Ukrainy, 1/16/8 34.

33. R. W. Davies, *Crisis and Progress in the Soviet Economy, 1931–1933* (London, 1996), pp. 185n.: Telegrams sent at the end of March 1933 by L. I. Lavren'tev and F. P. Gryadinskii to Postyshev, Kuibyshev and Chernov, and from R. I. Eikhe and Gryadinskii, complained of the dire state of food supplies to Kuznetstroi in West Siberia; telegram from F. I. Goloshchekin about food situation in Karaganda, telegrams from V. P. Shubrikov about the problems of reducing rations in Central Volga region in January–March 1933, pp. 276–7, 370; telegram from I. M. Vareikis, secretary of CBE, to Kaganovich on reducing ration lists, August 1932, p. 235.

34. Davies, *Crisis and Progress*, p. 141 (Sheboldaev), 258 (Khataevich).
35. O. V. Khlevnyuk (*et al.*) (eds), *Stalin i Kaganovich. Perepiska. 1931–1936gg.* (Moscow, 2001), p. 168 (Hereafter *SKP*).
36. *Bol'shevik*, No. 1–2, 1933, p. 23.
37. *SKP*, p. 210. RGASPI, 54/1/99, 45–7.
38. *Pravda*, 9 July, 1932; H. Kostiuk, *Stalinist Rule in the Ukraine* (London, 1960), p. 19.
39. *SKP*, p. 273. RGASPI, 54/1/99, 144–51.
40. RGASPI, 54/1/99, 167.
41. RGASPI, 54/1/99, 121–3.
42. *SKP*, p. 257.
43. Nobuo Shimotomai, 'A Note on the Kuban Affair (1932–1933): The Crisis of Kolkhoz Agriculture in the North Caucasus', *Acta Slavica Iaponica*, I, 1983, p. 46.
44. Conquest, *The Harvest of Sorrow*, p. 276.
45. R. Medvedev, *Let History Judge* (London, 1976), p. 93.
46. *XVII s"ezd*, p. 148.
47. *Pravda*, 30 November 1932.
48. *Pravda*, 24 November 1963.
49. *Materialy ob"edinennogo plenuma TsK i TsKK VKP (b)* (Moscow, 1933), p. 144.
50. L. M. Kaganovich, 'Tseli i zadachi politicheskikh otdelov MTS i sovkhozov', *Bol'shevik*, 1–2, 31 January 1933, pp. 12–37, and in *Partiinoe stroitel'stvo*, 3–4, 1933, pp. 1–22.
51. *KPSS v rezolutsiyakh*, Vol. 6, 1985, pp. 21–31.
52. *Partiinoe stroitel'stvo*, 12, 1934, pp. 1–3.
53. See E. A. Rees and D. H. Watson, 'Politburo and Sovnarkom', in E. A. Rees (ed.), *Decision-making in the Stalinist Command Economy, 1932–37* (London, 1997), pp. 12–4; E. A. Rees, 'Stalin, the Politburo and Rail Transport Policy', in Julian Cooper, Maureen Perrie and E. A. Rees (eds), *Soviet History 1917–53* (London, 1995), pp. 104–11.
54. *Istoricheskii Arkhiv*, 1994, No. 6, pp. 119–51. On 1 January 1934 Stalin met Sheboldaev, Ptukha and Evdokimov; on 4 July he met Khataevich, Evdokimov, Gryadinskii, Sheboldaev, Ivanov and Pramnek; on 4 July he met Kabakov, Putkha, Lavrent'ev, Mirzoyan; on 6 July he met Goloded, Ryndin, Razumov, Veger; on 16 July he met the Ukrainians: Kosior, Postyshev, Lyubchenko, Khataevich, Veger and Demchenko, evidently about the grain procurement targets; on 25 July he met Goloded and Gikalo of Belorussia. On 28 November he again met the Ukrainian leaders: Kosior, Postyshev, Petrovskii, Khataevich, Veger, Demchenko, Lyubchenko, Sarkisov and Chernyavskii; on 29 November he met Eikhe, Gryadinskii, Ptukha, Razumov, Evdokimov, Isaev and Mirzoyan; on 4 December he met Razumov, Eikhe, Gryadinskii, Mirzoyan and Shubrikov.
55. R. W. Davies, 'The Syrtsov–Lominadze Affair', *Soviet Studies*, XXXIII, 1981, pp. 29–50. On the Ryutin platform see R. W. Davies, *Soviet History in the Gorbachev Revolution* (Basingstoke, London, 1989), pp. 83–5. For the text of the Ryutin platform, see *Izvestiya TsK*, No. 6, 1989, Nos 3 and 8–12.
56. J. Arch Getty and O. V. Naumov, *The Road to Terror: Stalin and the Self-Destruction of the Bolsheviks, 1932–1939* (New Haven, London, 1999), pp. 55, 57.
57. *Bol'shaya Sovetskaya Entsiklopediya*, Vol. 20, p. 423.
58. Jeffrey J. Rossman, 'The Teikovo Cotton Workers Strike of April 1932: Class, Gender and Identity Politics in Stalin's Russia', *The Russian Review*, 56, January 1997, pp. 44–69.

59. Gijs Kessler, 'The Peasant and the Town: Rural–Urban Migration in the Soviet Union, 1929–40' (unpublished PhD thesis, European University Institute, Florence, 2001), esp. Chapter 5.
60. RGAE 700/1/839/82.
61. *Osnovnye ukazaniya k sostavleniyu Vtorogo Pyatiletnego Plana narodnogo khozyaistva SSSR (1933–1937)* (Moscow, 1932).
62. *Proekt Vtorogo Pyatiletnego Plana Razvitiya Narodnogo Khozyaistva SSSR (1933–37gg).* *Tom 2 Plan Razvitiya Raionov* (Moscow, 1934), p. 5.
63. Harris, *The Great Urals*, p. 150.
64. *Proekt Vtorogo Pyatiletnego Plana Razitiviya Narodnogo Khozyaisva SSSR (1933–1937).* *Tom 2 Plan razvitiya Raionov*, pp. 240–1.
65. *KPSS v rezolyutsiyakh*, Vol. 5, pp. 201–2.
66. Getty and Naumov, *The Road to Terror*, pp. 55, 57.
67. *SKP*, pp. 353, 360.
68. *Ibid.*, p. 421.
69. *Ibid.*, pp. 479–80.
70. *Ibid*, p 514.
71. *Ibid.*, pp. 549.
72. *Ibid.*, pp. 673–5, 687–8, 696–70.
73. R. W. Davies and O. Khlevnyuk, 'Stakhanovism, the Politburo and the Soviet Economy' (unpublished paper, delivered at the conference on Stalin's Politburo, 1928–53, at the European University Institute, Florence, 2000), pp. 14–9.
74. *Ibid.*, p. 28; Harris, *The Great Urals*, pp. 160–2, 167.

2
The First Generation of Stalinist 'Party Generals'

Oleg Khlevnyuk

Leadership Structure 1920s–1932 – republican and regional party secretaries

Stalin, addressing the Central Committee plenum in February–March 1937, described the top 3,000–4,000 leaders of the country as 'the general staff of the party (*generalitetom partii*)'.[1] The apex of this hierarchy of 'generals' comprised the secretaries of the republic, oblast and krai party organisations. On 1 January 1934 in the USSR there were eight Central Committees of national communist parties, 12 krai committees (kraikoms) and 15 oblast committees (obkoms), which were subordinated directly to the Central Committee of the CPSU. In addition there were 14 obkoms included in the republics and subordinated to the Central Committees of the national communist parties, and 29 obkoms included in the krais and subordinated to the kraikoms of the CPSU. This structure underwent significant changes in the following years. On 1 December 1938 there were 10 Central Committees of the national communist parties (with 44 republican obkoms subordinated to them), 6 kraikoms (with 13 obkoms subordinated to them) and 47 obkoms which were subordinated directly to the Central Committee of the CPSU.[2] The leadership of these party committees, above all the secretaries of the national communist parties, the kraikoms and obkoms, which were subordinated to the all-union Central Committee, will be the subject of this study.

These republican and regional party secretaries played an important role in the Soviet political system. They were much closer to local problems and, possessing significant powers, they were able quite quickly to resolve many urgent questions, to intervene as arbiters in interdepartmental disputes at lower level and to act as intermediaries in resolving the many issues which arose between central departments and local administrations and enterprises. Having direct access to the country's highest leadership they acted as conduits of regional interest. All this made the institution of the 'party generals' a key link in the Soviet party–state machine, ensuring the regime's vital capacity and activity.

The role and influence of the regional party secretaries must be studied on at least two, albeit interconnected, levels, first, from the point of view of the development of the *regions and their internal problems*, and secondly, on the level of *'centre–local'* relations. In the present work we will concentrate mainly on the second aspect of the question. We shall focus primarily on the principles on which centre–local relations were constructed in the Stalinist political system, the degree of independence enjoyed by the local leadership and their ability to influence the decisions that were taken in Moscow.

The regional party leaders attained the peak of their influence in the 1920s. Emerging victorious from the civil war the Bolsheviks were quick to enjoy the fruits of victory. The monopoly of political power, with the out-lawing of all other political parties, became a cornerstone of the new regime. For republican and regional leaders, most of whom were old Bolsheviks and professional revolutionaries, this meant not only the elimination of all major organised opposition in the country, it meant also a certain independence from the centre. The regional party leaders, who constituted the skeleton of the Central Committee and who to a large degree determined the composition of the delegations that were sent to the party congresses, acquired significant political weight. Following Lenin's death, the Moscow leaders, contending for power among themselves, strove to secure the support of the party 'generals', and in the process the centre's control over the regions was weakened.

The majority of the party's republican and regional secretaries backed Stalin and his Politburo allies in the struggle with the oppositions of the 1920s. They preferred Stalin, in the main not because of his control over appointments nor because they saw in him a cruel, powerful 'master'. In this power struggle Stalin had to tread carefully. As Stephen Cohen has rightly noted Stalin attained victory 'and became first among equals within the leadership not as an irresponsible author of "revolution from above" but under the guise of a careful statesman, who charted a "sober and quiet" course between the timidity of the right and the extremism of the left. For all his warfare rhetoric, he won in his familiar role of the twenties as the man of the golden middle, who had impressed fellow administrators with his pragmatic efficiency, "calm tone, his quiet voice."'[3]

To a significant degree it was pressure from the regional leadership that produced the sharp upward revision in the targets of the First Five-Year Plan.[4] This was a kind of reward dispensed by the Stalinist group in return for the political support that they had received in the struggle with the 'Right'. At the end of the 1920s the republican and regional party secretaries displayed a degree of independence of action, within the confines of official policy, in the territories under their control.

The Stalinist 'revolution from above' brought with it the destruction of the comparatively 'democratic' traditions of intra-party relations and the assertion of the autocratic power of the *vozhd'*. It also resulted in a new, more intense clash of interests between the centre and the regional leadership. This was graphically highlighted by the conflict between Stalin and the party secretaries at the beginning of 1930 in connection with the 'correction' of the course on full collectivisation. In his well-known letter 'Dizzy with Success' Stalin sought to shift the blame for the repression of the peasantry, and the consequent upsurge of peasant protests, onto the shoulders of local party workers. This evoked dissatisfaction among the regional leaders, who in letters to the Central Committee pointed out that they had acted on the basis of directives issued by the centre itself.[5]

Despite these accusation of 'excesses' regional leaders suffered no serious consequences. Only a few republican and regional leaders were transferred. Thus the 'example' which was made with the sacking in April 1930 of K. Ya. Bauman, secretary of the Moscow party committee and a candidate member of the Politburo, was soon followed by his appointment as first secretary of the Central Committee's Central Asia Bureau. Stalin, in discussing with Molotov Bauman's fate, stressed that Bauman had only displayed 'a conciliatory attitude' to 'leftist' distortions but was not himself allied to the deviationists.[6]

However, the sharply deteriorating situation in the country could not but further exacerbate relations between Moscow and the regional leaders. It was this which led S. I. Syrtsov, chairman of Sovnarkom RSFSR, speaking in October 1930 to a narrow circle of his fellows, to assert that a number of party secretaries (including A. A. Andreev, secretary of the North Caucasus kraikom, N. N. Kolotilov, secretary of the Ivanovo obkom, and R. I. Eikhe, secretary of the West Siberia kraikom) in a decisive moment 'might turn on Stalin'.[7] Syrtsov probably exaggerated the degree of opposition among the secretaries, but this statement reflected a definite mood among the regional party leaders.

The position of the secretaries was weakened by the sharp factional struggles which in the late 1920s and early 1930s infected many party organisations. A number of republican and regional party secretaries were challenged by groups of old party members who were dissatisfied with their position and who themselves nurtured leadership aspirations. N. M. Shvernik, first secretary of Urals obkom, was twice challenged by a dissident faction that was dissatisfied with his ability to defend the interests of the Urals metallurgical industry against the rival claims of Ukraine. In February 1928 the Central Committee backed Shvernik and removed a number of his critics from office. However, in January 1929, the Politburo acceded to the demands of the obkom, removed Shvernik, and appointed in his place as first secretary his arch-critic on the obkom I. D. Kabakov.[8] Shvernik was assigned to work in the party Secretariat and in 1930 became chairman of VTsSPS.

In Leningrad, at the end of 1929, a group of local officials demanded the removal of S. M. Kirov, accusing him of having cooperated with the liberal press in the pre-revolutionary period. In Moscow in 1929 a group struggle was waged between K. Ya. Bauman, first secretary of the Moscow party committee, and V. I. Polonskii, the committee's secretary. In West Siberia in the summer of 1930 a faction on the kraikom buro demanded that Moscow remove R. I. Eikhe, the kraikom's first secretary. The sharpest and most protracted dispute was that in Transcaucasus, where from 1928 to 1932 a struggle was waged both between various leading groups in the Transcaucasian republics (especially in Azerbaidzhan) and between the leadership of the Transcaucasus kraikom and the republican authorities. Similar examples could be cited.

In time, the conflicting sides in these disputes appealed to Moscow for support. Stalin in the first half of the 1930s as a rule adopted the line of strengthening of the principle of one-man management (*edinonachaliye*), lending his support to the existing regional leaders against their subordinates. The one notable exception was the conflict in Moscow, which remained in suspension for a certain time since Stalin would not allow Bauman to sack Polonskii. Stalin wrote to Molotov on 9 September 1929: 'Bauman must be disciplined sternly for trying to drag the organisation into a struggle, not over political views, but "over individuals." That is precisely why Polonskii should not be shifted (for the time being at least).'[9] In most cases the tendency was to consolidate the first secretary's power. Thus, after the question of Kirov was examined at a joint session of the Politburo and the Presidium of the Central Control Commission on 11 December 1929 Kirov's opponents were ousted from leading posts in Leningrad.[10]

The clash in Western Siberia was resolved with Eikhe's complete victory. Stalin resolutely supported Eikhe, and he accused his opponents of an 'attempt to deceive the Central Committee and create "their" own artel kraikom'.[11] The resolution of the long-running conflict among the Transcaucasian leadership was impeded by deep-rooted personal enmities. It was further compounded by the interventions in these conflicts by a number of Moscow leaders (most notably G. K. Ordzhonikidze) who had their own clients in the Transcaucasus. Consequently Stalin over several years sought to promote in the Transcaucasus a single, strong leader who could impose order. In the end he found his man in L. P. Beria. In order to clear the way for him Stalin step by step removed a large group of old respected Bolsheviks from leading posts in the Transcaucasus and transferred them to other regions of the USSR. L. I. Lavren'tev (Kartvelishvili) was removed as first secretary of the kraikom in October 1931, to be replaced by M. D. Orakhelashvili, who was then replaced by Beria in 1932.[12]

In East Siberia F. G. Leonov, the kraikom's first secretary, was at loggerheads with N. N. Zimin, the chairman of the krai ispolkom. In July 1932 the local newspaper published a speech by Zimin which sharply criticised the handling of grain procurement in 1931. On Leonov's orders these statements became a pretext for an attack on Zimin. In August 1932, while Zimin was on leave, the kraikom plenum was convened. The plenum censured Zimin, who was openly called a 'political bankrupt', and accused him of destroying the work of the krai's soviet apparatus. Not all krai workers were in agreement with these criticisms. The leaders of the krai Control Commission (krai KK) sent a detailed letter to Moscow on the dispute, and called the censuring of Zimin 'harmful' for the party organisation. One of Zimin's deputies wrote to Kaganovich and Molotov about the disorganisation of the krai ispolkom and requested that measures be taken to rectify the situation.[13] Early in September this letter was sent to the Central Committee. On 5 October Leonov and Zimin spent 3 hours in Stalin's office together with Molotov, Kaganovich, Postyshev, Gamarnik and Shkiryatov (a member of the Central Control Commission). On 9 October the Politburo by consultation (*oprosom*) drafted its decision. This released Zimin from his post, 'at his own request', and required Leonov in a fortnight's time to propose a new candidate as chairman of the krai ispolkom.[14] On 13 October the Politburo instructed Leonov to also replace the kraikom's second secretary, with whom, evidently, Leonov's relations were strained.[15] On 27 November Zimin was confirmed as the second secretary of the North Caucasus party kraikom.[16] Thus in this conflict, the Moscow leaders again supported the first secretary. Although Stalin backed Leonov, it seems that he remained dissatisfied with him and after a year demanded his removal (we will say more about this in detail later).

Moscow's preference for a policy of cadres' stability and the strengthening of *edinonachaliye* in the regions stemmed from various considerations. On the one hand there continued to operate the party tradition, by which honoured members of the party, if they did not participate in oppositions and 'deviations' had a right to a position within the ranks of the *nomenklatura*. On the other hand the intensifying crisis in the country demanded the consolidation of the administrative apparatus and the establishment of firm power in the regions. Moreover, Stalin by supporting the first secretaries, drew them still closer to himself.

As a result, despite certain transfers, the corpus of regional leaders at the beginning of the 1930s remained comparatively stable. It comprised mainly representatives of the old party guard. This is shown in the data concerning the length of party service (*stazh*) of 109 secretaries of obkoms, kraikoms and national communist parties (the information relates to 24 obkoms, kraikoms and national communist parties out of the 30 then existing) on 1 January 1933 (Table 2.1).

The intensifying conflicts in the republican and regional party hierarchies indicate that the old party guard was in crisis, which made easier the consolidation of Stalin's personal power. Caught between two fires, the regional leadership strove to surround themselves with their own people and expelled those who showed any tendency towards independent thinking

Table 2.1 Length of party membership (*stazh*) of party secretaries, January 1933

Joined the party	(%)
Before 1917	39.5
Between 1917 and 1920	55.0
Between 1921 and 1926	5.5

Source: RGASPI, 17/7/208   120.

from the posts in their territories. In this sense the position of the secretaries was even somewhat strengthened. However, despite having a comparatively safe 'tail' (*khvost*), the secretaries faced mounting pressure from the centre, which proved virtually impossible to resist. One of the decisive stages in Moscow's relations with the regional leadership was the shock of 1932–1933.

Intensification of contradictions between the centre and the regions in the period of crisis, 1932–3

Forced industrialisation and the coercive enforcement of agricultural collectivisation, including mass arrests, shootings and the deportation of the wealthier part of the peasantry, produced a deep socio–economic crisis, which came to a climax between the First and Second Five-Year Plans. The crisis culminated in the bitter struggles over the implementation of grain requisitioning and the ensuing mass famine of 1932–3.

Stalin and his circle sought to surmount the crisis by continuing the former policy of grain requisitioning, seizing as much grain as possible as part of the procurement process. In the face of sharp reductions of harvest yields in 1932, and growing peasant resistance, Moscow demanded unconditional fulfilment of the procurement plans. Regional leaders, who had actively carried through the policy of collectivisation and 'dekulakisation' felt sharply the growing critical situation in the localities. Confronted with the first signs of famine, the ruin of the productive capacity of the countryside, the complete unwillingness of the peasants to work for a meaningless labour-day payment (*trudoden'*), the regions' leaders attempted to introduce more flexible policies. While supporting the official line in words, in practice they attempted to reduce the procurement plans and strove to safeguard the production and consumption needs of the collective farms and their workers by creating seed funds, funding payment for *trudoden'* and other devices. In reality the regional leaders began to subvert or sabotage the centre's demands. Stalin and his circle saw this as a threat to state grain procurement and resolutely tried to halt all kinds of 'moderate' initiatives by the provincial authorities.

In this period Moscow's policy towards the regional leader combined two interconnected strands: the strengthening of central control and wide-ranging cadre transfers among the party generals. One of the first which fell under this blow was the leadership of Ukraine. Afflicted already in 1931 with the first signs of famine, the Ukrainian leaders attempted to correct the grain procurement plan. This drew Stalin's strong disapproval. On 2 July 1932 Stalin wrote to Kaganovich and Molotov, railing against S. V. Kosior, first secretary of the Ukrainian Communist Party, and V. Ya. Chubar', chairman of Sovnarkom Ukraine:

> Give the most serious attention to Ukraine. Chubar's corruptness and opportunistic essence and Kosior's rotten diplomacy (with regard to the CC of CPSU) and his criminally frivolous attitude towards his job will eventually ruin Ukraine. These comrades are not up to the challenge of leading the Ukraine today.[17]

He proposed that both Chubar' and Kosior be sacked. On 1 August 1932, after a series of new requests from the Ukrainian leadership for food aid,[18] Stalin again wrote to Kaganovich:

> Things in Ukraine have hit rock bottom. Things are bad with regard to the party. There is talk that in two regions of Ukraine (I think it is the Kiev and Dnepropetrovsk regions) about 50 raikoms have spoken out against the grain procurement plan, deeming it unrealistic. In other raikoms, they assert, things are no better. What does this look like? This is not a party, but a parliament, a caricature of a parliament. Instead of leading the raions, Kosior keeps manoeuvring between the directives of the CC CPSU and the demands of the raikoms – and now he has manoeuvred himself into a total mess . . . Things are bad with the soviet line. Chubar' is no leader. Things are bad with the GPU . . . Unless we begin to straighten out the situation in Ukraine, we may well lose Ukraine.[19]

The Ukrainian Communist Party, Stalin declared, contained 'many rotten elements'. He proposed to replace Kosior as Ukrainian General secretary with Kaganovich, to replace Chubar' with somebody from the central economic apparatus, and also to appoint V. A. Balitskii, deputy head of OGPU USSR, as head of the Ukrainian OGPU while retaining his all-union post. In the end Stalin was obliged to leave Kosior and Chubar' in their posts because of the difficulty of finding replacements.

Stalin's proposals, which were known to only a narrow circle of the highest leaders, provided the first hint of the coming assault on local elites. On 1 September 1932, on the report of P. P. Postyshev, the Secretary of the Central Committee, the Politburo considered a directive issued by the Lower

Volga kraikom regarding the implementation of the grain procurement plan and which had proposed the creation of kolkhoz seed and consumption funds. The Politburo issued a harsh resolution: to summon urgently to Moscow V. V. Ptukha, the first secretary of the Lower Volga kraikom, and demand that he explain himself before a commission comprising of Stalin, Postyshev and Kuibyshev.[20] On 4 September Ptukha spent half an hour alone with Stalin.[21] On 5 September in Stalin's office, Ptukha and members of the commission Postyshev and Kuibyshev had a further meeting.[22] As a result a resolution was drafted which the Politburo's members confirmed by consultation, which ruled the kraikom's directive to have been 'politically mistaken'. The Lower Volga kraikom was instructed that 'the first responsibility of the krai party organisation is the total fulfilment of the grain procurement plan' and not the creation of local funds. The Politburo, moreover, instructed all krai, oblast committees and Central Committees of national communist parties 'that copies of all their resolutions and directives, concerning grain procurement, are to be sent immediately after adoption to the CC and to the Committee for Agricultural Procurements (KomZag)'.[23] This marked a further strengthening of centralisation.

On 1 October 1932 the Politburo appointed to the post of second secretary of the Ukrainian Communist Party the energetic and harsh secretary of the Central Volga kraikom M. M. Khataevich (in his place V. P. Shubrikov was appointed as first secretary of the Central Volga kraikom).[24] On 9 October, on the proposal of the Ukrainian Central Committee, the new first secretaries for Dnepropetrovsk and Vinnitsa obkoms, V. A. Stroganov and V. I. Chernyavskii, were confirmed.[25]

As the crisis deepened the Moscow leadership tightened its grip on the regions with the dispatch of special emissaries with extraordinary powers to enforce grain procurement policy. On 22 October 1932 the Politburo commanded two groups of Moscow leaders: one, headed by Molotov, to Ukraine, another, headed by Kaganovich, to the North Caucasus.[26] These groups carried out mass seizure of grain and enforced repression against the peasants and against local party and soviet workers who were accused of sabotage and degeneration.

Exasperated by the failure of the Ukrainian authorities to meet their grain delivery quotas, despite having had the targets reduced three times, the Politburo on 24 January 1933 adopted a special resolution: 'Concerning the strengthening of the party organisations of CC CPUk.' The resolution declared: 'The CC CPSU considers it established that the party organisation of Ukraine is not coping with the party tasks laid on it in organising grain procurement and fulfilling the plan of grain purchasing, despite the three reductions of the plan.' To strengthen the leadership of the republic Postyshev, secretary of the all-union Central Committee and one of Stalin's closest colleagues, was appointed as second secretary of the Ukrainian Communist Party (in place of Khataevich) and simultaneously he became secretary of the capital (then Kharkov) obkom. Stroganov, recently appointed secretary of Dnepropetrovsk obkom, was removed and replaced by Khataevich. At the same time the Politburo replaced the secretary of Odessa obkom.[27]

On the eve of the crisis of 1932–3 the leaders of various other regional and republican organisations were transferred. On 9 October 1932 the Politburo acceded to M. D. Orakhelashvilli's request to be released from his post as first secretary of the Transcaucasus kraikom and appointed Beria in his place.[28] The long-running conflict in Transcaucasus was thus resolved. The party organisation of Kazakhstan was heavily purged. On 21 January 1933 F. I. Goloshchekin, the first secretary, was removed and replaced by secretary of the Urals obkom L. I. Mirzoyan.[29] On 7 March S. A. Bergavinov, first secretary of the Far Eastern kraikom, was released 'for poor work'.[30] On 18 October 1933 F. G. Leonov, first secretary of the East Siberia kraikom, lost his post for 'not coping with his work'.[31] On 30 September in a letter to Kaganovich, Stalin wrote:

> With Eastern Siberia things are bad. Leonov is weak. It is evident that the practical and organisational matters were transferred not long ago to Kozlov [second secretary of the kraikom] while he himself engages in 'high theory'. They are ruining things. It is necessary decisively to pre-pare replacement (replacement and not simple removal) of the present leadership [*verkhushka*].[32]

The leaders of a number of oblast organisations, included in the composition of krais or republics, also lost their posts.

It was the usual practice in this period for the Politburo to issue rebukes to secretaries of regional party organisations, to summon them to Moscow to give account and to dispatch innumerable commissions to the localities to carry out investigations. Streams of telegrams flowed from the centre to the regions issuing orders, and streams of telegrams flowed from the localities to the centre with requests.

One of the methods by which the Stalinist leadership sought to surmount the crisis of 1932–3 was through the organisation of the political depart-ments (*politotdely*) in the Machine-Tractor Stations (MTS) and sovkhozy. They represented extraordinary organs of administration in the countryside and were given extensive powers. The all-union Central Committee directly appointed and removed the heads of the *politotdely*. This created a situ-ation of dual power in the localities. The regional party secretaries had a 'fifth column' of Moscow appointees established in their rear, over which they had limited powers. A typical conflict which arose in the summer of 1933 is illustrated by the row between M. M. Khataevich, secretary of Dnepropetrovsk obkom, and Kisis, head of the Political Sector of the MTS of the oblast rural administration. Kisis accused the obkom leadership of ignoring the Political

Sector and its directives. The question was examined by the obkom buro, where Khataevich declared, as a Central Control Commission plenipotentiary reported to Moscow:

> The *politotdely* are subordinate to the obkoms; there cannot be two obkoms and I will not allow it. The non-fulfilment of the obkom's decisions by the Political Sector cannot be tolerated. From the Political Sector there arises the stench of counterposing the *politotdely* against the obkom, and in particular against me, Khataevich . . . I cannot allow this situation to continue.[33]

The question of the relations between Khataevich and Kisis was examined in Moscow, where they attempted to find a compromise, proposing that each make concessions and to carry on joint work.[34]

Friction between the politotdel and raikom leaders was widespread. The journal *Bol'shevik* in its lead article reported of the interrelationship between the local leaders and the heads of the *politotdely* of the MTS: 'Some opportunistic elements and people, reflecting localist moods, were very dissatisfied with the creation of the *politotdely*.'[35]

In the main, during the crisis of 1932–3 relations between the central and regional powers became increasingly strained. The regional leaders in full measure felt the precariousness of their position. Stalin, as in 1930, again sought to unload responsibility for the crisis onto the shoulders of the local officials.

Centre and local leaders in the period of comparative stability, 1934–6

As the crisis was surmounted and a certain stabilisation in the social–economic situation was achieved relations between Moscow and the republican and regional party secretaries underwent certain changes. In the historical literature of this period there exists the suggestion, based on memoir accounts, of an extraordinary attempt by a number of party secretaries at the XVII party congress in 1934 to remove Stalin from the post of General Secretary. R. A. Medvedev writes:

> At the XVII congress an illegal bloc was formed based on the secretaries of the obkoms and the CC of the national communist parties, who more than anyone else, had to bear and who realised the error of Stalinist policies. One of the instigators of this alleged bloc was I. M. Vareikis, secretary of the Central Black Earth obkom. Discussions took place in the Moscow apartments of several responsible workers, and in them participated Ordzhonikidze, G. I. Petrovskii, M. D. Orakhelashvili, and A. I. Mikoyan. A proposal was advanced to transfer Stalin to the post of chairman of Sovnarkom USSR or to TsIK USSR, and to elect Kirov to the post of General

Secretary of the CC CPSU. A group of congress delegates discussed this matter with Kirov, but he resolutely refused, and without his agreement the whole plan became unreal.[36]

N. S. Khrushchev in his memoirs and A. V. Antonov-Ovsenko in his book about Stalin both wrote about these events as though they were real. The latter names among the organisers of this conspiracy Kosior, Eikhe and Sheboldaev.[37] According to memoir accounts, many people were involved, and it is asserted that about 300 delegates at the XVII party congress voted against Stalin in the election of the new Central Committee.

The preconditions for an anti-Stalinist bloc certainly existed. After the famine crisis and its associated repression, including measures against high-standing communists, the secretaries undoubtedly desired to see at the head of the party a person who was more far-sighted and better disposed to the party generals. If some of the secretaries had indeed attempted to oust Stalin this would necessitate a fundamental reappraisal of the political role of the regional leaders and their capacity for concerted action in the 1930s. However, to date, no archival documents have been found which, directly or by implication, confirm the existence of any organised secretarial opposition to Stalin either at the XVII party congress or at any other time.

From 1934 to 1936 there emerged two clear tendencies in the centre's relations with the regional leaders. On the one hand there was a definite stabilisation of the position of the secretaries, but on the other their activities were subject to more intensive control and oversight from the centre.

The secretarial corpus at this time did not undergo serious change – the leading posts in the localities were occupied by an established group of leaders. However, as a result of the constant reorganisation in the administrative–territorial divisions of the country, many regional leaders were transferred from place to place. In 1934–6 many large administrative units were split up. Lower Volga krai was split into the Stalingrad and Saratov krais; the North Caucasus krai was split into the Azov–Black Sea and North Caucasus krais. The Ural oblast was split into the Sverdlovsk, Chelyabinsk and Obsko–Irtysh oblasts. The Central Black Earth oblast was split into the Voronezh and Kursk oblasts. The Ivanovo industrial oblast was split into the Ivanovo and Yaroslavskii oblasts. From the Gorky krai was formed as a separate independent unit the Kirov krai. From the Central Volga krai was formed the Orenburg oblast. From a number of raions of Western Siberia and East Siberia krais was formed the Omsk oblast and the Krasnoyarsk krai.

Several secretaries lost their posts, but almost all were appointed to other responsible positions. Thus, G. I. Broido, secretary of the Tadzhikistan Communist Party, was removed and appointed as deputy commissar of People's Commissariat of Enlightenment RSFSR.[38] Ptukha when released from the post of first secretary of the Stalingrad kraikom was appointed as second secretary of the Far Eastern kraikom.[39]

Conflicts and splits in their own ranks weakened the position of local leaders. These continued (although not in such an intense form as at the end of the 1920s and the beginning of the 1930s) into the period of stabilisation. Whereas Moscow earlier had resolved such conflicts in favour of one of the leaders, thus strengthening his power, in 1934–6 it pursued a policy of divide and rule: the central power preserved the conflict, demanding from the contending parties that they work together. This created an additional possibility for intervention by the centre in the activities of the regional secretaries. In precisely this way was resolved the conflict in Belorussia, between N. F. Gikalo, the first secretary of the communist party of the republic, and N. M. Goloded, the chairman of Sovnarkom of Belorussia.[40]

Similarly in the summer of 1936 the Politburo resolved the conflict between the first and second secretaries of Kharkov obkom, Demchenko and Kovalev. On 4 June Stalin summoned to his office a group of Politburo members (Molotov, Kaganovich, Ordzhonikidze, Voroshilov and Chubar') and the Ukrainian leadership (Kosior and Postyshev), and also N. N. Demchenko and Kovalev.[41] The Politburo required of Demchenko and Kovalev that they were 'to work together and to ensure friendly work'.[42] However, the conflict had gone so far that on 15 August the Kharkov obkom buro sacked Kovalev. The Politburo then dismissed the entire obkom buro. Demchenko was commanded to Moscow as first deputy commissar of NKZem USSR and Kovalev was made second secretary of Ivanovo obkom. An outsider, S. A. Kudryavtsev, second secretary of the Transcaucasus kraikom, was appointed first secretary in Kharkov.[43]

A significant shift in centre–local relations was the liquidation of the *politotdely* of the MTS. At the Central Committee plenum in November 1934, where the question was resolved, the regional leaders openly vented their dissatisfaction with the political departments. I. M. Vareikis, first secretary of Voronezh obkom, argued against a mere restructuring of the *politotdely*: 'It seems to me it is in the highest degree inexpedient and untimely to pose the question of the restructuring of the *politotdely* in the raikoms ... Because in recent times there were two centres.' Postyshev also spoke about the matter at the plenum.[44] The debate at the plenum shows that one of the reasons from the liquidation of the *politotdely* of the MTS was the pressure on the central authorities from the side of the regional party secretaries.

However, having been released from the oversight of the *politotdely*, the regional leaders remained subject to scrutiny by other officials, appointed as part of the central *nomenklatura*. By the party statutes, adopted by the XVII party congress, in the Central Committee there was created a special Department of Leading Party Organs (ORPO). ORPO carried out detailed accounting of all leading cadres. In 1935 the Central Committee transferred to its *nomenklatura* the first and second secretaries of the party city and district committees (gorkoms and raikoms); by the beginning of 1937 these numbered 5,275 individuals.[45] In the localities there was also a quite large group of other officials (heads of the transport *politotdely*, party organisers (*partorgs*) of the Central Committee in large enterprises and others) who were confirmed by the Central Committee and who could take their questions to Moscow. Although the majority of such *nomenklatura* posts were filled on the proposal of the local leaders or with their agreement, the strengthening of the *nomenklatura* system limited the rights of regional party leaders in resolving cadre questions. The *nomenklatura* itself was increasingly turned into an important device whereby the centre ruled the regions.

An essential aspect of the mechanism of control over the republics and provinces depended on the flow of information. Moscow had at its disposal a multiplicity of mutually independent channels of information. An important source of such information was the security apparatus. The NKVD systematically prepared reports (*svodki*) about the situation in the regions for the party and government leaders. Stalin and Molotov regularly received from the NKVD special reports on various regional problems.[46] All these *svodki* were prepared on the basis of reports from agents in the regions, which were then collated by the NKVD leadership in Moscow.[47] The security apparatus oversaw the regional party and soviet leadership with the help of agents in their circle. This is confirmed by an NKVD internal order, issued on 27 December 1938, which forbade the recruitment of agents from amid the responsible leading workers in the party, soviet, economic and social organisations, and workers of the Central Committees of the republican communist parties, kraikoms, obkoms, gorkoms and raikoms.[48]

The plenipotentiaries of the Commission of Party Control, which was attached to the Central Committee CPSU, and those of the Commission of Soviet Control, attached to Sovnarkom USSR, had direct access to the highest party and government leadership of the country and were also important sources of information. The regional correspondents of the central press, the officials of the various people's commissariats and departments also exercised a certain independence and provided a channel of communication which the centre used to monitor developments in the regions.

Attempts to evade central controls brought a swift response. Typical in this respect was the case involving the Saratov kraikom, which was widely publicised at the time. It stemmed from a conflict between the leadership of the kraikom (the first secretary A. I. Krinitskii, who was appointed to this post from the high position of head of the Political Administration of NKZem) and the plenipotentiary of the Commission of Party Control (KPK) for Saratov krai A. I. Yakovlev. Yakovlev's attempts to expose the errors committed by the krai leadership were rebuffed by the kraikom buro, which accused him of attempting to create a dual centre in the krai's leadership. On 13 June 1935 Yakovlev wrote to Stalin, detailing the failings of the krai authorities and complaining at their unwillingness to recognise their errors.[49] Stalin took heed; Krinitskii and the second secretary of Saratov gorkom, Shafranskii, were summoned to Moscow. On 21 June they were all given a hearing at a Politburo session. The Politburo supported Yakovlev. A special commission, chaired by Ezhov and including Zhdanov, Yakovlev, Krinitskii and Shafranskii, was charged within three days to prepare a draft resolution on the errors of the Saratov kraikom and to publish it in the press. The Politburo dispatched Zhdanov to Saratov krai to check on the kraikom's work.[50] On 23 June the Politburo approved a resolution, which was published in the press the following day.[51] Zhdanov's speech at the Saratov kraikom plenum early in July 1935, where he explained the import of the Central Committee's resolution, was also widely publicised.

The campaign organised around this affair illustrates the Stalinist leadership's policy in this period towards the local leadership. On the one hand Krinitskii was punished for the fact that he ignored several resolutions of the central organs, and for refusing to recognise the all-powerful representative of the KPK. At the same time Zhdanov in his speech issued a warning against 'exaggerations and excesses':

> If you find people who conclude, from the fact that the party kraikom have fallen out with the CC and won't listen to the krai party organisation, that its resolution need not be fulfilled–such people must be given a resolute rebuff . . . The CC does not wish to undermine the authority of the leadership, but on the contrary strengthen it on the basis of corrected mistakes and methods of leadership.[52]

Such an approach – strict control and criticism of local leaders, not going outside specified limits – was the basis of regional policy in the period 1934–6.

The same approach is illustrated in the conflicts that arose between central departments and local leaders. Indicative in this respect was the clash between the West Siberia party kraikom and the newspaper *Pravda*, which published on 9 July 1934 an exposé of abuses of power by the krai leadership (*verkhushka*) under the heading 'A nest of grafters and wastrels'. The article accused the West Siberia krai ispolkom's economic administration of waste and theft, and accused the local party leadership of protecting these crimes. The West Siberia kraikom buro on 17 July discussed the matter. In its resolution it acknowledged many defects, but it rejected *Pravda*'s basic proposition that the local party leadership had covered up these abuses. The same day Eikhe, first secretary of the kraikom, telegraphed the resolution to Moscow and requested authorisation for it to be published in the local press.[53] The Commission of Party Control examined the matter and referred it to the Politburo. On 31 July the Politburo ordered an on-the-spot investigation into *Pravda*'s allegations and prohibited its chief editor, L. Z. Mekhlis, from publishing any further material until the investigation was completed. The commission's membership included D. A. Bulatov, head of ORPO, Shkiryatov (KPK) and Eikhe. Bulatov was to go to Novosibirsk and there together with Eikhe to investigate the matter, and present to the Central Committee their proposals which they should agree beforehand with Shkiryatov.[54]

Evidently Eikhe and Bulatov failed to work out an agreed draft resolution. Matters were left suspended. On 26 August the Politburo summoned Eikhe to Moscow. On 3 September the KPK buro again examined the question. The resolution, which it adopted, bore a compromise character. On the one hand it noted that the economic administration had broken the law, and that the West Siberia kraikom buro had delayed adopting measures to eliminate the disorder. On the other hand the resolution made no mention of the allegations in the *Pravda* article against the kraikom buro. KPK resolved to bring to account a group of former workers of the economic administration and only two former leaders of the krai ispolkom (the responsible editor and the deputy chairman). The KPK agreed with the proposal of the West Siberia kraikom merely to rebuke the existing secretary of the ispolkom. The resolution finally ruled that the kraikom, despite some delay, adopted 'in the main correct measures' in this affair. On 5 September the Politburo confirmed the KPK resolution.[55]

Other provincial party leaders were treated in a similar manner. For example the Politburo rebuked E. I. Veger, the secretary of Odessa obkom, in connection with the mass repression of peasants in Novo-Bug raion Odessa oblast. Veger travelled to Moscow and on 5 July 1934 the Politburo revoked the rebuke.[56] The leadership of the Ivanovo obkom sought to defuse criticisms of their work by lobbying the central authorities. In August 1937 at the obkom plenum the head of the oblast administration of the militia M. P. Shreider spoke about this:

> We are witnesses with you, that in two years, beginning from August 1935, we were depicted in the pages of the central press not as an advanced oblast but as the most backward of oblasts. Comrade Nosov [secretary of the Ivanovo obkom] and his closest aides [*sotrudniki*] now unmasked as enemies, all scoffed at *Pravda*, they laughed after every signal from *Pravda*, they climbed aboard a train and went to Moscow, somewhere and spoke behind the scenes [*za kulisami*], the party organisation did not know, and if there appeared an answer from someone, this was only extracted with difficulty [*posle tyazhelykh rodov*].[57]

In general in this period in cases where Moscow detected any kind of local abuse of power, the republican and provincial party secretaries generally managed to escape criticism. At most, punishment was administered to the heads of the raikoms, gorkoms or even departmental heads. Evidently the highest leadership of the country, at least at this time, feared to breach cadre stability and to undermine the authority of the local leaders. Stalin with his own hand underlined from the draft slogans for 1 May 1934 the call: 'Against aristocrats [*bel'mozhy*] and "honourable fools", against red tape-bureaucratic methods of work'.[58] In March and then in December 1935 practically all party and soviet leaders of the republics, krais and large oblasts were awarded the Order of Lenin for successful work.[59] A definite political balance in the interrelationship of Moscow and the regional leadership created favourable conditions for strengthening the latter's activity in asserting local economic interests.

Petitions of the secretaries to the highest party and state bodies and the manner of their examination

The extraordinarily centralised system of administration that existed in the USSR meant that many, and not only the principally important but even secondary, questions were resolved or ratified in Moscow. The central departments were occupied in the distribution of resources, drafting plans and controlling their fulfilment in the regions and in individual enterprises. The *nomenklatura* system secured the centre's control over key cadre appointments. Not surprisingly, therefore, the archive files of the central party and government bodies overflow with various kinds of addresses, petitions and requests from the local party leaders. These communications constituted a vital part of the regime's nervous system, part of the two-way flow of information between the centre and the regions.

Local leaders were expected to show initiative in promoting the cause of their regions. Those secretaries who were considered too passive drew Moscow's attention and censure. For example in February 1939 A. A. Andreev, secretary of the Central Committee, and G. M. Malenkov, head of ORPO, in a note to Stalin proposed the removal of I. N. Karpov, the secretary of the Kalmyk obkom, on the grounds that 'comrade Karpov badly copes with his work. Leadership of the economy is unsatisfactory. Party work in Kalmykiya is neglected. Comrade Karpov does not pose questions before the CC CPSU. In leadership he does not show initiative.'[60]

The addresses of the republican, krai and oblast leaders to the central party–government bodies may usefully be divided into two groups. The first consists of addresses about resolutions on various questions, which the subordinate bodies were required (often purely formally) to adopt in agreement with the decisions taken by the highest bodies – decisions concerning cadres, which touched on the Central Committee's *nomenklatura*, and decisions about the implementation of major economic and political policies. The second group of addresses are requests and proposals concerning questions whose resolution required the assent of the central authorities. In regard to centre–local relations, it is the second group of documents which is the most interesting.

A significant part of these documents consists of various kinds of protests and complaints on current questions. The local party secretaries were responsible for the state of the economy, the fulfilment of the plans for agriculture and industrial production and for ensuring supplies to the population. The provincial secretaries were in constant contact with the economic commissariats and other central departments over the resolution of economic questions. If they could not obtain a satisfactory resolution there they turned to Sovnarkom or to the Central Committee.

The most numerous and frequent petitions from the localities in this period concerned agricultural deliveries to the state and the allocation of food reserves and seed supply from the central funds to the regions. The system of agriculture procurement involved the dispatch to the state of a significant part of the agriculture produce of the regions and its subsequent redistribution by the centre. These problems acquired special intensity in the early 1930s, in connection with the famine, whose consequence was still evident in many raions in 1934 and even 1935. In response to this crisis local leaders repeatedly sent requests to Moscow to reduce the procurement plans, to substitute one agriculture crop by another, to retain in the hands of the krai or oblast reserves for food supply or seed loans, to run down reserves, etc. In spite of the fact that the central power reacted with hostility to such addresses and repeatedly rebuked local leaders on this matter, the flow of such demands was not stemmed. There were also many addresses requesting tractors and vehicles for carrying out agricultural work.

Often the party secretaries performed the function of 'pushers' (*tolkachi*) securing essential supplies for the enterprises in their regions. Regional party secretaries sent a huge volume of telegrams to the government leadership concerning shortfalls in the supply of raw material and parts at this or that enterprise. Thus on 1 October 1933 Eikhe, secretary of the West Siberian kraikom, and F. P. Gryadinskii, chairman of the krai ispolkom, telegrammed Kaganovich and Molotov about a shortage of cement and requested they be assigned the necessary fund.[61] On 10 December 1933 Postyshev, second secretary of the Ukrainian communist party, telegrammed Molotov to report production hold-ups at the Kharkov bicycle factory caused by irregular supplies and sent a list of the materials it needed. Molotov the same day dispatched a telegram to NKTyazhProm: 'Comrade Ordzhonikidze. It is necessary to help. What answer to Postyshev.'[62] On 23 September 1934 Sovnarkom sent to I. P. Rumyantsev, secretary of the Western obkom, an answer from NKTyazhProm, which dealt with questions raised by Rumyantsev concerning material and equipment supplies for the construction of the Bezhit steel foundry.[63]

Leaders of the local organisations frequently protested to the Central Committee about the proposed transfer of workers, since it was precisely there that cadres questions were resolved. Regional leaders frequently objected to the transfer of their subordinates to other departments or other oblasts. Such cases generated a huge volume of correspondence and squabbling, which in a number of cases ended in the victory of the local secretary.

However, besides current questions the secretaries raised with the highest party and government bodies more complex questions relating to long-term problems: about the socio–economic development of the regions, prospecting for useful minerals, the creation of new industrial complexes, the building of roads, environmental management and amelioration measures. These addresses were especially numerous during the compiling and settling of the annual and the Five-Year Plans. Numerous requests were submitted to the central bodies in these periods about constructing new installations, about increasing the financing of existing construction projects, and about additional investment in housing, social and cultural amenities.[64] For example Sovnarkom USSR by the end of 1933 had received 13 notes (*zapiski*) from Beria, secretary of the Transcaucasus kraikom, in which he proposed to build a number of new works, railway links, pipelines and advanced schemes for the exploitation of lead, zinc, molybdenum and oil reserves.[65]

After the Second Five-Year Plan had been approved, local leaders competed in bidding for new enterprises designated in the plan. Thus, on 15 March 1934 A. K. Lepa, secretary of the Tatar ASSR, sent a request to Sovnarkom and Molotov for the projected optic equipment works to be sited in Kazan.[66] Sheboldaev, secretary of the Azov–Black Sea kraikom, in a letter to Stalin and Kaganovich, requested that the planned tyre combine be located in Krasnodar'. He based this request on both economic and political arguments (the need to strengthen in the krai's proletarian base, the weakness of which had made itself felt particularly in the course of the struggle with 'kulak sabotage' in 1932–3).[67] In 1934 Sheboldaev also contended with the Ukrainian leadership for the construction of the automatic-machine building works, as we shall see below.

This phenomenon had a fixed character. J. F. Hough, studying the activities of the Soviet local leadership in the 1950s–1960s, also noted the constant struggle among regional party secretaries for capital investment and for new industrial projects. In Hough's opinion this had various causes. Above all the constant raising of plan targets necessitated a broadening of productive capacity. The career considerations of local leaders also played its part; local leaders strove also to receive additional funds for the supply of their population, which usually accompanied great construction projects.[68] All these phenomena were already evident in the pre-war period. The assignment of new construction projects to the regions placed on the shoulders of the party secretaries of those regions new responsibilities and worries. On the other hand, these projects provided the regions with additional material and monetary resources. Secretaries of the major local party organisations competed with one another to get the largest slice of the industrialisation pie. Such activism also provided a political dividend, raising their profile in the eyes of their peers and of the Moscow leadership.

The various addresses from the localities to the central organs of power attained a huge volume. Sovnarkom USSR in just four months, from July to

October 1937, received 2,999 letters and 3,334 telegrams from the republics, krais and oblasts, which dealt with matters of material–technical supply, finance, housing–communal construction, etc.[69]

The examination of the petitions of local leaders figured prominently on the agenda of the highest party and government bodies. The Politburo itself examined the most important proposals. However, the flow of declarations was so great that on 30 April 1932 the Politburo, on Stalin's suggestion, adopted a resolution 'to resolve current questions on the demands of the localities' in the party Secretariat in consultation with the chairman of Sovnarkom, Molotov.[70] The party Orgburo examined many local questions, especially cadre questions. Many of these addresses from the local secretaries were referred for examination and resolution to the Central Committee's departments, Sovnarkom, Gosplan or to the corresponding commissariats. The *spravki* and expert *zapiski* which were compiled by Sovnarkom and the departments provide a wealth of material, which demonstrate how proposals were processed, and the mechanism of interrelations of local leaders and central bodies.

The regional leaders also attempted to resolve important questions through personal meetings in Moscow (see Chapter 1, p. 35 n54). Sometimes regional party secretaries and the heads of commissariats sought to jointly 'push through' questions of common interest. Thus in March 1934 M. O. Razumov, secretary of the East Siberia kraikom, and Ordzhonikidze, narkom of NKTyazhProm, jointly submitted a request for the inclusion of one of the krai's defence enterprises in a special list for workers' supply. In spite of the opposition of Mikoyan, who was responsible for the supply funds, Stalin supported the request and the Politburo confirmed the resolution.[71] Similarly in February 1934, despite Mikoyan's opposition, the Politburo approved proposals submitted by Khataevich, the obkom's secretary, with the support of Ordzhonikidze, to improve supplies to one of the construction projects in Dnepropetrovsk oblast.[72] It was with the support of some members of the Politburo that such complex questions as the releasing of industrial workers from military service were resolved.[73]

In cases where the interests of different regions clashed, their leaders strove to secure the support of influential central agencies. An example is provided by the discussion in July 1934 concerning the location of a new automatic-machine works. The all-union Central Committee resolved to support NKTyazhProm which proposed to build this works in Kiev, but the Azov–Black Sea kraikom, supported by Gosplan, proposed that it be built in Taganrog.[74] On 14 July 1934 the Politburo examined the note of the Ukrainian leaders Kosior and Postyshev. The question was resolved in their favour.[75] The Kiev variant was supported by some influential political voices. The secretary of the Azov–Black Sea kraikom, Sheboldaev, had difficulty competing with such influential politicians as Kosior and Postyshev, who were members of the all-union Politburo. Ordzhonikidze, the people's commissar of heavy industry, who often had a decisive say in resolving such interdepartmental disputes, supported the Ukrainians on this question.

Apart from the party secretaries, other officials were also involved in promoting local interests. Republics and provinces had their own permanent representatives in Moscow. These representatives and pushers were so numerous that the government from time to time adopted crude decisions forbidding mass business trips (*komandirovki*) to the capital. On 16 December 1932, for example, the Politburo, on Molotov's proposal, forbade the chairmen and deputy chairmen of Sovnarkom of the union republics and also krai and oblast ispolkoms (except RSFSR) to come to Moscow without the approval of the chairman of Sovnarkom USSR. Similar restrictions were placed on officials of the commissariats and the local soviet bodies. The Politburo proposed to institute a similar order for Sovnarkom RSFSR.[76] On 26 October 1936 Sovnarkom USSR adopted a special resolution about limiting the number of business trips (*komandirovki*) to Moscow on questions regarding the economic plan and budget for 1937. It stated that in Moscow there were 'excessively great numbers of representatives of the union and autonomous republics, krais and oblasts' (from the union republics alone, excluding the RSFSR, there were in Moscow over 200 representatives). Sovnarkom USSR demanded from the chairmen of Sovnarkom of the union republics and Sovnarkom RSFSR 'severely to cut the number of *komandirovki*'.[77]

All these warnings had little effect, since the existing system simply could not function without numerous 'pushers', who strove to overcome the obstacles, which were created by the clumsy and super-centralised bureaucratic apparatus. Moreover, such lobbying and bargaining between the centre and localities was considered a normal and necessary part of politics.

The Great Terror

The balance in relations between the centre and local leaders gradually became still more precarious. The campaign to check and exchange party documents, whereby many *nomenklatura* workers in the obkoms and kraikoms were dismissed, created serious problems for the regional secretaries. After August 1936 the attack on the secretaries was intensified. In the course of this campaign many individuals, who had been accused as 'Trotskyists' and 'Zinovievists', were arrested. Local leaders often strove to protect their people. As a result many of them were accused of 'political shortsightedness', and of 'protecting "enemies"'. The Stalinist leadership increasingly strove to turn the purge into an 'anti-bureaucratic revolution'.

In spite of certain changes in the first half of the 1930s the majority of secretaries on the eve of the Great Purges were either old party members with pre-revolutionary membership or activists who had been promoted in the years of the civil war. The data collected in February 1937 on 166 secretaries of the obkoms, provides a picture regarding length of party membership (*stazh*) (Table 2.2).

At the end of 1936 there is mounting evidence of Stalin's preparations for a large-scale purge of the higher party leadership. After the August trial of Kamenev, Zinoviev and other former oppositionists, many local party, soviet and Komsomol leaders were arrested. Correspondingly many first secretaries of the obkoms were accused of political shortsightedness. On this basis a new phase of cadre appointments was instituted. On 13 December 1936 the Politburo reshuffled the leadership of three large organisations: the Far Eastern krai, Stalingrad krai and Crimea oblast. L. Lavrent'ev was freed from the post of first secretary of the Far Eastern kraikom and sent to head the Crimean organisation in place of B. Semenov, who in his turn was sent as first secretary to Stalingrad kraikom, in place of I. M. Varekis who was transferred to the Far Eastern kraikom.[78] On 17 December S. K. Shadunts, first secretary of the Tadzhikistan Communist Party, was released from his post.[79] In January 1937 the blow fell on Postyshev, second secretary of the Ukrainian Communist Party and first secretary of Kiev obkom, and Sheboldaev, first secretary of the Azov–Black Sea kraikom, both of whom had earlier enjoyed Stalin's unquestioned confidence and support. Postyshev and Sheboldaev were accused of political shortsightedness and removed from their posts, while many of their closest co-workers were arrested. Postyshev was assigned to the less prestigious post of first secretary of Kuibyshev obkom (in place of Shubrikov who was removed in March 1937), and Sheboldaev was appointed first secretary of Kursk obkom in place of Ivanov who was dismissed the same day for 'unsatisfactory leadership of the economy'.[80] The Politburo in January–March 1937 reassigned to other posts the leaders of the Northern, Kharkov and Dnepropetrovsk obkoms, Belorussia and Kirgiziya SSR.[81]

This first wave of the purge in the secretarial corpus on the one hand hinted at Stalin's intentions, but on the other the 'party generals' still had some grounds for hope. Not one of them had so far been repressed, all those

Table 2.2 Length of party membership (*stazh*) of party secretaries, February 1937

Joined the party	(%)
In 1917 and earlier	38.0
Between 1918 and 1921	41.6
Between 1921 and 1923	7.2
Between 1924 and 1927	9.0
Between 1924 and 1929	2.4
Between 1930 and 1931	1.2

Source: RGASPI, 17/2/773 128.

removed received new leading posts. Moreover, Stalin may have feared a certain coordination of action of the alarmed secretaries. For example at the height of the transfers, on 25 January 1937, the Politburo sent to all oblast, krai and republican leaderships the following telegram:

> Noting that a number of party workers among the oblast leaders (for example comrades Krinitskii, Shubrikov, Veger, Razumov, Eikhe and others) have a tendency to spend their winter vacations in Moscow, where climatic conditions are no better than in their krais, nevertheless they remain too long in Moscow, isolated from the work in their krais. The Central Committee of the CPSU considers that it would be expedient, if this is not required by conditions of health, to spend their winter vacations not in Moscow but in their krais or in agreement with instructions of doctors–in the South, where the climate is warmer.[82]

This telegram might be seen as an attempt to obstruct contact between the secretaries of key party organisations on the eve of the fateful February–March Central Committee plenum. At the plenum Stalin sharply criticised Postyshev and Sheboldaev, and in his concluding words to the plenum, accused the local party leadership of political carelessness, conceit and complacency, and of desiring a quiet life. He spoke of family circles of mutual protection (*krugovaya poruka*) in the local organisations and the promotion of weak but compliant officials: 'People are sometimes selected not on political or practical principles, but from the point of view of personal acquaintance, personal loyalty, friendly relations, generally on indications of a narrow kind.' Stalin singled out for criticism Mirzoyan, first secretary of Kazakhstan Communist Party, and Vaionov, secretary of Yaroslav obkom. The first, according to Stalin, transferred with him to Kazakhstan from Azerbaidzhan and the Urals oblast, where he had previously worked, 30–40 of his people whom he placed in responsible posts. The second, when transferred from Donbass to Yaroslavl', took with him a select group of 'his' officials. Stalin saw in this a political threat:

> What does it mean to take with oneself a whole group of officials? . . . This means that we receive a certain independence from the local organisation and if you wish a certain independence from the CC. He has his group. I have my group, they are loyal to me.[83]

Stalin did not hold a very high opinion of the practical abilities of the old leaders. In his report to the plenum he noted the defects in the qualifications of the older generation of cadres, and observed that since the Shakhty affair in 1928 tens of thousands of technically qualified Bolshevik cadres had been trained. The wreckers and Trotskyists exerted influence through their ability to gain party cards and to gain positions in the institutions and organisations.[84]

Table 2.3 Level of education of party secretaries, February 1937

Cadre	Higher education (%)	Lower education (%)
Obkom secretaries	15.7	70.4
Okrugkom secretaries	16.1	77.4
Gorkom secretaries	9.7	60.6
Raikom secretaries	12.1	80.3

Source: RGASPI, 17/2/773 127.

On the eve of the plenum Malenkov, head of ORPO, sent Stalin a report on the party's leading cadres. Judging from Stalin's speech he was familiar with this report. From this it transpires that the proportion of party secretaries who had higher education was very low (Table 2.3).

Yet the level of education of the secretaries was not the only issue of concern. For Stalin, what was much more significant was the fact that the old leaders had lost their 'revolutionary' quality–energy, administrative fervour – and instead inclined to a quiet 'petty bourgeois' life. Stalin in his speech to the plenum criticised the prevailing 'mood of carelessness and self-satisfaction', 'atmospheres of triumphal procession and mutual congratulation' which 'demagnetised people', and the tendency for officials to 'rest on their laurels'.[85]

Mekhlis, one of Stalin's closest co-workers and someone well acquainted with the *vozhd*'s thinking, devoted almost all of his speech to an attack on the local leaders. Using numerous examples from local press reports he attacked the proliferation of 'toadyism and vozhdism', accusing in this the leaders of the largest organisations. In Gorky krai, Mekhlis asserted, there was published a paper entitled 'For the fulfilment of the instructions of comrade Pramnek' (E. K. Pramnek – first secretary of the kraikom). The kraikom halted its publication only after it was sharply criticised by *Pravda*. The newspaper *Chelyabinsk rabochii* published a report, that concluded with the words : 'Long live the leader of the Chelyabinsk workers comrade Ryndin!' I. D. Kabakov, secretary of the Sverdlovsk obkom, and others were also accused of encouraging localism and toadyism.[86]

To understand Stalin's attitude to the regional party secretaries, account must also be taken of the fact that many of them, who had had a difficult life and had borne a great work load, were in poor health. On 2 January 1936, for example, the Politburo granted a month and half vacation on the advice of the doctors to Ryndin, secretary of the Chelyabinsk obkom, and directed A. K. Lepa, first secretary of the Tartar ASSR, abroad for a month and half for his health.[87] On 31 January, Mirzoyan, first secretary of the Kazakh ASSR, was directed for a month and half for health reasons to Karlsbad.[88] On 15 October his vacation was extended by a month.[89] On 16 April 1936 the Politburo granted I. P. Rumyantsev, first secretary of the Western obkom, a two-month rest for his health. On 20 September he was granted a further month and a half vacation and was sent to recuperate in Vienna. The vacation was further extended until 30 November.[90] In October 1936 E. G. Evdokimov, secretary of the North Caucasus kraikom, received a two-month vacation for recuperation. Khataevich, secretary of the Dnepropetrovsk obkom, was also sent abroad to recuperate.[91]

Stalin, we may deduce, considered the promotion of young leaders to be the best means of strengthening the regime. They were better-educated, healthy, energetic and free from the routine of former 'revolutionary service' and bureaucratic family circles; they were in less measure tainted in the eyes of the people with responsibility for the former crimes and repressions. Their life experience and their rapid career advance served as the best guarantee of their loyalty to the *vozhd'*. But the upheaval associated with this cadre transfer was immense. The new generation of leaders, who stepped into dead men's shoes, was not one to be distinguished by its creativity or independence of thought.

At the end of the 1930s a major replacement of cadres became not only feasible but also came to be seen by the leadership as an urgent task. Sheila Fitzpatrick, in a special study of this question, showed that mass promotion and preparation of the new 'proletarian cadres' in the late 1920s and early 1930s created a 'potential problem; the promotees (*vydvizhentsy*), better qualified, than the old cadres and were on average only about ten years younger. In the natural course of things they would probably have had to wait a very long time for top jobs.'[92] Judging from Stalin's speech to the February–March plenum he recognised this problem: 'We have tens of thousands of able people, people with talent. All we need is to recognise them and in time to promote them, so that they are not left in the old place and don't begin to rot.'[93]

Stalin's speech to the February–March plenum and the beginning of investigation of local leaders testifies to the growing threat to their positions. However, in these conditions the party secretaries although they comprised the skeleton of the Central Committee members, proved unable (and moreover, did not even attempt) to oppose Stalin. Khrushchev in his famous report at the XX congress in 1956 declared that at the February–March plenum in 1937 the concept of a widespread conspiracy against the regime was 'forced on' the Central Committee, based on Ezhov's report. Khrushchev asserted that 'many members of the CC actually questioned the rightness of the established course regarding mass repression under the pretext of combating "two-facedness"'. If they did question it, they did so privately. The sole individual whom Khrushchev cites as having expressed doubts, Postyshev, did so obliquely by expressing his incomprehension that individuals who had supported the party in the most difficult period up to 1934 should then join the Trotskyites.[94]

In 1937–8 the first generation of Stalinist party secretaries was practically eliminated. In many oblasts and republics in a brief space of time several layers of the leadership were replaced. Consequently, by the beginning of 1939 (by the time of the XVIII party congress), of 333 secretaries of obkoms, kraikoms, and national communist parties only 10 had party *stazh* predating 1917. More than 80 per cent of the secretaries had entered the party in 1924–35. Over half of the secretaries (53.2 per cent) were between 31 and 35 years of age, while 91 per cent of them were between 26 and 40 years of age. In total there were just six who were over 46 years of age.[95] Some of the representatives of this second generation of Stalinist secretaries in fact ruled the country in the course of the succeeding decades, a few surviving until the early 1980s.[96]

The leaders of the local party organisations were one of the regime's chief props. Despite the activities of the innumerable plenipotentiaries and emissaries, who were sent from Moscow in the course of the various campaigns, it was precisely the obkom secretaries who in many regards determined the situation in the localities. There was a certain consolidation of their position and influence during the comparatively 'quiet' years, from 1934 into the first half of 1936. They constituted one of the main forces which could temper Stalin's personal power. They had a vested interest in the existence of a less terroristic, more predictable regime, as shown in 1935–6 when many attempted to limit the repression against communists. The question of the degree of political influence and power of the local leaders requires special study. An important part of this was facilitated by the close personal relations which some of the leading republican and regional party secretaries had with members of the Politburo.

Notes

1. 'Materialy fevral'sko-martovskogo plenuma TsK VKP(b) 1937 goda', *Voprosy istorii*, No. 3, 1995, p. 14.
2. Rossiskii Gosudarstvenyi Arkhiv Sotsial'no-Politicheskoi Istorii-RGASPI, 17/7/329 5.
3. Stephen F. Cohen, *Bukharin and the Bolshevik Revolution: A Political Biography, 1888–1938* (Oxford, 1975), p. 329.
4. H. Kuromiya, *Stalinist Industrial Revolution. Politics and Workers, 1928–1932* (Cambridge, 1988), pp. 20–1, 141.
5. See N. A. Ivnitskii, *Kollektivizatysiya i raskulachivanie (nachalo 30-x godov)* (Moscow, 1994), pp. 86–7.
6. Lars T. Lih, O. V. Naumov and O. V. Khlevnyuk (eds), *Stalin's Letters to Molotov* (New Haven, 1995), p. 199.
7. O. V. Khlevnyuk, A. V. Kvashonkin, L. P. Kosheleva and L. A. Rogovaya (eds), *Stalinskoe Politburo v 30-e gody* (Moscow, 1995), p. 97.
8. James R. Harris, *The Great Urals: Regionalism and the Evolution of the Soviet System* (Ithaca, London, 1999), pp. 82–3, 87–8, 93.
9. Lih *et al., Stalin's Letters to Molotov*, p. 178.
10. O. V. Khlevnyuk, *In Stalin's Shadow. The Career of 'Sergo' Ordzhonikidze* (New York, London, 1995), pp. 26–9.
11. Lih *et al., Stalin's Letters to Molotov*, p. 202.

12. Khrushchev in the 'Secret Speech' in 1956 recounted the bitter rivalry between Lavren'tev (Kartvelishvili), one of Ordzhonikidze's men, and Beria. In time, as Khrushchev recounts, Beria fabricated a case against Lavren'tev as a result of which he was shot in 1938. *Khrushchev Remembers* (trans. by Strobe Talbot, Introduction and Commentary by Edward Crankshaw) (London, 1971), pp. 602–3. On the tangled politics of the Transcaucasus, see Amy Knight, *Beria: Stalin's First Lieutenant* (Princeton, 1993).

13. RGASPI, 17/120/80 99–102.

14. RGASPI, 17/3/903 9.

15. *Ibid.*, 11.

16. RGASPI, 17/3/909 8.

17. O. V. Khlevnyuk, R. W. Davies, L. P. Kosheleva, E. A. Rees and L. A. Rogovaya (eds), *Stalin i Kaganovich: Perepiska. 1931–1936gg.* (Moscow, 2001), p. 210 (hereafter *SKP*); & RGASPI, 81/3/99.

18. *Golod 1932–1933 rokiv na Ukraini* (Kiev, 1990), pp. 183, 190.

19. *SKP*, p. 273; RGASPI, 81/3/99 144–51.

20. RGASPI, 17/3/898 5.

21. 'Posetiteli Kremlevskogo kabineta I.V. Stalina', *Istoricheskii arkhiv*, No. 2, 1995, p. 146.

22. *Ibid.*

23. RGASPI, 17/3/899 6.

24. RGASPI, 17/3/902 9.

25. RGASPI, 17/3/903 8.

26. RGASPI, 17/3/904 11.

27. RGASPI, 17/3/914 13.

28. RGASPI, 17/3/903 8.

29. RGASPI, 17/3/914 9.

30. RGASPI, 17/3/917 17.

31. RGASPI, 17/3/933 7.

32. *SKP*, p. 367; RGASPI, 81/3/99 25.

33. RGASPI, 17/120/106 44.

34. RGASPI, 17/120/106 46, 47.

35. *Bol'shevik*, No. 22, 30 November 1934, p. 16.

36. R. A. Medvedev, *O Staline i stalinizme* (Moscow, 1990), p. 295.

37. 'Materialy fevral'skogo-martovskogo plenuma TsK VKP(b) 1937goda', *Voprosy istorii*, No. 3, 1990, pp. 77–8; No. 4, 1989, pp. 93–4.

38. RGASPI, 17/3/954 16.

39. RGASPI, 17/3/961 24, 71; 17/3/964 38.

40. RGASPI, 17/3/949 22.

41. 'Posetiteli Kremlevskogo kabineta I.V. Stalinn' *Istoricheskii arkhiv*, No. 4, 1995, p. 26.

42. RGASPI, 17/3/978 34.

43. RGASPI, 17/3/980 3; 17/3/981 9.

44. RGASPI, 17/2/529 120–1, 134–5.

45. 'Materialy fevral'soko-martovskogo plenuma TsK VKP(b) 1937 goda', *Voprosy istorii*, No. 10, 1995, pp. 7–8 (report by G. M. Malenkov, head of ORPO, at the Central Committee plenum on 5 March 1937).

46. An example of such special reports is that signed by the deputy chairman of OGPU, L. G. Mironov and the head of the economic administration of OGPU, G. E. Prokof'ev for January–March 1933 about the shortfall in the supply of fuel

for Leningrad and the Stalingrad tractor works, about the difficult situation of the electrical power station in Belorussia, and also with the signature of the deputy chairman of OGPU, G. Yagoda, on 13 February 1934 concerning the non-fulfilment of the task of supplying tubes for tractors to the works at Stalingrad, Kharkov and Leningrad. See GARF R-5446/27/26 190–4; R-5446/15a/6 112–13.

47. See, for example, the agent reports about the situation in Rostov oblast, directed at the beginning of 1937 to the secretary of the CC CPSU, A. A. Andreev, in connection with his forthcoming visit to the oblast (RGASPI 17/120/284 129–49).
48. GARF, R-9401/2/1 10–11.
49. RGASPI, 17/120/187 5–9.
50. RGASPI, 17/3/965 2.
51. RGASPI, 17/3/966 2.
52. *V pomoshch' partinnomu rabotniku; Sbornik materialov* (Moscow, 1936), p. 91.
53. RGASPI, 17/163/1034 42–4.
54. RGASPI, 17/3/949 33.
55. RGASPI, 17/3/951 1, 35, 91–2.
56. RGASPI, 17/3/947 35; 17/3/948 20.
57. RGASPI, 17/21/1126 23. After some time Shreider, the destroyer of the Ivanovo leadership was also arrested, but survived, and published his memoirs *NKVD iznutri: Zapiski chekista* (Moscow, 1995).
58. RGASPI, 17/163/1020 61.
59. RGASPI, 17/3/961 23; 17/3/974 105–6.
60. RGASPI, 17/163/1214 23.
61. GARF, R-5446/82/22 292.
62. GARF, R-5446/82/33 21.
63. GARF, R-5446/14a/5 37–8.
64. See for example GARF, 5446/13/20 (protests by localities and departments against the 1932 control figures).
65. GARF, R-5446/82/25 258–60.
66. GARF, R-5446/27/24 99.
67. GARF, R-5446/27/26 338–40.
68. Jerry F. Hough, *The Soviet Prefects: The Local Party Organs in Industrial Decision-Making* (Cambridge, Mass., 1969), pp. 257–8.
69. GARF R-5446/34/1 38.
70. Khlevnyuk *et al., Stalinskoe Politbyuro v 30-e gody,* p. 24.
71. RGASPI, 17/163/1014 90.
72. RGASPI, 17.163/1000 44.
73. RGASPI, 17/163/1120 24; 17/163/1122 35.
74. GARF, R-5446/15a/5 69–70.
75. RGASPI, 17/3/948 48.
76. RGASPI, 17/3/911 2, 19.
77. GARF, R-5446/1/122b 79.
78. RGASPI, 17/3/982 77.
79. RGASPI, 17/3/982 79.
80. RGASPI, 17/3/983 14–16, 26, 110–12; 17/3/984 31.
81. RGASPI, 17/3/983 18–19, 43; 17/3/984 31, 36.
82. RGASPI, 17/3/983 46.
83. 'Materialy fevral'skogo-martovskogo plenuma TsK VKP(b) 1937 goda', *Voprosy istorii,* No. 11–12, 1995, p. 13.
84. *Ibid.,* No. 3, p. 8.

85. 'Materialy fevral'skogo-martovskogo plenuma TsK VKP(b) 1937 goda', *Voprosy istorii*, No. 3, 1995, p. 9.
86. *Ibid.*, No. 7, 1995, pp. 12–15.
87. RGASPI, 17/3/974 23.
88. RGASPI, 17/3/974 68.
89. RGASPI, 17/3/982 5.
90. RGASPI, 17/3/976 68; 17/3/981 36, 39; 17/3/982 48.
91. RGASPI, 17/3/981 67; 17/3/982 19.
92. Sheila Fitzpatrick, *The Cultural Front. Power and Culture in Revolutionary Russia* (Ithaca, London, 1992), p. 180.
93. 'Materialy fevral'skogo-martovskogo plenuma TsK VKP(b) 1937 goda', *Voprosy istorii*, No. 3, 1995, p. 14.
94. *Khrushchev Remembers*, pp. 575, 577. See in more detail O. V. Khlevnyuk, *Politbyuro. Mekhanizmy politicheskoi vlasti v 30-e gody* (Moscow, 1996), pp. 219–20; *Reabilitatsiya. Politicheskie protsessy 30–50x godov* (Moscow, 1991), p. 34.
95. RGASPI, 477/1/41 72–3.
96. On the composition of this new generation of Stalinist leaders, see Evan Mawdsley and Stephen White, *The Soviet Elite from Lenin to Gorbachev: The Central Committee and its Members* (Oxford, 2000).

3

Republican and Regional Leaders at the XVII Party Congress in 1934

E. A. Rees

Historians hitherto have examined the XVII party congress of 1934 primarily to shed light on the elusive question as to whether there were moves by provincial leaders to unseat Stalin from his post as party General Secretary.[1] By implication what was said in the corridors and in private meetings has been deemed far more important than what was said on the congress floor. Hard evidence of a conspiracy to remove Stalin and to elect in his place the Leningrad boss S. M. Kirov has not been found. This chapter examines how far it is possible to identify the operation of republican and regional lobbies at the congress, to examine the main lines of division among the leaders of the republics and regions, and to see how far the tightening of political and economic controls from 1929 onwards had transformed centre–local relations within the USSR.

The XVII party congress is of importance as the congress that immediately followed the famine, the congress that approved the Second Five-Year Plan, and the congress that preceded the Great Terror. The discussion on the congress floor was in no sense a real debate since no differences of principles were aired. There were many ritualistic statements of obeisance to the party leadership, and much rhetoric on unity, loyalty and achievement. This was the 'congress of victors', where, according to Stalin, it seemed that there was no one left to fight, no one left to argue with. Defeated oppositionists, including N. I. Bukharin and L. B. Kamenev, attended the congress to pledge their loyalty to the party and to declare their confidence in Stalin.

How far there was a gap between public protestations and private convictions remains uncertain. The proceedings, however, are not without interest and contain much information which can be sifted and analysed. The preceding two years had been extremely stormy, dominated by the famine. Within the party itself the opposition platforms of the Eismont–Tomachev–Smirnov group and that of Ryutin denounced official policy and demanded Stalin's removal from the General Secretaryship. They were the years which saw also an unprecedented concentration of power in Stalin's hands. For Stalin and the party leadership it was an opportunity to reassert their authority. For the delegates it was an opportunity to defend their record, to publicise their achievements, to promote local projects and identify issues of concern.

The congress met from 26 January to 10 February and was attended by 1,227 delegates with full voting rights and 739 delegates with advisory voting rights. The delegations, elected on the basis of party membership in each region, were dominated by representatives from the main industrial and urban centres. The top 12 regions, which accounted for 60 per cent of the delegates with full voting rights, in their order of importance were Moscow (178, 14.5 per cent), Leningrad (123, 10 per cent), Azov–Black Sea (57), West Siberia (49), Central Black Earth (48), Donetsk (48), Gorky (47), Ivanovo (47), Central Volga (44), Kharkov (36), Sverdlovsk (35) and Dnepropetrovsk (34). The party chiefs from these 12 regions plus the main republican party bosses constituted a major group of influential political leaders within the Stalinist political system. These regions, in the main, were the principal beneficiaries of the Second Five-Year Plan.

In terms of republican representation the congress was dominated by the RSFSR (including the ASSRs) with 891 delegates (72.6 per cent). Ukraine came second, with 195 delegates (15.6 per cent). Other republicans had a token representation, far smaller than the top 12 regions noted above. Out of a total of 136 speakers, 62 represented republican and regional interests, of whom 37 came from the RSFSR. The regions most strongly represented in terms of speakers were Moscow 8, Leningrad 9, Donetsk 4, West Siberia 3, and Gorky 3. The Central Black Earth oblast, Sverdlovsk, Dnepropetrovsk, the Western, Azov–Black Sea and the Far Eastern krai each merited two speakers (usually the first party secretary and the chair of the soviet executive committee).

In the 18 months preceding the congress the party leaders of a number of key republics and regions were ousted. In 1932 new party secretaries were appointed to the Transcaucasus (L. P. Beria) and Belorussia (N. F. Gikalo) and to three regions, Ivanovo, Northern and Central Volga. In 1933 new party leaders were appointed to Kazakhstan ASSR, East Siberia, Far East, North Caucasus, and to several Ukrainian oblasts (including Kharkov, Dnepropetrovsk, Donetsk, Odessa and Vinnitsa). Many of these personnel changes were directly related to the famine crisis.

The USSR in 1934 was a country of enormous imbalances. We have seen how in approving the Second Five-Year Plan certain areas were selected for concentrated development – Moscow, the Urals, Leningrad, West Siberia, North Caucasus, the Far Eastern krai, Kazakhstan ASSR and Gorky krai. But there were also those regions which were most severely affected by the famine – Ukraine, North Caucasus, Belorussia, Kazakhstan, Lower Volga and East Siberia. These regional variations had an important bearing on the conduct of republican and regional spokesmen at the party congress.

The administration of the republics and regions lay in the hands of a very tough generation of political leaders, who had been tempered by the experience of collectivisation and famine. But these leaders had also seen their powers significantly diminished after 1929, with the growing power of the central economic commissariats, and through the increasing power of the central party authorities to intervene, direct and control policy in their regions. Those who failed to meet the demands of the centre in 1932–3 had been unceremoniously removed.

The XVII party congress

Stalin's report to the XVII party congress underlined the growing military threat posed by Japan and Nazi Germany. He stressed the efforts made to develop the economies of the national republics and border regions. They had laid the foundation of a new metallurgical base in the East. The dominance of socialist forms in the economy, he argued, was the foundation of the USSR's internal stability and the 'basis of the firmness of its front and rear positions in the circumstances of capitalist encirclement'. The distinction between industrial and agricultural regions, Stalin asserted, was now 'obsolete'. Industrial regions were developing their own food supply bases, whilst agricultural regions were being industrialised. Consuming regions such as Moscow and Gorky had become major grain suppliers to the state. The irrigation of the Trans-Volga region would provide an additional 200 million puds of grain, which would give the government more room to manoeuvre domestically and on the international stage. This scheme was also intended to avert a repetition of the drought that had devastated the region in 1931.

In the section of his report 'Problems of Organisational Leadership', Stalin outlined 14 points concerning the strengthening of control and discipline. He issued a clear warning that 'incorrigible bureaucrats and office rats' who failed to implement official policy would be expelled:

> One of these types of workers are those who have rendered certain services in the past, people who have become 'aristocrats' (*bel'mozhi*) as it were, who consider that the laws of the Party and Soviets were not written for them but for fools... These swelled-headed aristocrats think that they are irreplaceable, and they think that they can flaunt the decisions of the leading bodies with impunity... They must without hesitation be removed from their leading posts, irrespective of the services they have rendered in the past and put in their places.[2]

Stalin played only a small role in drafting the Second Five-Year Plan; the details of the plan were left to Molotov and Kuibyshev. Molotov at the XVII party congress declared that the Second Five-Year Plan would be based on the objective of 'equably distributing industry throughout the territories of the USSR', of bringing industry closer to the sources of raw materials and power supply, of accelerating the economic and cultural development of the backward national republics and regions and advancing towards abolishing the antithesis between city and country.[3] He emphasised the need to develop local industries, highlighted the importance of economic integration and also warned of the dangers of 'gigantomania' in industry and agriculture.

The Second Five-Year Plan, Molotov declared, aimed to achieve a 'new regional distribution of capital construction'. The chief priority was the development of industry in the East that was dictated by economic and defence considerations. The key Urals–Kuznetsk combine (UKK) would receive a quarter of all capital investment during the plan period. Nearly half of all capital investment in new construction in heavy industry would be channelled to the Eastern part of the Soviet Union (the Urals, Siberia, Bashkiria, the Far East, Kazakhstan, Central Asia and Trans-Caucasus) with the object of developing iron and steel, coal, oil, machine-building and electrical power construction in these regions.[4] The area under grain cultivation was to be greatly extended. He drew attention to the need to resolve the problems of transport.

The report by Kuibyshev, chairman of Gosplan, outlined the main direction of development of each region.[5] The speech, which must have been eagerly anticipated by republican and regional leaders, indicated a big shift in investment to the east. First place in Kuibyshev's report was given to the Urals oblast, which was earmarked to become one of the most important and technologically advanced industrial regions of the country. A number of major centres were to be developed: the metalworks of Magnitogorsk, Nizhnyi Tagil, Bakal'skii, the Sredniural copper plant, the Ufa nickel complex and major engineering works such as Uralmashzavod, the Nizhny Tagil wagon works and the Chelyabinsk tractor works. Particular stress was laid on securing iron ore supplies for this region. The heavily overloaded rail system needed to be reconstructed, and the supply of electrical power increased.

West Siberia krai was also a major recipient of investment with the plan to transform the Kuzbass coalfield into a second Donbass and development of the Kuznetsk metallurgical works, and plans for the large-scale development of the coking/chemical industry. In Kazakhstan ASSR efforts were to be directed to developing the Karaganda coalfield output during the Second Five-Year Plan to increase it 9 times (to 7.5 million tons) and to develop the Pribalkash copper works.

Moscow during the First Five-Year Plan was assigned the role as the country's leading centre for high-technology machine-building, electrical engineering and chemicals, as well as traditional light industry. In the Second Five-Year Plan it had to help in reconstructing the economy of the rest of the country. Major investment was to be channelled into the Stalin motor works and the Novotula metal complex. Major efforts were to be directed to increasing the electrical power supply to Moscow. Moscow also benefited from several key transport projects: the Moscow–Volga canal, the Moscow–Donbass rail trunk line, the Moscow Metro and the electrification and reconstruction of Moscow suburban rail network.

Despite Kuibyshev's assurances that Ukraine SSR would preserve its position as one of the foremost centres of coal, metal and chemical production, and grain-growing and livestock-rearing, there could be no disguising the significant downgrading of the republic's ranking as a whole.

RSFSR

D. E. Sulimov, chairman of Sovnarkom RSFSR (1930–7), was a figure of some standing in the party, and a full member of the Central Committee. As first secretary of Urals obkom in 1926–7 he earned a reputation as a resolute defender of the Urals metallurgical industry in its constant battle with the metallurgical industry of Ukraine.[6] On his appointment to Sovnarkom RSFSR in November 1930 Sulimov was granted the right to attend the Politburo's closed sessions.[7] Sulimov was the most outspoken defender of the interests of the RSFSR against the claims of other republics in the USSR.

Sulimov welcomed the new importance attached to investment in the heavy industries of the RSFSR, underlined by Stalin's call for the development of the coal basins of Moscow, East Siberia, the Far East and the Urals. The UKK had since 1931 received 27 milliard rubles, i.e. 30 per cent of all investment in heavy industry. As a result, 'the geography of heavy industry in the USSR has changed significantly'. This would continue under the Second Five-Year Plan: 'The RSFSR's output of coal as a proportion of Union output will be raised from 36 per cent in 1932 to 48 per cent by the end of the pyatiletka [Period of the Five-Year Plan], for pig iron this rise will attain 44.5 per cent, for rolled metal about 48 per cent, and for iron ore it will reach 52.5 per cent.'[8]

Moscow and Leningrad

Moscow, which under Kaganovich was turned into a bastion of the Stalinist leadership, was also the chief beneficiary of the Second Five-Year Plan. The disparity between the treatment of Moscow and almost all other regions of the USSR was immense. The spokesmen for the capital and its oblast did not need to use the party congress as a platform to promote their claims. N. S. Khrushchev, second secretary of Moscow gorkom, confined himself to reciting their achievements in rebuilding the capital and its economy.[9] G. N. Kaminskii, chairman of Moscow oblast ispolkom, dwelt on the need to improve the quality of housing.[10] N. A. Bulganin, chairman of Moscow Soviet ispolkom, criticised Gosplan's Second Five-Year Plan for neglecting the production of urban communal heating equipment, trolley buses and other modes of urban transport as required by the Central Committee plenum of June 1931.[11] A. E. Badaev, chairman of the Moscow union of consumer societies and a full member of the Central Committee since 1925, noted a planned doubling in investment in Moscow from 900 million rubles in 1933 to 1,800 million rubles in 1934.[12]

Leningrad was another major beneficiary of official policy. S. M. Kirov, first secretary of Leningrad gorkom and gubkom, and a full member of the Politburo since 1926, was, like Kaganovich, one of the political heavy-weights in the party. Leningrad, although less favourably treated than Moscow, retained its industrial position, accounting for 14–15 per cent of the value of production of all Soviet industry. Kirov's speech highlighted the city's lack of energy resources, and its dependence on coal and oil that was transported over long distances on an unreliable rail network. He urged the development of the local peat industry to meet some of the city's energy needs.[13] It was essential, he argued, to resolve the problems of rail transport, and secure advances in water transport. He noted the importance of the new Belomor canal in the development of the north western region, paying tribute to the role of the Chekists in this work.

I. F. Kodatskii, chairman of Leningrad Soviet ispolkom and a member of the Central Committee, stressed the city's role as a major industrial and machine-building centre. However, he bluntly declared that they had no confidence in Kuibyshev's assertion that the energy needs of Leningrad would be satisfied. It was essential, as Stalin had indicated, to increase local energy supplies. Gosplan, however, had rejected Leningrad's proposal for a peat extraction target of 5 million tons, and had stuck to its target of 3.5 million tons. In addition to the planned Svir hydroelectric station it was necessary to build the Nevski station at the Ivanov rapids.[14]

P. I. Struppe, chairman of Leningrad ispolkom, stressed the importance of developing the mineral resources of the Far North and the Kola peninsula. The Central Committee was providing assistance. The new Belomor canal had opened up the region for development. Stalin, visiting Murmansk in July 1933, had foreseen the development of the fishing industry of the Barentsk Sea, but this required more trawlers. Leningrad could become the major fish supplier for the whole of the USSR. The planned reconstruction of the Mariinskii lock system, which Kuibyshev and Kirov had highlighted, would improve Leningrad's links with the Volga. This, he noted, was a 'colossal task', and one of national significance, and needed to be funded from the centre.[15]

European Russia

V. I. Ivanov, first secretary of the Northern kraikom and a Central Committee candidate member, had a distinguished record in regional administration as first secretary of Uzbekistan from 1924 and then of the North Caucasus kraikom. He boasted that timber exports from the krai in the preceding Five-Year Plan had earned 320 million gold rubles for the country.[16] He envisaged further improvements with the development of exports of high-value cellulose, rayon, spirit and other timber-chemical products. Not a word was said of the desperate problems of labour recruitment or of the industry's growing reliance on forced labour. Ivanov looked forward to development in livestock farming in the region to improve local food supplies.

The strikes and disturbances in the key textile region of Ivanovo in the spring of 1932, caused by food shortages, demonstrated the vulnerability of the regime in its industrial heartland.[17] N. N. Kolotilov, the long-serving party secretary and a Central Committee member was ousted, and replaced by I. P. Nosov. Nosov, in his report to the congress, cited the Central Committee's stern censure of the weakness of the local authorities. The Politburo had sent Kaganovich there to deal with the situation. Nosov reported that with the Central Committee's help they had corrected 'these colossal political mistakes'.[18] They were addressing the question of improving local food production. He noted also the intervention by Kaganovich and Postyshev in eliminating 'functionalism' in the administration of the textile industry.

A. A. Zhdanov, first secretary of Gorky kraikom and a Central Committee member, used his regional platform as a springboard to advance his career at national level. Gorky was a major engineering centre and one of the main beneficiaries of the First Five-Year Plan. Zhdanov boasted of large achievements in industry and agriculture: the krai had been turned from a consuming into a producing agricultural region, while in industry, great advances had been made in engineering, automobile, aeroplane and steam engine production. The Politburo had determined that the output of motor vehicles from the giant Molotov works was to rise to 50,000 in 1934, eventually rising to 300,000 per annum. Zhdanov noted that although the quality of lorries had improved, the quality of cars remained unsatisfactory. He proposed that the production of components should be concentrated in factories around the main works, so as to reduce reliance on 57 different suppliers.[19]

I. P. Rumyantsev, the long-serving first secretary of the Western obkom (1929–37) and a Central Committee member, noted strong peasant opposition to the policy of switching from food production to technical crops – flax, hemp and clover. The inadequate supply of fertiliser and of improved seed varieties from central agencies, he complained, also impeded this policy shift.[20]

V. P. Shubrikov, appointed first secretary of the Central Volga kraikom in 1932, berated Ya. A. Yakovlev, NKZem USSR and its associated body Sel'khozsnab, for shortcomings in the supply of spare parts for tractors and implements. He also dismissed Yakovlev's claim that two-thirds of kolkhozy had crop rotation as 'fictitious'.[21] V. V. Ptukha, first secretary of the Lower Volga kraikom – now renamed as the Stalingrad kraikom – had taken a hard line in defence of official policy during the famine that had devastated the region.[22] In his report to the congress he concentrated on the achievements of the Stalingrad tractor works and the Krasnyi Oktyabr works which in 1932 had experienced production difficulties, but which were corrected with the help of the Central Committee and the dispatch there of Voroshilov and Pyatakov.[23]

I. M. Vareikis, first secretary of the Central Black Earth obkom and a Central Committee member, another tough operative who had ruthlessly enforced collectivisation, welcomed the way in which the kolkhoz system was transforming these 'impoverished agriculture centres' of tsarist days, and was putting an end to 'the idiocy of rural life'.[24] E. I. Ryabinin, secretary of the CBE ispolkom, stressed the oblast's importance as one of the country's main agricultural producers, and called for further efforts to develop and mechanise the food processing industry. Like Vareikis, he noted the close involvement of the obkom with NKTyazhProm in building the Lipetsk metallurgical works. He stressed the huge potential for developing the iron ore reserves of the Kursk magnetic anomaly (KMA) as an ore supplier for European Russia, and which Kuibyshev had supported. But NKTyazhProm, he complained strongly opposed the obkom's proposals for the use of local ore and coke in the works. NKTyazhProm had also rejected the obkom's plans to build a slag-cement works in Lipetsk, which would make use of the waste from the metal works.[25]

The Urals and Siberia

I. D. Kabakov, first secretary of Urals kraikom and a Central Committee member, had a reputation as a capable administrator, with the krai being regarded as one of the best-managed regions in the USSR. The krai was another beneficiary of large-scale investment. Kabakov lauded Stalin as a 'theoretician of genius' and paid tribute to his decision at the XVI party congress to create a second industrial base in the Urals and West Siberia. The Urals, written off by many as a region in decline, was being transformed by the construction of the Urals–Kuznets combine (UKK), the Berezniki chemical combine, the Chelyabinsk tractor works, the Magnitogorsk steel works and the Ordzhonikidze heavy engineering works. Stalin had played an active role in resolving these policy questions. The development of the UKK, however, was held up by the weakness of the rail transport network in the Urals and West Siberia, which, Kabakov insisted, had to be improved as a top priority.[26]

Stalin and the Central Committee had censured the kraikom and Kabakov personally for their contemptuous and negligent attitude to agriculture. They had sent telegrams demanding corrections in policy. Kabakov claimed to have rectified this error. The local party organisation had been purged. Kabakov endorsed the Central Committee's decision of January 1934 to break up the Urals krai into three oblasts (Sverdlovsk, Chelyabinsk, Obsko-Irtush).[27] This decision was the clearest signal that the central authorities intended to clip the powers of the powerful Urals industrial and political lobby which had been so vociferous in promoting its interests. The party secretary of the new Chelyabinsk obkom was K. V. Ryndin, brought in from being party secretary in the Moscow party committee.

Ya. P. Ivanchenko of Sverdlovsk (Urals), one of the country's major producers of high-quality rolled metal, stressed their commitment to enforcing the Central Committee's resolution of September 1933 on improving the utilisation of the capacity of older non-ferrous metal works. The industry's development, however, he complained, was impeded by the poor mechanisation of timber operations for charcoal production, and by the poor transport system inside and outside the works, which NKPS and NKTyazhProm needed to urgently address.[28]

R. I. Eikhe, first secretary of the West Siberian kraikom and a Central Committee member, had ruthlessly imposed the government's policy of collectivisation. In 1933 he waged a fierce struggle against the regime's opponents, petitioning the Politburo in July 1933 to retain the power of the troiki in West Siberia to impose the death penalty.[29] He was also a strong advocate of severe measures to enforce labour discipline.[30] West Siberia, alongside the Urals, was a prime beneficiary of central policy, with investment being poured into the UKK. The highly mechanised Kuzbass coalfield would provide the fuel for the development of Siberia, and could, if NKTyazhProm provided the investment and cadres, become a major centre of the country's chemical industry.[31]

F. P. Gryadinskii, chairman of West Siberia krai ispolkom and a Central Committee candidate member, criticised Gosplan's plan to build three new car plants in the 'central part of the Soviet Union'. He urged that one of these plants be built at Stalinsk, where production costs would be lower. This would supply vehicles for Siberia, reducing the costs of their transport from the western part of the country. During the First Five-Year plan three combine-harvester works had been built in the central parts of the country. West Siberia had built its own combine plant at a cost of 26 million rubles, only to be told that it was not needed, and had to be converted to other production. They now had to bear the cost and inconvenience of bringing in combines by train from Ukraine and the North Caucasus. Kuibyshev's proposal to increase the acreage under wheat cultivation in West Siberia by 33 per cent, he observed, was a 'colossal task', particularly considering the requirement to further sharply raise yields.[32]

In East Siberia the situation in agriculture bordered on the catastrophic. In August 1933 the Central Committee censured the kraikom's work and in October it dismissed I. I. Kozlov, the kraikom secretary. E. M. Yaroslavskii and Ya. Gamarnik made several visits to the krai to assist in restructuring the party organisation. Over 22 per cent of party members of the krai were expelled. M. O. Razumov, the new party secretary, openly acknowledged the seriousness of the problems facing the region's agriculture. In his speech he also severely criticised shortcomings in the work of NKTyazhProm's glavki in exploiting the region's gold and precious metal reserves. He also censured shortcomings in the work of NKPS in providing supplies for the double-tracking of the Transbaikal railway.[33]

The Far Eastern krai was effectively under GPU and Red Army administration on account of the sensitive situation with regard to Japan and Manchuria. Razumov, of the East Siberian krai, stressed the importance of defence in the Far East, and its connection to internal security, with attempts by the Japanese to subvert the Kazakh population on the Soviet side of the border.[34] V. K. Blyukher, commander of the Red Army in the Far East, spoke of the preparedness of the region to repel any possible aggression.[35]

North Caucasus krai and Azov–Black Sea krai

Another region of difficulty in 1932–3 was the North Caucasus, headed by B. P. Sheboldaev, an ardent 'dekulakiser'. In August 1932 Sheboldaev was strongly censured by Stalin for his failure to enforce the policy of grain procurement in the North Caucasus.[36] In September 1933 Sheboldaev requested from the Politburo a reduction in the procurement targets for the kolkhozy of the region on account of harvest failure. The Politburo grudgingly acceded to the request.[37] He sought to make amends by enthusiastically enforcing the Politburo order of August 1932 on the use of capital punishment for the theft of collective farm property.[38] The high-powered Kaganovich commission visited the Kuban in November–December 1932 and ruthlessly enforced the deportation of kulak households.

In January 1934 the krai was split into two – the North Caucasus krai, headed by E. G. Evdokimov (head of the OGPU in the North Caucasus until 1932), and the Azov–Black Sea krai, headed by Sheboldaev.[39] Sheboldaev noted that in 1932/3 they had encountered the most intense form of class struggle, but that the central party leadership had corrected the kraikom's excessive liberalism.

V. F. Larin, on assignment in the Azov–Black Sea krai on behalf of the central party and government bodies, like Kuibyshev, stressed the central importance of industrial development in transforming this former White Guardist bastion. The creation of the giant Rostov agricultural implements works (Rostselmash), the Novocherkassk locomotive works and the development of the Shakhty coalmines were steps to the region's proletarianisation and Sovietisation.[40] The problems in the Kuban in 1932, it was asserted, stemmed from the absence of any proletarian centres.

Tatar ASSR and Bashkirya ASSR

G. G. Baichurin, first secretary of the Tartar ASSR, singled out for criticism three central commissariats: the People's Commissariat of Light Industry, which in the second year of the Second Five-Year plan in a period of 28 days had changed the plan targets for sewing and tanning no less than 10 times; the People's Commissariat of Water Transport, for its failure to move large quantities of freight laying idle on the quays of the Volga and Kama river; and the People's Commissariat of Communications, headed by Rykov, for its failure to develop the telephone and telegram network in this backward region.[41]

The planned construction of a major motor works in Bashkiriya ASSR in the southern Urals reflected the location priorities of NKTyazhProm and Gosplan. It had little to do with the political leverage of local authorities. The decision carried with it major implications for the ethnic composition of this autonomous region. Ya. B. Bykin, the newly appointed first secretary of Bashkiriya ASSR, in his speech complained that NKTyazhProm had not provided sufficient finance, materials or cadres, while the completion of the vital Ufa–Ishimbaev rail link was held up because of disputes between NKPS and NKTyazhProm. However, he welcomed the plans for developing the Izhimbaev oil field as the oil base for the East.[42]

Belorussia SSR

N. F. Gikalo was appointed first secretary of the Belorussia Communist Party in 1932 after extensive experience of party work in the North Caucasus, Uzbekistan, Azerbaidzhan and work in the Central Committee apparatus in Moscow. He noted the republic's crisis of grain procurement in 1932. In December 1932 they had reported to the Central Committee CPSU that the plan had been fulfilled only 46 per cent, and that there had been a mass exodus of peasants from the kolkhozy. The Central Committee instructed them to fulfil the target by 1 January 1933. Stalin and the Central Committee wrote to them accusing them of liberalism. This, he declared, had a galvanising effect, and the target was fulfilled on time.[43]

Belorussia was one of the republics conspicuously starved of industrial investment. N. M. Goloded, the long-serving chairman of Sovnarkom Belorussia (1927–37) and a Central Committee candidate member, like Kuibyshev, highlighted the importance of developing the republic's peat extracting industry in order to expand its energy base, and to boost the local construction materials industry and the expansion of light industry. He feebly requested that NKTyazhProm undertake more geological surveying work in Belorussia to uncover new raw material reserves.[44]

Ukraine SSR

The Ukraine posed the biggest headache for the Soviet leadership with the famine in 1932–3. In 1932 Stalin contemplated sacking the republics two leading figures, S. V. Kosior, General Secretary of the Ukrainian Communist Party, and V. Ya. Chubar', chairman of Sovnarkom Ukraine (see Chapter 1, pp. 23, 25, Chapter 2, p. 43). In the end he sought a different solution to the problem of ensuring effective central control over the republic. In 1933 P. P. Postyshev, who had worked in the Secretariat alongside Stalin and Kaganovich since 1930, and was a full member of the Central Committee, was sent to Ukraine as second secretary of the Ukrainian communist party, and first secretary of the Kharkov gorkom. In 1934 he was elected as candidate member of the Politburo.

Postyshev's role as the centre's representative in the Ukraine was spelled out in his speech to the congress, in which he castigated the Ukrainian party leadership for its 'great mistakes and blunders' in agricultural, industrial and nationalities policy.[45] There can be little doubt that Postyshev was speaking with Stalin's authority. Stalin himself rarely administered severe public rebukes to his colleagues, but left this to his deputies. In 1932, Postyshev declared, grain procurement had been worse than in 1931, despite the investment made in agriculture. The Ukrainian party leaders, he asserted, had ignored Stalin's warning at the XVI party congress and had relied on 'naked administrative and commanding' methods.[46] They had failed to check the influence of anti-Soviet elements in the kolkhozy and party–state administration, and they had failed to 'mobilise the class vigilance and revolutionary activism of the masses'. The republic's leaders had blamed failures of policy and 'excesses' on lower party workers. The interventions by Stalin and the Central Committee, he argued, had helped in effecting a major turn in the work of the Ukrainian party organisation. The counter-argument, that the crisis stemmed from errors of central policy – collectivisation, excessive procurement – was not even addressed.

Kosior offered no defence, but claimed that with the support of Stalin and the all-union Central Committee past errors in agriculture, industry and nationalities policy had been liquidated, but continued efforts were needed to improve matters.[47] Chubar', head of Sovnarkom Ukraine, adopted the same stance of self-criticism, but, taking his cue from Stalin, placed a part of the blame for the crisis in Ukrainian agriculture in 1932–3 on NKZem USSR and its leader, Yakovlev. This was a theme touched on also by Kosior.[48] Chubar' took comfort in the figures presented by Kuibyshev for investment in Ukraine during the Second Five-Year Plan, ignoring the clear evidence of a significant deterioration in the republic's economic ranking within the USSR.

The party stalwart G. I. Petrovskii, chairman of the Ukrainian TsIK (1919–39) also participated in this ritual of self-criticism. He welcomed the centre's intervention in correcting errors of policy in Ukraine. The Ukrainian GPU, now under V. A. Balitskii, had uncovered and destroyed the counter-revolution.[49] A. G. Shlikhter attributed the success of the Ukrainian party in overcoming its difficulties in agriculture to the close assistance provided by the Central Committee and Stalin and the dispatch of Postyshev to Ukraine.[50]

In 1933 M. M. Khataevich, an enthusiastic collectiviser and 'dekulakiser' as first secretary of the Central Volga kraikom, was promoted as first secretary of the key Dnepropetrovsk obkom and elected a member of the Ukrainian Politburo. His appointment was intended to strengthen the centre's control over the republic. Even by the standards of the XVII party congress, his speech was distinguished by its sycophantic praise of Stalin.

In September 1933 S. A. Sarkis [Sarkisov] was appointed as first secretary of Donetsk obkom.[51] Although tainted by a Trotskyist past he had won his way back into favour as a grain procurer. In 1933 in response to a major crisis in the coalfield, which NKTyazhProm and the obkom had failed to resolve, the central authorities had intervened over the heads of the Ukrainian authorities. The Central Committee resolution of 8 April 1933 instituted sweeping changes in the management of the industry, and the transfer of large numbers of engineering–technical personnel to underground work. Kaganovich led a Central Committee brigade to the Donbass to enforce the resolution, which had met strong opposition.[52] A commission, headed by N. M. Shvernik, instituted a major purge of the Donbass party organisation. These measures, Sarkis asserted, had brought a dramatic improvement in coal production. He reported that efforts were being made to improve food supply, which had been the cause of a big exodus of miners from the Donbass in 1933.[53]

I. G. Makarov, director of the Donetsk metallurgical works, demanded that NKPS improve the rail transport links with the region's works and mines. Ordzhonikidze's directive to improve the management of the works and to transfer white-collar workers to production had encountered strong opposition within the plant, he reported, but the obkom had acted firmly to enforce its implementation.[54]

V. Ya. Furer blamed the problems of the Donbass coal industry on poor leadership and anti-mechanisation attitudes. These supposedly were corrected after a telegram had been sent by Stalin, Molotov and Kaganovich to the Donetsk obkom. Efforts were being directed to improve food supplies and living conditions. The provision of kitchen gardens, he claimed, had had a beneficial effect on the attitude of 'backward' workers. Furer noted the importance played by Central Committee commissions and brigades, by the dispatch of new leaders, in ensuring that party policy was properly implemented.[55]

Transcaucasus SFSR

L. P. Beria, former head of the Georgian Cheka, was appointed first secretary of the Transcaucasus SFSR in 1932 on Stalin's initiative with the task of imposing order on the querulous political factions of the region. He quickly established a reputation as an assertive promoter of his region's interests. In his speech Beria took various all-union commissariats to task. He censured NKTyazhProm and its factories for failing to supply the oil industry with machinery and equipment on time; much of this equipment, he complained, was of poor quality. He demanded that NKPS and NKVodTrans urgently improve the transportation of oil to the region's customers throughout the USSR.[56] Beria also roundly criticised NKZem USSR for failing to implement two key Central Committee resolutions on the development of cotton and tea cultivation in Transcaucasus.[57]

G. Musabekov, chairman of the Transcaucasus Sovnarkom (1931–7) and a candidate member of the Central Committee, argued that the region's industrial development was impeded by its overdependence on the overburdened Transcaucasus railway line. He complained that the Second Five-Year Plan had no provision to complete the Baku–Dzhylfa line, on which tens of millions of rubles had already been spent; 200 km, had been built, and 120 km remained to be built, its completion would ease the burden on the Transcaucasus line.[58]

Central Asia

K. Ya. Bauman, sacked as first secretary of the Moscow party organisation for his excessive zeal in collectivisation, was made chairman of the Central Committee's Central Asian Bureau.[59] In his report he hailed the efforts of the region to fulfil the party's directive to make the country self-sufficient in raw cotton. By 1937 the production of raw cotton was to be increased by 60 per cent, mainly through increased yields. This, Bauman argued, required improved seed selection, and a huge increase in mineral fertilisers, and NKTyazhProm and Sovnarkom USSR should pay due regard to this.[60] Greater efforts were needed to mechanise irrigation work. They needed tractors from Leningrad, and vehicles from Moscow and Gorky. To these demands, Kaganovich wryly interjected that they had sent Bauman to Central Asia as Moscow's representative, not as a Central Asian lobbyist.

Kazakhstan ASSR was seriously afflicted by the famine of 1932–3, with half of the Kazakh population disappearing. In September 1932 the Politburo criticised 'leftist excesses' in the collectivisation of agriculture in the republic. L. I. Mirzoyan, brought in from the Urals party organisation, in January 1933 was appointed first secretary of Kazakhstan kraikom in place of F. I. Goloshchekin. In August and September 1933 Goloshchekin wrote to Stalin and Kaganovich complaining that Mirzoyan was unloading responsibility for past errors in economic and nationalities policy in the republic onto his shoulders.[61] He insisted that he had simply implemented official policy. Despite these protests Goloshchekin lost his seat on the Central Committee in 1934.

M. K. Amosov accused the former kraikom leadership, under Goloshcheikin, of 'serious political errors' in economic and nationality policy. From 1929 until 1933 there had been a 'catastrophic fall' in the size of the krai's livestock herd.[62] Mirzoyan and Amosov stressed Stalin's close involvement in resolving the crisis and the key role played by the Kaganovich commission. The republic had received 'huge aid' from the centre in the form of food, seed, cattle and tractors. The peasant exodus from the kolkhozy of 1932 had been halted, and in 1933 some 100,000 households had returned to the kolkhozy.[63]

Kazakhstan, Mirzoyan argued, had the potential to become a major industrial region. The kraikom was anxious to forge ahead in this field, but NKTyazhProm and other 'central economic organisations' were dragging their feet.[64] Amosov argued that the exploitation of the Emba oilfield required the speedy completion of the Orsk–Caspian pipeline. They urgently needed pipes from Ukraine, diesel motors and other equipment from Leningrad, Moscow and Gorky. They needed to build a railway line from Algaya to Gur'evsk and he urged the speedy completion of new rail links between Central Asia and the European part of the USSR.[65]

U. D. Isaev, chairman of Kazakhstan ispolkom and a Central Committee candidate member, complained of serious 'gaps and omissions' in Gosplan's Second Five-Year Plan for the region. This, he noted, was partly caused by the failure of the local authorities to prepare their submissions in time. He offered a number of 'corrections'. He proposed that the Karaganda coal basin should be expanded, at the expense of Kuzbass and Donbass, through investment in large-scale mines and coal enriching facilities. Rail links were needed to transport Karaganda coal to southern Kazakhstan and Central Asia. Isaev also criticised Gosplan's plan to invest 1.7 million rubles in the Emba oilfield by 1937, and urged that NKTyazhProm's target of 2.6 million rubles be adopted.[66]

A. I. Ikramov, first secretary of the Communist Party of Uzbekistan (1929–37), first secretary of Tashkent gorkom and a Central Committee candidate member, sought recognition for the republic's success in greatly extending cotton cultivation, raising yields and developing new specialised cotton varieties.[67] F. Khodzhaev, chairman of Sovnarkom Uzbekistan, supported by Bauman, advanced a radical scheme for developing the Khorezm oasis.[68] This required the building of a rail link to Khorezm, but in the meantime they needed 200–300 lorries to carry road freight.[69]

Relations between the regions and the all-union commissariats

While individual republican and regional leaders were largely immersed in their own concerns, on some matters there is evidence of a certain commonality of interests amongst these regional bosses. The speeches of republican and regional representatives at the XVII party congress point to acute tensions between them and the predatory and voracious all-union economic commissariats. This is evident in all branches of the economy–industry, agriculture, trade and transport.

From 1929 onwards Vesenkha and its glavki greatly extended their influence into the republics and regions, seizing control of the enterprises which previously had been under republican and local authority control. This was bitterly resented. Stalin proposed to 'unfetter local Soviet industry', to allow it greater initiative in producing goods of mass consumption, and to ensure it was provided with raw materials and funds. Molotov and Kuibyshev proposed to transfer more enterprises back to the control of krai and oblast authorities, and to provide these authorities with the resources and cadres to manage them.

Sulimov, chairman of Sovnarkom RSFSR, strongly criticised the stranglehold which NKTyazhProm and other all-union commissariats now exercised over industry. Between 1930 and 1934, he complained, the proportion of industry designated as of all-union significance in the Western oblast had risen from 31 per cent to 87 per cent and in the CBE from 77 per cent to 88 per cent.[70]

N. I. Pakhomov, chairman of Gorky krai ispolkom, complained that the huge potential of local industry was held back by the lack of essential materials and components, which were monopolised by the all-union commissariats. NKTyazhProm's glavki seized profitable republican and local enterprises, whilst enterprises which were crucially important for the economy but unprofitable, such as glass and building-materials' producers, were left to languish. Republican and local organs, he argued, should emulate the Moscow city authorities, and assume greater responsibility for housing construction and for providing communal services, over which the all-union commissariats showed little interest.[71]

E. K. Pramnek, second secretary of Gorky kraikom, noted that whilst giant enterprises such as Sormovo, Avtozavod, Izhevsk and Bumkombinat works, were working quite well, many medium and small-scale enterprises were working badly; the kraikom paid little attention to them, while the central commissariats scarcely knew of their existence.[72] Khataevich, first secretary of Dnepropetrovsk obkom, protested that NKTyazhProm and other all-union commissariats had taken over a vast number of enterprises of republican and local significance. Despite the strictures of Stalin and Molotov, he feared that the commissariats and glavki would obstruct the process of returning industries to republican and local control. He warned: 'Here, the opposition of the apparatus of the people's commissariats will undoubtedly be very great'.[73]

Kirov demanded an end to the 'anti-party' practice whereby industrial managers and local party secretaries colluded to agree on low production plan targets, which could be easily overfulfilled.[74] Party secretaries, he declared, should be more assertive in their dealings with managers, whilst managers should approach economic matters not simply from a technical standpoint but as party members themselves.

V. P. Shubrikov, first secretary of the Central Volga kraikom, noted major construction projects in Orsk raion – a new locomotive works, a metallurgical combine, a cracking plant for the Emba oilfield and a large meat-packing plant. Different departments of NKTyazhProm managed these projects, generating 'inter-departmental scuffles' over sites, resources and manpower and wasteful duplication of capacity. Shubrikov demanded that NKTyazh-Prom set up its own 'united planning leadership centre' in the locality to resolve these problems.[75] This reflected the weakness of territorial bodies as coordinating agencies in resolving inter-departmental, and particularly inter-commissariat, disputes.

The authorities in Moscow, Leningrad and the Urals faced particular problems in developing housing and communal services to cope with a rapidly growing urban population. However, the all-union commissariats and their enterprises carried out much of housing construction. Gryadinskii of West Siberia complained that too much construction was of a temporary nature, with the building of cultural facilities largely neglected.[76] I. F. Kodatskii, chairman of Leningrad Soviet ispolkom, complained that 'extreme central-isation' was inhibiting the development of local industry and the urban economy.[77]

In agricultural policy, the same pattern was evident. Official policy was not criticised. The party secretaries from the key agricultural regions all acknowledged the great impact of Stalin's speech to the Central Committee–Central Control Commission plenum in January 1933 'Concerning work in the countryside'.[78] Congress delegates, however, spoke of the catastrophic fall in livestock numbers in Kazakhstan, East Siberia, Transbaikal and Buryatiya. Mirzoyan, of Kazakhstan, and Razumov, of East Siberia, both lay the blame on the influence of kulaks and other hostile elements. But Bauman, head of the Central Asian Bureau, Mirzoyan, Razumov and Amosov argued that the crisis had also been caused by the attempt by local party authorities, contrary to the advice of the Central Committee in Moscow, to institute the artel form of collective farming.[79] The artel, under which all livestock was held in common, had provoked intense oppositions among the semi-nomadic herders, and had resulted in the mass slaughter of livestock. On the centre's advice they were now adopting the toz form of collective farming, which involved only the joint working of the land. Smaller work teams or 'links' were being created within the collective farm brigades, to increase a sense of identity between the peasants and the land and livestock. They were endeavouring to increase payment to the peasants. They were applying the all-union Central Committee's resolution, by which the number of livestock which peasants in the tozy and artel could privately own was raised. In this the centre was absolved of responsibility for the tragedy that had engulfed these regions.

Shubrikov, secretary of the Central Volga kraikom, and Ptukha, secretary of Stalingrad kraikom, both welcomed the plan, endorsed by Stalin and Kuibyshev, to irrigate the trans-Volga region and produce an additional 200 million puds of wheat. He demanded a pledge from Yakovlev and NKZem that the necessary equipment and machinery for this project would be forthcoming.[80] Amosov of Kazakhstan urged the scheme's extension into the southern Urals (Priural) region.[81] Chubar', of Ukraine, however, struck a note of dissent. Ukraine during the Second Five-Year Plan, he asserted, could produce an additional 200 million puds of wheat, without expensive outlays on irrigation, simply through the provision of additional fertiliser.[82]

In the wake of Stalin's criticism of NKZem and NKSovkhoz USSR, however, others like Kosior and Chubar' added their withering condemnations. Vareikis, of the Central Black Earth obkom, argued that the expansion of livestock-rearing in the CBE, Ukraine and Moscow oblasts was impeded by NKZem's failure to develop an adequate feed-fodder base.[83] This was hardly surprising under conditions of famine. Chubar' (Ukraine), Bauman (Central Asia) and Rumyantsev (Western oblast) complained about the shortage of mineral fertiliser for grain, cotton and flax cultivation. Voroshilov, commissar of defence, Chubar' (Ukraine), Amosov (Kazakhstan) and Gryadinskii (West Siberia) all condemned the policy of NKSovkhoz and other central commissariats in slaughtering young cattle to fulfil meat quotas. This provided the state with poor-quality meat and had a detrimental effect on the breeding stock.[84]

In the field of transport friction between the regional and republican bodies and the central transport commissariats was marked. The commissariat of rail transport (NKPS) was strongly criticised by republican and regional spokesmen, including Kirov of Leningrad, Beria of Transcaucasus, Kabakov of Urals, and by Chubar' and other Ukrainian delegates for major hold-ups of freight and the slow operation of trains.[85] Kuibyshev, Bauman of the Central Asian Bureau and Gryadinskii of West Siberia complained that the Turksib line was operating at only half capacity, creating serious holds-ups in the shipment of grain and timber from West Siberia. Gryadinskii urged fuller utilisation of the Turksib line through the construction of new feeder lines.[86]

The commissariat of water transport (NKVodTrans) was strongly criticised by a host of delegates – Chubar' and Sukhomlin of Ukraine, Beria of the Transcaucasus and Goloded of Belorussia. Chubar' criticised NKVodTrans and Gosplan for neglecting the development of the Dniepr waterway. Bauman and Khodzhaev criticised the failure to develop the water link with the Khorezm oasis. Gorky was a major port on the Volga, and a major shipbuilding centre. Zhdanov, first secretary of Gorky kraikom, called for a fundamental reconstruction of water transport. His deputy and protégé, Pakhomov, chairman of Gorky krai ispolkom, strongly censured NKVodTrans for failing to build shallow-draught vessels, and opening up unused waterways for navigation and thus easing the burden on the railways.[87]

These criticisms of NKTyazhProm and of the agricultural and transport commissariats had been anticipated by Stalin in his report to the congress. The republican and regional leaders took their cue from Stalin. In this way pressure on the commissariats was intensified. This was the prelude to some key personnel changes after the congress. In agriculture in April 1934 T. A. Yurkin, the commissar of NKSovkhoz, was demoted to deputy commissar and replaced by M. I. Kalmanovich. At the same time Ya. A. Yakovlev, commissar of NKZem USSR, was replaced by M. A. Chernov, and moved sideways to head the Central Committee's agricultural sector.

In transport A. A. Andreev survived as commissar of NKPS until 1935, but the commissariat remained under sustained attack and under close supervision of the Politburo's Transport Commission. In March 1934 Pakhomov, who had led the attack on the Commissariat of Water Transport at the congress was appointed its commissar, while Zhdanov, was appointed party secretary and made deputy chairman of the Politburo's Transport Commission with special responsibility for water transport.[88]

The regional leaders and the control organisations

Another source of tension within the state and economic apparatus was that between the republican and regional authorities on the one hand and the centrally administered control organisations on the other. From 1929 onwards there had been a significant strengthening of the role of the control agencies in ensuring the enforcement of central policy, through the work of the Central Control Commission NKRKI, the OGPU and the Procuracy. The control mechanisms were substantially strengthened with the creation of the political departments (*politotdely*) in agriculture in the spring of 1933, the purging of the party's ranks, and the moves which culminated at the XVII party congress to reorganise the system, of party–state control, and to tighten control from the centre over appointments to local party bodies.

The moves to tighten central control stemmed from what was perceived as the weakness of republican and oblast party authorities in controlling the work of the raikoms, especially during the famine of 1932–3. The republican and regional party leaders were closely tied to these agencies of control, and relied on their support in enforcing central policy, but they and their subordinates were also threatened by the growing power of these agencies. In June 1933 Khataevich, first secretary of Dnepropetrovsk obkom, was sharply criticised by Molotov over his attempt to defend the management of the 'Kommunar' works from harassment by the Procuracy.[89]

At the XVII party congress there was little hint of these tensions between regional authorities and the control agencies. None of the regional representatives criticised the newly established *politotdely*. Eikhe welcomed their establishment. Sheboldaev more cautiously noted the need to carefully define the respective rights and powers of the *politotdely*, and the kraikoms and their agricultural departments.[90] Kim, a *politotdel* official in the Far East, noted that L. I. Lavren'tev (L. I. Kartvelishvili), the newly appointed first secretary of the Far Eastern kraikom, had strongly supported the *politotdely*. The raikoms, however, had strongly opposed the *politotdely*. The kraikom dismissed a large number of raikom secretaries and adopted resolute measures to improve relations between them and the *politotdely*.[91] In November 1934, however, largely in response to local pressures, the Politburo abolished the *politotdely* in the MTS.

The nationalities question

A major shift in the direction of increasing central control and curbing the limited autonomy of the union republics was reflected also in the field of nationality policy. Stalin in his report continued to argue that 'Great Russian nationalism' represented as great a danger as 'local nationalism' but he signalled a new shift in emphasis. In Ukraine, Belorussia and other union republics, he argued, local nationalism had now become the chief danger on account of past failure to combat its influence, and on account of the power wielded in the past by local nationalists such as M. Skrypnik.[92]

Postyshev, acting as Stalin's mouthpiece, delivered a swingeing attack, denouncing the past failure of the Ukrainian party leadership to struggle against counter-revolutionary nationalism. The nationalist errors perpetrated by Skrypnik, he argued, and developed into a 'nationalist deviation'. Ukrainian nationalists had controlled the Commissariat of Enlightenment and had infiltrated the Commissariat of Foreign Affairs. Skrypnik and his supporters had opposed the creation in 1929 of NKZem USSR and the All-Union Agricultural Academy. Their objective, it was alleged, had been to detach Ukraine from the USSR, and to bring it under the sway of the imperialists. Some, such as Rechitskii, a candidate member of the Ukrainian Central Committee, were accused of perpetrating excesses in the countryside in order to discredit official policy. These defects, Postyshev argued, were being corrected with the Central Committee's help.[93]

The Ukrainian leadership had no alternative but to meekly accept these strictures. Chubar' felt compelled to assert that the Ukraine's relationship with the USSR was in no sense that of a 'colony'. Ukraine's rapid industrial development had been possible only in a 'free country' under the dictatorship of the proletariat, where Leninist nationality policy was enforced.[94] But A. G. Shlikhter complained that the Ukrainian party had been too slow in rebuffing the nationalist threat.[95]

Gikalo, first secretary of the Belorussia Communist Party, reported that nationalist, counter-revolutionary elements in the past had gained great influence in the republic's People's Commissariat of Enlightenment, Academy of Science, NKZem and Traktortsentr. Goloded, chairman of Sovnarkom Belorussia, claimed that with the help of the Central Committee the republic's economy was being transformed. Attempts by Belorussian nationalists, supported by foreign interventionist forces, to detach BSSR from USSR had been rebuffed. Efforts had been directed to mobilise the party, to purge its ranks and to raise revolutionary vigilance.[96]

Beria noted serious difficulties associated with agricultural collectivisation in the Transcaucasus in 1930–1, with strong kulak opposition, and increased activity by anti-Soviet parties, namely Dashnaks, Mussavets and the Georgian Mensheviks. Following direct intervention by Stalin and the Central Committee CPSU resolution of 31 December 1931 the local party began to correct these errors. In 1933 the agricultural procurement targets were overfulfilled.[97] Musabekov, chairman of the Transcaucasus Sovnarkom, stressed the federation's role in promoting the region's development, and in defusing inter-ethnic tensions.[98]

Bauman, chairman of the Central Asian Bureau, acknowledged the strong opposition of peasants and kolkhozniki to the extension of cotton cultivation in the region. Nationalists had exploited the situation, charging that the region was being given over to monoculture. They had succeeded in inveigling themselves into leading posts. Their leaders had been purged: Abdarakhmanov, chairman of Sovnarkom Kirghizia; Khodzhaev, chairman of Tadzhikistan Sovnarkom and Maksum, chairman of TsIK Kirghiziya.[99]

Ikramov of Uzbekistan rejected the allegations that Uzbekistan was being put over to cotton monoculture, converting it into a 'red colony', which was critically reliant on grain imports from West Siberia. Only large-scale collectivised cotton cultivation, he argued, could ensure prosperity for the population. Although the hopes of Uzbek separatist and nationalist counter-revolutionaries had been confounded, the nationalist mood, he admitted, remained strong amongst all sections of Uzbek society. Nationalist elements had infiltrated party and government bodies. In accordance with Stalin's words the republican party organisations would be 'bolshevised' in their struggle with the nationalists.[100]

Bauman (Central Asia), Khodzhaev (Uzbekistan), Isaev (Kazakhstan), Bykin (Bashkiriya), Goloded (Belorussia) and Musabekov (Trancaucasus) all spoke of their regions as 'former tsarist colonies' which were being transformed economically and culturally with the support of the centre.[101] This was intended to rebut the charge that these regions were being turned into new Soviet colonies.

The congress resolution

The XVII party congress did not fundamentally change the targets of the Second Five-Year Plan. In only one respect was it significantly changed. As a result of the intervention by Ordzhonikidze the annual growth rate for industrial production was lowered from 18.9 per cent to 16.5 per cent. Molotov, in closing the debate, stressed, there had been no changes to the plans for capital work.[102]

A high-level commission, including representatives of the main economic commissariat and the main regions was elected to draft the congress resolution.[103] The resolution confirmed the main outlines of the Second Five-Year Plan.[104] Following the congress there occurred some struggles between different regions over individual projects for which a location had not been designated. The plan was not finally approved until November 1934.

Kaganovich's report to the congress strongly criticised the poor management of agriculture.[105] The obkoms and kraikoms, he complained, had exercised ineffective control over the raions in the 'last two or three years'. On the basis of his report the congress abolished the Central Control Commission and the People's Commissariat of Workers' and Peasants' Inspection, and established two new separate control agencies – the Commission of Party Control (KPK), directly answerable to the Central Committee, chaired by Kaganovich, and the Commission of Soviet Control (KSK), directly answerable to Sovnarkom and chaired by Kuibyshev. These bodies were to ensure the full, effective and timely implementation of central party and government directives in the localities. The congress also approved the establishment of the Central Committee's Departments of Leading Party Organs (ORPOs) to deal with the selection and deployment of party cadres in the obkoms and raikoms.[106] These two key measures, which significantly weakened the power of republican and regional authorities, were approved without any dissent being expressed.

The impact of the republican and regional leaders in influencing policy at the congress was small. The main outlines of the Second Five-Year Plan had already been determined. Some items included in the plan, such as the Volga–Don canal, were not built. The building of the Baikal–Amur trunk line was delayed, and was far from completion in 1941. The scheme promoted for the development of the iron ore deposits of the Kursk magnetic anomaly came to nought, in large measures because of problems of impurities in the ore. Other schemes, included in the plan – such as the reconstruction of the Mariinskii canal system and the development of the Khorezm oasis in Central Asia – were delayed until 1935.[107]

The XVII party congress elected a new Central Committee of 71 full members and 68 candidate members. Of these 28 (39 per cent) were republican, krai or oblast leaders, and of the candidate members 29 (43 per cent) were republican and regional spokesmen. Amongst the full members of the Central Committee the representatives of the republics were: RSFSR (Sulimov); Ukraine (Kosior, Chubar', Petrovskii); Transcausacus (Beria); Central Asia (Bauman, Ikramov, Mirzoyan). The leadership of the two capitals were well represented: Moscow (Kaganovich, Khrushchev), Leningrad (Kirov, M. C. Chudov, Kodatskii). It included the leaders of the main krais and oblasts: Northern (Ivanov), Ivanovo (Nosov, N. I. Nikolaeva), Sverdlovsk (Kabakov), Chelyabinsk (Ryndin), West Siberia (Eikhe), East Siberia (Razumov), Far Eastern krai (Lavrent'ev), CBE (Vareikis), North Caucasus krai (Evdokimov), Azov–Black Sea (Sheboldaev), and the two main Ukrainian oblast Kharkov (Postyshev) and Dnepropetrovsk (Khataevich).[108]

After the XVII party congress the regional representation in the 10-man, all-union Politburo consisted of Kaganovich (Moscow), Kirov (Leningrad) and Kosior (Ukraine). Of the five candidate members, three were representatives of Ukraine – Chubar', Petrovskii and Postyshev. Following the congress, Zhdanov, party secretary of Gorky obkom, was transferred to Moscow as party secretary. In February 1935, Chubar' was made a full member of the Politburo, and Zhdanov and Eikhe were elected candidate members.

Conclusion

The proceedings of the XVII party congress highlight a number of important political trends. They confirm the evidence of the weakening of the influence of the republican and regional leaders as a whole. Criticism of official policy was muted, confined to particular details rather than general policy. What emerges very clearly is the way republican and regional leaders were highly dependent on the centre, particularly with regard to investment, production and procurement targets. In periods of crisis the centre demonstrated its ability to intervene directly in resolving problems in the regions. Regional leaders who failed were dismissed. The speeches of the republican and regional leaders were narrowly focused on their own concerns. There were no great issues to debate, and discussion revolved around practical matters.

The congress discussions underlined a new regional division of labour between the big metropolitan centres (Mosow, Leningrad), the major industrial regions, the agricultural regions and the regions supplying raw materials. Regional disparities in terms of levels of development and wealth remained great. From the vehement denials of official spokesmen it is evident that there was deep concern in Central Asia that they were being turned intro a region of cotton monoculture. Attempts by republican and regional spokesmen to modify the plan in favour of their own regions at the congress were simply ignored. The new emphasis on the development of the regions of the RSFSR coincided with a new Russian nationalist note in official policy, with the intensified attack on bourgeois nationalism in the non-Russian republics – Ukraine, Transcaucasus, Belorussia and Central Asia – from 1933 onwards.

As is clear from their speeches, regional and republican leaders were under intense pressure to enforce the centre's policies. They attempted to unload responsibility for failures onto the shoulder of others. There were enormous strains in relations between the territorial authorities and the all-union economic commissariats. Regional leaders did not criticise official policy, but were scathing in their criticisms of Gosplan, and of the main industrial, agricultural and transport commissariats. NKTyazhProm in particular was slated for its ruthless take-over of republican and local industries. These criticisms, however, appear to have had no impact in modifying the behaviour of these commissariats, although in some instances they may have contributed to their leadership being changed.

No attempt was made to inquire into the failures of collectivisation, or into the causes of the famine (the great unmentioned subject at the congress) or to bring those responsible for these policies to account. On the contrary it was these leaders – Stalin, Kaganovich and Molotov – unabashed and unrepentant, who led the drive to further tighten control and to find scapegoats for the failures of official policy in the laxness of local officials, in the pernicious influence of 'bourgeois nationalists' and the machinations of internal and external enemies. The republican and provincial leaders did not dissent. They were not the hapless victims of the centre's power, but rather ruthless accomplices in carrying through the party's policies. The central leadership and the republican and regional leaders were bound together primarily by self-interest, by a shared instinct to survive and prevail, and to a lesser extent by bonds of loyalty.

From the Central Committee–Central Control Commission plenum of January 1933 to the XVII party congress in February–March 1934 the centralisation of power in the party and state apparatus was relentless. At the XVII party congress, none of these steps, each of which seriously compromised the powers of the republican and provincial party organisations, were publicly questioned. Sensitive border regions were already placed under tight control, with the Far East regions already under Red Army and GPU control. The growing influence of the GPU was also reflected in the appointment of GPU personnel to head key regions: Beria in the Transcaucasus and Evdokimov in the North Caucasus.

Notes

1. R. Medvedev, *Let History Judge* (London, 1976), pp. 155–6; R. Conquest, *The Great Terror* (Penguin edn, 1971), pp. 63–5; R. Conquest, *Stalin and the Kirov Murder* (London, 1989), chapter IV.
2. *XVII s"ezd Vsesoyuznoi Kommunisticheskoi Party (b), 26 yanvarya-10 fevralya 1934g. Stenograficheskii otchet* (Moscow, 1934), p. 34.
3. *Ibid.*, pp. 369–72.
4. *Ibid.*, pp. 366–7.
5. *Ibid.*, pp. 399–412.
6. On Sulimov, see James R. Harris, *The Great Urals: Regionalism and the Evolution of the Soviet System* (Ithaca, London, 1999), pp. 24, 36, 44, 58, 66.
7. O. V. Khlevnyuk *et al.*, *Stalinskoe Politbyuro v 30-e gody* (Moscow, 1995), p. 178.
8. *XVII s"ezd*, p. 425.
9. *Ibid.*, pp. 145–7.
10. *Ibid.*, pp. 613–4.
11. *Ibid.*, pp. 489–90.
12. *Ibid.*, p. 80.
13. *Ibid.*, p. 256.
14. *Ibid.*, p. 422.
15. *Ibid.*, p. 99.
16. *Ibid.*, p. 96.
17. Jeffrey J. Rossman, 'The Teikovo Cotton Workers Strike of April 1932: Class, Gender and Identity Politics in Stalin's Russia', *The Russian Review*, 56, January 1997, pp. 44–69.
18. *XVII s"ezd*, p. 165.
19. *Ibid.*, p. 152.
20. *Ibid.*, p. 144.
21. *Ibid.*, pp. 190–1.
22. O. V. Khlevnyuk *et al.* (eds), *Stalin i Kaganovich Perepiska. 1931–1936gg.* (Moscow, 2001), p. 178 (Hereafter, *SKP*). In June 1932 Stalin proposed that Ptukha should be supported in his conflict with Pshchentsin, deputy chairman of the krai ispolkom. In January 1933 the chairman and deputy chairman of the kraispolkom were removed. In October 1933 G. E. Prokof'ev, Procurator, complained to Molotov that Ptukha, party secretary of the Stalingrad oblast, was retaining prisoners in his oblast for production work in violation of the Politburo's decision that all those sentenced to two years and more be sent to labour camps. *Sovetskoe rukovodstvo perepiska 1928–41* (Moscow, 1999), p. 263.

23. *XVII s"ezd*, p. 108.
24. *Ibid.*, pp. 93–4.
25. *Ibid.*, pp. 432–4.
26. *Ibid.*, p. 948.
27. *Ibid.*, p. 948. On the break-up of the Urals oblast, James R. Harris writes: 'Orders for the division of the Urals came directly from Stalin's office, and seem to have taken Urals officials by surprise', *The Great Urals*, p. 144.
28. *XVII s"ezd*, pp. 499–500.
29. Khlevnyuk *et al.*, *Stalinskoe Politbyuro*, p. 64.
30. R. W. Davies, *Crisis and Progress in the Soviet Economy, 1931–1933* (London, 1996), pp. 287–8.
31. *XVII s"ezd*, p. 44. Rukhimovich, director of the Kuzbassugol trust, welcomed Stalin's proposal at the congress that Kuzbass be turned into a second Donbass; *ibid.*, p. 491.
32. *Ibid.*, p. 415.
33. *Ibid.*, pp. 414–16.
34. *Ibid.*, p. 213.
35. *Ibid.*, pp. 629–30.
36. *SKP*, pp. 294, 298.
37. Khlevnyuk *et al.*, *Stalinskoe Politbyuro*, p. 138.
38. Davies, *Crisis and Progress*, p. 242.
39. On Evdokimov see Robert Conquest, *Inside Stalin's Secret Police: NKVD Politics 1936–39* (London, 1985), p. 25.
40. *XVII s"ezd.*, p. 479.
41. *Ibid.*, p. 296.
42. *Ibid.*, p. 50.
43. *Ibid.*, p. 72.
44. *Ibid.*, pp. 442–3.
45. *Ibid.*, p. 65.
46. *Ibid.*, p. 67.
47. *Ibid.*, pp. 197–201.
48. *Ibid.*, p. 418.
49. *Ibid.*, p. 141.
50. *Ibid.*, p. 88.
51. *SKP*, pp. 317, 326. Sarkis' appointment involved at least a modicum of consultation with the Ukrainian authorities. In September 1933 Kaganovich wrote to Stalin: 'Concerning Sarkis, I have reached agreement with the Ukrainians. We have already made him secretary of the Donetsk oblast committee. We did not put down Terekhov as second secretary because the Ukrainians said that neither he nor Sarkis would probably want that.'
52. *XVII s"ezd*, p. 162; N. Lampert, *The Technical Intelligentsia and the Soviet State* (London, 1979), p. 88.
53. *XVII s"ezd*, p. 162.
54. *Ibid.*, p. 57.
55. *Ibid.*, pp. 573–5.
56. *Ibid.*, p. 130.
57. *Ibid.*, p. 131.
58. *Ibid.*, p. 431.
59. R. W. Davies, *The Soviet Economy in Turmoil, 1929–1930* (London, 1989), pp. 103–4.

60. *XVII s″ezd*, p. 104.
61. *Sovetskoe rukovodstva perepiska 1928–1941* (Moscow, 1999), pp. 245–9, 258–9.
62. *XVII s″ezd*, p. 58.
63. *Ibid.*, p. 89.
64. *Ibid.*, p. 90.
65. *Ibid.*, p. 60.
66. *Ibid.*, pp. 437–8.
67. *Ibid.*, p. 83.
68. *Ibid.*, p. 104.
69. *Ibid.*, p. 481.
70. *Ibid.*, p. 425.
71. *Ibid.*, pp. 477–8.
72. *Ibid.*, p. 619.
73. *Ibid.*, p. 78.
74. *Ibid.*, p. 257.
75. *Ibid.*, pp. 190–1.
76. *Ibid.*, p. 415.
77. *Ibid.*, p. 423.
78. *Ibid.*, pp. 83 (Ikramov), 108 (Ptukha), 148–50 (Sheboldaev), 151 (Zhdanov), 164 (Nosov), 294 (Bauchurin), 585 (Kim).
79. *Ibid.*, pp. 58 (Mirzoyan), 60 (Amosov), 106 (Bauman), 213 (Razumov).
80. *Ibid.*, pp. 190–1, 108.
81. *Ibid.*, p. 60.
82. *Ibid.*, p. 418.
83. *Ibid.*, p. 94.
84. *Ibid.*, pp. 60, 416, 420.
85. *Ibid.*, pp. 301–2. See also the comments by K. V. Sukhomlin, V. Ya. Furer and I. G. Makarov, *ibid.*, pp. 57, 575.
86. E. A. Rees (ed.), *Decision-Making in the Stalinist Command Economy, 1932–1937* (Basingstoke, 1997), pp. 210–19.
87. *XVII s″ezd*, p. 477.
88. Rees, *Decision-Making*, pp. 243–4.
89. Khlevnyuk *et al.*, *Stalinskoe Politbyuro*, pp. 133–4.
90. *XVII s″ezd*, p. 150.
91. *Ibid.*, p. 586.
92. *Ibid.*, pp. 369–72.
93. *Ibid.*, p. 69.
94. *Ibid.*, p. 418.
95. *Ibid.*, p. 88.
96. *Ibid.*, pp. 442–3.
97. *Ibid.*, p. 130.
98. *Ibid.*, p. 431.
99. *Ibid.*, p. 106.
100. *Ibid.*, p. 84.
101. *Ibid.*, pp. 106, 480, 437, 50, 442, 431.
102. *Ibid.*, pp. 522–4.
103. *Ibid.*, p. 524. The commission members, as listed in the resolution, were Molotov, Stalin, Kaganovich, Kuibyshev, Voroshilov, Ordzhonikidze, Kalinin, Kirov, Kosior, Yakovlev, Lyubimov, Andreev, Pyatakov, Mezhlauk, Chubar', Goloded,

Isaev, Musabekov, Kabakov, Gryadinskii, Sulimov, Rakhimbaev, Ryabinin, Pakhomov, Gaister, Rudzutak, Shvernik and Yurkin.

104. *Ibid.*, pp. 660–9.
105. *Ibid.*, pp. 539, 542, 552–4.
106. *Ibid.*, p. 562.
107. *SKP*, pp. 565, 555.
108. Two republics, Belorussia SSR and Azerbaidzhan SSR, were represented only by candidate members of the Central Committee. Other regional administrations whose first secretaries were only Central Committee candidate members were: Central Volga krai, Bashkir ASSR, Crimea ASSR, Kalinin gorkom, Kursk gorkom, Odessa obkom, Stalingrad obkom, Donetsk obkom (Sarkis) and Kharkov obkom.

4
Moscow City and Oblast

E. A. Rees

Moscow in many ways occupied a unique position in Soviet politics, and as the capital it was highly visible domestically and internationally. For the Soviet leadership Moscow was a showcase, a demonstration of the regime's competence and of its control. On account of its proximity to the centres of power it enjoyed a position of unique advantage *vis-à-vis* other local author-ities. In the 1920s it was still overshadowed in many ways by the former imperial capital Leningrad (St Petersburg). By the late 1920s the regime faced the problem of defining the role of the capital city within the USSR and the form of urban development appropriate to a socialist state. The Moscow authorities had to deal with a rapidly growing population, which placed enormous strain of on supplies, housing, social amenities and trans-port.[1] Moscow and its surrounding oblast was also one of the country's most important industrial regions, it formed the central hub of the country's transport and communications network, and was the USSR's main cultural and educational centre. The development of Moscow in the 1930s casts important light on the nature of the Stalinist state and the way that that state determined its policy priorities.

On 14 January 1929 Sovnarkom established Moscow oblast, which embraced Moscow the capital city, as a single administrative unit. It com-prised the old Moscow guberniya and parts of Tula, Ryazan, Kaluga and Tver (Kalinin) guberniya. At the beginning of the 1930s it had a population of more than 10 million people. Apart from Moscow itself it included major urban and industrial centres such as Tula, Kalinin, Kolomna, Serpukhov, Podol'sk, Orekhovo–Zuevo, Ryazan' and Kaluga. With the growing complexity of administration at the beginning of 1931 Moscow city and Moscow oblast were given their own administrative bodies.[2] By the end of the 1930s Moscow city and oblast accounted for about one-fifth of all industrial workers and about one-quarter of all industrial production of the USSR.

The political leadership of Moscow

The Moscow party organisation was the largest and most prestigious in the country, with the strongest representation in party congresses. Its leader was almost invariably a member of the Politburo. L. B. Kamenev, one of the leading figures in Lenin's Politburo, was chairman of the Moscow Soviet, and deputy chairman of Sovnarkom RSFSR from 1922 to 1926. In 1926 he lost his post on the Moscow Soviet and was downgraded to candidate member of the Politburo as a result of his defeat in the power struggle with Stalin. N. A. Uglanov, who had been appointed first secretary of the Moscow party committee in October 1924, became the dominant figure in the capital. In 1926 he was made a candidate member of the Politburo. In 1928 Uglanov sided with the 'Right' against Stalin and was ousted. V. M. Molotov, Stalin's close ally, was briefly drafted in as first secretary, only to be replaced by K. Ya. Bauman, who was elevated to the position of candidate member of the Politburo.

The Moscow party organisation in the 1920s demonstrated a degree of independence in relation to the country's leadership. Various attempts were made to turn it into a base of opposition to the party leadership – Trotsky in 1923, the Joint Opposition in 1927, Uglanov in 1928. Stalin's efforts to find a dependable figure that could bring the Moscow party organisation to heel was protracted. Bauman as first party secretary proved during the collectivisation and dekulakisation drive of 1929–30 to be overly zealous. As part of the general retreat on collectivisation, signalled by Stalin's article 'Dizzy with Success', which blamed local officials for excesses, Bauman was sacrificed. On 18 April 1930 the Politburo relieved him of his post as secretary of the Moscow oblast party organisation, and appointed in his place L. M. Kaganovich.[3]

Stalin chose Kaganovich as first secretary of the Moscow Committee. In a telegram he sounded him out regarding the post. With such key appointments Stalin would normally have a meeting with the person concerned to make sure they understood what was expected of them. In his discussion with Kaganovich, Stalin stressed the need to stabilise the situation after the removal of Bauman, to reassert the authority of the party leadership, to unify the activists, purge the party's ranks, re-educate activists accused of leftist excesses, correct mistakes, and to prepare for new advance in collectivisation. On taking up his post Kaganovich addressed district party conferences, and meetings of activists in the enterprises. The Moscow party committee sent out large numbers of propagandists into the countryside in May–June, to strengthen the remaining kolkhozy after the mass exodus of peasants in the preceeding months. Hundreds of new workers and poor peasants were promoted in this period to party and soviet posts.[4]

Stalin needed a dependable person in Moscow. Kaganovich from 1922 to 1925 worked with Stalin in the Central Committee apparatus, in charge of cadres as head of the Organisation–Instruction department, and the Organisation–Distribution department. In 1925 he was appointed by Stalin to serve as General Secretary of the Ukrainian Communist Party, but was recalled in 1928, largely because of the dissatisfaction of other Ukrainian leaders with his authoritarian style. In 1928–9 he played an important role in the defeat of the Right opposition and in developing and implementing agricultural collectivisation. He became a full member of the Politburo in 1930, as well as a member of the Secretariat and Orgburo.

With the creation of separate city and oblast administrative structures in 1931 Kaganovich served as both secretary of the Moscow obkom and gorkom. Given his other party responsibilities much of the task of administering the capital fell on his deputies' shoulders.[5] He created his own team of loyal officials, including N. S. Khrushchev, K. V. Ryndin, N. A. Bulganin and G. M. Malenkov. Khrushchev was Kaganovich's protégé and their links went back to the Ukraine in the mid-1920s. Bulganin and Malenkov had links with Kaganovich which went back to Turkestan during the civil war. These three were to go on to make remarkable careers for themselves within the Soviet state. Kaganovich, according to Colton, packed the Moscow establishment with a personal coterie: 21 other ranking Moscow functionaries between 1930 and 1937 (11 who made it to obkom or gorkom secretary) can be identified as having earlier served with Kaganovich in Nizhny Novgorod, Voronezh, Turkestan, Ukraine and in the Central Committee's apparatus in Moscow.[6]

Between 1930 and 1935 Kaganovich was at the peak of his power, appearing almost to eclipse Molotov as Stalin's second in command and likely successor. He sat on a plethora of Politburo commissions, and in Stalin's absence from Moscow during his long summer vacations, he acted as his deputy in the Politburo.

Within the Stalinist political leadership Kaganovich occupied a position of immense influence. We have seen (Chapter 2) how Moscow became the leading beneficiary in terms of state investment during the Second Five-Year Plan. The powerful Moscow city and oblast party organisation was able to resist the trend from 1929 onwards whereby the central economic commissariats came to dominate the territorial administrative units. Kaganovich as Moscow boss and Stalin's second in command, had more political clout than Ordzhonikidze, head of the powerful Commissariat of Heavy Industry (NKTyazhProm). In this the Moscow party authorities occupied a position that was quite unique among the territorial units of the USSR.

Party organisation

One of Kaganovich's priorities in charge of the capital was to turn it into a loyal bastion of the ruling Stalinist group; to rectify the damage done to the party's reputation with the removal of Bauman and to wage an assault on the remnants of 'Rightist' support within the raikoms. In this, Kaganovich was assisted by the ruthless Ya. Kh. Peters, head of the Moscow party Control Commission. Some embers of resistance remained. At the XVI party congress in June 1930 Kaganovich accused Uglanov of retaining links with dissident elements within the Moscow party apparatus.[7] M. N. Ryutin, until 1928 secretary of the Krasnaya Presnaya raion, who in 1929 criticised Stalin to his face, was expelled from the party in 1930, and in 1932 during the famine crisis, circulated his platform in Moscow with its coruscating attack on Stalin and his policies.[8]

At the Moscow party conference in January 1934 many of the delegates stressed Kaganovich's role in turning the Moscow party organisation into one of the strongest bulwarks of the Central Committee, and a model organisation which other local party organisations should emulate. They had liquidated the remnants of the 'Uglanovshchina', and the 'leftist' deviation (*levatskyi peregib*) of Bauman. The Uglanovites were branded as 'tea-drinkers' (*chaepitchiki*) suggesting a certain idle gentility, an aloof detachment and an unwillingness to get involved in the direct tasks of management. Uglanov and his supporters attempted to turn the textile regions, especially Orekhovo–zuevskii raion, into their stronghold in their fight with the Central Committee. Under Uglanov, the raions felt themselves as separate 'fiefdoms' (*knyazhestva*), with the operation of family circles of mutual protection (*krugovaya poruka*).[9]

With Kaganovich's arrival these methods of leadership were changed, and by 1934 it was claimed that 'groupism' (*gruppovshchina*), familiarity (bat'kovshchina) and 'inter-intestinal war' between raions, such as that between Sokolnikii and Krasnaya Presnaya, had been eliminated. Whereas under Uglanov the administration was based on investigations and detailed reports (*doklad zapiski*) from the various local organisations, under Kaganovich the Moscow committee took a close interest in the work of all raikoms, displaying a detailed knowledge of the work of the local bodies.[10]

The transformation of Moscow into a loyal Stalinist bastion brought its own rewards, reflected in the new political weight which the Moscow party leadership wielded within the party's inner counsels. Kaganovich reported directly to Stalin on questions relating to Moscow. In the Stalin–Kaganovich correspondence from 1931 to 1936, however, there is only one written report from Kaganovich to Stalin, dated September 1931, on work in improving the organisation of the city's economy.[11] Questions of policy relating to Moscow often by-passed the more formalised processes of decision-making, and many appear to have been settled in private meetings. This reflected also the new importance accorded to the capital within the structure of the Stalinist state, and the profound shifts which occurred in centre–local relations in these years.

The economy of Moscow oblast

Industry

In the 1920s the industry of Moscow oblast was largely dominated by light industry, especially of textiles (cotton, woollen goods). Already under the First Five-Year Plan a significant shift in emphasis had been made in the direction of developing heavy industry. Moscow was turned into a major centre of machine-building, chemicals and electricity generation.[12] Moscow, like Berlin, had become a major centre for producing electrical equipment.[13] A major priority during the Second Five-Year Plan was to encourage a shift of heavy industry from the confines of the city out into the oblast, where in the past the textile industry had been predominant.

Moscow included some of the most important enterprises in the USSR: Dinamo, Elektrozavod, Vladimir Ilich, AMO, Gosnak, Serp i Molot, Tormoznoi, 24-i works, Krasnyi Bogatyr' and Kauchyk. Under Kaganovich's leadership heavy industry was given preferential treatment, and a number of 'model' factories were projected, either on entirely new sites or on the adapted premises of old plants such as Serp i Molot and AMO. In promoting the development of industry, and particularly defence industries, the Moscow party organisation coordinated its work with NKTyazhProm and NKVMDel. In the early 1930s Kaganovich was given responsibility for the rapid conversion of Moscow factories to tank production, and for conversion of factories to aircraft production.[14]

The Moscow authorities benefited from a close relationship with the NKTyazhProm, which was facilitated by the close friendship between Kaganovich and Ordzhonikidze. Kaganovich took initiatives in developing the metallurgical industry in Moscow oblast, particularly the development of the New Tula (Novotula) metallurgical combine, which had major defence significance.[15]

During the First and the Second Five-Year Plans the oblast was transformed into one of the main bases of industrialisation of the country. Radical reconstruction was undertaken at the Kolomenskoe locomotive-building works, the Mytishchinskii machine-building works, and the Lyuberetskii agricultural implements works, the Podol'skii spinning-machine works, and the Voikova factory producing central heating equipment and many other enterprises. The questions of quality of wagons for the metro to be supplied by the Mytishchinskii works drew the attention of Moscow gorkom bureau and Kaganovich's personal intervention.[16] There was a large-scale expansion of the chemical industry with the building of a number of new combines. The Moscow Stalin Motor Works (ZIS) produced 42 per cent of cars for the USSR, with its capacity being increased to 80,000 vehicles per annum during the Second Five-Year Plan. This one factory received during the course of the Second Five-Year plan an investment of 474 million rubles.[17] This was almost equivalent to the whole projected investment in heavy industry in the East Siberian krai under the terms of the Second Five-Year Plan and in reality, almost certainly exceeded what the oblast actually received.

The rapid development of the capital placed great strain on energy resources. In accordance with the plan of the Goelro project a number of electrical power stations were built around Moscow such as Kashira, Shaturskaya, Orekho-zuevskii and TETs, while others, such as Klasson were reconstructed. The development of the oblast's electrical power industry was given top priority during the Second Five-Year Plan the order to meet the growing needs of the city's industries and urban population, with the volume of electrical power generated being doubled between 1932 and 1937. On 26 January 1934 the Moscow party bureau examined construction work on the Stalinogorod hydro-electric power station. It charged Kaganovich to consult with Ordzhonikidze on the possibility of purchasing necessary parts from abroad.[18]

The draft of the Second Five-Year Plan referred to the 'gigantic development of heavy industry of Moscow oblast' and the problems which this would create. Priority was to be accorded to the development of the local fuel base in order to reduce the costs of transporting coal from the Donbass. Output from the Moscow coal basin was to rise from 2.8 million tons in 1932 to 10 million tons in 1937. The bulk of output by 1937 was to come from new shafts. The Gosplan target was evidently more modest than that proposed by the Moscow party committee. Kaganovich at one stage had envisaged by the end of Second Five-Year Plan an annual output of 20 million tons.[19]

Moscow oblast at the end of First Five-Year Plan was responsible for 40 per cent of the country's light industrial production. This was expected to decline to 28.2 per cent by 1937, notwithstanding an increase of 117 per cent in textile production during the period; 85 per cent of investment was allocated for modernising and expanding existing enterprises. Kaganovich intervened to resolve hold-ups in the textile industry, and to promote improvements in quality of production and to reduce waste. He delivered a report on low-quality production to the Moscow oblast conference in September 1933.[20] Despite this intervention a check of the textile industry in April 1934 revealed that the situation was largely unchanged.[21] The Moscow obkom bureau resolved to prepare a special note to the Central Committee.[22]

A major transport undertaking was the improvement of the Moscow–Donbass rail line, which carried coal to the central industrial region. Work commenced in 1932. Kaganovich was closely involved in monitoring progress on the line, with the Politburo being kept in close touch.[23] The work was to be finished in 1935. However, radical planners in NKPS and in the Moscow city administration, apparently with the backing of Kaganovich, pushed for the scheme to be upgraded, and for the Moscow–Donbass to be turned into a super-trunk line (*sverkh-magistral*). This scheme generated great controversy. In the end Stalin vetoed what he considered to be a wildly extravagant scheme. In September 1936 Kaganovich wrote to Stalin that NKPS had reworked its project for the line and had accepted 'Your instructions' that the line should not be a super-trunk but an ordinary line. The total cost of modernising the line was now set at 790 million rubles (of which 490 million rubles had already been spent) instead of the 1,170 million rubles projected for the super-trunk line. The work was to be completed in 1937. On 28 October the Politburo approved the revised project at a total cost of 780 million rubles.[24]

The electrification and reconstruction of the Moscow suburban rail network, by NKPS in collaboration with the Moscow authorities, was undertaken during the Second Five-Year Plan.[25] Kaganovich was involved in the reconstruction of the railway wagon building works at Kalinin.[26] The Kolomenskoe locomotive works, producer of the new IS (Iosif Stalin) locomotives failed to meet production target in 1932 and 1933. The matter was repeatedly discussed by the Moskow obkom with telegrams dispatched by Kaganovich warning of the consequences of non-compliance. Kaganovich had also tried to assist in limiting the high level of labour turnover.[27]

In 1934 an extraordinarily ambitious scheme to electrify part of the Soviet rail system was contemplated. This required the building of a giant electric locomotive works at Kashira, the capacity of which, according to G. N. Kaminskii, would exceed that of the biggest works of Westinghouse and General Motors in the USA, Braun in Italy and AEG in Germany together.[28] In reality, the scale of the project was to be drastically scaled down.

Agriculture and food supply

The retreat on the agricultural front in 1930 created a delicate situation for the Stalinist leadership. Kaganovich, as party boss of Moscow, did not tolerate public criticism of official policy. He publicly reprimanded Krupskaya when, in a speech to a conference of Bauman raion in Moscow in the summer of 1930, she declared that collectivisation had not been carried out in a Leninist manner.[29] His priority was to re-establish the party's authority and to restore order within the party. Addressing the Moscow oblast party plenum in December 1930 he called for Moscow oblast to be turned from a consuming into a producing region, to abandon the 'nihilistic, superficial, high-handed attitude to agriculture', and to ensure meat, milk and butter supplies for the urban population.[30]

The renewed collectivisation drive in the autumn of 1930, however, was predictably associated with a return to repression. Kaganovich, in a speech to the Moscow obkom plenum in February 1931, highlighted the intensification of the 'class struggle' in Moscow oblast. In the autumn of 1930, he reported, the OGPU had uncovered and liquidated 206 counter-revolutionary kulak groups (with 2,858 participants) which, he asserted, had been responsible for attacks on kolkhoz property and acts of terror (*terakty*). There had also been instances of anti-soviet groups at work in industry. He declared

'We Bolsheviks of course do not idealise the working class as a whole', emphasising the need to isolate hostile elements and to provide firm Bolshevik leadership.[31]

Moscow and Leningrad were both given privileged treatment with regard to food supply, although even they had their allocations cut from 1931 onwards. Moscow oblast as an agricultural region was quite atypical of the USSR. Partly because of its proximity to the large urban market provided by the capital and the availability of alternative employment, the living standards of the rural population was far above the norm. In 1931 the incomes of collective farm peasants in Moscow oblast was four–five times higher than that of peasants in the North Caucasus, Ukraine, Urals, Belorussia and the Lower Volga, a startling reflection of the persistence of huge regional variations in the distribution of wealth.[32] The peasants of Moscow oblast were also far better placed to gain access to manufactured and other goods.

Even this relatively privileged region was not immune to crisis, however. On 12 April 1932 Kaganovich visited Vichuga in neighbouring Ivanovo oblast, where acute food shortages had triggered popular protests and strike action. An OGPU detachment fired into the air to disperse the crowds. Hundreds were arrested and the strike movement was halted. The Central Committee dismissed the regional party secretary, and directed the Ivanovo obkom to resolutely purge its ranks of disloyal members. Sovnarkom took steps to improve food supply to the region.[33]

On 20 May 1932 the Politburo approved the legalisation of kolkhoz sales at market prices. This major concession was prompted by the disturbances in Ivanovo – and concern about acute food shortages. In the following months the policy was developed in a wave of legislative enactments.

Kaganovich in his speech to the oblast and city party conference in August 1932 outlined the role of the party in improving agriculture, in strengthening the kolkhozy and encouraging the peasants' private plots.[34] He rejected the views of those who believed that if the peasants had their own plots this would undermine the collective farms as 'nonsense'. The kolkhozniki should have each their own cow, and the collective farms should help them feed their animals. They should strive, at the same time, to strengthen the kolkhozy. This, he argued, was not a 'neo-NEP', as some 'opportunists' suggested.[35] It was necessary to develop markets, to stimulate artisan trades and to encourage the flow of goods to the bazaars. With this aim, a 50 km zone around Moscow was to be freed of state procurement and contracts, except for grain. It was necessary to increase the production of goods of mass consumption to stimulate trade.

Kaganovich's speech to the Moscow gorkom and obkom on 8 October 1932 again highlighted the need to increase the production of goods of mass consumption in order to bring more grain onto the market. He noted that the policy of directing consumer goods to the countryside had 'offended' the towns. He urged determined efforts to boost the region's artisan industries by reducing bureaucratic interference, with lower taxes, higher prices and increased incentives. He blamed the past neglect of this sector on a favourite bugbear, namely 'leftist' excesses and the underestimation of kolkhoz trade.[36]

The concessions went alongside more repressive measures to combat the 'theft' of collective farm property in August 1932. By the end of the year recourse was taken again to more direct measures to extract grain from the countryside. In the famine crisis of 1932–3 food supplies were secured for the capital as a top priority, in dramatic contrast to the tragic fate of Ukraine, North Caucasus, Lower Volga and Kazakhstan.

On 4 July 1933 Kaganovich delivered a report to the Moscow obkom and gorkom on strengthening the state sector in agriculture during the harvest and grain procurement campaigns and on overcoming the opposition of class enemies. The success of the spring sowing campaign, he argued, augured well for the future. He stressed the important role of the *politotdely* and Machine Tractor Stations (MTS) in ensuring political control in agriculture. The area of collectivised agriculture had increased from 50 to 65 per cent in Moscow oblast, with 2,250 new kolkhozy having being created. There was an increase in sown area and in mechanisation. Rural officials should regard individual peasants as 'tomorrow's kolkhozniki'. But he cautioned against the setting of exaggerated targets, and the need to repeat the errors, which in 1930 had forced the party to retreat.[37] With the establishment of the *politotdely* in the sovkhozy and MTS in 1933 Moscow provided one-third of the first 10,000 recruits.[38]

G. N. Kaminskii, chairman of Moscow oblast's soviet executive committee, reported to its plenum in July 1933 on the continuing problems in agriculture. Sovnarkom, the Moscow party committee and Moscow soviet executive committee had provided assistance by way of grain, seed, foodstuffs and a number of organisational measures to the worst affected districts.[39] Food resources were redistributed from the strong districts (mainly in the east) to the weak districts of the oblast (mainly in the south and south west).[40]

In September 1933, Kaganovich wrote to Stalin about the situation in Moscow oblast where 'as a result of unprecedented downpours that turned into a literal disaster, there has been a steep drop in grain yields'. He appealed as secretary of Moscow obkom, ('I ask You to help us') with the backing of M. A. Chernov, head of the Committee for Agricultural Procurements (KomZag), for a cut in the oblast's grain procurement target. Stalin approved.[41] Symptomatic of the situation in the autumn of 1933 was Kaganovich's visit to Efremov raion, where ruthless measures were employed to enforce grain procurement. As a result, Medvedev recounts, nearly half of the local population boarded up their huts and left Efremov raion, which had to import grain and potatoes for three years.[42]

Notwithstanding these difficulties, Khrushchev reported to the Moscow party conference in January 1934 that the task set of turning Moscow from a consumer to a producer in relation to vegetables and potatoes was already solved. A zone of 30 km around Moscow was turned over to vegetable-growing in 1933. All the new MTS, which served the kolkhozy and sovkhozy, were created within this zone. The road network in this zone had been greatly improved.[43] At the beginning of 1934 Moscow oblast was awarded, with four other oblasts, the Order of Lenin for their services in agriculture and their success in completing collectivisation.

However, the effective resolution of questions of agriculture was impeded in part by the extreme overloading of the whole system with endless orders and directives issued from above, including those from the Central Committee and Politburo. Plenipotentiaries were regularly sent to the localities to check on policy enforcement.[44] As a result the lower administrative links lost initiative or sought to evade these controls by increasing the resources at their disposal through the creation of secret funds and reserves whether of money, raw materials, fodder or seed or labour, and through devising new money substitutes.

In 1934 the newly established People's Commissariat of Food Industry (NKPishProm) took over a large number of republican and oblast enterprises. Kaganovich in September 1934 wrote to Stalin complaining that Moscow oblast, which had previously had a number of food-processing plants, had suffered particularly.[45] This was part of the general concentration of control over industry in the all-union commissariats. That Moscow oblast should also have suffered offers a remarkable insight into the balance between the branch economic commissariats and the territorial authorities.

The reconstruction of Moscow

Since the transfer of the capital during the civil war from Petrograd to Moscow, the urban development of the Soviet capital had been largely neglected. Under Kamenev, Uglanov and Bauman, lack of resources had impeded schemes for development. Moscow lacked the aura of a capital. It was still in many respects a medieval city, dominated by the Kremlin citadel, by monastic and church buildings, and by the houses of the nobility. Industrial development had been allowed to develop to a great extent unchecked within the capital itself. The task of the future role of Moscow as capital of the USSR was increasingly perceived as an urgent question.

In the late 1920s and early 1930s Russian and international architects advanced a series of fantastic schemes for the reconstruction of Moscow. These included N. A. Ladovskii's 'dynamic city', German Krasin's 'workers' colonies', the modernist visions of Le Corbusier, Ernst May and others. Other architects such as Moisei Ginsburg and L. M. Sabsovich advanced 'anti-urbanist' views, aimed at moving away from large urban population concentrations, whilst Kostantin Melnikov proposed the creation of a Green City.[46] Other architects argued for preserving old Moscow, and locating development elsewhere.

Three weeks after Kaganovich took over, the Central Committee on 16 May 1930 issued a resolution 'On Work at the Reconstruction of the Way of Life'. It denounced Sabsovich and Larin, criticising 'semi-fantastic' and 'utopian' theories about gaining socialism 'at a single leap'.[47]

From 1928 to 1933 Moscow city's population grew from 2.3 million to 3.6 million. The Politburo created a commission, including Stalin, and chaired by Kaganovich, to look into the reconstruction of Moscow and other cities. The Central Committee instructed the Mossoviet to build houses for half a million people in three years.[48]

Kaganovich's report to the Central Committee plenum in June 1931 'Concerning the socialist reconstruction of Moscow and the cities of the USSR', dealt with all aspects of the capital's urban economy. The city was to be transformed into a 'proletarian centre'. Kaganovich rejected any attempt to narrowly define what a 'socialist' city was. Russia's cities, he explained, had become 'socialist' the moment power was transferred to the Bolshevik government in 1917. He dismissed as 'nonsense' suggestions for the 'reduction or self-abolition' of large urban centres.[49] Greater order was needed in the development of the capital, to brake hyperurbanisation and to locate new factories outside Moscow. On Moscow's population Kaganovich volunteered only that it should neither decline nor be allowed to balloon out of 'tempting' thoughts of a Moscow of 10 million'.[50] The presentation was notable in that it included references to two major schemes – the Moscow–Volga canal and the Moscow metro. It was high time, Kaganovich declared, to bring Moscow up 'to the level of the technically advanced cities of Europe'.[51]

On the basis of Kaganovich's report, the Central Committee on 15 June 1931 approved its resolution 'Concerning the Urban Economy of Moscow and the Development of the Urban Economy of the USSR'.[52] It called for the development of a scientific plan for the development of Moscow's urban economy.[53] The plenum rejected all schematic approaches to the development of the capital, instead focusing on practical issues. Moscow should, however, avoid the excesses of development of capitalist cities, and in particular should avoid the excessive concentration of population in small areas.[54] The Central Committee also approved the resolution adopted by the Moscow gorkom, obkom, gorispolkom and oblast ispolkom: 'Practical Measures to Improve and Develop the Moscow City Economy.'

In July 1932 Kaganovich chaired a meeting of 150 specialists and officials and gave general guidance incorporating 'the direction for the future Moscow indicated by comrade Stalin'.[55] In his speech to the Mossoviet plenum in July 1934 be spoke of the importance of avoiding excesses (*krainost'*), such as schemes to 'ruralise' the capital or to turn into a giant metropolis. The emphasis was to be on modernising the city, expanding its population, but avoiding any excessive over-concentration of people. Apartment blocks were to be no lower than 6–7 storeys and no higher than 15 or 20 storeys. This, he stressed, was a policy which had Stalin's backing.[56]

Much of the work of supervising this reconstruction was entrusted to Kaganovich's deputies, Khrushchev and Bulganin. Khrushchev in his memoirs asserts: 'The huge task of overseeing all this was largely mine because Kaganovich was up to his ears in work outside of the Moscow Party organisation.'[57]

Kaganovich headed the Architectural-Planning Commission of Moscow gorkom and Mossoviet from 1933 to 1935. Thereafter it was headed by Khrushchev. The first plan was completed by the end of 1934, and was submitted at the beginning of 1935 to the Central Committee and Sovnarkom. On 10 July 1935 the Central Committee approved its resolution 'Concerning the Master Plan for the Reconstruction of the City of Moscow', which was co-signed by Stalin and Molotov. The plan revealed the city's future contours, aiming at a population of approximately 5 million. The main expansion, in accordance with Kaganovich's projection, was to be in the south west, beyond the Lenin Hills.[58]

The destruction of historical monuments in Moscow in the 1920s preceded Kaganovich's arrival, but on his appointment assumed a new scale. According to Medvedev: 'It was not Kaganovich but Stalin who played the decisive role and had the last say in the plans for the reconstruction of Moscow, and no large building within the capital's historical centre was razed or built without his approval.'[59] This is borne out by Stalin's correspondence with Kaganovich, with the former being kept closely informed, and his advice regularly solicited, as regards plans to change the architecture of the capital.[60] Much later Kaganovich, in his memoirs, recalled Stalin's close involvement in drawing up plans for the reconstruction.[61]

The modernisation of the capital was accompanied by the ruthless destruction of the symbols of the old order. Before the revolution Moscow had 460 Orthodox churches. On 1 January 1930 this was down to 224 and 1 January 1933 their number was further reduced to about 100.[62] In November 1935 the double-headed eagles were taken down off the Kremlin towers and replaced by the red stars. The matter was decided between Kaganovich and Stalin, with Stalin approving the design of the stars. Their decision was then confirmed by the Politburo, and presented to the public as a joint Central Committee–Sovnarkom USSR resolution.[63] In the 1920s and 1930s many of the buildings housing party and government departments were fundamentally reconstructed, whilst the GPU's Lubyanka building was greatly enlarged. The transfer of the Academy of Sciences from Leningrad to Moscow in 1934–5 was another important symbolic move.

On 25 May 1931, on a report from Molotov and Voroshilov, the Politburo approved as decision to build the Palace of Soviets on the site of the Cathedral of Christ the Redeemer.[64] On 5 June 1931 the Politburo, following a tour of the site by Stalin, confirmed the decision.[65] According to Kaganovich the order to destroy the cathedral was signed by Stalin, Molotov, Kaganovich, Kalinin and Bulganin.[66] It was duly blown up on 5 December 1931.

The Palace of Soviets was intended as an architectural wonder; standing higher than the Empire State building, crowned with a statue of Lenin 100 metres tall. As a project it stood alongside the metro and the Moscow–Volga canal as plans for transforming the capital. The scheme was dogged by constant problems concerning the foundations of the building. The project was included in the Third Five-Year Plan.[67] Construction work, however, was halted in 1941 and the project was finally abandoned in the late 1950s.

Other ancient monuments, including the Sukharev Tower, Kitaigorod's walls, the Passion Monastery and the Iversky Gates, were destroyed. Kaganovich is alleged to have advocated the demolition of St Basil's Cathedral and even of the Kremlin itself.[68] Kaganovich later denied these charges, and placed some of the blame for the destruction of Moscow's architectural monuments on Khrushchev, claiming that he himself had done much to preserve the city's architectural heritage.[69]

Building the metro

The question of building a metro system in Moscow (Metrostroi) had been discussed by the Moscow Duma in 1900. In the 1920s the Moscow party under Kamenev looked again at the feasibility of building it. The issue was revived in 1930. Even then it was a matter of considerable dispute. Some argued that the money should be spent on expanding other modes of transport in the capital. The scheme, Kaganovich later recalled, had also encountered some opposition from Gosplan on account of the high cost.[70]

Stalin, in his report to the Central Committee in June 1931, proposed that construction should begin without delay. Kaganovich was an energetic promoter of the project. At the height of the famine in March 1933 the Central Committee and Sovnarkom, on the proposal of Moscow organisation, approved the scheme.[71]

Leading mining specialist such as Rotert and Y. T. Abakumov were brought in from the Donbass, together with a large number of worker volunteers. Abakumov was closely associated with Khrushchev. Khrushchev took charge of construction, with Stalin's approval. Kaganovich, Khrushchev and Bulganin were closely involved in this work. Kaganovich regularly reported on this to Stalin and the Politburo. A key issue of dispute was whether the metro should be built by the German open-trench method, or by closed-tunnel method, which would be much deeper, and involve high investment in escalators. The dispute between Kaganovich and Rotert on this matter went to the Politburo, which supported the closed-tunnel method proposed by Khrushchev and Kaganovich.[72]

Kaganovich addressed Mossoviet on 29 December 1933 and announced that the party and government had set as a target the seventeenth anniversary of the October Revolution (7 November 1934) as the date for completing the first phase of the Metro. This was confirmed by a resolution passed by the Moscow obkom and gorkom aimed at speeding up progress.[73] In the event, this proved unrealistic.

The Second Five-Year Plan draft of January 1934 set a target of investment in Metrostroi of 1.2 milliard rubles, with the construction of 36 km of two-track lines by 1937. The January 1934 Central Committee resolution 'Concerning the Construction of the Metropoliten, first stage', it was claimed, had produced big improvements, with Moscow factories assigning their best engineers and workers to the metro. On a report from Kaganovich a new resolution was approved by Mossoviet 'Concerning the construction of the metropoliten' on 16 July 1934.[74]

An extremely close partnership developed between Kaganovich and Khrushchev. In building the metro Khrushchev reported regularly to Kaganovich on progress. Kaganovich visited Berlin *incognito* to study the metro there. Khrushchev reported to Kaganovich that he and Bulganin had attended a meeting of the Politburo on 4 May 1934, and had argued the case for an additional 23 million rubles capital investment in the metro, on top of the 100 million rubles already assigned for the current quarter. Some members of the Politburo had strongly opposed the proposal. Khrushchev and Bulganin had pressed their case and Stalin had intervened and set a compromise figure of 10 million rubles.[75]

On 14 May 1935 with a great fanfare of celebrations Stalin and Kaganovich opened the first 12 km of line connecting Sokol'niki and Gorky Park.[76] In this speech Kaganovich brought out the symbolic importance of this achievement: 'The Victory of the Metropoliten–The Victory of Socialism'.[77] It was a matter of pride that the metro had been built with Soviet equipment, by Soviet workers. The work had cost 700 million rubles. Kaganovich proposed that the metro be named in honour of Stalin. Stalin in a letter to the Moscow obkom proposed that it be named after Kaganovich in recognition of the latter's work on the project. This was confirmed by TsIK USSR on 13 May 1935.[78] The Moscow metro retained Kaganovich's name until 1955, when it was renamed in honour of Lenin.

Stalin's ability to concern himself in even relatively minor matters is illustrated by Kaganovich's note to him in September 1935 to secure his approval for reducing the fare on the metro from 40 to 30 kopeks. Stalin approved and the decision was then 'confirmed' by the Politburo.[79]

The Moscow–Volga canal

The largest construction projects undertaken during the Second Five-Year Plan was the building of the Moscow–Volga canal (Moskanalstroi).[80] On 15 June 1931 the Central Committee plenum, on a report by Kaganovich, accepted the need 'radically to resolve the task of replenishing the Moscow river by uniting it with the upper reaches of the Volga'. This was to double Moscow's supply of water by 1935.[81] The city's daily consumption rose from 8.5 million vedera in 1913 (1 vedro = 12.3 litres) to 16.7 million vedera in 1928, to 39 million vedera in 1933: a consumption of 60 million vedera was anticipated for 1935. Water shortages were frequent, and water cuts common.[82]

The project was considered in June 1931 by a Politburo commission, which included representatives of Moscow gorkom, Gosplan, and the People's Commissariat of Water Transport (NKVodTrans).[83] The project was opposed by NKVodTrans, with Gosplan also expressing reservations.[84] In March 1932 STO included the canal in the category of national 'shock' work.[85] It was to be three times as long as the Baltic–White Sea Canal. Water from the upper reaches of the Volga was to be diverted into the Moscow River and then returned to the Volga near Gorky.[86] The cost was estimated at 700 million rubles. At the end of 1932 construction was entrusted to OGPU.[87] The Moskanalstroi trust was set up. It was led by L. I. Kogan, who had previously headed the Belomor canal project. In 1933 many managers (GPU officials) and forced labourers were transferred from the completed Belomor project to the Moscow–Volga project.[88]

Two accounts claim that Stalin initiated the scheme,[89] any project of this scale required Stalin's approval. However, Kaganovich's role was central. As a member of the Politburo, Secretariat, Orgburo and head of the Central Committee's Transport Sector, he was an immensely powerful figure. Whilst he could advance proposals he was very careful not to cross Stalin. His prime concern, however, was with securing adequate water supply for Moscow, and only secondarily in improving water transport.[90]

On 1 June 1932 Sovnarkom adopted the Dmitrovskii plan, the least expensive of three projects submitted to it, and set the completion date as November 1934.[91] An important part in developing the project was played by academician S. Ya. Zhuk.[92] The project was nominally financed by Mossoviet, but the fact that Gosplan, NKTyazhProm and other commissariats were instructed to cooperate shows its national significance.[93] Construction work began in September 1932. On 5 December the Politburo approved the draft resolution, presented by the Kaganovich commission, on the course of the Moscow–Volga canal. It was to be completed by the end of 1935, with STO required in 1934 to provide 400 million rubles.[94]

This canal, 127 km long, was planned to be ready for navigation by the spring of 1936. Already in April 1934 Khrushchev reported to Kaganovich that at a meeting of the Politburo Kuibyshev, head of Gosplan, had proposed delaying its completion, apparently for financial reasons. Khrushchev and Bulganin had argued for sticking to the original completion date. Stalin also strongly opposed any delay, on the grounds that he thought it undesirable to retain a large number of convict labourers in Moscow oblast over an extended period.[95]

NKVD provided the project with labour, with the Dmitrov camp, headed by S. G. Firin, the main supplier. According to one British observer, Firin reported that 81,000 were engaged in the work in 1935, of whom nine-tenths were prisoners.[96] Lord Simon, who visited Moscow, observed the highly controlled nature of the work.[97] According to another source some 196,000 prisoners from the Dmitrov camp were involved in this project.[98] On 25 August 1936 the head of construction L. I. Kogan was replaced by M. D. Berman, head of NKVD Gulag.[99]

In 1935 the Politburo on various occasions discussed progress on the project.[100] A joint Sovnarkom–Central Committee resolution was issued, approved by the Politburo on 7 September 1935, concerning construction work and measures for bringing the canal into operation in 1937.[101] But prior to these decisions being taken by these bodies Kaganovich had secured Stalin's signature on the draft resolution, which had been earlier drafted by a Politburo commission.[102] The Politburo continued to monitor progress. In June 1937 the Politburo approved the Sovnarkom–Central Committee resolution on the completion of the project, which was named the Moscow Canal.[103]

The Moscow party conference of January 1934

The joint IV Moscow oblast and III city party conference met from 16 to 24 January 1934.[104] The conference, attended by 1,473 delegates, represented the party organisation from 146 raions of Moscow city and oblast. Kaganovich, as party secretary, presented the report of the Central Committee. Ryndin and Mikhailov reported on the work of the Moscow obkom, Khrushchev reported on the work of the gorkom and Kaminskii and Bulganin reported on the economic plan of Moscow oblast and city in the Second Five-Year Plan and the control figures for 1934.

Kaganovich hailed the 'leader of genius of the party and the working class, the great Stalin', who alone ensured the great victories achieved by the party, its internal and international might.[105] Kaganovich's report provided a wide-ranging review of both the international and domestic situation, highlighting the threats posed by Japan and Germany and the need for a strong Red Army. In general he argued; 'The Soviet Union will turn itself during the second pyatiletka into the most technically advanced state in Europe.'[106] The challenge of the class enemy in the kolkhozy, Kaganovich argued, had been thwarted, but he anticipated an intensification of the class struggle in the country and a further tightening of controls.[107]

Peters, head of the Moscow Party Control Commission (KK), at the Moscow party conference in January 1934, reported that they had brought to account 2,000 party members for 'Right' opportunist charges, and during the grain collection campaign in 1932 439 individuals had been brought to account of whom 70 per cent had been expelled from the party.[108] In 1933–34 only 10.4 per cent of membership of Moscow oblast were purged, lower than for any other oblast except Leningrad.[109]

The Moscow party conference saw the emergence of an extraordinary cult around Kaganovich, as the party chief of the 'red capital' (*krasnaya stolitsa*).[110] Kaganovich was presented as a Bolshevik 'superman', a man of boundless energy, a professional revolutionary, a theoretician, a practical administrator, a man who could turn his mind to almost any problem. His personal contribution in building the metro was highlighted. Leading industrial managers praised Kaganovich's role in promoting the reconstruction of existing works. I. A. Likhachev, director of the Stalin motor works, praised his role in ensuring the works' completion on time.[111] Kaganovich had actively promoted the production of aircraft motors at the Frunze works.[112] In 1935 the director of the Elektrostal' work recalled how Kaganovich involved himself in turning the works into an industrial giant, producing 45,000 tons of steel instead of 9000 tons.[113] Artyunyants, head of the construction of the Stalinogorsk chemical combine, asserted that construction was almost abandoned at the start of 1931, after 40 million rubles had been invested, because of a dispute concerning lack of water. Only with the intervention of Kaganovich was the issue resolved.[114] The two GPU chiefs charged with overseeing the Moscow–Volga canal project, Kogan and Berman, effusively praised Kaganovich's drive in overseeing the project, his intimate knowledge of technical questions and his contribution in solving practical problems.[115] He was lauded for his in-depth understanding of the problems of the urban economy, his intimate understanding of architecture and his interest in the problems of Soviet literature.[116] His role in promoting Moscow as a centre of education was highlighted, as was his role in promoting civil defence amongst the capital's population.[117] Two delegates posed the question of awarding Kaganovich the Order of Lenin.[118]

The Second Five-Year Plan for Moscow

The drafting of the Second Five-Year Plan for Moscow city and oblast began in the summer of 1932. A basic disagreement arose over the scale of planned investment. Gosplan USSR proposed to assign 2.669 milliard rubles for capital construction of heavy industry in Moscow oblast during the Second Five-Year Plan, while the Moscow oblast planning commission proposed 4.025 milliard rubles.[119] The working out of the details for the Second Five-Year Plan for Moscow oblast was extremely protracted. At a meeting of the oblast planning bureau in July 1932 was noted the 'complete disorderly phenomenon is represented by the circumstance that the union Gosplan completely excluded us from the first phase of work on these indicators, as for capital construction of a reconstruction character, reconstruction of the railway network, etc. From us they demanded only that we give them the freight turnover for the oblast and notes in the oblast of new railway construction.'[120]

The differences between Gosplan USSR and the Moscow authorities over the proposed investment level had been resolved by the start of 1934.

Kaminskii at the Moscow party conference in January 1934 noted: 'the plan for Moscow oblast in the second *pyatiletka* is an integral part of the Five-Year Plan for the whole Soviet Union.'[121] Kaminskii added 'We were led by the directives of L. M. Kaganovich that the pyatiletka for Moscow oblast was wholly agreed with Gosplan, so that this plan is not simply a local creation. The projected plan for the Novotula combine has been agreed with Gosplan.'[122] Bulganin insisted that the plan for the reconstruction of Moscow was based on the theses of Molotov and Kuibyshev for the Second Five-Year Plan: 'We agreed the basic information in the pyatiletka with the people's commissariats and with Gosplan USSR', but some details remained to be resolved.[123]

Moscow oblast in the Second Five-Year Plan emerged as a major economic region. In the plan period, Moscow oblast was to receive 10.7 milliard rubles capital investment, 10.9 per cent of a total capital investment of 98.8 milliard rubles. Moscow oblast and the Urals oblast were the two major recipients of capital investment, almost on a par with the Ukrainian SSR that received 16.8 per cent of total investment (see Chapter 1). For heavy industry Moscow was assigned 3.5 milliard rubles (9 per cent), rather closer to the figure proposed in 1932 by the Moscow party committee than that favoured by Gosplan. In most other fields Moscow oblast received the lion's share of investment: light industry (15.8 per cent), internal trade (8.3 per cent), water transport (36 per cent), communications (11 per cent), Tsentrosoyuz (15.9 per cent), housing cooperatives (20 per cent), housing fund of soviet executive committees (22 per cent), communal construction (15.4 per cent) and education (11.2 per cent).[124]

In the 1936 annual plan Moscow city and oblast were assigned 4,292 milliard rubles in capital investment (18.7 per cent of the total for the USSR as a whole). Ukraine SSR was to receive 3,342 milliard rubles (14.5 per cent of the total).[125] Large-scale investment was to go into improving energy supply, through the building of district electrical power stations, the development of peat reserves and the expansion of the region's coal industry. Priority was also given to housing construction, developing the food supply and distribution networks and expanding local industry. Moscow was turned into a major machine-building centre with substantial development of the chemical industry. At the same time the oblast retained its position as the main producer of textiles and shoes.

The total investment in Moscow city and oblast in 1935 and 1936 is unclear, but figures are available for what were listed as 'designated' construction projects. In 1935 Moscow oblast was to receive 2.503 milliard rubles capital investment (15.6 per cent for the USSR as a whole). This compared to 2.682 milliard rubles for Ukraine SSR (16.7 per cent). In practice in 1935, capital investment for the USSR as a whole was only about 75 per cent of that planned in the period January–November: Moscow oblast and city received 2.043 milliard rubles.[126] In 1936 Moscow oblast and city received 2.352 milliard rubles, while Ukraine SSR received 2.586 milliard rubles.[127]

The First and Second Five-Year Plans significantly changed the structure of industry in Moscow oblast. The heavy component in Moscow's industry grew from 20 per cent in 1927–8 to 43 per cent in 1932. During the Second Five-Year plan 70 per cent of investment in the industry of the oblast went on heavy industry. Development was concentrated in the technologically advanced sectors, with a stress on developing large-scale enterprises. Investment on projects of over 100 million rubles accounted for two-thirds of all investment. 1,362 milliard rubles was invested in the machine-building industry. Moscow oblast, Leningrad and the Urals were to be the technical base for the industrialisation of the Union.

Kaganovich's departure

In March 1935 Khrushchev was made first secretary of both Moscow obkom and gorkom. Kaganovich, who had been canonised at the Moscow party conference in January 1934, was now transferred to take charge of the People's Commissariat of Transport (NKPS). This was a sideways move, not a demotion, but one which in the longer term led to a weakening of Kaganovich's position within the leadership. By a decision of the Politburo of 10 March 1935 Kaganovich retained responsibility in the Politburo for Moscow city and oblast, but how long this remained in force is unclear.[128]

Khrushchev continued the main lines of policy developed under Kaganovich. The main change, reflecting the general trend, was the tightening up of political control. The checking of party documents in the Moscow party organisation in 1935 was directed against 'hostile' elements. Khrushchev played a central role in directing the repression in Moscow in 1937–8. In 1938 he was appointed first secretary of the Ukrainian Communist party and there continued the work of purging the republican organisation. In 1938 he was made a candidate member of the Politburo and the following year a full member.

In February 1938 A. I. Ugarov, formerly second secretary of Leningrad gorkom, was appointed first secretary of Moscow obkom and gorkom. In October 1938, however, on Stalin's orders, he was removed and blamed for the failure to deal with the problem of food supply for the capital.[129] The following year he was executed. He was replaced by A. S. Shcherbakov who had occupied various provincial party posts, including second secretary of Leningrad obkom, first secretary of Irkutsk obkom, and first secretary of Stalinsk obkom. He was made a candidate member of the Politburo in 1941. He remained as first secretary of Moscow obkom and gorkom from 1938 until his death in 1945.

As part of the general trend to break up the larger territorial administrative units Moscow oblast was reduced in size. In September 1937 Tula and Ryazan were split off into independent oblasts, and later Tver and Kaluga were also split off. As a result the territory of Moscow oblast came to approximate in size that of the pre-revolutionary guberniya. In the winter of 1937–8 Ezhov proposed to the Supreme Soviet that Moscow be renamed as Veliki Stalingrad, Stalingrad–Moskva, Stalinodar or simply Stalin. Stalin rejected the idea.[130]

Conclusion

Within the planning process Moscow under Kaganovich occupied a unique position. Moscow was far and away the most powerful of the regional authorities. It was provided with privileged access to the central party–government decision-making centres. As such it was in a position of considerable power *vis-à-vis* Gosplan and the main economic commissariats, such as NKTyazhProm. Many of the key decisions regarding the development of Moscow, including the reconstruction of the capital, the building of the Metro and of the Moscow–Volga canal, bypassed the process of drafting and approving the Second Five-Year Plan. These major projects were processed separately. They were given Stalin's blessing and support. Major economic projects in the Moscow oblast were approved with the agreement of the all-union economic commissariats. In this Moscow encountered few obstructions. The schemes for the building of the Novotula steel plan, the development of the Moscow coal basin were approved with NKTyazhProm. The building of the Moscow–Donbass trunk line was approved with NKPS.

Under Kaganovich from 1931 to 1935 the economy of Moscow city and oblast was transformed. In this period the city and its region swallowed up a very large proportion of state investment, far out of proportion to its population. From a centre of light industry it was turned into a major heavy industrial region, with rapid development of the defence industries and technically advanced and specialised sectors. From a consuming region for agricultural produce it was briefly turned into a producing region, although by 1938 the capital was again troubled with major problems of food supply. It was rapidly developed as a centre of specialist education. Moscow was reconstructed with the objective of turning it into a modern city. Symbolically the two great projects, the Moscow–Volga canal and the metro, underlined the new priority that the capital now commanded as a model for other cities of the USSR.

Kaganovich's role in this was central, but without Stalin's support none of these changes would have been possible. Kaganovich turned Moscow into a bulwark of the Stalinist regime. The new priority accorded to the capital reflected not just Kaganovich's influence. By 1930 the redevelopment of the capital had become a task which could not be long delayed. Moscow's pre-eminence also reflected the regime's changing conception of itself, and the creation of a much more centralised, unitary state. This reflected a dramatic shift in centre–local relations in the 1930s. It coincided with the attack on 'bourgeois nationalism' and the weakening of the powers of republican and regional units of administration; and it corresponded with the major shift of investment to the RSFSR, with Moscow a particularly privileged beneficiary. In this it can be seen also as part of the regime's shift in its search for a dependable base of social support, amongst the Russian population of the urban centres and within the capital above all.

Notes

1. Catherine Merridale, *Moscow Politics and the Rise of Stalin: The Communist Party in the Capital, 1925–32* (Basingstoke, 1990); Catherine Merridale, 'The Origins of the Stalinist State: Power and Politics in Moscow, 1928–32', in John Channon (ed.), *Politics, Society and Stalinism in the USSR* (London, 1998); Nobuo Shimotomai, *Moscow Under Stalinist Rule, 1931–34* (Basingstoke, 1991); Timothy J. Colton, *Moscow: Governing the Socialist Metropolis* (Cambridge, Mass., 1995); David Hoffman, *Moscow: Peasant Metropolis* (Ithaca, London, 1994).
2. *Rabochaya Moskva*, 27 February 1931 (Merridale, 1990, p. 97)
3. O. V. Khlevnyuk *et al.*, *Stalinskoe Politbyuro* (Moscow, 1995), pp. 116–18.
4. See Kaganovich's account in his memoirs L. M. Kaganovich, *Pamyatnye zapiski* (Moscow, 1996), p. 416.
5. N. S. Khrushchev, *Khrushchev Remembers* (London, 1971) (translated by Strobe Talbot, introduction and commentary by Edward Crankshaw), p. 57.
6. Colton, *Moscow*, pp. 839–40.
7. *Pravda*, 1 June 1930.
8. For the text of Ryutin's platform and declaration see *Izvestiya TsK*, No. 6, 1989, Nos 3 and 8–12, 1990.
9. *IV Moskovskaya oblastnaya i III gorodskaya konferentisii Vsesoyuznoi Kommunis-ticheskoi Partii (b), 16–24 yanvarya 1934g; Stenograficheskii otchet* (Moscow, 1934), pp. 470 (Tarasov), 363 (Kogan) 72 (Kul'kov), 202 (Ryndin), 463 (Enov), 328 (Shurov), 468 (Surin).
10. *Ibid.*, pp. 463, 465, 405 (Peskarev), 336 (Ryzhakov).
11. O. V. Khlevnyuk *et al.*, (eds), *Stailin i Kaganovich Perepiska. 1931–1936gg.* (Moscow, 2001), pp. 96, 97–8. (Hereafter, *SKP*).
12. *IV Moskovskaya oblastnaya i III gordskaya konferentsii*, p. 314 (Baskaev).
13. *Ibid.*, p. 242 (Alekseev).
14. R. W. Davies, *Crisis and Progress in the Soviet Economy, 1931–1933* (Basingstoke, 1996), p. 311.
15. *IV Moskovskaya oblastnaya i III gorodskaya konferentsii*, pp. 205, 446–8 (Gaidul'), 205, 370 (Sedel'nikov).
16. RGASPI, 17/21/3011 183.
17. *XVIII s"ezd Vsesoyuznoi Kommunisticheskoi Partii (b), 10–21 marta 1939: Stenograficheskii otchet* (Moscow, 1939), pp. 69–70 (Shcherbakov).
18. RGASPI, 17/21/3011 6.
19. *XVIII s"ezd Vsesoyuznoi Kommunisticheskoi Partii (b)*, p. 209 (Ryndin).
20. *Pravda* (Editorial), 22 September 1993.
21. RGASPI, 17/21/3011 87.
22. TsGAMO, 2157/1/927 54.
23. *Ibid.*, p. 237.
24. *SKP*, pp. 589–90.

25. *IV Moskovskaya oblastnaya i III gorodskaya konferentsii*, p. 506.
26. *Ibid.*, pp. 82, 224.
27. *Ibid.*, pp. 91–2 (Dorofeev), 220 (Ryndin), 406 (Peskarev).
28. *Ibid.*, p. 513.
29. R. Medvedev, *Let History Judge* (Nottingham, 1972), pp. 88–9.
30. *Ibid.*, pp. 248, 253.
31. L. M. Kaganovich, *Kontrol'nye tsifry tret'ego goda pyatiletki i zadachi Moskovskoi organizatsii* (Moscow, 1931).
32. Gijs Kessler, 'The Peasant and the Town: Rural–Urban Migration in the Soviet Union, 1929–40' (unpublished PhD thesis, European University Institute, Florence, 2001), Vol. 2, Statistical Appendices, Table C2 on Average Gross Household Incomes of Kolkhoz Households in 1931.
33. O. V. Khlevnyuk, *Politbyuro: Mekhanizmy politicheskoi vlasti v 1930-e gody* (Moscow, 1996), pp. 57–8. Davies, *Crisis and Progress*, pp. 189–90. O. V. Khlevnyuk, '30–3 gody Krizisy, Reformy, Nasilie', *Svobodnaya mysl'*, 17, 1991, p. 78.
34. L. M. Kaganovich, *Boevye zadachi Moskovskoi partiinoi organizatsii po pode'emu sel'skogo khozyaistva i ukrepleniyu kolkhozov* (Moscow, 1932); *Pravda*, 6 August 1932; *Rabochei Moskve*, No. 183.
35. *Pravda*, 6 August 1932.
36. L. M. Kaganovich, 'Ob itogakh sentyabr'skogo plenuma TsK i zadachakh moskovskoi organisatsii', *Partiinoe stroitel'stvo*, Nos 19–20, 1932, pp. 6–15.
37. L. M. Kaganovich, *Na putyakh k okonchatel'nomu prevrashcheniyu Moskovskoi oblasti iz potereblyayushchei v proizvodyashchuyu* (Moscow, 1933).
38. V. Markovich, 'Derevnya poluchila moguchii otryad bol'shevikov', *Partiinoe stroitel'stvo*, Nos 13–14, July 1933, p. 63.
39. TsGAMO, 2157/1/928 7.
40. TsGAMO, 2157/1/928 45.
41. *SKP*, pp. 338, 341.
42. Medvedev, *Let History Judge*, p. 347. R. Medvedev, S. Pavofenou and P. Khmelinskii, (Ekatovinburg, 1992) *Zheleznyi yastreb*, p. 64.
43. TsGAMO, 2157/1/928 265. Nedvetskii at the Moscow oblast ispolkom plenum in July 1933.
44. TsGAMO, 2157/1/927 39.
45. *SKP*, p. 495.
46. On the 'anti-urbanists' see S. Frederick Starr, 'Visionary Town Planning during the Cultural Revolution' in Sheila Fitzpatrick (ed.), *Cultural Revolution in Russia, 1928–1931* (Bloomington, London, 1978), pp. 207–40.
47. *Pravda*, 29 May 1930, p. 5.
48. L. M. Kaganovich, *Pamyatnye zapiski* (Moscow, 1996), p. 424.
49. Starr, 'Visionary Town Planning', p. 238. See L. M. Kaganovich *Socialist Reconstruction of Moscow and Other Cities in the USSR* (London, 1931).
50. *Pravda*, 4 July 1931, p. 4.
51. L. M. Kaganovich, *Za sotsialisticheskoi rekonstrukstiyu Moskvy i gorodov SSSR* (Moscow-Leningrad, 1931).
52. The resolution is in *Pravda*, 17 June 1931, pp. 2–3. Local implementing measures are in *Pravda*, 21–5 June 1931.
53. *KPSS v rezolyutsiyakh i resheniyakh s'ezdov, konferentsii i plenumov TsK, 1929–32*, vol. 5, pp 313–26.
54. *Moskovskie novosti*, No. 30, 28 July 1996, p. 11.
55. Bulganin, in *Vechernyaya Moskva*, 11 July 1935, p. 1.

56. *Pamyatnye zapiski,* p. 427.
57. Khrushchev, *Khrushchev Remembers,* pp. 63–4.
58. Colton, *Moscow,* p. 839, n. 55.
59. Roy Medvedev, reviewing Stuart Kahan's biography of Kaganovich, *Wolf in the Kremlin* (New York, 1987), in *Moscow News,* No. 52, 1988, p. 16.
60. *SKP,* p. 246.
61. *Pamyatnye zapiski,* pp. 423–31. F. Chuev, *Tak govoril' Kaganovich: Ispoved' stalinskogo apostola* (Moscow, 1992).
62. Colton, *Moscow* p. 268.
63. *SKP,* pp. 524, 527.
64. *Sovetskoe rukovodstvo perepiska 1928–1941* (compiled by A. V. Kvashonkin, L. P. Kosheleva, L. A. Rogovaya and O. V. Khlevnyuk) (Moscow, 1999), pp. 158–9.
65. RGASPI, 17/3/828 17.
66. F. Chuev, *Tak govoril' Kaganovich:* p. 47. On the Palace of Soviets see Colton *Moscow,* pp. 333–4, 365–7.
67. *XVIII s"ezd,* p. 434 (G. M. Popov).
68. Colton, *Moscow,* pp. 268–9.
69. Chuev, *Tak govoril' Kaganovich,* pp. 47, 51.
70. *Pamyatnye zapiski,* p. 430.
71. *Pamyatnye zapiski,* p. 434.
72. Khrushchev, *Khrushchev Remembers,* pp. 65–70.
73. L. M. Kaganovich, *Postroem pervuyu ochered' metro k XVII godovshchinee oktyabrya* (Moscow, 1934). The resolution of the Moscow gorkom and obkom is in *Rabochaya Moskva,* 7 January 1934.
74. L. M. Kaganovich, *O stroitel'stve metropolitena i plana goroda Moskvy* (Moscow, 1934).
75. *Sovestskoe rukovodstvo perepiska 1928–194,* p. 276.
76. Colton, *Moscow,* p. 257.
77. L. M. Kaganovich, *Pobeda metropolitena-pobeda sotsializma* (Moscow, 1935).
78. *Pamyatnye zapiski,* p. 440.
79. *SKP,* p. 582.
80. Shimotomai, *Moscow Under Stalinist Rule, 1931–34,* pp. 111–12, 11; E. A. Rees (ed.), *Decision-Making in the Stalinist Command Economy, 1932–1937* (Basingstoke, 1997), pp. 255–6.
81. *KPSS v rezolyutsiyakh i resheniyakh, s"ezdov, konferentsii i plenumov TsK, vol. 4* (Moscow, 1971), p. 545.
82. *Pamyatnye zapiski,* p. 440.
83. *Rabochaya Moskva,* 10 December 1931.
84. *Pamyatnye zapiski,* p. 443.
85. *Rabochaya Moska,* 27 March 1932.
86. L. S. Bykov and A. S. Matrosov, *Kanal imeni Moskvy. 50 let ekspluatatsii* (Moscow, 1987).
87. *Propagandist,* No. 16, 1934, p. 30.
88. *Pamyatnye zapiski,* p. 444.
89. *Vechernyaya Moskva,* 17 September 1934. *Izvestiya,* 9 September 1935.
90. L. M. Kaganovich, *Ob itogkh o"edinennogo plenuma TsK i TsKK VKP(b)* (Moscow, 1993), p. 17.
91. *SZ,* No. 44, 1932, p. 263, *Propagandist,* No. 7–8, 1933, p. 30.
92. *Rechnoi transport SSSR, 1917–1957,* p. 308.
93. *SZ,* No. 44, 1932, p. 263.

94. RGASPI, 17/3/935, topic 9.

95. *Sovetskoe rukovodstvo perepiska 1928–1941* (Moscow, 1999), p. 270.

96. W. Citrine, *I Search for Truth in Russia* (London, 1936), p. 80.

97. L. Simon, *Moscow in the Making* (London, 1937), pp. 224–5.

98. Khlevnyuk *Politbyuro*, p. 78.

99. RGASPI, 17/3/980 104.

100. RGASPI 17/3/963 III. RGASPI, 17/3/967, IV.

101. *SZ*, Nos 395, 396, 1935, *Izvestiya*, 9 September 1935; RGASPI, 17/3/971, 68.

102. *SKP*, p. 539.

103. RGASPI, 17/3/989 117; RGASPI, 17/3/989 238, 251, 280; *Pravda*, 15 July 1937.

104. *VI Moskovskaya oblastnaya i III gorodskaya kongerentsii Vsesoyuznoi Kommunisticheskoi Partii (b), 16–24 yanvarya 1934 g; Stenograficheskii otchet* (Moscow, 1934).

105. *Ibid.*, pp. 269, 58.

106. *Ibid.*, p. 43.

107. *Ibid.*, p. 197.

108. *Ibid.*, pp. 479, 475.

109. *Ibid.*, p. 364.

110. *Ibid.*, pp. 413, 428 (Kogan).

111. *Ibid.*, p. 178.

112. *Ibid.*, pp. 112–15 (Sudakov).

113. TsGAMO, 2157/1/1208 431.

114. *IV Moskovskaya oblastnaya i III gorodskaya konferentsii*, p. 120.

115. *Ibid.*, pp. 155–6, 427–30.

116. *Ibid.*, pp. 412 (Pavlov) 401 (Koldobskii), 427 (Kogan), 442 (Kolesova) 448 (Guidul'), 313 (Vasil'ev).

117. *Ibid.*, pp. 373 (Karpov), 137 (Eideman, head of Osovaviakhim).

118. *Ibid.*, pp. 440 (Kurnaev), 437 (Cherebadskaya).

119. RGASPI, 17/21/3012 209.

120. RGASPI, 17/21/3012 209.

121. *IV Moskovskaya oblastnaya i III gorodskaya konferentsii*, p. 503.

122. *Ibid.*, p. 515.

123. *Ibid.*, p. 549.

124. *Proekt vtorogo pyatiletnego plana razvitiya narodnogo khozyaistva SSSR (1933–1937), tom 2 Plan razvitiya raionov* (Moscow 1934), p. 240.

125. *Narodnokhozyaistvennyi plan na 1936 god: Plan razvitiya raionov* (Moscow, 1936), pp. 198, 325.

126. *Osnoynye pokazateli vypolneniya narodno-khozyaistvennogo plana po respublikam, kraiyam i oblastyam 1935* (Moscow, 1935), pp. 9, 25.

127. *Osnoynye pokazateli vypolneniya norodno-khozyaistvennogo plana po respublikam, kraiyam i oblastyam 1936* (Moscow, 1937), pp. 14, 38.

128. O. V. Khlevnyuk, A. V. Kvashonkin, L. P. Kosheleva and L. A. Rogovaya (eds), *Stalinskoe Politbyuro v 30-e gody*, p. 143.

129. *XVIII s"ezd Vsesoyuznoi Kommunisticheskoi Partii (b), 10–21 marta 1939: Stenograficheskii otchet* (Moscow, 1939), pp. 69–70 (Shcherbakov).

130. *Istochnik*, 3, 1994, p. 128. 'Kak Moskva chut'ne stala Stalinodarom', *Izvestiya TsK KPSS*, No. 12, December 1990, pp. 126–7.

5
The Karelian ASSR

*Nick Baron**

Introduction

This chapter seeks to suggest a novel approach to the study of Stalinist decision-making. It does so with a view to overcoming the dichotomy between agent-centred and structure-dominated historiographies that for so long has weakened conceptual innovation in this field. Emphasis on agency, characteristic of the so-called 'totalitarian' historians, has pushed most popular historiography – and much serious work – towards an untenable methodology of unbounded voluntarism. On the other hand, emphasis on the causal primacy of structure tends towards a faceless functionalism. Neither approach is able to capture the reciprocal and dynamic interaction between human deeds and the contexts in which they are embedded that characterises historical change. A more fruitful framework of analysis is suggested by 'structuration' theory, which concentrates the researcher's attention on the sources, character and consequences of this creative interaction, while situating the decision-making agent's mediation of cultural, psychological, material and other prior 'structures' within a field of competing power interests. Such an approach seeks to 'find in each successive state of the phenomenon under examination both the result of previous struggles to maintain or modify it, and the principles...of subsequent transformations.'[1]

The focus of the present chapter is the transformation of Soviet economic space during the second decade of Soviet rule. Specifically, it examines the spatial dimension of Stalinist decision-making in relation to the negotiation, elaboration and implementation of the Second Five-Year Plan in the Karelian Autonomous Soviet Socialist Republic (ASSR). In doing so, it touches on a complex of questions suggested by the structurationist approach: how conflicting conceptualisations of this region's economic role derived from various territorial, institutional or sectional interests with diverse predispositions and prejudices, and embodied their struggles to maintain or modify the state's economic geography; how changing power relations and alignments or oppositions of interest promoted or precluded the realisation of these competing spatial visions; and how the material transformation of Soviet economic geography produced new ways of seeing its constituent space, new configurations of power and new strategies of expansion or retrenchment.

In conclusion, an argument will be presented for the adoption of a dynamic model of Stalinist totalitarianism, conceived as both function and consequence of the regime's chosen mode of development.

The geographies of Soviet Karelia

Following the failed Finnish and successful Russian revolutions, the necessity of defending Bolshevik power within Russian borders, and enthusiasm for exporting it beyond, prompted Soviet leaders to establish a unified, autonomous, national territorial unit on the Soviet Russian–Finnish frontier, the Karelian Labour Commune (KTK), formed on 8 June 1920 by decree of the All-Russian Central Executive Committee of Soviets (VTsIK). The initiative for this dramatic experiment in national autonomy came from an émigré Finnish social democrat, Edvard Gylling. In an interview in mid-1920, Gylling had convinced Lenin that a prosperous socialist republic on the border of Finland would act as a magnet for exiled Finnish communists and an inspiration for progressive minds in Finland and northern Europe. At the same time, the pragmatic Bolsheviks were concerned to conciliate the Finnish government, with whom they were in urgent peace negotiations, and to preclude the 'Karelian question' from acting as either an obstacle to peace or a stimulus for anti-Soviet propaganda. To this end, the Soviets reluctantly agreed to append to the Soviet–Finnish Peace Treaty of October 1920 a Declaration guaranteeing the integrity of Karelia's self-government. Gylling, in the hope of translating these paper rights into real and lasting autonomy, secured a series of decrees from the Russian centre granting the KTK exceptional freedom of economic activity, including the right to dispose of 100 per cent of revenue produced on its territory, and to retain 25 per cent of all hard currency earnings realised from the sale of its timber abroad.

Soviet Karelia (from 1923, an ASSR) was able to sustain its fiscal privileges throughout the 1920s, primarily by appealing to Lenin's personal role in its formation, and to its propaganda significance for Russia's foreign policy. The Karelian government's ambition to ensure maximum economic progress for a territory established on the basis of its national specificity, however, contained within itself an inherently irresolvable problem: how to reconcile optimal economic space with narrower ethno-linguistic borders. The Finnish leaders of Karelia, antagonistic towards any manifestation of separate Karelian (as opposed to Finnish) nationalism, compromised the territory's national integrity from the start by demanding the inclusion within its borders of ethnically mixed and non-Karelian areas, in effect privileging economic over national criteria of spatial structuration.[2] This set an inauspicious precedent. Then, in 1923, at the behest of disgruntled Russians from the dissolved Olonets government leadership (the old regional administration of southern Karelia, most of whose territory had already been transferred to the KTK in 1920), and against Gylling's wishes the Karelian population was reduced to a minority in its own republic by the incorporation within the territory of 60,000 Russians in Pudozh district (uezd), east of Lake Onega. The Karelian population was further diluted during the 1920s by an influx of Russian settlers and seasonal migrants, attracted by the burgeoning regional timber industry.

The underlying conception of Soviet space which informed Karelian planning activities in the 1920s was that of a loose federation of regions and national territories enjoying extensive autonomous rights, especially in economic decision-making. Gylling himself was clear where Karelia's natural place lay on the map: the Soviet state's western border with Finland was an anomaly of history, artificial and provisional, and Karelia would sooner or later be unified with a post-revolutionary socialist Finland. In the meantime, Gylling conceived of the territory as a 'dual periphery', oriented as much towards Scandinavia as towards the Soviet centre, and pursued his objective of gradual, balanced, sustainable and autarkic regional development.

During the mid-1920s, the Soviet leadership supported Gylling's ambitions for Karelian autonomy within the framework of its New Economic Policy (NEP) and a nationalities policy which promoted the welfare of minority ethnic groups. Thus, the leadership subordinated Gosplan's project for the optimal economic 'regionalisation' of Soviet territory to the interests of the autonomous national republics. Consequently, the Karelian ASSR (145,000 km^2 in area) retained its autonomous status and economic privileges when the mighty Leningrad Region (oblast) was established in 1927, extending 341,000 km^2 over most of the north-west of European Russia, and including the Kola Peninsula north of Karelia.[3] Later in the decade, however, the Soviet centre's ideological shift towards intensified planning of the economy signalled the incipient transformation of its territory into an increasingly unitary space of decision-making, within which branch or functional priorities counted for more in the field of central power relations than negotiating resources grounded in geographical specificities, national particularities or distant internationalist aspirations. In the face of these levelling forces, the Finnish leadership of Karelia clung with suicidal tenacity to its own national policy, its transnational perspectives and its claims to privileged status.[4]

Already in the early years of the First Five-Year Plan, Karelia was forced *de facto* to cede its special economic rights to Union and Russian centres of authority. The republic's loss of budgetary independence and control over locally operating economic trusts (especially Karelles, the main regional timber-felling organisation), meant that it now depended for all heavy industrial funding, and most of the funding for felling and wood processing, on the Union and Russian ministerial centres. At the same time, it became increasingly dangerous to assert specialised territorial knowledge as a negotiating resource in the centre as this could be interpreted as resistance to central directive and 'bourgeois' localism. Karelia's strategic border role burdened it with responsibility without power, which proved a dangerous and double-edged commodity.

The Karelian Second Five-Year Plan

It would be inaccurate to speak of a coherent Second Five-Year Plan determining Karelian economic development during the years 1933–7. There never was such a plan. Instead, there were several varying, often conflicting, visions of Karelia's role in Soviet economic space. These visions were derived from diverse conceptualisations of economic, political, national and strategic geographies, and embodied both the consistent policy priorities of different interests and the impulses of exigency.

Archival sources permit us to distinguish four generally discrete institutional visions of Karelia's role in Soviet economic space: those of the Karelian government, of the NKVD, of the Leningrad authorities and of the Union centre.

The Karelian vision

Planning for the Second Five-Year Plan in Karelia began at the end of 1931. During the next two years, Karelia constantly modified its plan perspectives in line with changing central policy priorities and plan variants, new economic conditions and revised limits for current investments. In particular, the opening of the Belomor–Baltiiskii Water Route (BBVP), constructed in 1931–3 with forced labour, offered up the perspective of radically expanding the scope of Karelia's spatial relations by uniting the White Sea ports, the Kola Peninsula and the Arctic passage through a single water transport network with Leningrad's port on the Gulf of Finland (via the river Svir, Ladoga canal and river Neva) and with the Russian interior (via the Mariinskii Water System).[5] Formerly the ASSR's inter-regional ties had been limited to receiving cellulose from Leningrad for the Kondopoga Paper Factory in southern Karelia, and sending timber back to Leningrad for export, or into the interior for processing.[6] Now, Karelian planners hoped, the new cheap transport system would provide the stimulus to effect a fundamental transformation of the structure and size of the republican economy.[7]

In December 1931, the Karelian Gosplan (Karplan) Commission on the Second Five-Year Plan presented the Karelian government (Sovnarkom) and the Karelian People's Commissariats with its first set of 'Basic Directives for Compiling Orientations for the Industrial Development of Karelia, 1933–1937'. This document outlined a scheme for the 'maximum rational' exploitation of the republic's natural resources. In particular, it envisaged combining existing and projected new Karelian enterprises into industrial complexes to process local raw materials and their waste products on the basis of regional hydroenergy resources. The 'correct geographical location of new enterprises', stated the report, should ensure their greatest proximity to material and labour resources, energy and transport. Furthermore, branch administrations should consider 'demand in the market' for their product when formulating plans.[8]

A February 1932 Karplan report entitled 'Perspectives of Development' outlined the Karelian vision of its prospective economic transformation.[9] Whereas (according to this document) the ASSR's First Five-Year Plan had been based almost uniquely on timber felling and processing, its Second Five-Year Plan would promote hydroelectricity production and utilisation, as well as the exploitation of its new transport capacities. The construction of 15 major hydro-electric power stations (GES), requiring 273.5 million rubles of investment (43 per cent of all planned republican industrial and timber capital investment), would enable Karelia by 1937 to produce one thirty-fifth of the Soviet Union's total electricity output: 55 major new industrial enterprises would be developed on the basis of this massively expanded energy base and the region's new transport links. Planners envisaged the construction of a huge industrial combine at Kandalaksha, in the north of Karelia, to be supplied with appatite from the Kola Peninsula, for the production of chemicals and aluminium for Leningrad. In central Karelia, they planned another major plant producing aluminium for Leningrad, and to utilise shungite ores discovered in Pudozh district (*raion*) for the processing of heavy metal (vanadium) and the generation of energy for the Leningrad metallurgical industry. In southern Karelia, the report envisaged mineral extraction and further light metal-processing for Leningrad, the construction at Kondopoga of a cellulose plant and the expansion of the existing paper factory, plus major new food production plants to permit Karelia, traditionally a food importer, to achieve a greater degree of autarky. The report asserted that Karelia's output of paper (projected for 1937 at 66 thousand tonnes annually), and of aluminium and shungite, would for the first time make the ASSR a significant contributor to the Union economy in sectors other than timber (Table 5.1).

In early 1932, Gylling declared to the Karelian Central Executive Committee of the Soviets (TsIK) that 'by the end of the Second Five-Year Plan, Karelia will be unrecognisable!'[10] Karelia's plan figures reflected his vision: according to an August 1932 Karplan project, whereas in 1932 new enterprises yielded 10 per cent of production, by 1937 they would account for 80.5 per cent; instead of the present 27 enterprises on republican territory there would be 84, with an eight-fold increase in gross output (by value in 1932 prices); and most of these new plants would be producing energy, machines, metals and chemicals.[11] If Karelia could realise this vision, its economic structure would indeed undergo fundamental transformation (see Table 5.2).

Table 5.1   Top three Karelian industrial sectors, 1928–9 to 1937 (% of total industrial output by value, incl. energy and timber-processing, excl. felling)

Sector	1928–9 (actual)	1932 (actual)
Timber industry	66	43
Machine construction	18	11.7
Mineral extraction	8	15.6
	1933 (forecast)	*1937 (forecast)*
Chemical production	22	28.4
Timber industry	20.8	16
Mineral extraction	16.1	14.8

Source: NA RK 700/1/839/10ob.

Table 5.2   Top three Karelian industrial sectors, 1932 and 1937 (% of output of major enterprise of NKTyazhProm, NKLegProm and NKSnab)

Sector	1932 (actual)	1937 (forecast)
Spirits production	38.4	–
Mineral extraction	23	–
Machine construction	19.7	23
Chemical production	–	26
Metallurgy	–	16.7

Source: GAOPDF RK 3/2/751/8.

Karplan's overwhelming focus on energy and industrial construction meant that it provided for only relatively modest growth in republican timber-felling, from 6.9 million fest-metres (f/m) achieved in 1931 to 18.3 million f/m for 1937. On this point, however, local and central views of Karelian development absolutely diverged. In February 1932, central planning agencies announced that the 1937 target for Karelian felling would be a stunning 35.5 million f/m.[12] To add insult to injury, the bulk of this timber would be redirected from export to the internal market.[13] By the end of May, Karplan had correspondingly revised its figure up to 24.5 million f/m in an attempt to meet Union demands halfway.[14] However, it was already clear that Karelia's vision of its own future was irreconcilable with the Union centre's planning priorities (see Table 5.4, p. 132).

In Moscow, the Council of People's Commissars of the Soviet Union (Sovnarkom USSR) issued a decree on 25 March 1932 setting a timetable for the compilation of the Second Five-Year Plan.[15] On this basis, the Karelian Sovnarkom and Karplan issued timetables for their subordinate organisations. Preliminary plans were to be presented by the Karelian Sovnarkom to

Gosplan RSFSR and Gosplan USSR by the end of June, with the final plans to be ready for presentation by mid-November.[16] The Karelian government and party obkom published a series of further decrees in the course of the year urging faster work, threatening department heads and enterprise directors with disciplinary action, and mobilising the Komsomol to fight 'bureaucratism' in the planning departments and organisations.[17] This last measure, together with the almost continuous purging of staff which Karplan had suffered over the previous 18 months (over half their apparat had been declared unsatisfactory), did nothing to improve the efficiency of planning preparations.[18] It was always a problem to attract qualified personnel to Karelia, and the centre was not willing to help. In September 1932, deputy head of Karplan G. D. Tyuvaev visited the Moscow oblast planning office and enviously compared their 246 officials, who were in everyday contact with Russian Federal (RSFSR) and Union planners, with his remote and isolated Karelian staff of 40. However, when he then applied to the Cadres Section of Gosplan USSR for additional staff, he was informed that graduates were sent only to 'more important peripheries and regions [*kraya i oblasti*]'.[19]

During the same visit, Tyuvaev investigated the progress in central planning organs of work relating to the Karelian plans. At Gosplan RSFSR he visited G. I. Smirnov and other officials, including a certain Lobov,who held the position of 'Curator for Karelia', but found that no-one was working at all on Karelia since no-one had received any of the relevant information from the individual RSFSR commissariats.[20] The Russian Federal planners' task was complicated, he was told, by the fact that plans for some Karelian sectors (heavy metallurgy, aluminium production and geological exploration) were in fact compiled as part of Leningrad oblast plans; and planning for Leningrad oblast (as for Moscow, the Urals, the Lower Volga and Siberia) was conducted not in the Russian Gosplan and ministries, but by the corresponding Union agencies. On then visiting Gosplan USSR, Tyuvaev discovered the officials there were similarly ignorant and inactive. The division of responsibility between Russian and Union agencies in the centre, Tyuvaev wrote back to Karelia, caused a great deal of 'extra red-tape', delays and confusion. As a result, directives issued by Gosplan USSR, Gosplan RSFSR and the Union commissariats frequently contradicted each other. In Karelia, enterprises directly subordinated to Union commissariats ignored directives issued along the Gosplan line altogether, while Karplan had no knowledge of directives transmitted down ministry lines.[21]

In fact, each national territory had a permanent representative attached to the presidium of the All-Russian Central Executive Committee of Soviets (VTsIK), whose duty it was to ensure policy and planning coordination between centre and periphery. The representatives liaised on a wide range of issues with the central authorities, directed all petitions by the republics to the appropriate central agencies and monitored all visits by republican officials to the capital. During the 1920s, the Karelian representative played a major role in Karelian relations with Moscow, promoting with some success Karelian interests in Russian and Union decision-making bodies.[22] However, the role of this office diminished during the 1930s, as information increasingly began to bypass the Karelian government, flowing along ministry lines directly between central agencies and their subordinate trusts or plenipotentiaries in Karelia.

In December 1932, Tyuvaev paid another visit to Moscow to investigate central procedures and the progress of the Karelian plan. He sent a long and reflective memorandum back to the chair of Karplan I. A. Danilov.[23] Soviet planning for capital investment, Tyuvaev complained, suffered in general from great 'instability' (*neustoichivost'*), but this was especially bad in relation to Karelia. While planning agencies at Karelian, Russian and Union levels were debating control figures, the limits within which they had to work were constantly changing. Commissariats challenged Gosplan figures, and Gosplan USSR disputed figures presented by its Russian counterpart (currently, it was refusing to accept Russian plans for the Kandalaksha Chemical Combine). Gosplan USSR, in fact, did not inspect any plans in detail: it seemed usually to accept figures submitted by the branch sectors of the Russian planning agency, but to reject figures submitted by its territorial sectors and subordinate regional agencies, unless they were presented with exhaustive explanatory notes and justifications.

In relation to the Karelian plan, Tyuvaev reported that he was experiencing problems getting its limits confirmed both in Gosplan USSR's branch sectors and in its Northern Group. Union planners were not only universally reducing capital investment allocations, but specifically believed Karelia's funding requests to be exaggerated or inadequately justified. Tyuvaev had therefore informed the presidium of Gosplan RSFSR of Karelia's disputes with its Union counterpart, and Gylling had submitted a petition to Sovnarkom RSFSR requesting their support.

The divergence between the Soviet centre and Karelia on fundamental principles of the ASSR's future development was already clear. The character and outcomes of budgetary and organisational conflicts during 1932 and 1933, which lie outside the scope of this chapter, confirmed the new balance of power between the Union and Russian centres and the Karelian national periphery and determined whose vision would ultimately prevail.

The NKVD variant of Karelian development

In mid-1933, the Soviet political police (OGPU) completed the most challenging section of the BBVP, the canal through central Karelia linking the White Sea and Lake Onega, and commenced construction on this territory of an industrial combine, the Belomor–Baltiiskii Kombinat (BBK). As we noted above (pp. 119–23), this event prompted politicians and planners concerned with Karelia – in both the centre and the periphery – fundamentally to reconsider their conceptions of future regional development. A 1933 report submitted by the BBK to Karplan and the Karelian obkom declared that 'the opening of the Belomor-Baltiiskii Water Route...to the greatest extent has changed the economic geography of the North'.[24]

The BBK, established by a Sovnarkom USSR decree of 17 August 1933 and placed under the jurisdiction of the OGPU (from 1934, the People's Commissariat for Internal Affairs, NKVD), had the task of developing the economy of the recently constructed canal and its adjacent forests. The Combine was freed from taxes until 1936, and given *khosrashchet* status.[25] Its own statement of purpose declared that:

> In an exceptionally short period the BBK OGPU must fulfil the gigantic work of assimilating and exploiting the natural resources of Karelia and putting to maximum use those wide opportunities which the Belomor–Baltiiskii Water Route opens for the region, must create a series of new large-scale hydrotechnical installations, hydroelectric power stations and industrial enterprises, develop mining and extraction of mineral resources, construct socialist towns etc.[26]

The Combine would operate independently of Karelian republican authority, but the founding decree stipulated that it should agree its economic plans with the Karelian Sovnarkom before presenting them via OGPU headquarters in Moscow to the Union centre for ratification. In practice, the OGPU was unlikely to submit its activities to such oversight by the local civil authorities. Already for more than a decade there had been constant friction between the political police and Karelian economic organisations over the use of forced labour on contract from OGPU's Solovetskii Camp of Special Designation (USLON). During the mid-1920s, the Karelian government had sought to put a stop to the hiring of prison labour from OGPU. This move, however, had not stopped agencies outside Karelian jurisdiction, in particular the Murmansk railway, whose own felling trust Zhelles carried out lumber work in over 1.6 million hectares of Karelian territory, from using convicts for felling and other heavy work.[27] At the end of the decade, with the First Five-Year Plan straining Karelia's own labour resources far beyond capacity, and with recruitment and resettlement policies yielding feeble results, local organisations had also begun hiring labour from USLON, though not without incessant disputes over the high prices charged by the enterprising Chekists.[28]

After the establishment of the BBK, relations between the political police and civil authorities were not improved by the novelty of working together, by the alienation to BBK jurisdiction during 1933–5 of vast swathes of forest in central Karelia (2.9 million hectares comprising the entire territories of four *lespromkhozy* – the economic units organised for administering the timber industry – and sections of three others), or by the transfer to the BBK of several People's Commissariat of Transport (NKPS) timber factories, which Karelia had been coveting since the dissolution of Zhelles in 1930.[29] In October 1933, the Karelian Sovnarkom sought to encourage cooperation by issuing a decree proposing measures to establish 'businesslike relations, reciprocal information exchange and the regulation of current questions'.[30] As early as February 1934, however, Karplan complained about the impossibility of formulating its own plans when it received no information from the Planning–Economic Department of the BBK.[31] At the 1937 Karelian Party Conference, the Head of the Karelian Statistical Administration (UNKhU) Ivanov declared that it was easier to get materials directly from Gulag central administration in Moscow than from the BBK in Karelia. In 1935, he lamented, the Combine had refused even to reveal its gross output statistics for Karelia's report to VTsIK on the occasion of the ASSR's fifteenth anniversary. Yet without BBK data, he maintained, it was impossible fully to describe the condition of the Karelian economy or to plan its development. Scornfully, the leader of the BBK, Almazov, replied that

> Some Karelian organisations – Gosplan and others – are offended by the BBK, but what is it to them how many prisoners we have? And yet still they ask us 'How many prisoners do you have?' and I reply 'You don't need to know how many, it isn't interesting.'[32]

This stance concealed, of course, the assiduous record-keeping of the OGPU–NKVD, for whom the number and composition of their workforce was of prime significance. For the BBK leadership, the fundamental purpose of the camp was economic production. An order of the Combine authorities in 1935 declared that the 'first duty...and honour' of all camp administrators was to ensure 'the use of the supply of workers, at the fullest stretch and with maximum attention to achieving the most effective indicators, while at the same time...retaining the 'full value' [*pol'notsennosti*] of the work force.' Needless to say, the transport to Karelia of hundreds of thousands of workers and specialists to operate not only the BBK's own felling and industrial enterprises, but also to work under contract in local industry, was also of the greatest interest to Karelian economic administrators.[33]

Despite their mutual suspicion, the BBK and the Karelian authorities had common interests and shared visions of the ASSR's potential role in the Union economy. Both believed Karelia's future lay in developing its energy resources and utilising new transport opportunities as the basis for large-scale and complex industrial construction. In 1934, planning of the diversion and damming of central Karelian rivers (to boost their potential hydro-energy capacities) was transferred from the Leningrad Division of the People's Commissariat of Heavy Industry (NKTyazhProm) Hydro-Electricity Planning Administration 'Gidroelektroproekt' to the Leningrad Bureau of the BBK.

In April, Karelian and BBK officials and experts (including 'specialist' prisoners) convened to discuss the project, and to formulate a proposal which they would jointly submit to the Union centre. Of two variants, the meeting selected the one which took better account of the location of energy consumers and the construction of transmission networks, although its initial cost would be 30 million rubles higher than the rival plan. This initially higher cost was justified on the basis that 'economics here should be subordinated to energy as a stimulus for the development of the region's industry and cultural life.' The meeting also emphasised that this variant would directly benefit not only Karelia, but also Leningrad, since its implementation would raise the level of lake Onega, and hence boost the output of the Svir and Neva GES, several hundred kilometres to the south of the BBK's territory in Leningrad oblast.[34]

On the basis of this decision, the Karelian Sovnarkom issued a decree to develop a joint project with the BBK on industrial construction in central Karelia.[35] The BBK leadership submitted a report to the Karelian Sovnarkom in June which confirmed their acceptance of the joint project, but pointed out that nothing could start until their respective requests for funding had been ratified by the central organs.[36] The plan was discussed by NKTyazh-Prom's Chief Administration of Energy, 'Glavenergo', in August and confirmed by the head of this agency on 30 September 1934.[37] Gylling wrote directly to Molotov in December petitioning for the release of funds to cover the Karelian share of construction within the project.[38] The BBK petitioned for their funds via Gulag NKVD in Moscow.

Although the BBK's conceptualisation of regional economic space to a great extent coincided with the Karelian vision, there were two major divergences of interest. Firstly, BBK planners focused their attention only on that territory of central Karelia between the White Sea and Lake Onega through which the canal passed and which was under their administration, whereas the Karelian government planned for the whole of Karelia. On these grounds, for example, the BBK was antagonistic to Karelian plans to develop an aluminium factory in Kandalaksha, arguing that such production would be better located in their own central zone.[39] The BBK submitted a request for 51.7 million rubles for the construction of an aluminium factory adjacent to the canal: their petition was accepted, although they were allocated only 30 million rubles in the 1934 draft variant of the Second Five-Year Plan, and the construction was later abandoned when the centre refused to release even this sum.[40]

Secondly, the Karelians planned to use local energy to stimulate the exploitation primarily of their own raw materials, together with appatite from the Kola Peninsula to supply Kandalaksha, whereas the scope of the BBK's vision was far more grandiose. While Karelia saw the new water transport system as an opportunity primarily to increase freight capacity to Leningrad and the interior, BBK projects emphasised the significance of the wider 'inter-regional transport network' to import resources from the Far North, where the OGPU–NKVD had developed raw material extraction operations in Vaigach, the Pai Khoi range and Novaya Zemlya. Moreover, the NKVD believed that in consequence of the centre's decision to exploit the Great Northern Sea Route, Karelia had the potential to become not only the 'gateway to the North' but also to the Pacific, and to develop a powerful manufacturing industry based on processing incoming raw materials from the Arctic and Far Eastern NKVD labour camps into products for the internal Soviet market.[41] According to the NKVD's inflated vision of Karelian development, only the ASSR's transformation into an industrial transit zone between Pacific, Arctic and central Russia would justify the investment required 'geographically to combine the materials, fuel and energy of the whole region on the model of the Urals–Kuznetsk Combine'. Almost as an afterthought, it added 'on a smaller scale' (Table 5.3).[42]

Total capital investment requirements for the central Karelian development project were estimated by the Leningrad Bureau of the BBK in mid-1935 at 514.6 million roubles (see Table 5.3). This, it should be noted, was equivalent to 80 per cent of all economic investment in Karelia according to the final published Gosplan USSR Second Five-Year Plan.[43] However, the scale of the NKVD's ambitions for Karelia could not be reconciled with central planning priorities. Although Gosplan's published Second Five-Year Plan had envisaged funding for the BBK's aluminium factory and for a new Timber–Paper–Chemical Combine in Segezha, it had made no provisions for associated construction of power plants (the plan had allowed only 31.6 million for electrical construction, to be directed towards Karelia's civil project on the river Suna).

Table 5.3 Planned BBK capital investment in Central Karelia, 1934–7 (excl. housing construction)

Object	Investment (million rubles)
Aluminium factory	51.7
Zinc factory	15.5
Cryolite production*	4.0
Sulphuric acid production	5.0
Lower Vyg Timber–Chemical Combine	12.5
Segezha Timber–Chemical Combine	175.0
Medvezh'egorsk Timber–Chemical Combine	194.0
Povonets Timber–Chemical Combine	14.5
Heavy metallurgy (shungite–vanadium)	42.4
Total	**514.6**

Note: *Used as a flux in the electrolytic production of aluminium.
Source: NA RK 700/1/1425/2.

The BBK decided to interpret this omission as an oversight, and requested that supplementary energy construction, being necessary for the implementation of the approved industrial development projects, should be considered 'implicit' in the plan, and that the requisite number of extra GES in central Karelia should be included on central lists.[44] NKTyazhProm seem to have responded to this argument less than enthusiastically: not only did it refuse to include in its 1935 titular lists the construction of the largest GES planned by the BBK at Matkozha (although it had already been approved by NKTyazhProm's Glavgidroenergo), but even failed to release the finance already allocated in the published plan for the construction of the Matkozha aluminium factory (partly, we assume, because the centre had adopted the BBK's own logic that the GES was a prerequisite of the factory).[45]

Like the Karelian civil authorities, the BBK administration was supposed to concentrate on timber-felling and processing. Thus, while a special series of Sovnarkom USSR and Council of Labour and Defence (STO) USSR decrees permitted the NKVD to launch construction of its Segezha Paper–Pulp Combine and allocated generous funding for this purpose, the BBK was forced to suspend work on its aluminium factory, and on the planning of further projected enterprises dependent for energy on the Matkozhnenskaya GES. In January 1935, the BBK Leningrad Bureau's report on central Karelian development noted that if the GES, aluminium factory and other subsidiary objects were not included in 1936 lists, these projects should be considered postponed until the Third Five-Year Plan.[46] In June 1935, the BBK party committee warned that 'the sharp reduction in capital investment in the BBK for 1935 will not permit work to be continued in this year at such tempos... as would ensure realisation of all tasks given to the Combine by the party and government on its establishment'.[47] To some extent, the BBK was a victim of its own initial success on the labour-intensive canal project. In mid-1935 Gosplan USSR suggested transferring more Karelian forests to the Combine on the grounds that using its forced labour in felling offered the possibility of 'significant results with relatively insignificant capital investment'.[48]

In 1936, the BBK again failed to obtain its requested allocations.[49] It was therefore forced to postpone its grandiose plans for central Karelia, and focus almost exclusively on expanding its felling output, on the construction of the Segezha timber processing combine and on its light manufacturing activities, which played an increasingly important role in the regional economy.

The view from Leningrad

A major report on perspectives for the Karelian economy, commissioned by the Karelian government in 1933–4 from the Leningrad Section of the Communist Academy and compiled under the editorship of Ya. K. Berztys, declared that 'the Leningrad oblast is hugely important to the Karelian economy as a consumer of raw materials, and of the semi-manufactured and finished products of the mineral extraction and processing industry'.[50] As we have seen, some of the oblasts sectoral plans (heavy metallurgy, aluminium production and geological exploration) included Karelia in their projections and control figures. Although the Leningrad oblast plans for other sectors did not include Karelia, the Leningrad planning agencies invariably took the potential of the Karelian economy into account.

This was especially true in three related sectors for which the wider regional economic area could not be conceived without consideration of Karelian space. Firstly, in transport. Since 1927, Karelia had been an enclave in Leningrad oblast, mediating between Murmansk's raw materials and Leningrad's industry, and the oblast therefore shared an interest both in the construction (and subsequently, in the projected deepening) of the BBVP, and in the planned electrification of the Murmansk railway through Karelia. Secondly, in energy construction. In the north the construction of the Niva GES in Kandalaksha would serve not only the Karelian Northern Chemical Combine but also Murmansk's extraction industry centred on Khibinogorsk on the Kola Peninsula. The Leningrad–Karelian project to divert major rivers in its central area (which later became, as mentioned above, a joint Karelian–BBK project) would both enable the railway to be electrified in this section and, by increasing the flow on the Svir river (on the southern boundary between Leningrad oblast and Karelia), raise the capacity of the Svir GES, the second largest in the oblast. Thirdly, in lumber. Not only were Karelian trusts the major suppliers of felled timber and sawn timber products to Leningrad industry, but timber-felling and extraction in the Pudozh district were administered directly from Leningrad.

In other sectors, too, Leningrad was interested in the development and performance of Karelian industry. The Kandalaksha Combine would receive raw materials from the Kola Peninsula and produce aluminium and chemicals for Leningrad industry. The BBK's projected aluminium factory in central Karelia would provide light metals. Shungite extraction in Pudozh would supply energy and rare heavy metals (which formerly had to be imported) to the Leningrad metallurgical sector and nascent electronics industry. Minerals and building materials extracted and cement manufactured in southern Karelia would be transported to Leningrad. Fish from the White Sea (some processed in a large canning factory in Kandalaksha) would supply Murmansk and the Kola Peninsula with food.[51]

Organisationally, Leningrad drew Karelia increasingly under its control during the Second Five-Year Plan. The Karelian party organisation had already in mid-1928 been subordinated to the Leningrad obkom, which monitored its activity and despatched guiding directives both on general economic development (especially in timber) and on specific projects (especially those in which Leningrad had its own keen interest, such as the supply of firewood, paper and building materials). In June 1933, the Leningrad obkom criticised Karelia for its 'insufficient attention to timber,' and called it to take action, among other things, against class alien and hostile elements in its administration calling for a 'so-called consistent and balanced use of forests' (in other words, an ecologically sustainable felling programme, such as Gylling had envisaged in the previous decade).[52] Leningrad had the prerogative of veto over most important economic appointments in Karelia; to some posts, such as MTS directorships, Leningrad obkom first secretary Sergei Kirov made direct appointments from among his own personnel.[53] The Leningrad party authorities frequently lent their weight to Karelia's petitions to the centre, and on the most important issues, Karelian party secretaries requested Kirov to intervene in Moscow on their behalf. Additionally, Leningrad sent to Karelia workers and qualified cadres (many Leningrad factories and institutes exercised half-hearted patronage over enterprises in Karelia), a majority of whom either never turned up, or, having arrived and seen the primitive living conditions in the republican capital Petrozavodsk, refused to go any deeper into the forested wilderness and promptly returned to the metropolis.

In mid-1933, the Karelian Sovnarkom established a Permanent Representative in Leningrad. Officially, the representative's functions were to coordinate planning with Leningrad institutions, and to establish contacts and win contracts with Leningrad enterprises which received goods from Karelia or supplied the ASSR with heavy machinery for its new construction projects. In practice, the representative spent most of his time chasing up late deliveries or payments to Karelia by Leningrad factories, trying to lure Leningrad workers and specialists to the chilly north, and keeping a watchful eye over the antics of Karelian students in their Leningrad hostel.[54]

Moscow's perspectives on Karelian development

All Soviet central interests agreed on one point: that Karelia should as a priority specialise in timber production and processing, and curb its grander industrial pretensions. However, to speak of a single central conceptualisation of the wider economic space within which Karelia existed, without taking account of different territorial, production and political interests would be an oversimplification. The course of Karelian negotiations in 1932–4 with the Union and Russian authorities (see pp. 119–23) clearly demonstrated that different central agencies held different conceptions of the ASSR's spatial role and relations.

For one thing, the Sovnarkom USSR–Central Committee directives for the Second Five-Year Plan specifically promoted the development of national republics. For the Union centre, this meant primarily the Central Asian republics, in line with its strategically motivated policy of shifting industry eastwards. The relationship between the Union and Russian centres was in this respect ambiguous, since the RSFSR wished to promote the interests of its constituent national territories, but at the same time was reluctant to expend disproportionate sums of its own resources on their development. Hence the Russian centre frequently rebuffed the appeals of its own national peripheries for higher allocations, while supporting the same requests within Union bodies. Conversely, Karelia could often only get what it wanted from Russia by appealing directly to the Union government or party centres.

Secondly, individual central bureaucracies, at both Union and Russian Federal level, inevitably promoted the development of their own branches of production or sectoral interests. When it came to the distribution of funds, however, most agencies sought to have as many as possible of their projects included in the titular lists of other administrations, so as to leave room within their own limits for their own favourite projects. These, invariably, were unrelated to Karelia. We have already considered an example of this form of behaviour when NKTyazhProm's Glavenergo backed the joint Karelian–BBK project of energy construction (see p. 126), but NKTyazhProm's collegium subsequently refused to finance some objects conceived within that project and reduced funding on other objects included within Glavenergo's limits (realising, we suspect, that by refusing to construct GES it could also save itself money on enterprises planned to consume this energy).[55] This strategy of financial pass-the-parcel, even among administrations of the same ministry, was especially common when several organisations were involved in the same construction object. An example of this was the project to expand the Kondopoga Paper Factory and construct a cellulose factory on a neighbouring site. M. I. Kalinin later called this construction the 'timber–paper Magnitostroi,' apparently without irony.[56] Both projects were dependent upon increasing the generating capacity of the Kondopoga GES, which itself relied upon a major river diversion and dam-construction project, Sunastroi. All central bodies agreed on the urgent political priority of increasing Karelia's output of newsprint paper, and Karelian and branch-centre plans for Kondopoga therefore won repeated approval in principle at the highest levels. Nevertheless, throughout the Second Five-Year Plan both NKLes and NKTyazhProm consistently refused, reduced, or deferred allocations of funding, which placed all these inter-related projects and their administrations under great strain.

The military was another institution which was extremely interested in the development of Karelia, especially in the development of communications and transport networks in its isolated western border districts. However, while the General Staff and the People's Commissariat for Defence readily supported repeated petitions from the Karelian and BBK NKVD authorities for funds to implement their construction plans they, too, were reluctant to reallocate their own funding.

The Union centre elaborated the first draft of the Second Five-Year Plan in 1932. In the course of this year, it became clear that the extremely ambitious targets initially considered (such as the Karelian 1937 felling target of

Table 5.4   Projected timber-felling targets for Karelia, 1937 (million fest- metres)

Variant	Target
Karplan February 1932[a]	18.3
Gosplan USSR and NKLes, February 1932[b]	35.5
Karplan May 1932[c]	24.5
Karplan 1934[d]	14.5/15.0
Gosplan USSR Second Five-Year Plan[e]	16.5
Annual Plan 1937[f]	12.877
Realised 1937[g]	9.465

Sources: [a]NA RK 700/1/839/7ob; [b]NA RK 682/1/195/5; [c]NA RK 700/1/839/105; [d]lower figure from NA RK 700/1/1086/44ob, and higher NA RK 682/1/195/25; [e]*Proekt vtorogo pyatiletnego plana razvitiya narodnogo khozyaistva SSSR (1933–1937), Tom II. Plan razvitiya raionov* (Moscow, 1934), p. 308, confirmed in final Gosplan version, see NA RK 690/3/613/29; [f]Calculated from NA RK 700/1/1588/27; [g]Ibid., ll. 48–51.

35.5 million fest-metres, compared to 6.5 million achieved in 1931, see pp. 119–23) would have to be substantially reduced (see Table 5.4).

In September 1932, Gosplan USSR sent a letter to the Karelian Representative in Moscow stating that the Northern Group in Gosplan had learned that some local organisations were compiling their Second Five-Year Plans on the basis of the 1932 annual plan. This was entirely incorrect, admonished the central planning authority, as it led to 'formalistic, unfounded projections for 1933 and the Second Five-Year Plan'. Instead, the Plan must be 'organically linked to the factual fulfilment of the First Five-Year Plan' and with the expected (i.e. not projected) results of 1932. During 1933, planners in the centre (insofar as they concerned themselves with Karelia at all) were occupied in revising their ideas to take account, on the one hand, of the new perspectives opened by the BBVP and the BBK, especially in the sphere of energy construction, and on the other (in contradiction to the first) of the need drastically to reduce overall investment levels against a background of deepening economic crisis and famine. As we have already seen (pp. 123–8), the latter consideration largely prevailed. Both a draft Second Five-Year Plan published in advance of the XVII Party Congress at the start of 1934, and a 'final' variant ratified by the Congress and published soon afterwards, envisaged that Karelia would 'retain the character of its basic specialisation in the sphere of the timber and paper industry'. As a lesser priority, the ASSR would also develop new industries 'closely related to the tasks of assimilating the Belomor–Baltiiskii Water Route.'[57]

Karelia's final published territorial plan allocated a total of 651 million rubles to the Karelian economy, distributed by sector, as in Table 5.5.

What is, at first glance, astonishing in Gosplan's post-congress version of the Karelian plan is the proportion of investment assigned to heavy industry,

Table 5.5 Major capital investment in the Karelian Second Five-Year Plan
(million rubles, 1933 prices)

Total	651	(%)
NKTyazhProm	236.8	41.3
Energy construction	31.1	
Light metals (aluminium)	30	
Machine-building	13.5	
Chemicals	127	
NKLes	208	32
NKLegProm	10	1.5
NKSnab	9.6	1.5

Source: *Vtoroi pyatiletnii plan razvitiya narodnogo khozyaistva SSSR (1933–1937gg). Tom II. Plan razvitiya raionov* (Moscow, 1934), pp. 19–22.

despite the same plan's statement that Karelia would retain the 'character of its basic specialisation.' Gosplan's omission from its earlier draft plan of the Nivastroi and chemical-construction projects in the northern Karelian district of Kandalaksha, however, hints at an explanation of this: it is likely that Gosplan believed that Kandalaksha, with its close links to the Khibinogorsk appatite works, was located in Murmansk region (and was therefore part of the Leningrad, not the Karelian, regional plan).[58] Four years later, Karelia did indeed surrender this economically significant district to the newly established Murmansk oblast.

Following the publication of Gosplan's final variant, regional planning authorities were instructed to present their revised plans to the centre by late March.[59] The Karelian government decided to 'consider realistic' the target of 16.5 million fest-metres for 1937 felling.[60] They were not satisfied, however, with Gosplan USSR's absolute rejection of their proposed control figures for investment, and petitioned the centre for alterations to some of the plan's sections.[61]

Karelia's own planning work was held up by problems of liaising with the BBK's Planning–Economic Department and with the NKLes representative in Leningrad oblast.[62] After Karplan with some delay submitted its plans to the centre, the republican authorities waited for a response. A few months later in Moscow, the Karelian representative reported to Gylling that Gosplan USSR was still working on the republic's new proposals. His letter was profoundly pessimistic.[63] Gosplan's Sector for the Timber Industry had reportedly presented a report on the allocation of labour to the lumber industry which had not included any provision at all for Karelia. Although the Sector for Light Industry (promoting branch interests) had looked favourably on Karplan's projects for expanding light industry in the ASSR, the Northern Group (promoting wider territorial interests) had rejected all of Karelia's industrial proposals, claiming that because of 'inadequate raw materials and poor transport' (it was evidently not as impressed by the BBVP's possibilities as other regional interests were), the ASSR should solely concentrate on timber. The Karelian representative had also filed a protest with the deputy chair of Gosplan USSR at the exclusion of light industry in the sectoral volume of the published final plan from the branch control figures for the republic (although, confusingly, the published regional volume of the plan did include a 10 million rubles allocation for light industry, as we saw above). However, the Karelian official wrote, he believed that there was little chance that the ASSR's proposals for light industrial construction would be accepted. Pragmatically, he suggested that Karelia should not pursue its plans for this sector. Instead, the republic should try not to lose the 10 million rubles that – according to the regional plan, at least – it had been allocated, by presenting alternative projects for its use more in line with the Northern Group's emphasis on timber. In this way, Karelia's resistance to specialisation was progressively worn down not so much by peremptory central dictate as by bureaucratic deadlock, and the vestiges of its economic autonomy expunged.

Rapidly changing economic circumstances, however, rendered Gosplan's published control figures and output targets obsolete within a few months. On 20 June 1935, M. I. Kalinin directed scathing criticism at Karelia for the fact that it still had 'no overall complex ... perspective plan, but only separate outlines of separate branches of the economy'. Kalinin then offered a clear statement of the centre's conception of Karelia's economic role, deriding the republic's aspirations to promote new industrial sectors, and proclaiming that it should concentrate all its efforts on maximising output of timber. This sector, he asserted, should account for 70 per cent or more of Karelian production![64]

There was never, in fact, a definitive, let alone coherent, Second Five-Year Plan for Karelia. The Union and Russian planning agencies and ministries issued Karelia with a series of annual and quarterly control figures and limits, along both branch and territorial lines, often mutually contradictory, and rarely matched by the appropriate funding. This made unified regional planning and administration impossible. The Second Five-Year Plan as a means of directing the Karelian economy was, to all intents and purposes, a disruptive fiction.

Implementation of the Second Five-Year Plan in Karelia, 1935–7

The year 1935 was a watershed in Soviet Karelian history. Prompted by new foreign policy and security concerns in the Baltic region, the centre on the one hand took measures to ease the ASSR's increasingly critical economic situation, and on the other hand tightened political control over the republic. Crucial to the emergence of both these tendencies was the appointment of Andrei Zhdanov to head the Leningrad party organisation in December 1934, following Kirov's murder. Zhdanov was determined both to enforce party discipline and to enhance the defensive capability of the regional border. In the autumn and early winter of 1935, Zhdanov removed Gylling and most of the Finnish communists from the Karelian leadership on the grounds of nationalist deviation (they had stubbornly ignored a series of Leningrad obkom resolutions on nationality policy over several years), and appointed his own official P. Irklis to the top Karelian party post. Another Leningrad official, P. I. Bushuev, was sent to preside over the Karelian Sovnarkom. From this time, is difficult to distinguish an independent Karelian position in economic policy-making. Indeed, Karelian officials grumbled that the ASSR was turning into a 'colony' of Leningrad.[65]

Controlling the Karelian Economy, 1935–6

At the same time, a multiplicity of Union, Russian Federal and Leningrad organisations increased and intensified their levels of supervision over the implementation of directives in the republic. The party organisations themselves, their control organs and the security police had always closely watched activities in the economic sphere: in the Stalinist state nothing fell outside the scope of politics, and political control was the regime's defining characteristic. All directors of enterprises and most economic administrators were, of course, also party members and therefore subject to party discipline. The Leningrad obkom exercised control either directly by despatching its own 'instructors' to Karelia or through the Karelian party, which was increasingly transformed into the local executive arm of Leningrad. The Commission of Party Control (KPK) for Leningrad oblast also came to play an important role in monitoring policy implementation. In September 1935, the Leningrad KPK was directed to supervise the Karelian party organisation, and the Karelian collegiate of the KPK became a Central Committee field agency directly subordinated to and controlled by the central KPK attached to the Central Committee.[66] The Karelian NKVD, which was by now absolutely subordinated to the Leningrad Administration of the NKVD (UNKVD), ominously also stepped up its intervention in economic activities.

After 1935, the supervision exercised by these organisations over economic administration became not only increasingly intrusive, but also increasingly unfettered by considerations of economic rationality or efficiency. The absence of realistic planning to govern or guide productive activity in the ASSR naturally created a context conducive to this arbitrary interventionism. The Karelian authorities and enterprise directors had usually to manage their activities on stop-gap allocations, short-term loans or their own internal savings. They invariably lapsed deeply into debt, both to suppliers and workers. Moreover, chaotic planning created wide scope for – indeed, often necessitated – recourse to statistical trickery, false reporting, rent-seeking, violation of regulations and legislation, illicit bargaining, corruption and cliquism, if managers were to achieve high central plan targets with minimal central funding. Intensifying repression universalised illegitimate behaviour in the Soviet economy, transforming resourcefulness and ingenuity into strategies for survival.

In February 1935, for example, the Karelian NKVD investigated and compiled a report on 'abnormal relations' between the administration of a major Karelian construction site, Sunastroi, and the local militia. During 1934, tensions had developed as a result of the management's 'malicious infringement' of the passport laws when recruiting its workforce. The local militia had issued temporary passports to migrant workers and twice agreed to renew them so as not to disrupt construction. But henceforth, the NKVD declared, it would no longer tolerate the administration's persistent violation of the law, or its practice of such politically irresponsible recruitment methods, even for the sake of fulfilling the economic plan.[67] At this stage, however, the Karelian obkom evidently desired to retain the director of its largest and most important project, and for the time being Sunastroi director P. N. Travkin remained in his post.

In December 1935, the Leningrad obkom commissioned an investigation by the Leningrad UNKVD on lumber work by Karelles. The report was highly unfavourable: progress in felling was unsatisfactory, plans remained unfulfilled by large margins, and the workforce was well under strength, mainly because of lack of food (there were cases of starvation), the appalling living conditions and heavy wage arrears. The report noted numerous strikes in Karelian timber stations, although far more frequently the workers simply deserted (often after they had collected their advance wages). The administration of the trust, the report continued, was riddled with class aliens and criminal elements. When the director of one *lespromkhoz*, indebted to its workers for 149,000 rubles, finally received 4,000 rubles in October, he spent 800 rubles on a three-day drunken spree. Another director spent 470 rubles on an accordion while his workers went unpaid. The Karelian party committee was warned to 'take serious steps to improve the situation'.[68]

Another such report, compiled by a special party investigator from Moscow visiting the Kondopoga Paper Factory, originally sent to A. A. Andreev and N. I. Ezhov in the Central Committee in March 1936, detailed production collapse, political negligence, financial chaos and lack of leadership from NKLes, the NKLes Chief Administration of the Western Paper Industry (Glavzapbumprom) and the factory administration. Living conditions, the report noted, were disgraceful: in the living quarters up to 10 men slept in rooms of 15 m² among 'stench, dirt, ice, lice, bedbugs, and the sick.' There was alarming dissatisfaction among the workers, widespread drunkenness, hooliganism, fighting, gambling, and 'until recently', the report noted wryly, 'prostitution was doing a thriving trade in the women's barracks'.[69]

Such investigations prompted Leningrad and Moscow to issue a stream of directives demanding immediate steps to rectify shortcomings in the enterprises and felling organisations. However, most problems resulted from insufficient financing by the Russian and Union centres. Instead of extra funding, the authorities increasingly applied administrative, party disciplinary and judicial measures against economic officials, which served only further to disrupt their performance. The tendency towards repression was given added momentum by foreign policy developments. Since 1933, despite the Soviet–Finnish Non-Aggression Pact and Finland's declared neutrality, the Soviets had become increasingly concerned by their neighbour's apparent pro-German orientation. This fear dictated a new policy towards the 1,000 km Karelian borderland. Repression was not new in the border zone. As early as 1925 the OGPU had staged a series of show trials of inhabitants of the border districts. In 1933, the Karelian NKVD had fabricated the 'the Finnish General Staff conspiracy' in Leningrad and the southern Karelian border districts. Arrests continued during 1934 of border area residents for alleged spying and wrecking activities. From 1934, measures were taken to tighten security along the border, including the introduction of a special passport regime, the vetting of workers sent to felling operations in 'Group A' districts (those closest to the state border), the clearance of villages and the expulsion from the area of political unreliables.

From 1935, however, repression began to bite even deeper into economic activities. Karelian organisations had been subject to almost continuous administrative purging since the beginning of the decade, but in mid-decade, in connection with the verification of party documents, leadership changes and the widespread arrests and exiling of political undesirables from the border zones and from Petrozavodsk, the rate of turnover of officials and workers increased considerably. In February–March 1935 alone, a purge of Karelles resulted in the dismissal of 18 officials from the central administration and 183 from the 18 *lespromkhozy* (including 48 accused of being kulaks, and 37 of having participated in the White Army and the Finnish incursions of 1921–2).[70] The entire leadership of the Kem' felling enterprise was declared anti-soviet and removed, causing predictable disruption to its activities. In October 1935, the NKLes Chief Administration of Northern Timber 'Glavsevles' in Moscow wrote to Karelles, sending a copy of the letter to the Karelian party committee. The Chief Administration noted that the Karelian timber trust still claimed a deficit in cadres of over 400 persons, although Moscow and Leningrad institutes had despatched more than 350 specialists to Karelia over the previous two years. Glavsevles therefore attributed the deficit to specific regional factors, notably Karelia's terrible living conditions, and 'the frequent and usually unjustified dismissal of specialists and their arrests.' It instructed Karelles to petition the

Karelian obkom to order local party committees and militia to desist from dismissing and arresting leading timber workers and specialists without prior agreement from both the trust and the obkom.[71]

Strengthening the Karelian economy, 1935–6

At the same time, during late 1934 and 1935 the centre's concern to strengthen its external border prompted it to adopt, alongside increased measures of administrative purging and repression, a more generous attitude towards the Karelian economy. Zhdanov also played a key role in promoting this policy in the centre. Government, security police, party organisations and the military at all levels had long been calling for increased expenditure on the border districts, especially on supplies, communications and transport, to tie the remote villages more closely to their district centres, and the peripheral districts to the republican centre. It was also hoped that border development would discourage cross-border smuggling, encourage settlement by reliable Red Army kolkhozniki and stem the demographic collapse aggravated by forced resettlement and rising mortality rates (the high number of suicides in these areas was the subject of a number of NKVD and party reports).

For the first time since the early 1920s, Moscow's dealings with Karelia were distinguished by an attitude other than total ignorance, disdain or hypocrisy. In mid-December 1934 Karelian party boss, Kustaa Rovio and Gylling sent another of their exhaustive tirades to Stalin and Molotov (this would be their last), demanding additional resources for creating a permanent timber workforce, raising salaries, improving supplies of food and consumer goods, especially to border districts, and building roads. They also requested guarantees that they would be permitted to receive all their statutory budgetary income and to use all available funds for construction and exploration within their plan, even when this exceeded their capital expenditure limits. Molotov scribbled in green pencil across the top of this letter: 'To Chubar' and Mezhlauk. We must turn our serious attention to Karelia. Must be discussed at the Zams.'[72] The letter was duly passed to the Conference of Deputy Commissars. At the same time, the Karelian leadership sent a separate letter to Voroshilov, pleading a similar case, but expressed in terms of improving Karelia's defence capability. They also lobbied the Commissar of Heavy Industry. In February 1935, Ordzhonikidze called Stalin's attention to a personal letter from Gylling and Rovio requesting the use of 17.5 million rubles for the Kandalaksha construction, which they claimed they could source in Karelia's 1934 budgetary surplus. Stalin forwarded the letter to Molotov with the note (in brown pencil) 'What should we do?'[73]

Once Molotov had indicated his interest in Karelia, central agencies set to work with unprecedented energy elaborating a project to meet the ASSR's requests. In early February, Mezhlauk sent his conclusion on the Finns' letter to Stalin and Molotov, stating that 'Gosplan USSR considers that in view of the special situation of the Karelian Republic as a border territory and the character of its natural conditions, it is appropriate to carry out measures which will ensure its more rapid economic growth and the full use by the Karelian Republic of its special rights to revenue'.[74] He suggested that Karelia should be allowed to use an extra 21 million of its 1934 surplus to recruit timber workers and for construction projects. In the next two months, the Karelian representative in Moscow attended several rounds of talks in Gosplan USSR co-chaired by V. I. Mezhlauk with K. K. Abolin of the Commissariat of Finance (NKFin USSR), while Gylling telegrammed Molotov, and Rovio wrote to the Central Committee requesting a speedy settlement of this question.

By late April, however, Gosplan USSR commission, while leaving most specific funding items untouched, had slashed the overall 1935 Karelian budget from 202.5 million rubles to 150.5 million. By early May, after D. Z. Lebed' (representing Russian Federal interests) had subjected the Union draft to extensive editing at a meeting of the Conference of Deputy Commissars, the Gosplan commission agreed to reduce it further to 110.5 million.[75] Lebed' also insisted on excising two points articulating the principles on which the Karelian budget was formed: their inclusion, he noted, would 'reiterate the fact of their violation by the Russian government, or anticipate the possibility that these rights will not be observed'.[76]

On 17 May, Molotov submitted this version of the Sovnarkom USSR resolution to the Politburo, requesting its ratification in view of the 'significance' of the projects involved. The supreme party organ approved the draft on 21 May, and it was issued as a secret governmental decree the following day.[77] The Karelian budget thereby regained some of its privileged status, though without regaining any autonomy. Above its statutory income (already high *per capita* in comparison to other Russian national territories), it was to receive a proportion of NKLes income from timber felled on its territory (this was meant also to act as an incentive to improve the organisation and performance of the lumber trusts in Karelia); it was to be freed from the statutory deduction of Union and Russian Federal expenses; it was to receive 38 million rubles from the Union budget; and its capital investment limits for 1935 were raised by 21 million rubles for resettlement, agriculture, geological research, road construction, municipal amenities and for the already long overdue completion of Sunastroi.[78]

In September 1935, following the replacement of the Karelian party leadership, the new first party secretary Irklis and the Leningrad second secretary M. C. Chudov travelled to Moscow for talks with Ezhov and Molotov about financing further measures to aid the border republic's development, which had been elaborated earlier in the year in Leningrad. After the Politburo had approved these projects at the end of the month, Sovnarkom USSR issued a decree on 5 October granting Karelia a number of additional privileges specifically designed to strengthen its border districts.

Specialists' salaries were raised, collectivised peasants in five border areas were freed entirely from agricultural taxation for three years and tax rates were lowered in four others districts, and 10 more MTS were established. Three secret clauses instructed Gosplan USSR to revise Karelia's 1936 plan with a view to ensuring increased mechanisation of felling, the creation of a permanent workforce, more extensive road construction and the improvement of cultural–economic development in the border districts.[79] No-one in Karelia expected such generosity: the republican Commissar of Agriculture is reported as declaring 'Oh my God! What am I going to do now! Another ten MTS is going to make life difficult!'[80] Further Union decrees in 1936 and 1937 extended Karelia's privileges and intervened in the planning process to raise the ASSR's limits for construction in strategically important sectors and districts.[81]

Repression in the Karelian economy, 1937

During 1936 and 1937, most of the economic work of the ASSR was geared to fulfilling these decrees. The timber industry in Karelia, however, failed to improve its performance. In terms of plan fulfilment, 1934 was the peak year and in 1936 and 1937, the republic met only 73 per cent of its annual plans (see Table 5.6). Most of Karelia's absolute increase in output of 25.6 per cent in 1936–7 was accounted for by the BBK (Karelles increased production by 9.3 per cent, the BBK by 51.9 per cent).

Delays in Sunastroi slowed down the construction of the planned second stage of the Kondopoga GES, and in turn the Kondopoga Paper–Pulp

Table 5.6   Timber-felling output in Karelia, 1932–7 (thousand fest-metres)*

	1932	1933	1934	1935	1936	1937
Karelles	3,180	3,675	4,097	4,215	4,401	4,852
– of which Medvezh'gorsk,						
Povenets, Vygozero LPKhs[†]	1,859	1,264	983	442	–	–
BBK	–	123	734	1,130	1,676	3,486
Total Karelian	6,439	6,010	6,810	6,849	7,043	9,465
BBK as % of total	–	2	14.4	16.5	23.8	36.8
Total as % of Second Five-Year						
Plan targets	–	82.3	94	90.1	73	73.5

Notes:
*Totals exclude Kandalaksha district, transferred from the Karelian ASSR to Murmansk oblast' in 1938. Other active felling organisations were Pudozhles (formerly Sevzaples, Lenles), NKLes KASSR, Oboronles (from 1936), plus Karpromlessoyuz and the Rugozerskaya railway.
† These LPKhs were transferred to the BBK between 1933 and the end of 1935.
Source: 'Results of the Karelian Second Five-Year Plan,' dated 1938–9, in GARK 700/1/1558/27, 48–51.

Combine received insufficient energy to increase its production (construction progress in the latter two was delayed in any case). Between 1932 and 1936 the output of paper actually fell, although there was an atypical rise in production measured in m^2 in 1935, seemingly achieved by the simple ruse of reducing the thickness of the paper.[82] In 1937 the Combine fulfilled only 75 per cent of its capital construction programme.[83]

Such weak results at a time when the international situation was becoming more tense and the internal political environment increasingly paranoid triggered a devastating assault on Karelia's economic administrators.[84] In early 1937, the Leningrad party leadership, both directly and through its clients in the top posts of the Karelian organisation, launched the attack in conjunction with the local NKVD, which itself acted on directives both from Leningrad and from its Moscow centre. In the late summer of 1937, however, Irklis and the Leningrad officials in Karelia themselves fell victim to the purges on charges of 'rightist' deviation (this was related to a purge of the Leningrad party organisation) and conspiracy with Karelian bourgeois nationalists (such as Bushuev, who was an ethnic Karelian from Tver Province). At the same time, the Karelian party organisation was subordinated directly to the Moscow Central Committee and entered a period of ferocious self-destruction that lasted just over a year. During this time the NKVD, having already taken deliberate steps to destroy the Karelian judiciary and procuracy, worked supremely unhindered in its destruction of Karelian administrative cadres, according to its own central quotas and plans.[85]

Many of the leading officials in Karelian commissariats and enterprises were Finnish survivors from the time of the previous leadership. They were now implicated also by their association with Irklis, the 'rightists' and the Karelian nationalists.[86] It is quite clear that the high turnover of officials in 1935–7 and the pressures of operating with constant interference from the NKVD and KPK further contributed to weak performance indicators. This meant that officers of the security organs did not have to strain their imaginations to create pretexts for arrests, or to weave from denunciations and forced confessions their own fantastic cartography of the centres and peripheries of counter-revolution, espionage and treason. Often, as with Travkin of Sunastroi, they already had files of compromising material (*kompromat*) waiting to be put to use.

As early as November 1936, Karelian obkom officials had subjected the Sunastroi administration to criticism.[87] In April 1937, a report submitted by a party investigator accused Travkin and his deputy Rogozhin of embezzlement, mismanagement and suppressing criticism. 'The apparat does not serve the state', wrote the party official, 'it serves Travkin'. On the previous year's May 1 meeting, loyal engineers had greeted their bosses with the slogan 'Long live the genius-construction leaders Travkin and Rogozhin'. On the other hand, there had been something resembling a violent insurgence among workers in protest at the administration's neglect of their welfare.[88] In August 1937, Travkin sent a letter to the Karelian obkom bureau complaining that constant accusations of wrecking against him and his personnel had rendered it impossible for them to carry out their economic tasks since the previous year.[89] Despite an attempt by the party chiefs to rein in attacks on him, accusations by the ambitious, antagonistic or fearful among his subordinates and rivals continued unabated.

The Karelian local newspaper, *Krasnaya Kareliya*, on 29 September 1937, published a vitriolic report on wrecking in Sunastroi. Travkin, wrote the newspaper's special investigator, had created his own 'fiefdom', wherein he had ruled since 1932 as 'absolute lord and master'. He had surrounded himself with suspicious characters, neglected workers' living conditions, failed to use machinery efficiently, permitted a high turnover of the workforce and falsified annual reports.[90]

It was presumably an indication of the importance of the Sunastroi project that Travkin was allowed to continue in his post through 1937 until construction neared completion. On 17 January 1938, however, Travkin was arrested by the Kondopoga district NKVD and on 21 March he was shot on charges of counter-revolutionary sabotage and conspiracy according to a decree of the troika of the Karelian NKVD. Rogozhin was arrested five days after his boss' execution, and sentenced in April to 10 years 'deprivation of freedom' on charges of counter-revolutionary sabotage.[91] Unsurprisingly, all the earlier problems in the construction persisted. Although the new director sought to overcome the shortage of workers by contracting labour from the NKVD, disputes with the BBK administration over their wages and numbers meant that in the first eight months of 1938 only 33.1 per cent of the annual capital investment plan was fulfilled.[92]

The purges particularly ravaged Karelia's timber industry. In July–August 1937 alone, 10 'diversionary-wrecking organisations' were liquidated in Karelles; 33 officials were arrested in total from the trust's administration including nine engineers, seven directors of mechanical bases, six directors of *lespromkhozy*, and two deputy leaders of the trust. The majority being Russian, they found themselves implicated in the purge of the NKLes USSR 'rightists' under Lobov and Al'bert in their branch centre, rather than in local Finnish or Karelian nationalist counter-revolutionary conspiracies or espionage, though the NKVD inevitably found means of tying together these diverse oppositional 'centres'.[93] A former head of Karelles and a plenipotentiary of NKLes in Karelia were shot soon afterwards. Almost the entire administration of the Kondopoga Combine was arrested and shot on charges of having participated (according to nationality) either in a 'spying-diversionary-wrecking organisation' established in 1935 by a Czech specialist working for the German secret service, or in allied groups established in the

Combine by Finnish bourgeois nationalist conspirators and spies.[94] It would hardly be an exaggeration to claim that a large proportion of the ASSR's leading cadres, including a majority of its senior economic personnel, perished in the purges of 1937–8.[95]

Results of the Karelian Second Five-Year Plan

We have already briefly considered Karelia's weak performance during the Second Five-Year Plan with regard to the material output of its most important sector, the timber industry (Table 5.6). But regional interests had intended to achieve more than higher timber production. To what extent did implementation of the Plan alter the structure of the regional economy? At the start of the chapter, we outlined Gylling's vision of the transformation of the economy during the period under survey (Tables 5.1 and 5.2). Table 5.7, offers a picture of the actual change in its composition during these five years.

What is striking at first glance is that the contribution of timber production (excluding paper) to gross Karelian output by value had fallen from 72.7 per cent to 53.1 per cent (the converse of what Kalinin had demanded in 1935). Instead, sectors which increased their share of output were: metal-working and machine-building (thanks to the reconstruction of the Onega Factory, which first manufactured machinery for the Belomor canal's construction and exploitation, and later for NKLes); food production

Table 5.7 Actual distribution of output in Karelian industry, 1932–7 (% of gross output in 1926/27 prices)*

Branch	1932	1937
Electricity stations	0.8	1.3
Timber-felling and floating	51.8	35.9
Timber chemical	0.1	0.1
Building materials	8.3	6.2
Metal-working	1.5	3.7
Machine-construction	7.1	9.8
Wood-manufacture	0.9	4.2
Timber-sawing	19.0	13
Paper-manufacture	5.6	4.3
Food-manufacture	3.4	7.5
Sewing	0.4	11.3
Leather, fur and footwear	0.2	2.1
Printing	0.3	0.5
Total	**99.4**	**99.9**

Notes: *These figures exclude Kandalaksha. (and therefore chemical production).
Source: Calculated from TsUNKhU KF-SSR report, presented after January 1941, in NARK 1411/2/360/10–11, reproduced in *Vavulinskaiy, Narodnoe khozyaistvo Karelii 1926g – iiun' 1941g.*, p. 27.

(in line with the aims of Second Five-Year Plan, the Petrozavodsk Bread Factory was expanded, and fish production increased, largely by BBK prisoners and exiles); leather, fur and footwear manufacturing; and, most dramatically, sewing, which increased its share of the Karelian economy by a factor of almost thirty. These last enterprises, in fact, had been almost non-existent in Karelia at the start of the decade, and their establishment and growth were entirely the work of the BBK, which needed to find lighter work for its female and invalid population.

As well as wholly representing the leather and sewing sectors, the Combine played a dominant role in road construction (not included in the Table 5.7) and fishing, had sole responsibility for operating the Belomor canal, contributed nearly 40 per cent of the republic's felling output, had medium-sized ship-building workshops in Pindush and, by 1937, was close to completing the major Segezha Paper–Pulp Combine (this list excludes, of course, its additional economic activities in the Murmansk region). The Gulag's felling, sewing and leather output alone accounted for over 28 per cent of republican output by value. Table 5.7 therefore reveals clearly that by the end of the Second Five-Year Plan, the Karelian economy had undergone quite extensive structural change in unforeseen directions, much of which was owing to the increasingly powerful regional role of the forced labour authorities.[96]

Conclusion

The loose form of 'structuration' theory that informs this chapter's analysis of economic–spatial decision-making invites a redefinition of 'totalitarianism', an indispensable but abused – and therefore justifiably criticised – theoretical construct of the Stalinist system. The sociologist Edward Shils claimed that in the totalitarian state the expansion of the modernising centre into the periphery, although accompanied by a *show* of diffusing authority (for example, through mock elections, constitutions, and propagandistic declarations of democracy), in fact concentrates ever-increased power at its own locus.[97] In terms of the preoccupation of the present chapter to elucidate the processes and principles of Stalinist spatial structuration, totalitarianism may thus be redefined as a drive to realise a unitary centralist conception of space through the total synthesis of the centre–periphery dualism. It is equally important to note, however, that the achievement of this objective is, of course, logically impossible. Totalitarianism thus entailed not only an impulse to total control, but also the ever-more vicious response to its own necessary failure.

What has been mistaken by some 'revisionists' in the past as forms of peripheral power, or even as forms of pluralism, may in this light be considered as phenomena of *résistance* (in the Foucauldian sense, i.e. not countermanding, but constitutive of power relations) at the points of peripheral contact with central interventions.[98] Karelian *résistance* derived from the region's own manifold peripherality in Union and Russian space: both in metaphorical terms of its national, cultural, linguistic and economic specificities, and in physical–spatial terms of its frontier situation and its remoteness and relative inaccessibility from Soviet centres. In the planning and implementation of economic decision-making, the distance from the centre to sites of implementation occasioned the 'normal' administrative problems of centre–local relations in a field of overcentralised power which we have recurrently observed throughout this chapter: conflict between branch and territorial bureaucracies at all levels; alliances among central field agencies (such as the Gulag) and regional interests; the exploitation by the periphery of differences among central institutional interests; imperfect information flows and the superiority of local knowledge; weakness of policy implementation and oversight; and cumulative radicalisation resulting from the establishment of competing control agencies at all levels.

The particular ferocity of the Karelian repressions derived from what may be described as the *spatial paradox of Stalinist power*. On the one hand, the Stalinist centre sought to enforce its own conceptualisation of a unitary and uniform Soviet space through subsuming the periphery into the centre. On the other hand, strategic concerns dictated the need to strengthen Karelia as an important frontier region. This meant, in effect, conceding its peripheral status, not solely by the closure and fortification of the state border and increased military mobilisation, but also by reinforcing the ASSR's economic and political resilience against foreign subversion.

It was, of course, impossible to enforce central control by repression without weakening the periphery; and yet undermining the periphery – especially when the state's territory was encircled by enemies – would necessarily endanger the integrity of the centre. Stalinist terror precluded its own success. Instead of enhancing central authority, state strategy reproduced further *résistance* in conditions of chaos and fear, and in this way sharpened its own spatial paradox. Ultimately, Stalinism in the late 1930's collapsed both spatial logic and distinctions between *résistance* real and perceived. Confronted by Karelia's national, cultural and linguistic specificities, its diplomatic and strategic significance and the problems arising from its remoteness and inaccessibility, the Stalinist centre, its prefects and field agents, re-imagined the periphery as a liminal space populated by proliferating anti-Soviet (anti-central) 'centres' of fascism, bourgeois nationalism, counter-revolution, spying and wrecking. The spatial paradox thus generated and sustained a dynamic of terroristic intervention which in its purpose, scope, intensity and its fantastic, self-defeating irrationality may justifiably be termed 'totalitarian'.

Notes

*I am grateful to the Economic and Social Research Council (ESRC) for funding the research on which this chapter was based.

1. Pierre Bourdieu and Looc J. D. Wacquant, *An Invitation to Reflexive Sociology,* (Cambridge, 1992) p. 41.
2. For a detailed examination of the establishment of Karelia's borders, see Nick Baron, 'Soviet Karelia, 1920–1937. A Study of Space and Power in Stalinist Russia', unpublished PhD thesis; University of Birmingham, 2001, Chapter Two.
3. See Baron, 'Soviet Karelia, 1920–1937', Chapter Two.
4. For an analysis of Soviet spatial planning during the First Five-Year Plan and the Karelian response, see Baron, 'Soviet Karelia, 1920–1937', Chapter Four.
5. For the construction of the Belomor Canal (the northern section of the BBVP in central Karelia), see Nick Baron,'Conflict and Complicity: The Expansion of the Karelian Gulag, 1923–1933', *Cahiers du Monde russe*, 42(2–4), April–December 2001.
6. National Archive of the Republic of Karelia (NA RK) 700/1/839/7.
7. State Archive of Socio-Political Movements and Formations of the Republic of Karelia (former Karelian party archive, GAOPDF RK) 3/3/39/7.
8. NA RK 700/1/569/30–30ob.
9. NA RK 700/1/839/7–10ob.
10. E. Gylling, 'Kareliya pered vtoroi pyatiletkoi', *Sovetskaya Kareliya*, Nos 1–2, 1932, p. 8.
11. GAOPDF RK 3/2/751/8.
12. NA RK 682/1/195/1–6.
13. I.V.Pervozvanskii, 'Ekspluotatsiya lesa v Karelii vo vtoroi pyatiletke', *Sovetskaya Kareliya*, Nos 1–2, 1932, p. 61.
14. NA RK 700/1/877/43.
15. NA RK 700/1/839/82.
16. NA RK 700/1/870/153.
17. For example, NA RK 700/1/870/107 and GAOPDF RK 3/2/751/1–4.
18. On the 1931 Karplan purge, see *Sovetskaya Kareliya*, Nos 3–4, 1931, pp. 9–12, Nos. 5–7, pp. 1–10.
19. NA RK 700/1/819/5ob.
20. The document does not indicate Lobov's initials.
21. NA RK 700/1/819/6–7ob.
22. NA RK 690/3/435/5.
23. NA RK 700/1/824/195–207.
24. GAOPDF RK 3/3/39/9. For a detailed discussion of the BBK, its impact on the economic geography of the North and its economic tasks, see Baron, 'Soviet Karelia, 1920–1937,' Chapter Five, and *idem*, 'Production and Terror: The Operation of the Karelian Gulag, 1933–1939', *Cahiers du Monde russe*, 43(1), January–March 2002.
25. NA RK 865/36/1/35–36.
26. NA RK 865/1/51/190–191 published in V. G. Makurov (ed.), *Gulag v Karelii. Sbornik Dokumentov i materialov 1930–1941*, (Petrozavodsk, 1992), p. 91.
27. NA RK 690/1/27/65.
28. GAOPDF RK 3/2/445/25–25 ob. For more on the development of the Karelian Gulag in the 1920s, see Baron, 'Conflict and Complicity'.
29. Russian State Economic Archive (RGAE) 432/32/776a/1–4 and NA RK 865/36/1/2.

30. NA RK 865/36/1/13.
31. NA RK 690/3/613/15–18.
32. Russian State Archive of Social–Political History (former central party archive, RGASPI), 17/21/1914/187.
33. For more details on the population of the BBK in the 1930s, see Baron, 'Production and Terror'.
34. NA RK 520/1/28/1–22. The two variants are described in detail in NA RK 700/1/1425/17–39.
35. A. A. Kolpakov, 'Energeticheskoe ispol'zovanie vodnykh resursov srednei Karelii', *Belomorsko Baltiiskii Kombinat*, No. 5, 1935, pp. 3–6.
36. NA RK 520/2/29.
37. NA RK 700/1/1425/38–39.
38. NA RK 711/1/4/25.
39. NA RK 700/1/1425/4.
40. *Proekt vtorogo pyatiletnego plana razvitiya narodnogo khozyaistva SSSR (1933–1937), Tom II. Plan razvitiya raionov* (Moscow, 1934), pp. 18, 310.
41. BBK Project 1935, NA RK 700/1/1425/24 and the BBK 1937 report on central Karelian development in the Third Five-Year Plan, NA RK 865/36/2/3–57.
42. NA RK 700/1/1425/24.
43. *Vtoroi pyatiletnii plan razvitiya narodnogo khozyaistva SSSR (1933–1937gg), t. 2 Plan razvitiya raionov* (Moscow, 1934), pp. 19–22.
44. NA RK 865/41/753/1.
45. *Ibid.*, 1–3, and 865/756/63.
46. NA RK 865/41/753/1.
47. GAOPDF RK 38/1/1/33ob-34.
48. State Archive of the Russian Federation (GARF) 5446/16a/1330/5.
49. The bulk of Gulag funding went to the Moscow–Volga canal construction, see NKVD titular lists for 1936, June 1936, in GARF 5446/18a/637/212, 215.
50. NA RK 700/1/1318/125.
51. NA RK 700/1/569/112 and 700/1/1318/125–6.
52. GAOPDF RK 3/3/1/8ob.
53. For example, in 1933 Leningrad ratified the appointment of the head of the Kandalaksha Chemical Combine construction, GAOPDF RK 3/3/1/2.
54. NA RK 711/1/3/1 and 711/1/4/57–60.
55. For example, in October 1934 the Glavenergo titular list funding for a major Karelian energy project was reduced, and then only partially released, which Karelia claimed was illegal, NA RK 690/3/629/285–291.
56. Quoted in Yu. S. Fridlyand, and M. Ya. Eiger, 'Puti elektrifikatsii AKSSR vo vtoroi pyatiletki', *Sovetskaia Kareliya*, No. 6, 1934, p. 29.
57. *Vtoroi pyatiletnii plan*, pp. 19–22.
58. Berztys also noted this possibility, referring to some anomalous Gosplan calculations concerning regional electricity capacity, NA RK 700/1/1318/132.
59. NA RK 690/3/613/34.
60. NA RK 690/3/613/29.
61. NA RK 690/3/613/54–55.
62. NA RK 690/3/613/15–18 and 21.
63. NA RK 690/3/613/56.
64. NA RK 689/5/65/232–233.
65. GAOPDF RK 3/3/2994–2.
66. Decree of KPK pri TsK VKP (b), 3/9/1935, GAOPDF RK 16/3/48/4.

67. GAOPDF RK 16/3/51/1–5.
68. GAOPDF RK 3/3/299/83–89.
69. GAOPDF RK 3/4/56/5–15.
70. GAOPDF RK 3/3/314/35–36.
71. GAOPDF RK 3/3/299/48–49.
72. State Archive of the Russian Federation (GARF) 5446/16a/567/4–5, 15–18.
73. GARF 5446/16a/567/74.
74. GARF 5446/16a/567/19–20.
75. GARF 5446/16a/567/66–108.
76. Letter of Lebed' to Mezhlauk, 7 May 1935, in *ibid.*, l. 48.
77. RGASPI 17/163/1063/143–147.
78. GARF 5446/1/102/44–46.
79. GARF 5446/1/108/27–30.
80. GAOPDF RK 3/3/299/41.
81. See GARF 5446/1/113/179–181 and 5446/1/132/165–167.
82. NA RK 2034/1/16/23 and L. Kert, 'Kondopoga', *Karelo-Murmanksii Krai*, Nos 1–2, 1934, p. 47.
83. NA RK 2034/1/10/1.
84. For a detailed examination of the origins, process and consequences of the purges in the Karelian economy, see Baron, 'Soviet Karelia, 1920–1937', Chapter Six.
85. See Baron, 'Soviet Karelia, 1920–1937', pp. 310–27.
86. Archive of the Federal Security Agency of the Russian Federation in the Republic of Karelia (Arkhiv FSB RF po RK), fond of the secretariat, opis 1, poryadka 82, delo of year 1938, list' 13.
87. RGASPI 17/21/1965/151.
88. GAOPDF RK 3/4/378/34–35.
89. GAOPDF RK 3/4/378/46–47.
90. *Krasnaya Kareliya*, 29/9/1937, p. 3.
91. Response to enquiry submitted to Director of Arkhiv FSB RF po RK, 17 September 1997 ('Arkhivnaya spravka po fondu ugolovnikh del na lits, snyatykhs operativno-spravochnoi kartoteki').
92. GAOPDF RK 3/5/1833/27.
93. GAOPDF RK 3/4/265/87.
94. For example, GAOPDF RK 3/4/265/38–50,71–95, and Arkhiv FSB RK po RK secretariat/1/82/year 1938/15.
95. Karelian Party Secretary, N. I. Ivanov, reported to the Fourteenth Karelian Obkom Conference, 13–14 June 1938, that there had been 1,167 new promotions in Karelia to senior bureaucratic posts during 1937 and the first half of 1938 (it is not clear how many of these *vydvyzhentsy* were themselves purged and then replaced), in RGASPI 17/21/1918/39–40.
96. In 1936, the BBK received the equivalent of almost a third of total investments in the republic, see GARF 5446/18a/637/212, 215 and *Narodnokhozyaistvennyi plan na 1936 god. Chetvertyi god vtoroi pyatiletki. Tom II. Plan razvitiya raionov* (Moscow, 1936), p. 289.
97. Edward Shils, *Centre and Periphery* (Chicago, 1975).
98. See Michel Foucault, *The History of Sexuality. Vol. 1. An Introduction* (New York, 1990), p. 95.

6
The Donbass

Hiroaki Kuromiya

The Donbass, or Donets Basin, straddles south-eastern Ukraine and south-western Russia on the northern shore of the Sea of Azov. It was (and still is) a peculiar place.[1] It was one of the most important industrial (steel and coal) centres in the country, so important a source of energy supply for the whole country as to be called the 'all-union stokehold [*vsesoyuznaya kochegarka*]'.[2] Yet it was a perennial trouble spot for the economic administrators. For Moscow the Donbass remained rather unmanageable throughout much of Soviet history. The unmanageability stemmed in part from the difficulties of running the coal-mining industry (the dominant industry in the Donbass) in general. Yet the problem was caused at least as much by the fact that the Donbass remained an attractive haven for all sorts of fugitives who sought freedom in the anonymity of the dark, unreachable underground of the mines. Thus, Moscow suspected that the Donbass was a nest of hidden 'enemies' of the Soviet government. The Donbass case demonstrates well how in the 1930s Moscow essentially attributed economic and political difficulties to the matter of 'human material', a favourite expression of the Bolsheviks. This, in turn, explains the context within which one of the most momentous events of the period of the Second Five-Year plan, the Great Terror, took place. The Donbass case may be extreme, but it is a case extremely revealing of centre–local relations in the 1930s.

The historical background

A land larger than the state of Massachusetts but smaller than Indiana, the Donbass is located quite far from Moscow or St Petersburg (or, for that matter, the two capitals of Ukraine, Kyiv and L'viv). Part of the Donbass came to be administered by the Don Cossack Host during the Muscovite period, but its southern and western parts became incorporated into the Russian Empire only in the late eighteenth century under Catherine II. This southern steppe land belonged to what used to be called 'the wild field [*dyke pole, dikoe pole*]', a no man's land where many powers (Muscovite,

Polish–Lithuanian, Turkish and many others) contested for domination. It was a frontier area sandwiched between two Cossack (Zaporozhian and Don) lands and, like the Cossack lands, it traditionally attracted many fugitive serfs, criminals and others who wanted freedom and fortune. The steppe was thus synonymous with freedom, i.e. freedom from exploitation, persecution and oppression.[3] This historical heritage often posed a political problem to the metropolises.

The frontier land was also multi-ethnic. This fact, of course, reflected the history of a land criss-crossed by many migrating individuals and groups who were then encouraged to settle to secure the southern frontiers of the Russian Empire. Although the western part of the Donbass has always been predominantly Ukrainian, and the eastern part predominantly Russian, the Donbass has always been ethnically complex and its ethnic composition in flux. Its population grew very rapidly from approximately 700,000 in 1897 to 4.5 million in 1937.[4] In 1926, the ethnic composition (by self-identification) of Stalino okrug in the administratively Ukrainian part of the Donbass was as follows: Ukrainians 53.22 per cent, Russian 34.18 per cent, Greeks 5.12 per cent, Germans 2.19 per cent, Jews 1.97 per cent, Belorussians 0.97 per cent, Tartars 0.90 per cent, Poles 0.48 per cent, and so on.[5] It is not known whether the multi-ethnic nature of the area posed any serious challenge to Moscow. Yet the potential threat of Ukrainian separatism was real in the eyes of Moscow, and the presence of other ethnic groups, such as Germans, posed some challenge to Moscow in times of external crisis, such as during the First and Second World War.

One peculiarity of the Donbass is that after the southern frontier had been closed by the Russian conquest of the area in the eighteenth century; modernity transformed the Donbass into a symbolic frontier land again. The coming of modern industry (mainly coal-mining and steel production) to the Donbass is symbolised by the foundation in the 1870s of the New Russia Coal, Iron, and Rail Producing Co. in what came to be called Yuzivka (Yuzovka) after its founder, the Welshman John Hughes.[6] Attracted by the opportunities created by modern industrial development, which made the Donbass into a major industrial centre of the empire, people began to migrate *en masse* to the Donbass, leading to the very rapid, sustained increase in its population. Although it was not free of periodic economic depressions, the Donbass continued to suffer from labour shortage and thus to remain an attractive haven, or refuge, for whoever needed employment. The Donbass, with its well-developed system of underground mines, was an ideal hiding place for criminals, fugitives, and sometimes revolutionaries hounded out of the cities and towns. By attracting such people and providing a certain freedom for them, the Donbass began to function as a new 'frontier' in a symbolic sense: it became a land far removed from the political metropolis, where the latter's power was severely limited and people found ample opportunities to live a new life.[7]

The Donbass, like any other frontier land, was a land of contradictions and did not necessarily live up to the romantically idealised image of freedom attributed to it. The presence of many ethnic groups meant ethnic strife, and popular anti-Semitism was a fact of life. Industrial operation involved an unprincipled exploitation of labour. Sharp social rifts, seen in the Russian Empire in general, were manifest in blatant form in the Donbass, accentuated further by the contrast between the bright and safe surface where the bosses worked and the dark and dangerous underground where the rank-and-file toiled. Like many other mining communities in Russia and elsewhere, life in the Donbass was harsh and often very violent.[8] For all the brutality of everyday life, however, the Donbass continued to attract people, much as the New World, a land of 'freedom and opportunities', with all its widespread crime, racism and exploitation, still continues to attract people from all over the world, as though, from a global perspective, it were still a frontier land.

Politics in the Donbass were unstable and unpredictable. It was notoriously difficult even for the Marxists to organise labour, which tended to be uprooted, mobile and unruly. The 1917 revolutions and the ensuing civil war did not establish the Donbass as a whole as politically reliable for the Bolsheviks. It is true that the Bolshevik party won the civil war in the Donbass (which changed hands dozens of times in the three years of bitter battle) in part because of the support of its working people. Yet the seemingly proletarian Donbass did not blindly follow the Bolshevik line. The isolated mining towns and settlements were surrounded by vast steppe lands the political loyalty of whose residents (particularly Ukrainian-speaking peasants and Don Cossacks) was always suspect in the view of the Bolsheviks. Even after civil peace was restored the Donbass was plagued, probably more than any other industrial centre, by numerous strikes.[9]

The Donbass that the Bolshevik regime had inherited from imperial Russia describes an area of central importance economically but with an unwieldy working people who were difficult to manage. This latter legacy did not always militate against the Bolshevik government, however. The traditionally great gulf between rank-and-file workers and engineering–technical personnel, which was even made wider and deeper by the revolutions and civil war, kept anti-specialist feelings (or 'specialist-baiting' [spetseedstvo]) extraordinarily strong and alive among Donbass workers. It was, therefore, no accident that the famous 1928 Shakhty affair (a case of 'economic counter-revolution' against mining specialists, which marked the beginning of Stalin's 'revolution from above', a process that broke opposition to the rapid industrialisation drive and the wholesale collectivisation of agriculture) took place in the Donbass. The trial against the alleged remnants of 'class enemies' was closely orchestrated by Stalin and in fact the trial itself took place not in the Donbass but in Moscow, an indication of the significance Moscow attached to this affair.[10] Yet the Shakhty affair was only one of many other similar incidents, large and small, against 'bourgeois' experts (i.e. those educated before the revolution) that took place in the Donbass in the 1920s.[11] These deliberate political acts and the Donbass workers' anti-specialist attitudes reinforced each other, providing Moscow's fight against its alleged 'enemies' with a degree of popular political support.

Nevertheless, the Donbass remained a grave trouble spot throughout much of the Stalin era. Anyone who studies Soviet industrialisation will realise sooner or later that again and again the Donbass was to be a bottleneck for Moscow's relentless drive for industrialisation: production and productivity in the mines often failed to rise as fast as Moscow expected, jeopardising the growth of other branches of industry. Stalin and the Politburo in Moscow therefore frequently intervened directly in Donbass affairs. The Shakhty affair was merely one of the first such incidents.

Technology and human material

The case of the Donbass illustrates how closely connected the two preoccupations of the Bolsheviks – technology and 'human material' – were. The Bolsheviks, as Marxists, believed that material forces were responsible for the progress of human society.

Technology, which drove capitalist development, occupied a central place in their thinking. Vast and rapid industrialisation, with the 'latest word in technology' (another favourite expression of the Bolsheviks), was supposed to solve the contradiction posed by the revolution: a 'proletarian revolution' in a still predominantly agrarian society – or, as Antonio Gramsci put it, 'revolution against *Das Kapital*'. During the Second Five-Year Plan, Moscow demanded an immediate and dramatic return on the huge investment it had made in the preceding five years. It was not reasonable, however, to expect an immediate and dramatic return on the mechanisation of coal-mining in general.[12] Impatient, Stalin and other political leaders insisted that the economic difficulties were due largely to the scarcity of people ('cadres') who were capable of maximising the use of technology. Hence in 1935 came Stalin's famous slogan, 'Cadres decide everything', which replaced his earlier slogan, 'Technology decides everything'.

Historians have demonstrated that Stalin's adoption of the slogan was a signal for a new offensive directed against the engineering–managerial cadres whom he held responsible for the perceived economic woes of the country. (In fact, the years 1934–6 marked 'the three 'good' years' in which there was a dramatic increase in industrial production.[13] Stalin wished for even more dramatic improvement.) They have also shown that the famous (or infamous) Stakhanovite movement, which originated in a carefully arranged norm-busting initiative in 1935 by the Donbass collier Aleksei Stakhanov, was the first concrete manifestation of this offensive and that the movement led to extensive and violent removals of cadres in the Donbass and in industry in general as part of the Great Terror.[14]

Yet the case of Ukraine and the Donbass suggests that this shift in emphasis from technology to cadres began somewhat earlier and that Moscow's interest in 'human material' concerned much more than the narrowly defined industrial cadres. Of critical importance was the shift in the image of enemies from 'class enemies' to 'enemies of the people' which took place at the time of the grave famine crisis in 1932–3. Studies of other areas of the country (the Urals, Siberia, Kazakhstan, the Northern Caucasus [which includes part of the Donbass], for example) will illustrate a similar shift. Still the case of Ukraine and the Donbass in particular is especially revealing.

The mortal enemy of the dictatorship of the proletariat was the 'class enemy', who signified the international 'bourgeoisie', the remnants of the domestic 'bourgeoisie' such as the 'kulaks', and those deemed as the lackeys of the former industrial bourgeoisie such as old (or 'bourgeois') engineers and technicians. This last group was singled out as the most dangerous enemy in the industrial sector because the actual industrial 'bourgeoisie' had largely disappeared (emigrated) abroad. The Shakhty affair was thus merely one of a series of show trials Moscow staged against those alleged to be still serving class enemies, both external and internal. Another prominent case was the 'Industrial Party' trial in 1930.

By the time of the famine of 1932–3, which hit Ukraine particularly hard, Moscow began to portray new images of its enemies. In 1931, once a breakthrough had been wrought in the matter of creating new, Soviet (as opposed to old or 'bourgeois' specialists) and the 'elimination of the kulak as a class', Stalin played down the theme of the danger of the 'class enemy'.

This retreat from the 'class war' rhetoric may have been part of what has been usually described as the 'Great Retreat', a retreat from revolutionary rhetoric and practice in general and particularly within social and cultural spheres. Still 'bourgeois' specialists were arrested and persecuted. Yet from 1931 onward when engineers and technicians were accused of wrecking and other political crimes, they tended not to be referred to as 'bourgeois', but merely as engineers and technicians. (This suggested that card-carrying members of the Communist Party were also among the accused.) Simultaneously, impatient with slow returns on the huge investment the government had made during the First Five-Year Plan, party and government officials began to portray Communist managers and bosses as 'enemies' who secretly sabotaged and wrecked government policies.[15]

As already indicated, the impatience of Stalin and his associates was unreasonable, all the more so because, at the time, the workers were hungry and as poorly prepared for mechanised production as the Communist managers were. Yet Moscow did not hesitate to deal with the industrial crisis in the Donbass by open attacks upon managerial and technical cadres whom they assailed not only as incompetent or inept bureaucrats (as many had been) but as 'anti-mechanisers', 'saboteurs', 'enemies of the people' and 'counter-revolutionary' elements. It was made patently clear that carrying a party card did not make one immune to the punishing hand of the party and the secret police. The change in the image of 'enemies' as portrayed by Moscow, marked an important turning point in Moscow's dealings with local party and industrial bosses, a fact often overlooked by historians.[16]

This subtle shift was politically necessary and expedient because if tried and tested Communists were to be politically condemned, it could not be as 'class enemies'. Therefore, a new, class-neutral 'enemy' crept into the political discourse of the time. Indeed, at the time of the famine, at least in Ukraine and the Northern Caucasus, Communists in responsible positions were treated just like the old 'class enemies'. In November 1932 the Politburo of the Ukrainian Communist Party sanctioned the 'immediate arrest and trial' of certain Communists in responsible positions who were 'politically dangerous'.[17] Thus, among the many arrested officials of collective farms in Ukraine were a large number of Communists. From October to November 1932 nine party members were sentenced to death.[18] (How many non-party officials were sentenced to be shot is not clear. In Dnipropetrovsk oblast', for example, 59 kolkhoz officials were sentenced to capital punishment in the same period. In one district of Donetsk oblast' alone, 20 were given the death sentence.)[19] At the beginning of December 1932, according to the Central Committee of the Ukrainian Communist Party, 327 Communists stood trial. They were to be deported north along with the 'kulaks'.[20] In the Donbass many party members were in fact arrested alongside kulaks.[21] Class distinction was no longer apparent or meaningful in these cases. Indeed, from the famine crisis onward the secret police began to hunt 'enemies' actively within the party.[22] In October 1933 a newspaper article labelled five mining officials in the Krasnodon coalfield accused of deliberately cutting workers' wages 'Enemies of the people'.[23]

Nor were 'ordinary' people immune to enemy-hunting. As the famine crisis loomed large, Stalin found it convenient to revert in part to the earlier rhetoric of 'class enemy', but now he implied that the nature of enemy action had changed. In January 1933 Stalin declared that

> the last remnants of moribund classes – private manufacturers and their servitors, private traders and their henchmen, former nobles and priests, kulaks and kulak agents, former White Guard officers and police officials, policemen and gendarmes, all sorts of bourgeois intellectuals of a chauvinist type, and all other anti-Soviet elements – have been tossed out.

> But tossed out and scattered over the whole face of the USSR, these 'have-beens' have wormed their way into our plants and factories, into our government offices and trading organisations, into our railway and water transport enterprises, and, principally, into the collective farms and state

farms. They have crept into these places and taken cover there, donning the mask of 'workers' and 'peasants', and some have even managed to worm their way into the party.

What did they carry with them into these places? They carried with them hatred for the Soviet regime, of course, burning enmity towards new forms of economy, life, and culture.

Then Stalin emphasised:

We must bear in mind that the growth of the power of the Soviet state will intensify the resistance of the last elements of the dying classes. It is precisely because they are dying and their days are numbered that they will go from one form of attack to another, sharper one, appealing to backward sections of the population and mobilising them against the Soviet regime...This may provide fuel for a revival of the activities of defeated groups of the old counter-revolutionary parties: the SRs, the Mensheviks, and the bourgeois nationalists of the central and border regions...the Trotskyites and Right deviationists...This is why revolutionary vigilance is the quality most needed by the Bolsheviks at the present time.[24]

Three months later A. Ya. Vyshinskii, Stalin's 'grand prosecutor', stated that having lost the battle, the enemy now resorted to 'methods known as quiet sapping' rather than direct frontal attack, and that the enemy sought to conceal its wrecking acts with all sorts of 'objective reasons', 'defects' and the contention that the incidents did 'not seem to be caused by malicious human intent'. Therefore, Vyshinskii emphasised, the enemy 'becomes less detectable and hence it becomes less possible to isolate him'.[25]

One can detect here genuine fear of the enemy on the part of Stalin and Vyshinskii. It would appear to be absurd not to fear the ghosts of those who had died *en masse* during collectivisation, industrialisation, dekulakisation and famine, and to fear the revenge of those of their families who had survived state terror by fleeing to the cities, factories, mines, construction sites and elsewhere. To them must be added, as Stalin made clear, political enemies of all sorts. Because the famine crisis coincided with the rise of Adolf Hitler to power in Germany, it was logical that Stalin questioned whether in case of war these people would support him and his government,

There was more to it, however. Stalin was a past master of political manipulation. In this case, too, Stalin was actually promoting a political vigilance campaign by implying that enemies were hidden everywhere, even within the party. Vyshinskii's remark that it had become less possible to isolate the enemy suggests that mass repression would become inevitable. One can detect here the political logic that it would be better to 'isolate' one hundred people in the hope of finding one enemy among them than to leave that one at large. This is of course dangerous logic. According to the testimony made in 1937 by G. G. Yagoda, then chief of the secret police – the GPU – in 1932–3 some of his officials opposed the vigilance campaign: 'Any talk of counter-revolutionaries is nonsense.'[26] Yet, there were others who were eagerly vigilant, and the campaign went on all the same.

Amid this vigilance campaign, the Donbass, with its reputation as the 'free steppe', became even more politically suspect than before. Testimony after testimony shows that it was very easy for people, even fugitives (the dekulakised, the clergy, and other disenfranchised, or 'former people' – *byvshie lyudi*) to find 'freedom' in the Donbass, i.e. to find living and employment (by changing one's identity if need be).[27] The dark anonymity of the Donbass underground seemed to protect anyone who needed freedom. Yet this impression (which was to a large extent real) gave the Donbass the appearance of a nest of 'enemies' of the Soviet government.

Neither the industrial commanders nor the rank-and-file workers were free of accusations of wrecking. Mining was dangerous work and the miners were, after all, highly prone to accidents. Accidents were attributed to deliberate wrecking by 'enemies'. Before 1931, the authorities could (and did) blame 'class enemies' ('bourgeois' specialists), leaving the Communist managers and workers usually safe from wrecking charges. Thereafter, however, no one, including the 'ordinary' worker (who might be a dispossessed kulak or a fugitive priest), was immune, as Stalin implied in his January 1933 speech. The Donbass press, particularly *Sotsialisticheskii Donbass* for 1932–3, was replete with such accusations against 'enemies'.

Enemy-hunting spread to the service sector as well. Poor catering, for example, prompted many vigilantes to see enemy activity in workers' cafeterias which, under famine conditions, often became the only source of subsistence. In the Donbass, 80 per cent of the staff of Donnarpit (Donbass Public Catering) were said to be disenfranchised people. In none of the Donnarpit cafeterias were either soap or towels available. The only 'redeeming' factor was that the Donnarpit office was next to the GPU: it was easy to drag Donnarpit officials there.[28] Indeed, many seem to have been dragged to the GPU; in December 1932, for example, 20 men were indicted for disrupting the catering of the Smolianka, Rutchenkove and Budenivka mines in the Stalino district by a systematic misappropriation of foodstuffs. The defendants were allegedly former kulaks, merchants, bakery owners and a former army officer. Two were sentenced to be shot as 'enemies of the people'. Five others were given 10 years' imprisonment. The press reported that 'The Enemies of the People Have Got What They Deserved'.[29] There followed many similar cases in 1933. In the summer of 1933, for example, a group of people working in the catering service in Makiivka (Makeevka) was arrested for stealing millions of rubles' worth of foodstuffs. The group included 'people with a party membership card in their pockets'. They were branded as 'enemies of the people'. Four were sentenced to death.[30] Even when workers were fed, the food was often spoiled and resulted in food poisoning. Most likely, the caterers were not responsible: there was no soap, no towels! Yet the press published calls for death sentences for the 'enemies of the people'. Death sentences ensued.[31]

The Great Terror and centre–local relations

It is no surprise that the Bolshevik government in Moscow reduced economic issues to those of 'human material' in as much as an economy is run by humans. Nor is it particularly remarkable that the government poorly understood economics: it was bent on destroying old economic relations and building a new, centrally planned economy, about which there was no textbook from which to learn. Yet the extent to which Moscow attributed economic problems to human issues was extraordinary. Even in its January 1933 secret circular, clearly not meant for campaign or 'public relations' purposes, the Ukrainian Communist Party Politburo stated categorically that the mass exodus of people to Russia and Belorussia (Belarus') from Ukraine was 'organised by the enemies of the Soviet government, SRs and Polish agents agitating, "through peasants", in the northern areas of the Soviet Union against collective farms and the Soviet government'.[32] In other words, the exodus was due not to the famine but to 'enemy' agitation.

The preoccupation with 'enemies' was much more than political expediency. It had to do with the fact that the regime had driven all critical political thinking underground: people did not or could not speak their minds freely; there was no easy way of identifying the 'enemies', as Stalin and Vyshinskii complained in 1933. As there were no 'independent' means (such as free elections, free mass media, or opinion polls) of gauging the 'political mood of the population' (a set phrase used by the secret police), surveillance and intelligence became virtually the only means.[33]

In his 1985 book on the Great Terror, J. Arch Getty has argued that 'the party bureaucracy was chaotic rather than totalitarian, and that local officials had relative autonomy, within a considerably fragmented political system'.[34] Getty's thesis on Soviet centre–local relations in the 1930s has shifted the attention of scholars away from the paradigm of the totalitarian school and toward the localities whose officials had to dirty their hands in carrying out the brutal policies of the centre. Getty's book has influenced much of Western discussion on the Soviet 1930s.

The case of the 'free', unmanageable Donbass tends to support, to an extent, the Getty thesis that the centre's hold on the localities was far from total or complete (I will argue below, however, that the Donbass case also adds some important twists). Now that at least some of the documents of the Politburo are available, one can see the great extent to which it involved itself in what appeared to be the most mundane and minute matters of little political significance. Still this did not mean that the Politburo maintained control of everything. For example, it was never able nor could it even make a serious attempt to get the migration of the population under tight control. Even though it arrested and incarcerated millions of people and sought to control tightly the influx of people into major cities (such as Moscow, Leningrad, Kharkiv and Kyiv), even the seemingly almighty Politburo could not control spontaneous movements of people. This was particularly true outside the major cities, although it was far from the case that the authorities were in complete control of the influx into them. Nor did the labour market ever cease to operate in the centrally planned economy. The coal-mining industry, of which the Donbass was by far the most important centre, registered almost invariably the highest labour turnover in the industrial sector. The Donbass was thus the epitome of a land far from the centre and free of central control (of course, 'free' in a relative sense of the word).

The limited control exercised by the centre over the localities may in fact be part of a much larger problem of the political centre's very limited ability to gauge and measure the 'political mood of the population', as discussed above. Even when the centre was able to control to an extent the actions of the officials and people (for example, by incarceration and other means of punishment or by limiting residence in the cities), it was not able to control the minds of the people. So long as the Soviet regime meant to remake human material in its own mould, it destroyed suspect human material as irredeemable. This logic was apparent in Stalin's 1937 utterance. According to G. Dimitrov's notes on his conversations with Stalin in November 1937, Stalin said that the Russian tsar did one good thing: the building and uniting of a huge state. Now the enemies of the people wished to sell Ukraine to Germany, Belorussia to Poland, the Maritime Province to Japan and the Donbass to France. Stalin declared that anyone who 'threatens the unity of the socialist state by deed or by thought, yes, by thought too, will be destroyed mercilessly'.[35] Stalin's categorisation of the Donbass alongside Ukraine, Belorussia and the Maritime Province indicates the significance he attached to it.[36]

Yet how could Stalin determine who would 'threaten the unity of the socialist state...by thought'? He could not. Hence came the necessity of more extensive surveillance and enemy-hunting than ever. This posed a dilemma for the political leaders. The secret police had every institutional reason for exaggerating critical thinking and 'enemy' forces; otherwise its very *raison d'être* would be called into question. The centre knew that intelligence reports could not be taken at face value. One might well remember the complaint Molotov once made about the Soviet intelligence reports that every day he used to spend half a day reading them, but he still could not trust them.[37] It is still not clear how and what information Stalin and his associates used in making important decisions.

Yet it seems to be evident that they were guided by a belief that in implementing important policies and mobilising bureaucracies and people, moderation was more dangerous than excess. Such was the case with the First Five-Year Plan drives for industrialisation, collectivisation and dekulakisation.[38] Once a breakthrough was wrought, the centre could easily shift the blame for the excesses to the local officials who had to implement the policies of the centre. The enemy-hunting operations during the Second Five-Year Plan were no exception.

The enemies Stalin portrayed were nearly devoid of class content; now the enemies were the class-neutral 'enemies of the people', fifth columnists and German and Japanese spies and agents (labels such as 'Trotskyites' and 'Zinovievites' became synonymous with foreign agents and spies). As already discussed, no one, including a card-carrying Communist Party member, was safe from state terror because he might entertain the 'thought' of overthrowing Stalin's regime (how could one tell, as Stalin and others often asked, whether a breakdown of a machine was the result of accident or sabotage?)

From the point of view of the centre the so-called 'free steppe' of the Donbass appeared to be infested with such hidden 'enemies'. As Stalin made clear, the economic significance of the Donbass to the country played a major role here; had the Donbass been an inconsequential hinterland, it might not have mattered much. The hidden 'enemies' had to be identified and destroyed, as Stalin intimated. No one was safe from state terror, but certain groups were more vulnerable than others. For example, ethnic Germans and Poles, i.e. the diaspora nations of the western border states, became politically suspect as potential fifth columnists. Soviet officials expressed much fear that money and other forms of aid from Germany to ethnic Germans in Ukraine, begun at the time of famine crisis, was in fact an 'open fascist campaign'.[39] In 1934 the secret police uncovered 'Fascist cells' in many German colonies in the Donbass. They were accused of conducting 'counterrevolutionary agitation to disintegrate the collective farm system and undermine the Soviet government'.[40] Eight days after the murder of Kirov in Leningrad on 1 December 1934, the Ukrainian Communist Party Politburo, in response to a circular of the Central Committee of the party in Moscow, sent a special secret telegram to the oblasts, ordering an elaborate review of German and Polish districts in Ukraine, threatening deportation abroad or to remote areas of the country for 'the slightest attempts at anti-Soviet activity or propaganda'.[41]

After the Kirov murder many foreign political refugees were considered tantamount to enemies. Several hundred Polish refugees, both Communists and non-Communists, were arrested in Ukraine between December 1934 and 1936.[42] The Donbass hosted many such refugees and was hard hit by anti-Polish and anti-German repression. The refugees were repressed as 'spies' and 'fascist agents'.[43] From late 1934 to 1936 at least 10 German 'counterrevolutionary' organisations were liquidated by the Donbass NKVD: 'Prolog', 'Renegaty', 'Filial', 'Segment', 'Redaktor', 'Pereplet', 'Azovtsy', 'Kolltso', 'Pochtamt', 'Zheleznyi krest', etc.[44]

Ethnic Ukrainians, unlike ethnic Russians, became politically suspect by default, although there is little compelling evidence that ethnic Ukrainians were much harder hit by Stalin's terror than ethnic Russians who were repressed for other reasons. P. Lysenko, for example, a Donbass miner who was arrested in 1932 as a 'Ukrainian insurgent', testified to being tortured by secret police officials in Ordzhonikidze (formerly Yenakiieve).[45] Ukrainians from Galicia (then under Polish rule) became as suspect as ethnic Poles and Germans.[46] In the Donbass mines, workers were arrested for reading Ukrainian nationalist literature. In 1935 some Ukrainians in Kadiivka [Kadievkal were repressed for protesting against the use of the Russian language in meetings and for allegedly contending that 'Ukraine is under a [Russian] yoke'.[47]

People who came from the border area were met with suspicion. For example, a Ukrainian born in Bukovina who had moved to the border on the Soviet side, came to the Donbass in the mid-1930s to work as a 'common labourer'. 'Unfortunately at that time an arms factory was being built and the GPU was interested in newcomers, paying special attention to their place of origin. When they found out where this man had lived, they arrested him. He was held in prison for four months and then sent to labour camps.'[48]

By all indications, Ukraine was hit hardest in the country in the political repression of the mid-1930s: in 1935, for example, by far the largest numbers of 'spies' were arrested in Ukraine.[49] In Ukraine, the Donbass was subject to the most intense crackdown: as of 1 December 1935, in connection with the verification campaign of party documents, 560 people in Donetsk oblast, 408 in Dnipropetrovsk oblast, 350 in Kharkiv oblast and 264 in Kiev oblast were arrested by the NKVD as 'spies', 'Trotskyites', 'nationalists', 'fascists and terrorists', etc.[50] In the process, party membership in the Donbass was halved between 1933 and 1936 (from 166,000 to 83,000).[51]

Viewed in the political context of the mid-1930s enemy-hunting in the Donbass, the Great Terror (which, as Getty has correctly noted, decimated local elites) appears to have been more than the result of centre–local tensions or of Moscow's attempts to control recalcitrant regions by centralising political power. Had there been no centre–local tensions and had the regions been completely subjugated to the centre, the enemy-hunting would still have been necessary in as much as it was impossible to know who was harbouring anti-Soviet feelings.[52] The terror operation was a trial of conscience to secure internal security, staged by a regime faced with the threat of external war.[53]

Afterthoughts of Stalin's closest associates at the time of the Great Terror support this view. According to L. M. Kaganovich for example, Stalin, if alive, would have admitted his mistakes. 'We were to blame for going too far [peresolili], thinking that there were more enemies than there actually were.' Yet the Great Terror was justified, Kaganovich implied, because there were fifth columns and, had they not been eliminated, the Soviet Union would have been beaten by the Nazis.[54] In an almost identical vein,

V. M. Molotov also insisted that 'Stalin played safe (Stalin perestrakhoval)'. There was no hard evidence that, for example, the Red Army leader Tukhachevskii was a German agent, but he was 'dangerous', and 'we were not sure whether he would stay firmly on our side in a difficult moment'. Evidence was not so important, Molotov suggested, because 'there is no smoke without fire'. Molotov justified Stalin and himself: 'Let an extra head fall and there will be no vacillation at the time of war and after the war.' The terror of this period was necessary and inevitable, Molotov maintained, and 'it was impossible to conduct it without mistakes'.[55]

Conclusion

The Donbass was a symbolic frontier land where all sorts of people fled to change their identities and live new lives. Many did succeed in so doing, because the Donbass was in constant need of Workers and readily provided employment and shelter to whoever needed it. One witness, for example, who was dekulakised in Kirovohrad in 1929 and fled to the Donbass in 1930, has given this testimony: '[I]f no one who knows you notices you, then you can work [in the Donbass], only keep silent about who you are, where you are from. This was never spoken. This was all locked up in the individual. People worked in this way. As soon as someone notices, then you become frightened and wonder where to hide, because if someone notices you, then people will know that you are there. So people leave.'[56]

It is not that the Donbass was truly unique in providing 'freedom', but that it was the favoured place because of its reputation, to which it often lived up, as the free steppe. It was a much safer place to live than the major cities; employment was easy to find; and few people cared about the identities of others because they had backgrounds of their own to hide. The Donbass was attractive even though work, particularly mining, was a dangerous trade, working and living conditions were horrendous and the possibility of wrecking charges, in case of an industrial accident, was very real. The centre had good reason to suspect that the Donbass was a 'nest' of enemies and in fact often intervened directly in its affairs. Sometimes, however, a degree of economic realism prevailed. The following case is instructive. In 1933, an internal passport system was introduced in an attempt to control the population movement. In Stalino, for example, 220,661 passports were issued, while 10,465 persons were denied a passport; 45 per cent of those denied passports were said to be kulak-fugitives, 19 per cent 'parasites' and 14 per cent the disenfranchised and former criminals. There were at least 1,896 colliers and 1,150 metal workers among the 10,465 who were denied passports. Of these workers, however, 906 were allowed to remain in Stalino because of their exceptional importance to industry. This extraordinary permission symbolised the 'freedom' the Donbass had long signified to outlawed members of society.[57] Still, despite its economic exigencies, or perhaps because of them, the centre continued to be preoccupied with enemies, precisely because they were difficult to unearth. One could go so far as to contend that the anonymous Donbass underground symbolically embodied the last, imaginary frontier the centre could not conquer: that of the human mind and critical thinking.

State terror in the Donbass was extensive. As the 1935 party records suggest, it was probably one of the areas hardest hit by Stalin's terror. Any statistics on the Great Terror are incomplete and therefore provisional. Yet in 1937–8 up to one-third of the total executions in Ukraine appear to have taken place in the Donbass, which accounted for only about 16 per cent of the population of Ukraine in 1937.[58] At some point, a degree of economic as well as political realism had to be restored in order for the centre not to destroy the Donbass (and other provinces). This was what happened in 1939.[59]

Notes

1. Some of the material of this essay is derived from my book, *Freedom and Terror in the Donbas: A Ukrainian–Russian Borderland, 1870s–1990s* (Cambridge, 1998).
2. In 1917, the year of revolutions, the Donbass produced 87 per cent of the country's coal output, 70 per cent of pig iron, 57 per cent of steel, more than 90 per cent of coke and more than 60 per cent of soda and mercury, Yu. V. Afonin, 'Monopolistychna burzhuaziya Donbassu v 1917g.', *Ukrains'kyi istorychnyi zhurnal*, No. 9, 1990, p. 45. In 1929 the Donbass still accounted for 77.3 per cent of the country's coal production and for 60.8 per cent in 1938, *Sotsialisticheskoe stroitel'stvo Soyuza SSR (1933–1938gg.): Statisticheskii sbornik* (Moscow, 1939), p. 47.
3. Note, for example, N. Gogol's description of the 'limitless, free [vol'naya], beautiful steppe', N. V. Gogol, *Polnoe sobranie sochinenii*, Vol. 2 (Moscow, 1937), p. 60. I owe this citation to Judith Deutsch Kornblatt, *The Cossack Hero in Russian Literature. A Study in Cultural Mythology* (Madison, 1992), p. 54. Note also Mykola Cherniavslkyil's 'free sons of the steppe [*Villnykh stepu syniv*]', quoted in Vadym Olifirenko, *Duma i pisnia. Dzherela literaturnoho kraieznavstva* (Donetsk, 1993), p. 125.
4. Petro Lavriv, *Istoriya pivdenno-skhidnoi Ukrainy* (Kyiv, 1996), p. 173, and *Vsesoyuznaia perepis' naseleniya 1937 g. Kratkie itogi* (Moscow, 1991), p. 45. The 1937 figure concerns the Ukrainian part of the Donbass only. Statistical comparison is difficult because there was no distinct administrative unit called the Donbass, but in 1937 probably more than 1 million people lived in the administrative Russian part of this coal-mining industrial centre.
5. *Vsesoyuznaya perepis' naselenyia 1926 goda*, Vol. 11 (Moscow, 1929), p. 30.
6. See Theodore H. Friedgut, *Iuzovka and Revolution*, 2 vols (Princeton, Oxford, 1989–94).
7. This transformation was not entirely unique to the Donbass. For similar reasons 'New Russia', of which the Donbass was part, underwent a similar transformation. See Terry Martin, 'The Empire's New Frontiers: New Russia's Path from Frontier to Okraina 1774–1920', *Russian History*, Nos 1–4, 1992. The Donbass symbolised this transformation in a dramatic fashion.
8. For life in the Donbass, see Friedgut, *Iuzovka*, and Charters Wynn, *Workers, Strikes, and Pogroms: The Donbass–Dnepr Bend in Late Imperial Russia, 1870–1905* (Princeton, Oxford, 1992).

9. See H. Kuromiya, 'Donbass Miners in War, Revolution, and Civil War', in Lewis H. Siegelbaum and Ronald Grigor Suny (eds), *Making Workers Soviet: Power, Class, and Identity* (Ithaca, London, 1994), and Kuromiya, *Freedom and Terror in the Donbass*, Chapters 3, 4.
10. See H. Kuromiya, 'The Shakhty Affair', *South East European Monitor*, 4(2), 1997, which utilises Soviet archival documents unavailable to researchers until recently.
11. The most prominent was the 1924 Kadiivka (Kadievka) coalfields trial of engineers and technicians charged with 'economic espionage'. See *Kochegarka*, 16, 17, 18, 19, 22 and 23 July 1924, and *Pravda*, 16, 18, 19, 20, 22 and 23 July 1924.
12. See H. Kuromiya, 'The Commander and the Rank and File: Managing the Soviet Coal-Mining Industry, 1928–33', in William G. Rosenberg and Lewis H. Siegelbaum (eds) *Social Dimensions of Soviet Industrialization* (Bloomington, 1993).
13. Naum Jasny, *Soviet Industrialization, 1928–1952* (Chicago, 1961), p. 142.
14. Lewis H. Siegelbaum, *Stakhanovism and the Politics of Productivity in the USSR, 1935–1941* (Cambridge, 1988); Robert Maier, *Die Stachanov-Bewegung 1935–1938. Der Stachanovismus als tragendes und verschiirfendes Moment der Stalinisierung der Sowietischen Gesellschaft* (Stuttgart, 1990); Gábor T. Rittersporn, 'Heros du travail et commandants de la production. La campagne stakhanoviste et les stratégies fractionelles en URSS (1935–1936)', *Recherches*, No. 32/33; Robert Thurston, 'The Stakhanovite Movement: The Background to the Great Terror in the Factories, 1935–1938', in J. Arch Getty and Roberta T. Manning (eds), *Stalinist Terror: New Perspectives* (Cambridge, 1993); and Francesco Benvenuti, 'Stakhanovism and Stalinism, 1934–38', Unpublished Discussion Papers, SIPS, No. 30 (University of Birmingham, Centre for Russian and East European Studies, 1989). O. V. Khlevnyuk, *Stalin i Ordzhonikidze. Konflikty v Politburo v 30-e gody* (Moscow, 1993), p. 58 calls this assault 'political pogroms'.
15. See Kuromiya, 'The Commander and the Rank and File'. For a more detailed analysis of the general economic crisis, see R. W. Davies, *Crisis and Progress in the Soviet Economy, 1931–1933* (London, 1996).
16. See Kuromiya, 'The Commander and the Rank and File'. Note also the 1934 attempt by the Commissar of Heavy Industry, Sergo Ordzhonikidze, to curtail the repressive measures by the Procuracy against managerial and technical personnel. See Khlevnyuk, *Stalin*, pp. 34–5 and his essay in E. A. Rees (ed.), *Decision-Making in the Stalinist Command Economy, 1932–37* (Basingstoke, 1997). This invoked Stalin's wrath.
17. *Holod 1932–1933 rokiv na Ukraini: ochyma istorykiv, movoiu dokumentiv* (Kyiv, 1990), p. 265.
18. *Ibid.*, p. 285.
19. *Ibid.*, p. 281, and T. Bespechnyi and T. Bukreeva, 'Te tri koloska', *Sotsialisticheskii Donbass*, 14 February 1991. For similar cases in the Northern Caucasus, see E. N. Oskolkov, *Golod 1932/1933: Khlebozagotovki i golod 1932/1933 goda v Severo-Kavkazskom krae* (Rostov on Don, 1991), pp. 47–51.
20. *Holod 1932–1933 rokiv na Ukraini*, p. 293.
21. T. Bespechnyi, 'Golod 1932–1933 godov v Donbasse', *Sotsialisticheskii Donbass*, 13 December 1989.
22. In July 1933, for example, the chief of the Donets'k oblast' GPU, V. Ivanov, compiled the political profiles of 175 suspect party members under surveillance. This is a truly interesting document. (Derzhavnyi arkhiv Donet'skoi oblasti [DADO], R-835/1sch/79 201–26). A party member and an engineer, E. M. Andreev, for

instance, was reported to have said on the anniversary of Lenin's death: 'It'd be better if Stalin died. No one would be sorry for him... 'War's inevitable in the [Far] East. I'm confident that the workers will kill everyone off, including the GPU. We engineers cannot stand aside. We have first of all to destroy the GPU because they are guilty of things such as have never been witnessed before on this earth.'

23.   *Sotsialisticheskii Donbass*, 12 October 1933.
24.   I. V. Stalin, *Sochinenyia, Vol. 13* (Moscow, 1961), pp. 207, 212.
25.   H. Kuromiya, *Stalin's Industrial Revolution: Politics and Workers, 1928–1932* (Cambridge, 1988), p. 318.
26.   Quoted in O. V. Khlevnyuk, *1937-i: Stalin, NKVD i sovetskoe obshchestvo* (Moscow, 1992), p. 24.
27.   Note the many testimonies in James E. Mace and Leonid Heretz (eds), *Oral History Project of the Commission on the Ukraine Famine*, 3 vols (Washington, DC, 1990), *passim*. See also Dmytro Solovey, *The Golgotha of Ukraine* (New York, 1953), pp. 11–15, 17–20; Vladimir A. Bohdan, *Avoiding Extinction. Children of the Kulak* (New York, 1992), p. 78, Antonina Khelemendyk-Kokot, *Kolhospne dytynstvo i nimets'ka nevolia. Spohady* (Toronto, 1989), pp. 61, 82; and Jochen Hellbeck (ed.), *Tagebuch aus Moskau 1931–1939* (Munich, 1996), pp. 81, 87. This phenomenon may not have been peculiar to the Donbass, particularly after industrialisation changed the labour market from a buyer's to a seller's market. The cities, particularly Moscow, St Petersburg (Leningrad), Kiev and Kharkiv, also provided a degree of anonymity to their residents, but residency in the capitals and other major cities was tightly controlled by the police during the Soviet period. So, as a rule, it was far more difficult and hence much less attractive for people who wanted anonymity to live in these cities than in the Donbass. Siberia, which also symbolised freedom, may have been as attractive as the Donbass in this respect, but Siberia embodied hell as much as heaven. See Galya Diment and Yuri Slezkine (eds), *Between Heaven and Hell. The Myth of Siberia in Russian Culture* (New York, 1993). Even though Siberia had attracted many settlers (including Ukrainians) before the revolution, after the revolution it became more a symbol of exile, convict labour and death, particularly for Ukrainians who preferred to try their luck in the more proximate Donbass. Stephen Kotkin, *Magnetic Mountain: Stalinism as a Civilization* (Berkeley, 1995), presents a more heavenly picture of the Russian east (despite a hellish climate and all the horrors of everyday life), but for Ukrainians, particularly the dekulakised, the Donbass was a temporary refuge from which one day they hoped to return to their native villages, whereas Siberia was too distant and too hellish for them to entertain hopes of one day reclaiming their home lands.
28.   GARF, 7416/1/202 63.
29.   *Sotsialisticheskii Donbass na protsesse vreditelei rabochego snabzheniia*, No. 2, 25 December 1932, and *Sotsialist icheskii Donbass*, 26, 28, 29 and 30 December 1932.
30.   *Sotsialisticheskii Donbass*, 26 June and 8 July 1933.
31.   DADO, R-835/1/51 76–79, R-835/1sch/117 2zv. and *Sotsialisticheskii Donbass*, 11 January, 30 August and 11 September 1933.
32.   Tsentral'nii derzhavnii arkhiv gromads'kikh ob'ednan' Ukraini (TsDAGO) 1/16/9 115–6.
33.   In this sense, I think that speaking of 'public opinion' under Stalin without qualification is misleading.
34.   Arch Getty, *Origins of the Great Purges: The Soviet Communist Party Reconsidered, 1933–1938* (Cambridge, 1985).

35. Anatolii Latyshev, 'Ryadom so Stalinym', *Sovershenno sekretno*, no. 12, 1990, pp. 18, 19. For the same speech by Stalin on 8 November 1937, see also Robert C. Tucker, *Stalin in Power. The Revolution from Above 1928–1941* (New York, 1990), pp. 482–3. Tucker's analysis is based on a 'verbatim record'.

36. His statement about 'enemies' selling the Donbass to France referred to the fact that the French capitalists had owned very substantial capital in the Donbass coal and steel industry before the Bolshevik Revolution and lost it after the revolution. Like Stalin, Adolf Hitler attached much significance to the Donbass. According to General Eric von Manstein, the Donbass 'played a fundamental part in Hitler's operational calculations as far back as 1941, for he considered possession of it to be of vital importance to the outcome of the war'. See Erich von Manstein, *Lost Victories* (ed. and trans. by Anthony G. Powell, with a Foreword by B. H. Liddell Hart) (London, 1958), pp. 399, 412.

37. *Sto sorok besed s Molotovym. Iz dnevnika F. Chueva* (Moscow, 1991), pp. 31–2.

38. See Kuromiya, *Stalin's Industrial Revolution*.

39. *Natsional'ni vidnosyny v Ukraini u XX st. Zbirnyk dokumentiv i materialiv* (Kiev, 1994), pp. 212–6. As early as 1934, as a result of the Nazis coming to power in Germany, the Central Committee of the Communist Party decided to have full and accurate data collected on all Germans working in industry and in administrative bodies, and to see to it that this survey should not be publicly known. According to one who collected this data, already at the end of 1934, the party 'had before it the most precise data on the numbers and occupations of all the Germans living in the USSR. All the secret service work and repressions carried out later were guided by the data we collected and arranged.' Ingeborg Fleischhauer and Benjamin Pinkus, *The Soviet Germans: Past and Present* (New York, 1986), pp. 34, 91.

40. DADO, 326p/1/290 21.

41. Eight days later another telegram followed declaring a purge of 'anti-Soviet elements' from the border military zones. (TsDAGO, 1/16/11 294–5, 323). Throughout 1935 tens of thousands of people 'disloyal to the Soviet government', particularly ethnic Poles and Germans, were deported from the western border areas (TsDAGO, 1/16/12 *passim*).

42. *Istoricheskii arkhiv*, No. 1, 1992, pp. 114–17. In December 1935, P. Postyshev, then the Ukrainian party leader, contended categorically that 90 per cent of the so-called political emigrants were Polish agents. RGASPI, 17/2/561 162.

43. TsDAGO, 1/1/469 126 and RGASPI, 17/120/181 85–6, 120–2.

44. *Vechernii Donetsk*, 23 February 1990.

45. P. Lysenko, *The Black Deeds of the Kremlin. A White Book. Vol. 1. Book of Testimonies* (Toronto, 1953), pp. 118–9.

46. See, for example, RGASPI, 17/120/181 74 and 17/2/561 162.

47. DADO, 424p/la/183 23, 27. For other cases, see, for example, DADO, 424p/1a/183 37–8 and *Sotsialisticheskii Donbass*, 4 February 1935.

48. Lysenko, *The Black Deeds of the Kremlin*, p. 119.

49. RGASPI, 17/120/181 251.

50. RGASPI, 17/120/84 1. See also *ibid.* 17/120/181 73.

51. *Sotsialisticheskii Donbass*, 9 October 1936.

52. For a similar argument, see Oleg Khlevnyuk, 'The Objectives of the Great Terror, 1937–1938', in Julian Cooper, Maureen Perrie and E. A. Rees (eds), *Soviet History, 1917–53: Essays in Honour of R. W. Davies* (London, 1995).

53. For an excellent analogy to the Inquisition, see Kotkin, *Magnetic Mountain*, pp. 336–8.

54. Feliks Chuev, *Tak govoril Kaganovich. Ispoved' stalinskogo apostola* (Moscow, 1992), pp. 35–6, 101.
55. *Sto sorok besed s Molotovym*, pp. 36, 392, 397, 413, 416, 418.
56. Mace and Heretz (eds), *Oral History Project*, Vol. 2, pp. 1136–7. According to Hans Koch, a German counter-intelligence officer in charge of Ukrainian religious affairs during the Second World War, 'Priests were 'exhumed', but the demand far exceeded the supply; yet more than I had expected did turn up – many had spent years as workers in the Donbass, had sung as basses in factory choirs, etc.', in I Harvey Fireside, *Icon and Swastika. The Russian Orthodox Church under Nazi and Soviet Control* (Cambridge, Mass., 1971), pp. 153–4.
57. DADO, R-835/1sch/78 7–10. In some mines, nearly 20 per cent of workers were unmasked as kulaks (DADO, R-835/1sch/106 192–3).
58. Kuromiya, *Freedom and Terror in the Donbas*, Chapter 6. Ethnic Germans, Poles, and Greeks alone accounted for as many as 9,367 executions in Stalino oblast.
59. Many Donbass residents believed that Moscow would have wiped out the Donbass had it been possible to do so without destroying its industry. Numerous Donbass residents with whom I have talked expressed this view. One interviewee, born in 1913 in the Donbass and dekulakised in 1929, suggested that the Donbass was saved to some extent by its having too many former kulaks. He fled from exile to the Donbass and managed to find a job. Adam Ulam lists as one of the still unanswered questions about Stalin's reign: 'At what point did he [Stalin] say to himself: "If I have another 50,000 miners shot, there won't be any coal production . . . And so on"' (G. R. Urban (ed.), *End of Empire. The Demise of the Soviet Union* (Washington, DC, 1993), p. 174).

7
Vinnitsa Oblast

Valery Vasil'iev

Introduction

Vinnitsa oblast in the 1930s occupied a great part of Podolya, which was one of the regions of Right-bank Ukraine, lying to the south-west of the river Dniepr. The name 'Podolya' begins to appear in manuscripts in the second half of the fourteenth century for designating the land between the rivers Southern Bug and Dnestr.[1] In 1793 as the result of the partition of Rechi Pospolitoi between Prussia, Austria and Russia this territory under the name of Podolskaya province (guberniya) was incorporated into the Russian Empire. The province extended over 40,000 km^2. To its north lay Volynskoi, to the north-east Kiev, to the south Kherson and to the south-west Bessarabia province.[2] Vinnitsa was one of the USSR's most agricultural regions. It illustrates some of the common problems encountered by rural oblasts in their relations with their republican and all-union authorities. As a region situated on the border with Poland and Romania, it also had important security significance for the Soviet leadership.

According to the 1897 census Podol'skaya province had nearly 3 million inhabitants and it occupied second place in European Russia, after Moscow province, for population density. There were 7,207 settlements, of which 17 were towns and 120 small towns. The urban population numbered about 40,000, the majority of whom were Jews, Ukrainians and Russians. Ukrainians comprised 81 per cent of the population. They were primarily employed in the cultivation of winter and spring wheat, oats, buckwheat, sugar beet, technical crops, and market gardening. Local industry was mainly taken up with processing agricultural products and supplying the peasants' needs. In the province there were 46 sugar refineries, 83 distilleries, 68 tanneries, 272 potteries, 14 copper-iron and bell works and 40 cloth works.[3]

During the revolution and civil war, the province witnessed intense fighting, not only between various armies but also between army detachments and the peasants of Podolya. By 1921 the province's economy lay in ruins.[4] The majority of the population regarded the Red Army, Soviet Power and the

Bolsheviks as an alien and unlawful presence. In the early 1920s Communist rule in the province rested on institutional power not popular consent. At the end of the civil war the Red Army, including many elite detachments, retained a strong presence in the region. The Red Army was assigned the task of suppressing 'political banditry', i.e. fighting the remnants of the military detachments of the army of Simon Petlyura, which continued a partisan war against Soviet power until 1925.

The GPU was also closely involved, with the military, in the struggle with 'political banditry'. The GPU also oversaw the collection of the tax in kind (prodnalog) and the 'surrendering of weapons' of the population. During the famine of 1921–2, which afflicted large parts of Russia, southern Ukraine and Crimea, there was a substantial extraction of grain from the comparatively good harvest of Podolya. In 1922 the peasants provided 272,000 tons of grain under the prodnalog, plus additional 'voluntary' food aid. The collection of the prodnalog, was in effect requisitioning under another name. This enflamed the anti-Soviet attitudes of the villages of Podolya and created the base for peasant resistance.

The organs of soviet power remained largely unformed in the districts (volosts) and villages.[5] In Podolya and other rural provinces the Communist Party operated through the poor peasants' committees (nezamoshniki) that were created in 1920. These were similar to the committees of poor peasants created in Russia in 1918, but the Russian poor peasants' committees were liquidated in 1920. In March 1923 there were 1,883 of these committees, uniting 108,000 people.[6] The activists in the villages carried out land redistribution, struggled with the kulaks and 'banditry', helped in fulfilling requisitioning and the prodnalog. In 1921–4 thousands of communists from Donetsk and Ekaterinoslav and also from the Red Army were sent to the province. Significantly, only a quarter of the 4,606 members in the province's party organisation in 1924 came from Podolya.[7]

Bitter disputes between the various organs of power in the province, and the difficult political–economic situation in the region, resulted in a mass exodus of party workers. In the first half of 1920s the all-union and Ukrainian Central Committees repeatedly had to resolve conflicts between the provinces' party committee (gubkom), the revolutionary committee (gubrevkom), the soviet executive committee and the GPU, and to assign new cadres to the province. Between 1920 and 1925 the secretary of Podolya gubkom was changed 12 times.[8]

The crisis of grain and collectivisation, 1923–33

The New Economic Policy (NEP) was implemented in Podolya only from the beginning of 1923. Although this was intended to end the use of repressive measures, it initially caused a worsening of the economic situation. The agricultural tax for 1923–4 imposed a great burden on the peasants. Thousands of peasant households were compelled to sell livestock and property and to lease out their land. In May 1924 the X province party conference called on the central authorities to provide substantial economic support, to reduce the tax burden for 1924–5 and to increase assignments, in order to restore the region's agriculture.[9]

In 1924, on petition by Podolya's leaders, the agricultural tax for the province was reduced from 208,000 tons to 144,000 tons of grain. At the same time the Ukrainian Central Committee increased the province's budget from 6 million rubles to 11 million rubles. This made it possible to raise the wages of the chairmen of village soviets, teachers, doctors and agronomists, and to modestly fund the schools and hospitals.[10] The province's budget was increased by additional funding from the 'centre' and also by means of new local taxes. At this time there was also a significant decentralisation of administration. The All-Ukrainian Central Executive Committee (VUkTsIK) on 3 June 1925 abolished the provinces (guberniyas) and divided the territory of Ukraine into 41 okrugs and 624 raions.[11] Podolya province (guberniya) was divided into Vinnitsa, Kamenets–Podolskii, Mogiliev–Podol'skii, Pros-kurovskii, Tulchinskii and Shepetovskii okrugs.

In the autumn of 1927 the situation with the grain-purchasing campaign in Podolya became critical. The secretary of the Tul'chinskii okrugkom, Marchernko, reported in January 1928 to L. M. Kaganovich, general secre-tary of the Ukrainian Communist Party, that in carrying out grain seizures they had resorted to 'harsh repressive measures' against private traders.[12] The all-union and Ukrainian Central Committees sent telegrams to the okrugkoms demanding full implementation of the plan of grain purchasing. Already on 10 January 1928 a member of the Mogilev–Podol'skii okrugkom buro, in discussing the question of grain purchasing, noted 'increasingly the Ukrainian Central Committee's directives are changing in tone. The CC now poses the question of grain purchasing much more acutely than was ever done in one single directive in previous years.'[13] The resort to compul-sion prompted some communists in the okrugs and raions to criticise the 'regime of excesses', the return to the methods of War Communism, and the attempt to lay the blame for excesses on local party workers.[14]

The resort to repression involved the application of Article 127 of the Criminal Code, by which 'kulaks' found guilty of hoarding grain were to be deprived of their liberty for one year and their property confiscated. More-over, from January 1928 the okrugkoms assigned party activists to work in the villages on a semi-permanent basis.[15] Okrug and raion organs in 1928–9 also dispatched various plenipotentiaries to the villages. This was consolidated into a system of administration in the following years.

The Politburo was divided, and a retreat in policy was initiated. The Central Committee–Central Control Commission plenum in April 1928 criticised the methods adopted in the grain-purchasing campaign, which in fact meant 'going onto the rails of requisitioning (prodrazverstka)' – the illegal confiscation of grain reserves, prohibiting the 'free' grain market, establishing grain-seizing detachments, searches etc.[16] The central authorities, in blaming local officials for the resort to administrative measures, created the impression that it was possible to fulfil the increased plans of grain-purchasing without such methods.

The collectivisation of agriculture transformed relations between the central and local authorities. This policy was launched by Stalin and his supporters at the Central Committee plenum of November 1929 under the pretext of the mass entry of the peasantry into the kolkhozy. In reality the percentage of collectivised households in this period only rose in a few regions (Central and Lower Volga, the steppe okrug of Ukraine). Despite the efforts to promote the campaign, there was no mass entry of peasants into the kolkhozy. In Ukraine from June–October 1929 the number of collectivised households increased by 5 per cent, by which time just 10.4 per cent of all households were in the kolkhozy.[17] To the cautious appeals of certain speakers for more detailed preparation and planning, Stalin curtly responded: 'Do you think that everything can be organised in advance?' Those who raised the question of 'difficulties' were accused of 'opportunism'.[18]

The insistent demands for forced tempos of collectivisation prevailed. S. V. Kosior, the general secretary of Ukrainian Communist Party, in addressing the Central Committee plenum, enthusiastically supported the new policy. The Ukrainian Central Committee plenum, which began its work less than 24 hours after the ending of the all-union plenum, set the local leaders still higher targets. Declaring that for Bolsheviks nothing was impossible, Kosior proposed to increase in 1930 the sown area for the sovkhozy twofold, and for the kolkhozy 3.5 times. 'These figures at first glance are completely astounding', Kosior conceded, but added, 'it seems to me that these figures can not only be fulfilled but over fulfilled'.[19]

In carrying out collectivisation, leaders at various levels sought to become 'record-breakers' in competition with one another. The first secretary of the North Caucasus kraikom, A. A. Andreev, at the all-union Central Committee plenum, declared that his region would complete collectivisation by the autumn of 1930. Kosior, not to be outdone, pledged that the Ukrainian steppe okrugs would be fully collectivised by the spring of 1930.[20] The spirit of competition was reflected in the pages of the Moscow and Kharkov press, in which leading articles and declarations by party leaders welcomed the speeding up of collectivisation.

The okrug and raion officials sought to keep up with their leaders in this developing political campaign. In December 1929 the Tul'chinskii okrugkom plenum adopted a resolution to collectivise all poor and middle peasant (bedniak and serednyak) households of the okrug in two years, and by the spring of 1930 to socialise 50 per cent of all cultivated land. The Shepetovskii okrugkom buro resolved to collectivise by May 1930 50 per cent and by October 75 per cent of all cultivated land. The okrugkom requested from the Ukrainian Politburo that the okrug be listed among those to be fully collectivised. Its secretary, Pilipenko, petitioned the Ukrainian Central Committee on this question, and reported to the buro of the okrugkom that he had received its support.[21]

Thus the wishes of the Communist Party's leadership were harmonised with the mood of the local party officials and their attitude to the tempo of collectivisation was further radicalised. Social tensions in the Ukrainian villages – disputes over landholdings, caused by overpopulation (especially on the Right-bank), demands for land redistribution – were inflamed by rural activists and communists in their attacks on the stronger peasant households. This created favourable social conditions in the villages for collectivisation, a component part of which was dekulakisation and the plundering of the property of its victims.

In the winter of 1930 okrug and raion party–soviet workers were sent to the villages as plenipotentiaries to implement collectivisation and dekulakisation. They were assisted by worker 'twenty-five thousanders' (192 workers from Lugansk, Odessa, and Vinnitsa were assigned to Vinnitsa okrug) and also by rural activists and communists. The number of collectivised households rose from 10.4 per cent in October 1929 to 64.4 per cent by 10 March 1930. In the okrugs of Right-bank Ukraine the level of collectivisation attained a staggering 72.6 per cent.[22]

The force and threats which were directed at the peasants in the course of creating these 'paper' kolkhozy, provoked united and violent resistance. In various regions of the USSR, including Ukraine, there rose a tide of peasant anti-collectivisation protests. In the first three months of 1930 the GPU registered 3,129 peasant protests in Ukraine, in which 950,620 people participated. These demonstrations reached a crescendo in March when 877,610 individuals participated.[23]

The character and scale of the protests in Ukraine's border regions were especially alarming for the government. In Tul'chinskii, Mogiliev–Podolskii and Vinnitsa okrugs the peasant disturbances affected 343 village soviets. As a result, Soviet power was liquidated in 73 villages, and the GPU recorded 81 armed incidents. V. A. Balitskii, chairman of the Ukrainian GPU, in an armed train, with the support of a GPU cavalry detachment, put down the rebellions.[24]

The Soviet leaders, fearing a new civil war, ordered a halt to mass collectivisation. On 2 March 1930 Stalin's article 'Dizzy with Success' was published, and on 14 March the Central Committee adopted its resolution 'Concerning the struggle with distortions of the party line in the kolkhoz movement.' Stalin's article placed all the blame for the excesses of collectivisation on the local party workers, summoning them to correct their mistakes, while the Central Committee's resolution obliged local party organisations to halt the practice of using compulsory methods of collectivisation.

The all-union Politburo in Moscow on 17 March 1930 dispatched G. K. Ordzhonikidze to Ukraine to investigate the situation. He visited a number of okrugs and in his notebook gave the following assessment of the situation:

> Ukraine set itself the aim of achieving this spring 100 per cent collectivisation. There, senselessly, naked administrative pressure was applied as a matter of course. As a result the countryside reacted very strongly, risings of peasant women common, and in three okrugs: in Tul'chinskii, Shepetovskii and Mogilev there were real peasant uprisings. The uprisings were put down with force, firing of bullets and in several cases of artillery. Dead and shot 100, wounded several hundred. This is a region with an overwhelming population of poor peasants. In other raions (Kosostenskii, Vinnitsa, Krivoi Rog, Kharkov, Melitopol) there were also risings [bunty]. The reasons: rash collectivisation, the race for percentages, the shedding of blood, fierce pressure in the collection of seed, pronouncements concerning religion and the church. Threats, removal of roofs, floor coverings, ovens etc. Here the apparat played a dirty trick. Had we not had Stalin's article, the CC's resolution, without any doubt we would have had a very strong complication in Ukraine.[25]

On 20 March 1930 the Ukrainian leadership criticised the poor leadership provided by okrugkoms during collectivisation and censured those workers who had committed excesses. All officials were called to heed the Central Committee's resolution of 14 May 1930 and work to preserve and strengthen the kolkhozy.[26]

The officials who in Ordzhonikidze's terms had committed grave disorder (*podlozhili svinyo*) began to be brought to legal and party account. By 29 March 1930 in Ukraine 4001 had been called to account, of whom 478 were arrested and 328 were brought to court.[27]

Following Stalin's article the peasants began en masse to leave the paper kolkhozy. The percentage of collectivisation in Ukraine fell sharply. On 29 March 1930 Kosior attributed the speedy collapse of the collective farms to 'panic, vacillation of the lower level officials'. He demanded that the mass bringing of officials to account be halted and he proposed 'that those who have discredited themselves be transferred to other work in other okrugs'.[28]

The mood among lower-level party–soviet officials is reflected in letters, information gathered by raion and okrug party organs, in the stenographic reports and resolutions of the buros and the plenums of the raikom and okrugkoms.[29] The feeling of vacillation, which arose among local workers after reading Stalin's article 'Dizzy with Success', changed into resentment and an unwillingness to implement the Central Committee's resolution of 14 March 1930. Ordzhonikidze mentioned this in his notes.[30]

The local workers refused to take the blame for the failure of the first wave of full collectivisation and the mass anti-collectivisation outbursts of the peasants. Instead they blamed kulaks, counter-revolutionary, anti-Soviet elements, religious believers and activists of the Association for the Liberation of Ukraine (spilka vyzvolenia ukrainy, or SVU) for undermining the campaign. Many 'sub-kulaks' (podkulachniki) and strong middle peasants, it was claimed, had joined the kolkhozy in order to obtain the best land and to 'undermine' the kolkhoz from within. The tendency among the lower officialdom to seek explanations for failure in an elaborate 'enemy syndrome', was to shape future events.

The Moscow and Kharkov leadership sought to deal with the incompetence and weakness of the lower workers in Ukraine through major administrative changes. Thus in June 1930 the okrug administrative tier was abolished, and a decentralised two-tier administrative system was established in its place: republic–raion. The reform was intended 'to turn the raion into the key point of socialist construction in the village'.[31] By October 1930 more than 500 raion party committees (*raikoms*) had been created in Ukraine. As a result the number of communists in the rural raions grew by 33 per cent from 1 October 1930 to 1 July 1931.[32] Six, and then 10, territorial sectors within the Ukrainian Central Committee oversaw the work of the raikoms. Leading and coordinating such a large number of bodies inevitably proved extremely complicated. This reform was subsequently blamed by the Moscow authorities for disorder in Ukrainian agriculture, which contributed to the famine of 1932–3.

In the autumn of 1930 the authorities again attempted to re-launch collectivisation by force. Thousands of officials, party activists and workers from the towns were sent to the villages. In this period 5,700 recruiting brigades, who were occupied in collectivisation and the grain procurement campaign, were created in Ukraine.[33]

On 25 December 1930 the Ukrainian Politburo, in a resolution based on the ruling of the all-union Central Committee plenum, declared: 'The central fighting task of work in the village is now the preparation of the spring sowing campaign, which must attain collectivisation of 70 per cent of the sown area in Ukraine and on this basis the liquidation of the kulaks as a class.' Targets were set for the collectivisation of various regions: Steppe 83 per cent, Left-bank 66 per cent, Right-bank 63 per cent and Poless 32 per cent. The resolution included provision to train 200,000 tractor drivers, brigadiers, drivers, and agro-specialists from among the collective farm shockworkers. It also planned 'to dispatch 2,000 workers into the villages' and to send in worker repair brigades.[34]

However, this new offensive encountered intense opposition from the Ukrainian peasantry. On 27 January 1931 the all-union Politburo reduced Ukraine's target for grain procurement from 544,000 tons to 400,000 tons. On 1 February V. M. Molotov visited Ukraine, and at a session of the Ukrainian Politburo demanded categorically that the new target be fulfilled. The Ukrainian Central Committee, in a resolution adopted the same day, urged the local workers unconditionally to fulfil the plan. It also proposed that 'for the non fulfilment of these firm targets by kulak households to apply to them all authorised repressive measures'.[35]

In response to these directives the raion workers, having experienced the first wave of mass collectivisation, immediately began to arrest those peasants who refused to enter the kolkhozy and to supply grain, labelling them as 'kulaks', 'sub-kulaks' and 'anti-Soviet elements'. In the first half of March 1931 the Ukrainian Central Committee daily received requests from the localities about what to do with arrested kulaks, and when they should be dispatched into exile. The Ukrainian Politburo on 12 and 15 March examined the matter. It decreed that 'kulaks, who have been arrested by village soviets and raiispolkoms are to be released and transferred for resettlement within the borders of the raion'.[36]

At this time the Ukrainian leaders became acquainted with the work of the commission, headed by A. A. Andreev, set up by the all-union Politburo to organise the deportation of kulaks.[37] They reported to the all-union Politburo about the demands of their raion party organisations. The Ukrainian Central Committee's resolution of 23 April 1931 declared: 'Taking into account that the current growth of collectivisation will in fact achieve full collectivisation of the steppe and wooded steppe, to consider it possible to carry out dekulakisation with the transition to full collectivisation.'[38] The resolution envisaged that after the spring sowing, 40,000 kulak households would be expelled from Ukraine. However, Moscow reduced the figure. On 3 May 1931 Postyshev, a secretary of the all-union Central Committee, reported to Kosior, the Ukrainian party leader, the centre's decision to deport 30,000 kulak households from Ukraine to the Urals.[39] On 15 May the Andreev commission confirmed this decision.[40] This deportation was completed between 1 June and 15 July 1931.[41]

This did not improve the economic situation. Raikom workers naturally exaggerated the success of the spring sowing campaign. The GPU's reports, however, revealed that there were 200 collective farms (20 of them in the Podol'skii raions) where the sowing was done very badly. This was blamed on mismanagement.[42] In addition, the deportations created panic among the kulak households who had been compelled to join the kolkhozy. The economic situation was exacerbated by the export of 439,000 tons of grain from Ukraine, which on the insistence of Stalin and Molotov was shipped out from Odessa in January–February 1931.[43]

The annual grain procurement campaign in 1931 encountered resistance from the kolkhozy and the individual households (*edinolichniki*) who were reluctant to surrender their grain to the state. The threat of famine stalked the Ukrainian countryside. The centralised supply of grain to the towns was sharply cut. In the autumn of 1931 Stalin and Molotov dispatched numerous telegrams, directives and resolutions, demanding that the Ukrainian authorities fulfil the plan. The Ukrainian leadership in turn issued stark warnings to the raikom leadership that 'all non-fulfilment of plans inevitably leads to expulsion from the party and to being brought before the courts'.[44] This was no idle threat. The Ukrainian Politburo between 1 November 1931 and 10 February 1932 dismissed 31 raikom secretaries. A still wider scale of repression was applied to other categories of lower party–soviet workers.

As a result, the raion officials again reverted to methods of mass pressure on the peasantry. In the villages of Podolya revolutionary staffs, revolutionary committees and towing columns, made up of urban workers and rural activists, were set up. A war situation was created in the villages: peasants were subject to mass resettlement, peasant property was plundered and sold, peasants were arrested and killed. In the majority of cases the plan for grain procurement in the villages was realised in one night, and the peasants were left not only without grain stocks but in some cases even without food.

In January 1932, in Podolya, as in Ukraine generally, signs of famine became manifest. The peasants left the kolkhozy in droves, taking with them property which had been socialised. The number of terrorist acts increased. In the face of growing discontent among all groups in Ukrainian society, the authorities resorted to further administrative reform. The evident failure of the June 1930 reform had to be corrected. A new three-tier administrative system (republic–oblast–raion) was created. On 27 February 1932 the Kharkov, Kiev, Dnepropetrovsk, Odessa and Vinnitsa oblasts were established. In July the Donetsk oblast was formed, and in October the Chernigov oblast was set up. In 1935–6 the Kamenets–Podol'skii, Mogilev–Podol'skii, Proskurovskii and Shepetovskii border okrugs were created.

The new Vinnitsa oblast embraced 47,580 square kilometres. It was divided into 66 raions, which are included in the composition of present-day Vinnitsa, Khmelnitskoi, Zhitomirskoi and Odessa oblasts. The population in 1934 approached 4 million people, of whom 92 per cent lived in rural areas.[45] It was the most agricultural oblast of Ukraine, and it specialised primarily in sugar beet. In the 1930s the oblast produced between 30 and 40 per cent of Soviet sugar. There was also some grain and livestock farming, with fruit and vegetable cultivation in certain raions.

The depth of the crisis in Ukrainian agriculture was underlined by the fact that the grain procurement campaign of the autumn of 1931 continued into the spring of 1932. Despite evidence of famine conditions the grain procurement target was raised several times. The peasants were in a physically weakened state. The loss of horses meant that cows were widely used for the spring sowing, which was completed only in July 1932. The oblast leadership did everything to fulfil this plan, but encountered strong resistance from officials at the raion level. At the III All-Ukrainian Party Conference in July 1932 delegates openly expressed their view that the plans for grain procurement were unrealistic.

Molotov and Kaganovich, who attended the conference as representatives of the Politburo, blamed the deteriorating situation on the mistakes and weakness of the Ukrainian Communists. Molotov insisted that no concession on procurement targets would be allowed. V. Ya. Chubar' after his speech was accused of 'lack of political vigilance'. The conference, having had the views of the representatives of the Moscow leadership spelled out to them, unanimously voted for the proposed text of the resolution of the conference. In its greeting to the all-union party leadership it acknowledged that the Ukrainian Communist Party had committed a number of mistakes in agriculture, but these, it asserted, had been exposed and subject to merciless 'Bolshevik criticism'.[46]

Stalin and his supporters remained dissatisfied with the situation in Ukraine. By 1 November 1932 just 136 million puds of grain, against a plan of 356 million puds, had been procured in the republic.[47] Stalin sought a way out of this situation by increased repression and intensified central control over the localities. At the end of October 1932 an extraordinary commission, headed by Molotov and Kaganovich, was sent to Ukraine.[48]

At the same time the oblast leadership was changed. In October 1932 Vladimir Ilich Chernyavskii, secretary of the Dnepropetrovsk obkom, was appointed first secretary of Vinnitsa obkom. He replaced M. A. Alekseev who was appointed first secretary of Kharkov gorkom. Chernyavskii was an old Bolshevik, born in 1893 in Odessa into a Jewish family. From March 1921 he worked in leading posts in Vinnitsa, Ekaterinoslav and Kiev provinces. He was well connected, and was on close terms with P. P. Lyubchenko, and with L. M. Kaganovich, who acted as his patron. In November 1927 Chernyavskii was elected a member of Ukrainian Central Committee. In 1929 he worked as secretary of the Kiev okrugkom, then as head of the Ukrainian Central Committee's organisation–instruction department, and in September 1930 he was appointed secretary of the Ukrainian Central Committee. In the same year he was elected as a candidate member of the Ukrainian Politburo.[49]

At this time a new chairman of the oblast ispolkom, A. L. Trilisskii, was appointed. He was born in 1892 in Volyna. He had higher agronomic education. In the years of revolution he was a prominent activist in the Borot'bists, a Ukrainian Marxist–Nationalist party. In 1920 he joined the Ukrainian Communist Party. He was a close and long standing friend of P. P. Lyubchenko, and it was on his recommendations in 1927 that he was appointed as chairman of Odessa okrug party committee, where he worked together with Chernyavskii. In February 1930 he was appointed first deputy commissar of the Ukrainian Commissariat of Agriculture (NKZem Ukraine) and in March 1932 he became commissar. In January 1932 he was elected as member of the all-union Central Committee and in October 1932 was sent to Vinnitsa oblast.[50]

Chernyavskii brought with him several officials whom he placed in key posts. Thus the first secretary of the Vinnitsa gorkom was Levinson – a friend of Chernyavskii from Odessa. Chernyavskii's assistant was Lerman, who had previously worked with him in Dnepropetrovsk. In the oblasts such people were know as Chernyavskii's tail (khvost). Trilisskii also had his own network of clients. In Vinnitsa distinct leadership cults developed around Chernyavskii and Trilisskii. Kolkhozy, sovkhozy and schools were renamed in honour of these local dignitaries. Their portraits were carried in demonstration, and were displayed on the walls of offices and homes.

The new oblast leadership in 1932 immediately set about fulfilling the plan for grain procurement. In this it was assisted by Lyubchenko, a secretary of the Ukrainian Central Committee, and K. V. Sukhomlin, member of the Ukrainian Central Committee, who were commanded to Vinnitsa oblast by a Ukrainian Politburo resolution of 30 October 1932.[51]

The strong resistance of the starving peasants to grain procurement was broken by the application of harsh repressive measures. On 18 November 1932 the Ukrainian Politburo adopted a secret resolution for the liquidation of 'the main kulak and Petluraist counter-revolutionary nests'. This also foresaw the 'removal to the towns of ideologists and organisers of kulak sabotage, evil accountants and bookkeepers of the kolkhozy'. The resolution paid special attention to 'kulak terror' in Kiev, Khar'kov and Vinnitsa oblasts. The leaders of these oblasts were required to intensify repression against so-called kulaks and other counter-revolutionary elements, imposing 'the most severe punishment in cases of terrorist acts [*terakty*], arson, squandering of state and social property'.[52]

The Central Committee–Sovnarkom USSR on 14 December 1932 called on the party and soviet organs 'resolutely to uproot... counterrevolutionary elements' by means of arrest, confinement in concentration camps, not shrinking from the use of the death penalty. It called for the repression of 'saboteurs with party cards in their pockets' and of unreliable kolkhoz aktiv. The Ukrainian Central Committee and Sovnarkom were instructed to correct errors in implementing the policy of Ukrainisation and to 'remove Petluraists and other elements from the party and soviet organisations'.[53]

On the basis of this resolution Vinnitsa obkom adopted a policy of extensive repression, and was the first to fulfil the grain procurement plan in the Ukraine.[54] The oblast GPU for November–December 1932 claimed to have liquidated 121 'counter-revolutionary groups' comprising 546 members.[55] In December 1932 *Kommunist*, the theoretical journal of the Ukrainian Central Committee, published 'Report of a Vinnitsan concerning the completion of the plan of grain procurement'. This exercise in self-promotion, however, was ill-timed and evoked irritation in Moscow and Kharkov. The Ukrainian Politburo censured the journal for having publishing the article without its authorisation.[56]

The difficulties in securing grain led to still more drastic measures. The Ukrainian Politburo, under pressure from Stalin and Kaganovich, was obliged to revise its resolution of 18 November 1932 which had excluded the sowing seed fund of the kolkhozy from the grain procurement plan. At the same time the leadership of Vinnitsa were instructed: 'You will have the right to report after you have fulfilled the plan for seed loan, for technical crops and also for the sovkhozy.'[57]

In these conditions Stalin and the Ukrainian Politburo in January 1933 attempted to strengthen control over the activities of oblast and raion party workers. Firstly, new first secretaries were appointed to Kharkov, Dnepropetrovsk, Odessa and Crimea obkoms in the persons of P. P. Postyshev, M. M. Khataevich, E. I. Veger and B. A. Semenov. Secondly, the Central Committee plenum approved the creation of the *politotdely* of the Machine Tractor Stations (MTS) and sovkhozy. The main task of these extraordinary bodies was to 'purge the kolkhoz of class alien-hostile elements', to struggle against 'saboteurs with party cards in their pockets' and to strengthen the organisational and economic work of the kolkhoz.

The *politotdely* were led by the Political Administration of NKZem USSR, which answered directly to the all-union Central Committee's Agricultural Sector, which at this time was headed by Kaganovich. The heads of the *politotdely* were approved by the Politburo. The heads of the *politotdely* MTS were made members of their respective raikoms, and the heads of the political sector of oblast and krai rural administration were made members of the bureaus of the party obkoms and kraikoms. The *politotdely* were set up in Vinnitsa oblast in March–April 1933. A hundred political workers (politruky) from the Red Army were dispatched to work in them. GPU workers were appointed as deputy heads of the *politotdely*.

In Vinnitsa oblast a report compiled by the *politotdely* workers, issued under the name of L. Papernyi, head of the political sector of the oblast rural administration, provides a graphic account of the situation in the countryside. It reported that in the villages up to 50 per cent of the kolkhozniki were afflicted by starvation, whole streets had died, and that local party workers acted mainly by methods of administrative pressure on the peasantry. Such a situation encouraged mass passive resistance of the peasants against the authorities and strengthened their desire to flee the countryside.

The senior Ukrainian leader G. I. Petrovskii visited the oblast in March 1933. He advised Chernyavskii to inform Stalin directly about the situation. However, Kosior advised Chernyavskii against taking such a step.[58]

At this time the MTS *politotdely* commenced the spring sowing campaign. They encountered opposition from the starving population and they began to purge 'class-alien and anti-kolkhoz elements, who occupied various economic and leading posts in the kolkhozy'. According to incomplete information in 1933 the *politotdely* expelled 13,847 people from their posts in the oblast, including more than half of the chairmen of the kolkhozy. At the same time 2,808 individuals were expelled from posts in the MTS.[59] In April–May 1933 a further 2,000 individuals were expelled from the oblast party organisation on the demands of the *politotdel* officials.[60]

As a result relations between the raikoms and the *politotdely* of the MTS sharply deteriorated. Chernyavskii and the obkom leadership attempted to temper the high-handed actions of the *politotdely* and to defend the raion leaders. The *politodel* workers in a letter to Stalin, Kaganovich and Postyshev accused the obkom leadership of political errors and of paying insufficient attention to itself. The Ukrainian Central Committee intervened and instructed the obkom to normalise relations with the *politotdely*. Despite some improvements, relations remained tense. At the end of 1933 Papernyi, head of the *politotdely*, wrote to Moscow: 'Unfortunately I cannot consider the apparent improvement sufficiently firm, since I am sure that the recon-struction from the side of the obkom bears formal "manoeuvre" character.'[61]

The raikoms and the obkom, while avoiding conflict with the *politotdely*, kept an eagle eye on their activities, and immediately reported to the central organs even the smallest errors in their work. These tensions persisted until the MTS *politotdely* were abolished in November 1934. A clear example of this rivalry dates from August 1934. In the course of the grain procurement campaign the head of the political sector of the oblast rural administration, Koltypin, issued a directive to the *politotdely* of the MTS and sovkhozy not to engage in record breaking in surrendering grain to the state. The party obkom quickly rescinded it and Chernyavskii reported the directive to the Ukrainian Central Committee.

On 5–6 September 1934 Kaganovich and Kosior hastily visited the oblast and summoned meetings of party workers in Vinnitsa and Tul'china and expounded on the 'harmful and criminal' directive of Koltypin. On 9 September the Central Committee censured Koltypin. He was removed from his post and then expelled from the party.[62]

The Moscow leadership also sought to control the situation in the localities through the purge of the party ranks. In 1933 in Vinnitsa oblast 8,745 (27 per cent) out of 33,000 communists were expelled.[63] In certain raions as few as 10–15 communists were left after the purge. The Ukrainian Central Committee and the obkoms had to direct communists to the kolkhozy and MTS to reinforce the party's ranks.

In general, the local leaders supported the attempt by Stalin and his supporters to find a way out of the famine crisis by recourse to increased repression. In March 1933 Chernyavskii in a letter to Kosior proposed that some of those 'purged' from the kolkhozy should be assigned to public works (road-construction, peat-cutting, quarrying) and 'clear enemies of the people, provocateurs, potential diversionists, Petluraists–fascist agents and kulaks should be quickly expelled from the oblast and sent to the north, adopting measures which had proved effective in the North Caucasus'.[64]

Curbing of repression, 1933–4

In the spring of 1933, however, there was a certain softening of the political line. On 17 March 1933 the Ukrainian Politburo resolved to free the sale of grain in Ukraine. On Chernyavskii's request, the Ukrainian Politburo on

27 March 1933 assigned Vinnitsa oblast an additional 30–40 tractors, 500,000 rubles credit and additional supplies of industrial goods. Economic organisations were required to settle their debts with the kolkhozy and an appeal was sent to the all-union Politburo for additional supply of seed as a loan. On 17 April the oblast received 150,000 tons of grain.[65] At this time Chernyavskii sent a letter to Kosior outlining a number of measures to assist individual peasants in those raions afflicted by food shortages.[66] The tone and content of this dispatch differed markedly from his previous address to Kosior only a few weeks earlier.

In April 1933 Vinnitsa obkom complained to the all-union Central Committee's Agricultural Sector about 'artistic [*khudozhestvennyi*] planning' of sown area by NKZem Ukraine, which in three successive revisions had each time enlarged the plan for sown area for the oblast.[67] As a result the target exceeded the amount of land in the oblast. Although the Ukrainian Central Committee had modified the plan, it still proved wholly unrealistic. The very fact that the obkom should appeal against NKZem Ukraine to the all-union Central Committee was highly indicative of the changing climate.

The softening of the political line and the curbing of repression, which Stalin must have authorised, was reflected in the Central Committee–Sovnarkom USSR resolution of 8 May 1933 which demanded a halt to the 'the adoption of mass resettlement and acute forms of repression in the countryside'. The instructions established limits to the resettlement of peasants for various regions of the USSR; for Ukraine it was resolved to resettle 2,000 peasant households.[68] Nevertheless, repression continued. The head of the oblast GPU Sokolinskii declared at the Vinnitsa obkom plenum in June 1933: 'There was almost not one counter-revolutionary organisation discovered in our Union that did not have a major off-shoot on the territory of our Vinnitsa oblast'.[69]

On the other hand, in response to the unending requests for help from the Ukrainian Central Committee and obkoms, Stalin (having received advice from Postyshev and Kosior, as is evident from the text of the secret resolution of the Ukrainian Politburo) attempted to normalise the situation, and dispatched additional funds of grain and food supplies to Ukraine.

The help provided was extremely small. Vinnitsa oblast from the middle of April to the middle of June received just 13,496 tonns of grain, which for 4 million starving people was just a drop in the ocean. Peasants of the border raions attempted to flee from the famine into Romania or Poland. M. A. Trilisser, a member of the party's Central Control Commission, who visited the Slavutskii raion of Vinnitsa oblast, reported to Kaganovich and Kosior that he had seen masses of peasants crossing the border into Poland. The Polish border guards photographed them, questioned them, registered them and sent them back. As a result of this report the Ukrainian Politburo reprimanded Chernyavskii and Trilisskii, and removed the heads of the Slavutskii raikom and raiispolkom from their posts.[70]

The Vinnitsa leadership attempted to rehabilitate itself by being the first in Ukraine to fulfil the state plan of grain procurement. They succeeded in doing this, but the oblast was again left without grain. In the following weeks the same situation emerged in other Ukrainian oblasts. Only then did Postyshev and Kosior convince Stalin of the need to reduce Ukraine's general target for grain procurement. Kaganovich was charged with reducing the procurement targets for those kolkhozy which were suffering grain shortages, with the transfer of arrears to 1934.[71]

In the evolving political–administrative system, the personal links which oblast leaders had with workers of the republican and central organs acquired great significance. Chernyavskii was promoted by Kaganovich, and he sent the most important documents and requests to Kaganovich, who took a close interest in the problems of sugar production. He spent a lot of time in Moscow in 1934–5, and received the support of A. I. Mikoyan, head (narkom) of the People's Commissariat for Food Industry USSR (NKPishProm), to improve the work of the oblast's sugar and food-processing industries. Chernyavskii was a member of the Ukrainian Politburo and was closely connected with the republican leadership. His connection with Kosior dated back to Kiev in 1917. He was bound to Lyubchenko by personal and close family ties. From 1935 onwards he established good relations with Khataevich, and used all these contacts in his efforts to resolve the problems of the oblast.

The Soviet organs in the oblast, and the economic enterprises under the control of the commissariats, were in the charge of Trilisskii. In 1931–2 as head of NKZem Ukraine, he established personal contact with G. F. Grin'ko, head of the powerful Commissariat of Finance of the USSR. Grin'ko, was a former Borot'bist, who had occupied senior positions in the Ukrainian government until 1926, when he was transferred from the republic for being too nationalistic. As a result of a visit to Grin'ko in Moscow Trilisskii succeeded in increasing the budget of Ukraine in 1931 and 1932 by 2 and 3 million rubles, respectively.[72] In 1933–4 a number of workers of NKZem Ukraine, who had formerly worked under Trilisskii, namely Marnevich, Skalyga and Drok, were transferred to NKZem USSR. Trilisskii maintained good relations with these officials, and NKZem Ukraine continued to regard them as their own people.

Chernyavskii and Trilisskii at the XII congress of the Communist Party of Ukraine (18–23 January 1934) defended their record during the famine of 1932–3, emphasising their loyalty to Stalin and to the 'general line'. Chernyavskii sought to absolve himself of responsibility for the failure to fulfil the sugar beet harvesting plan. In 1933 a target yield of 100 tsentners per hectare was set, but was then increased to 120 tsentners on Chernyavskii's request. The actual yield was about 70–80 tsentners per hectare.[73] In 1934 the all-union Central Committee set a target for sugar beet yield in the oblasts of 122 tsentners per hectare, and at the end of the Second Five-Year Plan of 200 tsentners per hectare. Chernyavskii at the Ukrainian Communist Party congress declared that this figure was not very great and that by the end of the Second Five-Year Plan the oblast should double it.

Chernyavskii in his speech noted that on account of the inadequate work of the local leadership the oblast's tractor park was utilised only 50 per cent of its capacity. Trilisskii complained of the shortage of spare parts for tractors and proposed that they be produced in the oblast. At the end of his speech Trilisskii, a former Borot'bist, highlighted the need to struggle with Ukrainian nationalism.[74] Both Chernyavskii and Trilisskii argued in favour of creating an industrial base in the border regions of Ukraine at the expense of building processing works. This was intended to create 'strong proletarian centres' in the border regions. At the congress Chernyavskii and Trilisskii retained their positions; they were re-elected to the Ukrainian Central Committee, and Chernyavskii remained a candidate member of the Ukrainian Politburo.

However, at the XVII congress of the CPSU (26 January–10 February 1934) the Vinnitsa leadership came under pressure. Stalin, without naming names, criticised the poor yields for sugar beet. A still sharper criticism was outlined in Kosior's report.[75] Chubar', head of the Ukrainian government, argued for more resources for Ukrainian agriculture. He also argued for greater attention to be paid to the mechanisation of sugar beet harvesting, a matter of keen interest to Vinnitsa.[76] During the congress, Chernyavskii and Trilisskii met with members of the Politburo and Stalin, who voiced his dissatisfaction regarding their failure to fulfil the targets for sugar beet yields, which they had taken upon themselves. Chernyavskii spoke about this at the Vinnitsa obkom plenum after the congress.[77]

Following Stalin's criticisms of NKZem USSR and NKSovkhoz USSR, many delegates argued for changes in the way agriculture was managed.[78] Utilising this opening Chernyavskii in 1934–6 at the Ukrainian Central Committee plenums repeatedly criticised the state of affairs in agriculture, and lobbied for increased allocations of implements, seeds and fertiliser. He resolutely protested against the practice whereby NKZem USSR distributed tractors and implements directly to the okrugs over the heads of the oblast leadership.

Up to December 1934 the oblast leadership supported a more balanced and moderate agricultural policy. The high point in this course came in November 1934 at the Vinnitsa obkom plenum where the activity of the *politotdely* was sharply criticised. I. Starobin, a close ally of Chernyavskii, and head of the obkom's agricultural department, declared:

> The adoption of repression in essence is a result of poor work, the result of an inability to lead. Extensive repression is a sign not of strength but a sign of weakness, an inability to lead. To whom is repression applied? To the partorg, to the chairman of the village soviet, the chairman of the kolkhoz. But in fact these are the best that we have. We have no others. Can we push aside this party organisation and receive from somewhere a 'new' party organisation? We must with these people carry through in

this field the party's decisions. It is precisely these people whom we must educate, whom we must help to grow.[79]

However, local leaders were often pushed by central policies into attempting to resolve agricultural problems through pressure and repression. Chernyavskii sent a number of letters to the centre, with requests to raise NKZem's plans for the sown area in the oblast, taking account of the perspective provided by collectivisation. This led to constant upward revisions of plans for the kolkhozy.

The Vinnitsa leadership encountered considerable difficulties in compelling individual peasants to give up their grain to the state. The oblast leadership sought to resolve the problem by further extending collectivisation. Thus, in 1934, Chernyavskii advocated collectivising the peasant households in the oblast's border regions. However, implementing this proved very complicated because of its implications for border security. A way out was found in the resettlement of individual peasants, described as 'malicious withholders of grain', outside the border of Ukraine. In October 1934 Kosior sent such a request to Kaganovich. As a result the Ukrainian Central Committee, on 31 October 1934, adopted a resolution for the resettlement of 500 families of individual peasants from the villages of Vinnitsa, Chernigov, Khar'kov and Kiev oblast. Thus a new wave of deportations was set in train.

Renewed repression, 1934–7

After Kirov's assassination on 1 December 1934 the deportation of members of minority nationalities from the oblast began. On 9 December 1934, after receiving a telegram from the all-union Central Committee, the Ukrainian Central Committee adopted a resolution concerning the resettlement of the Polish and German population. On 17 December a border regime was introduced into 11 border raions of Ukraine. In March 1935 the first contingent of Poles and Germans were sent to the eastern part of Ukraine for resettlement. In 1935–6 8,403 Polish and German families were deported from the oblast.[80]

Simultaneously, the land of individual peasants was compulsorily collectivised. As a result about 10 per cent of peasant households of the oblast by the spring of 1935 were left without land. They faced the choice of joining the kolkhoz, being resettled, or dying from starvation. The latter was not an exaggeration. In 1933–5 there were cases of swellings, starvation and death, and instances of cannibalism. A submission, prepared by Vinnitsa obkom's agricultural department in February 1933, revealed that more than half of all kolkhozy in the oblast issued to the kolkhozniki for each 'labour day' (trudoden') a mere 0.5–1.5 kilograms of grain. As a result more than 20 raions of the oblast, it noted, suffered mass starvation.[81]

The high grain procurement targets which were set for the 1935 harvest were fulfilled with difficulty. Chernyavskii ordered Lerman to ensure the 'pulling together' of reports (*svodki*) concerning grain supplies to the state together with Shelemen'tev, the Committee for Agricultural Procurements plenipotentiary for Vinnitsa, and Bondarev, the head of the oblast office of 'Zagotzerno'. With some statistical sleight of hand it was claimed that the oblast had fulfilled the plan for grain procurement on 1 September 1935 ahead of schedule. In reality the plan was not fulfilled for another two months.[82]

The Stakhanovite movement in Vinnitsa oblast, which commenced in September 1935, took the form of a movement of 'five-hundreders' and 'thousanders', that is of links and brigades of kolkhozniki who attained a yield of 500–1,000 tsentners (50–100 tons) of sugar beet per hectare. The obkom played the main role in promoting the movement. In December 1935 it adopted three resolutions on this question. In the raions norm-setting brigades were set up, for whom the best conditions of work were created. The Vinnitsa leadership proudly publicised the achievements of the 'five-hundreder' M. Demchenko and the border zone of Yampol'skii raion, which attained an average yield of 200 tsentners per hectare. This created the impression that the target of 200 tsentners per hectare set by the Central Committee by the end of the Second Five-Year Plan would be attained.

The Kremlin noted Vinnitsa's 'success' in this work by conferring government awards on 72 Stakhanovites of the oblast.[83] Kosior, Lyubchenko and other Ukrainian leaders, including Chernyavskii, received the Order of Lenin. In the greeting of the obkom to Chernyavskii it was asserted that the order was given to the whole oblast organisation in recognition of its fulfilment of the tasks assigned to it – to achieve the first place in the USSR in the development of agriculture.[84]

The Soviet leadership sought to use this movement to increase labour productivity and achieve a new 'great leap forward' in the economy.[85] In 1936 the agricultural procurement targets for Vinnitsa oblast were sharply raised. Chernyavskii, in discussion with Goryanoi, the secretary of Mogiliev–Podol'skii okrugkom, complained that the Central Committee paid no heed to the problems of Vinnitsa as a border oblast. Goryanoi was given the task of collecting data on the state of the kolkhozy with the aim of achieving a reduction of the targets. A similar task was assigned to Shelemet'ev. As a result Vinnitsa's plan for grain procurement was reduced by 16,000 tons.[86]

Such actions could not but provoke the censure of Stalin and the Politburo. Control over the oblast leadership was tightened up. Thus, when the raikom and obkom authorities reported in August 1936 that Starokonstatinovskii raion had fulfilled its plan for grain procurement, Moscow sent a Sovnarkom USSR plenipotentiary for grain procurement to the oblast. He reported that the plan had not been fulfilled. As a result Borshch, the raikom secretary, was dismissed.[87]

In August 1936, Chernyavskii seriously clashed with Postyshev over the question of refining sugar beet. Postyshev insisted on immediately setting nine refineries in Vinnitsa oblast in operation. Chernyavskii urged delay, arguing that the summer drought had not allowed the beets to mature sufficiently for the best extraction of sugar. Moreover, all vehicles had been commandeered for the grain harvest campaign. Lyubchenko, chairman of the Ukrainian Sovnarkom, supported Chernyavskii. Postyshev, however, insisted that his orders be carried out. The all-union Politburo supported Postyshev and required the Vinnitsa leadership to end the harvesting of beet by 10 October.[88] Chernyavskii and Starobin secretly instructed the raikom secretaries not to speed up the harvesting of beet. On 13 September 1936 the Vinnitsa obkom telgrammed the all-union and Ukrainian party and government leadership claiming that, in spite of the 'exceptionally unfavourable conditions' caused by drought, the oblast had supplied the state with 43.5 million puds (696,016 tons) of the highest quality grain. It pledged every effort to achieve a high target for the sugar beet harvest.[89]

However, the sugar beet harvest proved very difficult. In October 1936 the raikoms, with the tacit support of the obkom, increased the number of Stakhanovite links and brigades, as a way of providing incentives for the kolkhozniki. The bonuses which were paid to the so-called Stakhanovites was a source of envy amongst the half-starving kolkhozniki. Rank-and-file kolkhozniki wrote to Moscow and Kiev complaining that so called 'thousander' links had failed to achieve even 500 tsentners per hectare. Checks showed that 19 out of 28 such links had failed to attain 1,000 tsentners per hectare.

These measures strengthened the unwillingness of the kolkhozniki to gather in the harvest. The digging and carting of beets continued till March 1937. Recalcitrant peasants were subjected to illegal penalties: the withholding of wages, expulsion from the kolkhoz, assault and mockery. At the beginning of 1937 a Ukrainian Central Committee brigade was sent to the oblast to investigate. The brigade noted cases of mass pressure on the peasants in Chechel'nitskii and Lipovetskii raions and in Shepetovskii okrug. Consequently, in a special resolution, the Ukrainian Central Committee accused the Vinnitsa leadership of breaching socialist legality.

The plan for autumn ploughing was not fulfilled. This seriously reduced the grain harvest in 1937. The digging and carting of beets in conditions of rain and snow created serious difficulties. Some 50 per cent of the oblast's horses and 80 per cent of the tractor park of the MTS were unsuitable for work. There were serious problems in feeding the oblast's livestock.[90] In 1937 the economy of Vinnitsa oblast, like other Ukrainian oblasts, was again in crisis. The targets for the Second Five-Year Plan clearly would not be attained. Stalin placed the blame for this state of affairs on the leadership of the various levels.

The tide of repression grew in the wake of the Kirov assassination on 1 December 1934. The Ukrainian NKVD arrested Yu. Mazurenko, one of the leaders of the Ukrainian Communist Party in the early 1920s. N. Lyubchenko, the brother of the Ukrainian prime minister, confessed to having organised a counter-revolutionary organisation of Borot'bists, headed by himself, Khvylei and Trilisskii. In March 1935 it was reported that a counter-revolutionary SRs-Borot'bists organisation had been uncovered.[91]

In 1935 *Pravda* published several pogrom-style articles concerning Trotskyists in Dnepropetrovsk. Khataevich, first secretary of Dnepropetrovk obkom, in conversation with Chernyavskii at the Ukrainian Central Committee, voiced his displeasure with these articles, declaring 'they beat people without caring'.[92] In 1935–6 R. Begailo, the second secretary of Vinnitsa obkom, attempted to stem the flow of expulsions of communists from the party associated with the exchange and checking of party cards. In his safe he kept files with compromising material on several communists and would not release them. In August 1936 he was dismissed, and until his arrest he worked in Kiev oblast as director of a sugar refinery.

Attempts were made to stem the growing tide of repression. In August 1936 S. Goryanoi, during the discussion of the closed letter of the all-union Central Committee 'Concerning the terrorist activity of the Trotskyist–Zinovievist counter-revolutionary bloc', at a meeting of the Mogiliev–Podol'skii okrugkom buro, declared that the members of the bloc should not be shot. Chernyavskii when informed of this did all in his power to ensure that information concerning Goryanoi did not reach Kiev.[93] Early in November 1936 an official of the obkom's agricultural department, Burov, directly asked his superiors, Starobin and Lerman, why Chernyavskii did not smash the wreckers and enemies who were active in the oblast's agriculture. To this Lerman, taking Burov aside, said: 'Take note, we smash nobody, since our people form a circle, we have confidence in them, they do our general work.'[94]

At this stage no leading figures in the oblast were accused of wrecking. However, the oblast NKVD began making arrests at the end of 1936. By May 1937 some 600 people had been arrested in the oblast, some of whom testified against Chernyavskii. At the same time material was prepared against Trilisskii, who together with Khvylei and Lyubchenko, was made the leader of a counter-revolutionary nationalist organisation of Ukrainian Borot'bists.

Soon after, Starobin and Trilisskii were arrested. Chernyavskii attempted to defend Trilisskii. He was elected candidate member of the Ukrainian Politburo at the XIII Congress of the Ukrainian Communist Party (May– June 1937), but in August 1937 at the Ukrainian Central Committee plenum he was attacked and accused of creating a circle of 'enemies of the people' in Ukrainian agriculture. Kosior, at the Vinnitsa obkom plenum on 16–17 August, repeated these accusations. According to his account 16 members of the obkom had been expelled from the party and arrested.

On 1 September 1937 Chernyavskii was arrested. He was accused, together with Khataevich, of creating a rightist organisation, which allegedly aimed to destroy the kolkhozy, and plotted to eliminate the Soviet leadership with Stalin at its head. Chernyavskii was allegedly connected, via Trilisskii, with the Ukrainian Borot'bists headed by Lyubchenko who, it was alleged, had attempted to restore the bourgeois order in Ukraine, to separate it from the USSR and to create an independent state. To this end, Lyubchenko maintained contact with I. Ye. Yakir, head of the Ukrainian military command, and Trilisskii, and with the commander of the military corps of Vinnitsa oblast. At the end of 1937 Trilisskii and Chernyavskii were shot.

Thus the political responsibility for the failure of Stalin's economic policy in 1936–7 was laid on the republican and regional leadership. The Stakhanovite movement and the new attempt at a 'great leap forward' preceded a wave of wide-scale repression, which still further complicated the situation in the economy and led to the promotion of a new strata of leaders in the localities. In general the political leadership sought to overcome the economic crisis in the Soviet economy between the First and Second Five-Year Plans by further centralising the system of administration and transferring administrative functions from local to central organs.

Conclusion

The Vinnitsa political elite, formed in the conditions of economic crisis and famine in Ukraine in 1932–3, did not play any decisive role in the shaping of economic policy. The oblast leadership was strictly dependent upon the 'centre', which closely controlled its activity. Control was exercised in the form of the *politotdely* of the MTS, the party purge of 1933–4, the dispatch to the oblast of union and republican leaders, special plenipotentiaries and brigades of the highest political organs, as well as by the representatives of the GPU–NKVD. Centre–local relations were shaped by the growing resort to repression in resolving economic problems in 1932–3 and again in 1936. Initially, the 'centre' made a decision (collectivisation, dekulakisation), which promoted a new wave of repression, then the lower officials in the oblasts and raions broadened the scale of repressive policies. This was accompanied by corresponding requests to the central organs, after which the centre itself was compelled to rein in the repression lest it get out of hand. Thus the 'centre' played the main organising and controlling role. In this a leading part was played by the GPU–NKVD, whose influence grew progressively over time.

The main task of the Vinnitsa leadership in the years of the Second Five-Year Plan was the fulfilment of government plans of supply of agriculture produce. The problem of reducing plans and securing as much as possible by way of funds, tractors, vehicles, fuel, mineral fertiliser and seed comprised the basic inter-relationship of the oblast leadership with the central organs of power and administration both in Ukraine and the USSR. In these inter-relationships the all-union and the Ukrainian Politburos acted as arbitrators, resolving conflicts and problems between oblast leaders and the all-union and republican commissariat of agriculture. The Vinnitsa leadership also utilised its personal connections in the commissariats and higher party organs to press the interests of the oblast. In the period of the apparent softening of the political course this mood gained serious support at the oblast level. However, the abnormality and errors of economic policy in agriculture often pushed the Vinnitsa leadership into adopting methods of repression. The oblast's leaders attempted to stem the growing tide of repression in 1936–7. However, the new economic crisis intensified the repression that was directed against the oblast elite, which was held responsible for the non-fulfilment of the tasks set by Stalin at the XVII congress of the party.

Notes

1. *Sbornik svedenii o Podol'skoi gubernii*, Vyp.1 (Kamenets–Podol'skii, 1880), pp. 1–3.
2. *Narisi istorii Podillya* (Khmel'nits'kii, 1990), p. 115.
3. *Entsiklopedicheskii slovar'. Izdateli F. A. Brokgauz', I. A. Efron'* (St Petersburg, 1898), pp. 96–8.
4. *Istoriya mist i sil URSR, Vinnits'ka oblast* (Kiev, 1972), p. 43.
5. Even in July 1922 delegates at the VIII Podol'skoi party conference spoke of the absence of organs of power in the volosts and villages. See *Gosudarstvennyi arkhiv Vinnitskoi oblasti* (hereafter, GAVO), P-1/1a/23 39.
6. GAVO, P-1/1a/56 50.
7. *Narisi istorii Vinnits'koi oblastnoi partiinoi organizatsii* (Odessa, 1980), p. 110; GAVO, P-1/1a/6 58.
8. *Ibid.*
9. GAVO, P-1/1/5 40ob.
10. GAVO, P-1/1/7 35.
11. *Zbirnik uzakonen' URSR*, 1925, No. 29–30, p. 435.
12. GAVO, P-35/1/772 62
13. GAVO, P-31/1/371 26.
14. GAVO, P-31/1/370 33; P-31/1/371 36. See the reports of the buro of the Mogiliev–Podolskii okrugkom of 29 January 1928, and of the Mogiliev–Podolskii okrugkom plenum in March 1928.
15. GAVO, P-33/1/722 71.
16. *Kommunisticheskaya partiya Sovetskogo Soyuza v rezolyutsiyakh i resheniyakh s"ezdov, konferentsii i plenumov TsK* (Moscow, 1984, 9th edn), pp. 317, 319.
17. *Tsentral'nii derzhavnii arkhiv gromads'kikh ob'ednan' Ukraini* (hereafter, TsDAGO Ukraini), 1/20/3153 67.
18. R. W. Davies, *The Socialist Offensive* (London, 1989), p. 158. See also Rossiskoi Gosudarstvennyi Arkhiv Sotsial'no-Politicheskoi Istorii-RGASPI, 17/2/441 tom. 1, 32, 69–70; tom. 2, 3–18, 33, 40, 42, 50, 56, 61, 64–72.
19. *Ibid.*, pp. 161–4. See also TsGAOO Ukrainy, 1/1/331 12.
20. *Ibid.*
21. TsDAGO Ukraini, 1/22/3154 1–2, 24–25.
22. TsDAGO Ukraini, 1/22/3153 67.
23. See Lynne Viola, *Peasant Rebels under Stalin. Collectivisation and the Culture of Peasant Resistance* (New York, 1996), pp. 139–40; Victor Danilov and Alexis Berelowitch, 'Les documents de la VCK-OGPU-NKVD sur la campagne sovietique', *Cahiers du Monde russe*, 25(3), July–September 1994, p. 673.

24. TsDAGO Ukraini, 1/20/3184 62.
25. RGASPI, 85/1/c/125 2–20b.
26. GAVO, P-29/1/577 141–1480b.
27. TsDAGO Ukraini, 1/20/3153 70.
28. GAVO, P-29/1/577 137.
29. This is based on an analysis of the documents of Tul'chinskii, Bratslavskii, Kryzhopol'skii, Sobolevskii, Dzhurinskii, Yaltushovskii, Trostyanetskii, Ladyzhinskii and Bershadskii raikoms of the party and also Mogilev–Podol'skii, Tul'chinskii and Vinnitsa okrugkom. See GAVO, P-33/1/1012 81–6; P-33/1/1013 1, 76, 81–2, 100–1, 104–5, 174, 214–18; P-31/1/563 246–8, 256–60, 276–82, 286–8, 363–5; P-40/1/153 89–90, 99; P-40/1/156 1–3; P-2325/1/89 5–7; P-2325/1/90 3–6; P-29/1/609 31–43.
30. RGASPI, 85/1/c/125 2–2ob.
31. TsDAGO Ukraini, 1/20/4162 4.
32. TsDAGO Ukraini, 1/20/4370 28.
33. N. A. Ivnitskii, *Kollektivizatsiya i raskulachivanie (nachalo 30-Kh godov)* (Moscow, 1994), p. 152.
34. GAVO, P-45/1/93 360. On 13 January 1931 the Ukrainian Politburo adopted a secret resolution to double the level of collectivisation in Ukraine during the spring sowing campaign. See TsGAOO Ukrainy, 1/16/8 9.
35. GAVO, P-51/1/447 56.
36. TsDAGO Ukraini, 1/20/4277 20, 24.
37. On the work of the Andreev commission see Ivnitskii, *Kollektivizatsiya*.
38. TsDAGO Ukraini, 1/16/8 75.
39. TsDAGO Ukraini, 1/16/8 86.
40. RGASPI, 17/162/10 54.
41. TsDAGO Ukraini, 1/20/4277 43.
42. TsDAGO Ukraini, 1/20/4282.
43. TsDAGO Ukraini, 1/20/4312 44.
44. TsDAGO Ukraini, 1/20/4354 7.
45. GAVO, P-136/7/3 6.
46. See *Tretya konferentsiya KP(b)U: Stenog. zvit* (Kharkiv, 1932). For an analysis of the stenographic report of the conference, see Yurii Shapoval, *Stenogrammy i protokol III konferentsii KP(b) U yak dzherelo vivchennya golodu 1931–1932 rr i golodomoru 1932–1933 rr. Golodomor 1932–1933 rr v Ukraini: prichini naslidki. Mizhnarodna nau-kova konferentsiya* (Kiiv, 1995), pp. 149–56.
47. *Komunistitichna partiya Ukrainy: z'izdi i konferentsii* (Kiivv, 1991), p. 153.
48. See *Golod 1932–1933 rokiv na Ukraini: ochima istorikiv, movoyu dokumentiv* (Kivv, 1990), pp. 45–8.
49. GAVO, P-6023/4/4725, tom 2, 227–8: *Stroinki istorii Kompartii Ukrainy: zapitannya i vidpovidi* (Kiiv, 1990), pp. 452–6, 468, 473–4.
50. GAVO, P-6023/4/4593, tom 1, 20, 23, 46, 61.
51. *Golod 1932–1933 rokiv na Ukraini*, pp. 41–2.
52. TsDAGO Ukraini, 1/16/9, 59–60.
53. Cited in *Golod 1932–1933 rokiv na Ukraini*, p. 45.
54. GAVO, P-136/1/29 48.
55. GAVO, P-136/1/27 42.
56. TsDAGO Ukraini, 1/16/9 86.
57. TsDAGO Ukraini, 1/16/9 86–7.
58. See *Golod 1932–1933 rokiv na Ukraini*, pp. 57–9.

59. Calculations by the author. See GAVO, P-137/1/59 72–3.
60. GAVO, P-137/1/59 40.
61. GAVO, P-137/1/59 52.
62. GAVO, P-136/7/5 37.
63. GAVO, P-137/1/59 39.
64. GAVO, P-136/6/228 21. Concerning the events in the North Caucasus see E. Oskolkov, *Golod 1932–1933 gg v zernovykh raionakh Severo-Kavkazskogo Kraya: Golodomor 1932–33gg. v Ukraini: prichini i naslidki. Mizhnarodna naukova konferentsiya* (Kiiv, 1993), pp. 113–23.
65. TsDAGO Ukraini, 1/16/9 199, 296, 326.
66. GAVO, P-136/6/ 228 22–6.
67. GAVO, P-136/1/27 49.
68. GAVO, P-137/1/26 5-5ob.
69. GAVO, P-136/1/29 146. For the Ukraine as a whole in 1933 the GPU 'unmasked' four major mythic counter-revolutionary organisations. See V. A. Zolotar'ov and Yu. I. Shapoval, 'Kolivan' u providenni linii partii ne bulo '(Storinki biografii K. M. Karlsona – zastupnika narkoma vnutrishnikh sprav URSR)', *Ukrainskii istorichnii zhurnal*, No. 1, 1996, pp. 96–7.
70. TsDAGO Ukraini, 1/16/10 106–7.
71. TsDAGO Ukraini, 1/16/10 249, 260–1.
72. GAVO, P-6023/4/4593 tom 1, 220.
73. GAVO, P-6023/4/4593 tom 1, 58, 212; t. 2, 1. 296.
74. *XII z'izd Komunistichnoi partii (bil'shovikiv) Ukraini, 18–23 sichnya 1934 r. Stenografichnii zvit* (Kharkiv, 1934), pp. 76–9, 351–4.
75. *XVII s'ezd Vsesoyuznoi Kommunisticheskoi Partii (b), 26 yanvarya-10 fevralya 1934 g: Stenograficheskii otchet* (Moscow, 1934), pp. 20, 200.
76. *Ibid.*, p. 420.
77. GAVO, P-136/1/95 48–9.
78. O. V. Khlevnyuk, *1937: Stalin, NKVD i sovetskoe obshchestvo* (Moscow, 1992), p. 36.
79. GAVO, P-136/7/97 157.
80. TsDAGO Ukraini, 1/16/11 294–5, 316, 323; 1/16/12 39, 45, 314, 342, 346; 1/16/ 13 49; GAVO, P-136/ 1/191 37. The question as to why political repression acquired a nationalist colouring requires special study.
81. GAVO, P-136/7/179 4–6.
82. GAVO, P-6023/4/4725, tom 1, 78–9.
83. *Narisi istorii Vinnits'koi oblasnoi partinoi organizatsii* (Odessa, 1980), p. 153.
84. GAVO, P-136/8/68 30.
85. O. V. Khlevnyuk, *1937: Stalin, NKVD i sovetskoe obshchestvo*, pp. 57–8.
86. GAVO, P-6023/4/4725 tom 1, 52–3, 62.
87. GAVO, P-6023/4/4725 tom 1, 68.
88. GAVO, P-6023/4/4725 tom 1, 35.
89. GAVO, P-136/7/318 30.
90. GAVO, P-6023/4/4725, tom 1, 35, 63, 69.
91. GAVO, P-6023/4/4593 tom 2, 262–65: V. A. Zolotar'ov, Yu. I. Shapoval, 'Kolevan' u provedenni linii partii ne bulo', p. 98.
92. GAVO, P-6023/4/4725 tom 1, 10.
93. GAVO, P-6023/4/4725 tom 1, 38.
94. GAVO, P-6023/4/5921 84–5.

8
The Great Purges and the XVIII Party Congress of 1939

E. A. Rees

The Great Purges that swept the USSR in 1936–8 fundamentally transformed the Stalinist regime. The causes, mechanisms and consequences of this upheaval still remain imperfectly understood. Here we shall seek to elucidate some aspects of the purge process as they impinged on centre–local relations in the USSR. We shall look briefly at the way in which the purge was conducted and then focus on the XVIII party congress of 1939. This provides a comparison with our study of the XVII party congress in 1934 (Chapter 3). In neither congress can it be said that any real debate occurred on substantive policy matters. However, by examining the statements of delegates we can get some indication of the impact which the terror had on centre–local relations, and on the extent to which terror inhibited the expression of critical opinion. We can also get a better picture of what were the enduring features of centre–local relations in the Stalin era, and the way in which these relations were influenced by the regime's growing reliance on repression and terror.

The purge process

The purge process was initiated in July 1936 when the Central Committee dispatched a secret letter, 'Concerning the terroristic activity of the Trotskyist–Zinovievist Counter-Revolutionary Bloc', to all republican, provincial and regional committees of the party. From the outset it appears that the purge was intended to embrace all administrative levels throughout the country. Following the trial of Zinoviev and Kamenev in August and the appointment of N. I. Ezhov to head the NKVD in September, arrests and dismissals of officials in the regions and republics grew apace.

In January 1937 the first shot in the attack on the regional leaders was fired, with two prominent regional party leaders – namely Pavel Postyshev (second secretary in Ukraine and first secretary of Kiev) and Boris Sheboldaev (first secretary of the Azov–Black Sea kraikom) – coming under attack. Both were accused of failings in their political leadership of their regions and of tolerating Trotskyist infiltration of their organisation. At this stage, both were simply demoted to lesser regional posts.[1]

The Central Committee plenum of February–March 1937 instituted a decisive escalation of the terror. Stalin in his speech to the plenum criticised the 'cults' of local leaders, family circles and private cliques.[2] This gave the party secretaries independence from the local party apparatus and from the central authorities in Moscow. Stalin sought to rein in the provincial leaders, and at the same time pose as defender of little people and of party democracy. He emphasised the failure of political leadership, lack of vigilance, which had allowed economic sabotage, conspiracy and plots to assassinate Soviet leaders to develop unchecked.

On Ezhov's request, the main regional NKVD chiefs attended the plenum as observers. Zhdanov's report to the plenum provided the basis for the re-elections of party secretaries in May 1937 by secret ballot as part of the campaign to mobilise pressure from below. How far the purge would go remained unclear. According to G. M. Malenkov's speech to the plenum the Central Committee in 1935–7 had expelled just 35 obkom deputy heads (8.8 per cent of the total checked); 111 gorkom deputy heads (5.5 per cent), 63 instructors (3.9 per cent), 184 gorkom and raikom secretaries (3.5 per cent) and 3,212 cell secretaries (3.4 per cent).[3]

The attack on the republican and regional party leaders in the first half of 1937 was still held in check. The execution of Tukhachevskii and the other military commanders in June 1937 was followed by a major extension of the purge. Arrests and executions of party and state officials reached new heights, with the NKVD apparatus in the regions being further strengthened. The leaders of the Belorussian Communist Party, headed by V. F. Sharangovich (first secretary) and Deniskevich (second secretary), were removed as enemies of the people and executed. In the second half of 1937 nearly all of the 80 regional party leaderships, as well as the party leadership of the union republics, were arrested and most were shot as traitors.[4]

The purges in the regions followed a remarkably similar course. In 1937 Stalin dispatched his deputies to the localities to investigate and initiate the purge process, through the convening of local party meetings, at which leading officials were criticised and voted out of office, and were then arrested by the NKVD. A. A. Andreev visited Voronezh, Chelyabinsk, Sverdlovsk, Kursk, Saratov, Kuibyshev, Rostov and Krasnodar. L. M. Kaganovich visited Ivanovo, Smolensk, Donbass, Yaroslavl' and Chelyabinsk. A. A. Zhdanov visited Leningrad, Orenburg, Bashkiriya and Tatary. A. I. Mikoyan went to Armenia. In 1938 N. S. Khrushchev, having purged the Moscow party organisation, was then dispatched to Ukraine as first secretary to carry out the same cleansing operation.

From 2 July 1937 onwards the purge entered a new phase, with the Politburo's directive for a mass operation by the NKVD against 'anti-soviet elements' (Order No. 00447). This order set quotas for each regions of the country for the arrest, imprisonment and execution of 'ex kulaks'. Three-man commissions, the troiki, were set up for each region, comprising the party first secretary, the head of the Procuracy and the head of the NKVD, with the power to impose the death sentence. Similar orders for campaigns against other anti-Soviet elements, including members of national minorities and criminals, followed.[5] The system of quotas encouraged local officials to come forward with upward revisions of the targets.[6]

These local initiatives, demanding upward revisions in the quotas for arrests and shootings of 'anti-Soviet' elements, reflected not merely a desire on the part of local officials to demonstrate their zeal and vigilance, it reflected also deeply ingrained attitudes among local party bosses, who were only too pleased to be given their head by the centre in eliminating what they regarded as troublesome elements. Local party bosses might have in the past fallen foul of the centre on issues of economic performance, mismanagement, corruption and cliquishness, but on the question of their resolve to wage war against the 'anti-Soviet' elements in society they were often as keen to demonstrate their implacable hostility to these people as the centre. The republican and regional leaders were neither more 'liberal' nor more 'hardline' than the leaders in the centre.

Almost all the republican and regional leaders, including long-standing figures who had played a central role in carrying through the 'revolution from above', fell victim to the purge. Stalin informed the Central Committee on 12 October 1937 that eight full members of the committee had been arrested as 'enemies of the people'. These included prominent regional leaders and those with strong regional connections: D. Z. Lebed' (chairman of Sovnarkom RSFSR, 1930–6); I. P. Nosov (first secretary of Ivanov obkom, 1932–7); M. M. Khataevich (first secretary of Dnepropetrovsk, 1932–7, then second secretary); A. I. Ikramov (first secretary of the Uzbekistan Communist Party, 1929–37); A. I. Krinitskii (first secretary of Saratov kraikom and gorkom); I. M. Vareikis (first secretary of the Central Black Earth obkom, 1928–34, Voronezh obkom, 1934–5, Stalingrad kraikom, 1935–6, Far East kraikom, 1937).[7]

Stalin also informed the Central Committee that a further 16 candidate members had been arrested and found to be German, English and Japanese spies. These included: G. F. Grin'ko (narkom of NKFin USSR, a former Borot'bist); P. P. Lyubchenko (chairman of Sovnarkom UkSSR, 1934–7); N. N. Demchenko (first secretary of Kiev, then Kharkov obkom, 1936 commissar of NKZem USSR, NKSovkhoz); A. S. Kalygina (secretary of Voronezh gorkom, 1936–7 then commissar of NKLegProm); B. A. Semenov (first secretary of Stalingrad obkom from 1936); V. P. Shubrikov (secretary of Central Volga kraikom, Kuibyshev obkom, 1932–7, second secretary West Siberia kraikom, 1937); F. P. Gryadinskii (chairman of the West Siberia kraikom, 1930–7); S. A. Sarkis (first secretary of Donetsk obkom, 1933–7, head of the Donets coal trust); Ya. B. Bykin (first secretary of Bashkir obkom,

1934–7); A. K. Lepa (first secretary of Tatar obkom, 1933–7); N. F. Gikalo (first secretary of the Belorussian Communist Party, 1932–37, then first secretary of Kharkov obkom); V. V. Ptukha (first secretary of Stalingrad kraikom, 1934–5, second secretary of Far East kraikom, 1935–7); 13 candidate members of the Central Committee were promoted as full members.[8]

The Politburo on 4 December approved the ousting of a further 10 Central Committee members, including M. E. Mikhailov (first secretary of Kalinin obkom, Voronezh obkom, 1937); K. V. Ryndin (first secretary of Chelyabinsk obkom); V. I. Ivanov (commissar of NKLes and former first secretary of Northern kraikom). In January 1938, P. P. Postyshev was finally removed as first secretary of Kuibyshev obkom.

In January 1938 indications were given of a slackening of the purge, only for the purge process to be again intensified. In the summer of 1938 three Politburo figures with strong republican and regional links were purged: S. V. Kosior (Ukrainian General Secretary), V. Ya. Chubar' (chairman of Sovnarkom UkSSR, 1923–34) and R. I. Eikhe (former first secretary of West Siberia kraikom) were arrested and subsequently executed. L. P. Beria's appointment as deputy narkom of NKVD in July 1938 brought a slackening of the terror. The Politburo order of 15 November on liquidating the troikas and Ezhov's removal as head of NKVD some days later marked the end of mass terror.

The changing balance in centre–local relations

Historical studies of the Great Purges reveal a very clear division of opinion, between those who emphasise the importance of central directives and those who emphasise local initiatives. This division of opinion reflects fundamental differences in interpretations of the Stalinist state.[9] Those who emphasise central directives argue that the limited autonomy exercised by republican and regional leaders in the 1920s had already been drastically reduced by 1932. Local initiative had not been wholly extinguished, nor could it ever be, but after 1932 the localities acted largely in response to central directives. Those who emphasise local initiative argue that the powers of the centre remained weak even after 1932, and that often local initiative had the effect of shaping central policy, even of generating developments which went beyond what the centre desired or sought.

J. Arch Getty and Oleg Naumov argue that up to 1936 the centre's control over the republican and regional leadership was in many ways weak. Even by early 1937 the Central Committee *nomenklatura* list included only 5,860 officials of a national stratum of party secretaries and officials numbering well over 100,000.[10] Whether this was weakness is debatable. The 5,860 officials listed constituted what Stalin called the 'general staff of the party' (see Chapter 2, p. 37). The mechanisms of central control, Getty and Naumov argue, were often ineffective; even central agencies of control such as the NKVD and KPK often fell under the control of local cliques. Yet from the autumn of 1936 the NKVD's regional leadership was fundamentally overhauled.

Since the late 1920s, Getty and Naumov argue, provincial party leaders had been turned into powerful 'feudal barons', with their own political machines and regional personality cults.[11] In 1936 Stalin desired only to administer a warning to these officials: 'Stalin wanted to hold the regional secretaries' heels to the fire without setting the whole house ablaze.'[12] Some time in 1937, Getty and Naumov argue, perhaps triggered by the so-called 'military conspiracy', Stalin decided on a thorough purge to eliminate the republican and regional leaders.[13]

Notwithstanding the evidence of Stalin's frustration with the republican and local leaders – the charges of cliquishness, corruption and incompetence which were laid against them – there is little evidence to suggest that they constituted in any sense a threat to his position or that they had conspired against him. There is little evidence either that they were capable of acting collectively or that they dissented with the centre on fundamental questions of policy. The charges, which were laid at their door – of conspiracy, espionage and wrecking – appear to be wild calumnies. At the same time, the absence of evidence of dissent and opposition does not mean that it did not exist.

What is clear is that centre–local relations were often extremely abrasive, and that behind the façade of unity, there were bitter mutual recriminations and a deep sense of distrust. On repeated occasions – in 1930, in 1932–3 and again in 1936–7 – the local leaders were made the scapegoats for the centre's policy failures. They were under intense pressures to meet plan targets, and had been pushed into enforcing repressive measures against the local population and against their own cadres. The plethora of control mechanisms developed by the centre, which were calculated to instil fear and insecurity, typified an administrative system which distrusted its subordinates. The isolation of republican and regional leaders from their own subjects placed them in a peculiarly vulnerable position, whereby pressure from above, combined with pressure from below, could and was used to dislodge them.

The relationship between the centre and these local leaders was based less on loyalty than a common, instrumental view of self-interest. Stalin calculated the advantages and disadvantages of retaining the current generation of leaders in their posts. By 1936 he calculated that the disadvantages outweighed the advantages, and that a rising generation of leaders was available to be promoted. The removal of the existing leaders either by electoral means or by forced retirement would have been complicated and protracted. Their replacement by purge was the other option available.

Stalin's disdain and distrust of many of the republican and regional leaders was heightened by his own suspicious nature and by the nature of the state which he had created. It was a state which operated by central commands; in which policy failures were off loaded on to subordinates who were denied any effective say over policy; in which open debate had become impossible and in which subordinates were required to trumpet their praises of an infallible leadership. It was a system calculated to foster among subordinates various strategies of deception and duplicity, and to engender feelings of contempt and hatred of their superiors. It was a system where the only realistic forms of dissent were passive resistance, evasion, conspiracy and intrigue. Passive resistance and evasion strategies were endemic. How widespread conspiracy or intrigue was remains a matter of supposition. The Great Terror was also shaped by Stalin's calculation that in a major crisis, such as war, he could not rely on these subordinates, and that the regime needed to be replenished with new, more energetic cadres.

The regime's control of the economy was in many ways imperfect and crude. Most of the criticisms for economic failings fell on the economic commissariats. But republican and regional authorities were also held responsible for economic problems, the failure to meet plan targets, high levels of waste and the high accident rates. But the charge made by Stalin at the Central Committee plenum in February–March 1937 was that party officials were devoting not too little but too much attention to economic matters, and that they were neglecting their political responsibilities, losing their revolutionary vigilance. To justify the sweeping purge of the country's ruling elite something more than accusations of economic incompetence was necessary. The charges of treason and conspiracy levelled against them served to justify their elimination and to galvanise mass opinion.

The purges in the localities, as Khlevnyuk has demonstrated, were controlled and directed from the centre at each stage, through the setting of quotas for arrests and executions, through directives and telegrams and through the organisation of show trials. This is not to deny the existence of local initiatives. Divisions within local ruling cliques also came to play an important role in the developing campaign, through scapegoating, mutual recriminations and blame-shifting. Major economic failures, corruption and incompetence became the basis of new investigations, new charges and executions.

The importance of these local initiatives does not in any way diminish the role which the centre, and Stalin personally, played in orchestrating the purges. From July 1936 onwards a number of unmistakable signals were issued from the centre as to what was expected. The terror developed through a series of steps: the Central Committee's letter of July; the Kamenev–Zinoviev trial in August; the appointment of Ezhov to head the NKVD in September; the Kemerovo trial in November; the Central Committee plenum in December; the trial of the Zinovievist–Trotskyist bloc in January 1937; the Central Committee plenum of February–March 1937; the convening of the meetings of party cells in March–April 1937; the trial of Tukhachevskii and the other military commanders in June. Stalin alone could have halted this mounting campaign, yet at every stage he lent his support for its intensification.

Sometimes he feigned reluctance, allowing others to make the running. To argue that Stalin was caught up by this campaign, that he was persuaded by the waves of denunciation unleashed by the campaign to intensify and extend the repression, is to see Stalin as a rather simple soul, who knew not what he was doing.

The Great Terror of 1936–8 was organised as a campaign, and displays remarkable similarities to the campaign methods that Stalin had used in consolidating his power and reorienting the party–state apparatus in 1928–32. The terror combined elements of mass mobilisation, purge and mass promotion, and features of an anti-bureaucratic revolution akin to those of the 'revolution from above'.[14]In both periods Stalin utilised a combination of central directives with local initiative in his attack on what he perceived as entrenched institutional interests.[15]

The purges evoked incomprehension among its victims, as reflected in their many appeals to Stalin. Khrushchev in his 'secret speech' in 1956 noted the widespread falsification of cases by the NKVD against provincial leaders, such as the so-called 'Ural uprising staff', supposedly headed by I. D. Kabakov, first secretary of Sverdlovsk obkom. Khrushchev added:

> The investigative materials of that time show that in almost all krais, oblasts and republics, there supposedly existed 'Rightist Trotskyite, espionage-terror and diversionary-sabotage organisations and centres' and that the heads of such organisations as a rule – for no known reason – were first secretaries of oblast or republic Communist Party committees or Central Committees.[16]

Khrushchev revealed that other leading provincial chiefs, such as Robert Eikhe, had been tortured and then executed on such trumped-up charges.[17]

Khrushchev in his memoirs notes that in 1937 the party lost its guiding role, and fell under the supervision of the NKVD. Candidates for nomination to gorkom and obkom posts had to be screened and sanctioned by NKVD.[18] During the terror NKVD officers were in fact appointed in a limited number of cases as local party secretaries.[19] In 1937–38 no one dared voice such scepticism; all were required to subscribe to the belief that such conspiracies were widespread, however exaggerated or absurd the accusations may have seemed.

The development of central–local relations within the USSR was in part shaped by developments in the country's relations with the outside world. The question of external security and internal security were seen historically to be intimately connected; military failure in 1904–5 and 1917 was the prelude to revolution, while revolutionary crisis and internal disintegration in 1918–20 was associated with foreign intervention. Stalin and his deputies were acutely conscious of this inter-relationship. The shift in centre–local relations after 1928 was shaped in part by the dictates of the planned economy, but also by broader internal security and defence concerns.

Silvio Pons describes the way in which from 1936 onwards Stalin confronted the prospect of an 'inevitable war' and the way this shaped both foreign and domestic policy. Internally it led to the creation of a state of siege or what Pons calls 'the total security state'.[20] This was what impelled Stalin to take preventative action to remove the possible sources of internal disintegration and to impose a new internal regime, in the words of Hélène Carrère d'Encausse to impose 'order through terror'.[21] It is in this regard that Khlevnyuk's view of the terror as a 'prophylactic purge' has to be seen.[22] The republican and regional elites were purged as part of a conscious and deliberate strategy to contain the dangers posed by the centrifugal forces within the state.

Stalin and other official spokesmen stressed the positive effect which the Soviet order and central planning had had on the economic and cultural development of the backward republics and regions of the USSR.[23] This was a very one-sided view. On the other side the legacy of revolution and civil war, the impact of collectivisation and famine, the destruction of traditional elites and social structures and the imposition of the centre's development priorities on these regions had created immense strains in centre–local relations, especially in the non-Russian regions. All competitor states of the USSR were extremely conscious of these internal weaknesses, and drew up strategies to exploit them as and when the need might arise.

Whereas in drafting the First and Second Five-Year Plans a token recognition was paid to the regional dimension in planning, in drafting the Third Five-Year Plan there was no attempt to involve republican and regional representatives. Gosplan and the entire planning apparatus were thrown into turmoil by the terror. The Third Five-Year plan had no section devoted specifically to regional development, although stress was again laid on the importance of location policy for economic and defence needs. Whereas in the annual plan for 1936 the RSFSR was organised on the basis of existing administrative units (12 krais, 11 oblasts and eight ASSR) in the Third Five-Year Plan the data provided for the RSFSR was organised on the basis of nine regions (European north, North-west, Central, Lower Volga, North Caucasus and Crimea, Urals, West Siberia, East Siberia and the Far East).[24] This reflected the continuing trend towards the creation of what was in effect a unitary state, underpinned by a unified economy.

The purge coincided with a fundamental reorganisation of the territorial administration and of the economic commissariats. In both cases the intention appears to be the same, namely to break up the larger administrative bodies into smaller, more manageable ones, which would be closer to their subordinate units. The economic commissariats were charged with inattention to the needs of the republics and regions, administrative remoteness and the pursuit of large grandiose development schemes, denounced as 'gigantomania', which placed a huge burden on the rail transport system.[25] The intention was to ensure more effective central control over these units. But the effect was to create enormous problems for the centre in ensuring effective coordination between these different levels.

In September 1937 in the RSFSR alone 11 new oblasts were established: Krasnodar, Orlov, Novosibirsk, Tula, Smolensk, Ryazan, Archangel, Tambov, Vologda, Irkutsk and Chitinskaya. In October 1938 the Far Eastern krai was split into the Primorskii and Khabarovskii krais, and the Perm oblast was also created. In February 1939 the Penza oblast was created. On 22 September 1937 four new oblasts were formed in Ukraine: Poltava, Nikolaev, Zhitomir, and Kamenetsk–Podolsk. In June 1938 Voroshilovgrad oblast was formed, and in January 1939 Zaporozhe, Sumskaya and Kirovograd oblasts were set up. On 15 January 1939 Belorussia was reorganised into five oblasts. At the same time, Uzbekistan SSR was organised into five oblasts.

The enormous power that the NKVD gained over the regional party bodies in 1937–8 did not prove permanent. From November 1938 onwards, as the purge was wound down, the power of the regional party leaders *vis-à-vis* the NKVD bodies in their territories was strengthened. On 14 November 1938 a Central Committee directive, signed by Stalin, was sent out to all the regional party authorities to carry out a check (*proverka*) on NKVD officials in their regions. This was done in cooperation with the central party author-ities of ORPO. Charges were lodged with the central authorities against abuses of power perpetrated by NKVD officers. In some instances NKVD officers were purged, although the majority appear to have escaped censure. Stalin, in checking the power of the NKVD, had no intention to disarm it. Party workers were drafted into the NKVD to replace those purged. This to some extent restored a measure of equilibrium in the local party's relations with the NKVD.[26]

This provided the background to the XVIII party congress. The check on the power of the NKVD allowed local party officials some measure of security, and allowed them some freedom to exercise their responsibilities. Restoring the morale of these officials was important in returning the system of local government to some normality. The convening of the party congress was intended also as an unmistakable sign of the central leadership's intention to restore authority to the party. But the moves to check the power of the NKVD should not be exaggerated. As a result of the purge the NKVD, now under Beria, occupied a position of formidable power, as a constant presence.

The XVIII party congress

The XVIII party congress marked a fundamental break with its predecessor. The Communist Party itself had been greatly weakened since 1930. As Khrushchev revealed in 1956 out of 1,966 delegates who attended the

XVII party congress, 1,108 were arrested on charges of anti-revolutionary crimes. Out of 139 members and candidates of the Central Committee elected by the XVII party congress 98 were arrested and shot.[27]

The XVIII party congress, which met from 10 to 21 March 1939, was attended by 1,570 delegates with full voting powers and 395 delegates with advisory voting powers. The break-up of party territorial organisations was reflected in the make-up of the delegations. Whereas at the XVII party congress there were 41 republican and regional organisations represented, at the XVIII party congress there were 99 republican and regional organisations represented.

The regional party organisations at the congress represented a great range of bodies of varying weight in the party, with one delegate being elected per 1,250–1,500 members. The ranking of party organisations according to the number of delegates, revealed a very clear hierarchy: Moscow, Leningrad, Stalinsk, Rostov, Dnepropetrovsk, Kiev, Kharkov, Ivanovo, Gorky, Krasnodar, Voronezh, Sverdlovsk, Stalingrad, Yaroslavskii, Kalinin and Voroshilovgrad. These 16 top regional organisations accounted for just over half of the voting delegates. The RSFSR accounted for nearly 70 per cent of all delegates. Out of 122 speakers at the congress, 57 were republican or regional spokesmen. The ranking of regions in terms of numbers of speakers was Moscow four, Leningrad three, with two each for Stalinsk, Ivanovo and Gorky.

The republican and regional party secretaries were recent appointees, and had been in office, in many cases, not more than a few weeks or months. They were relatively young, mostly in their mid-thirties and had been suddenly catapulted into positions of power. This was hardly the background, even with the easing of the terror and reassurances of stability, which would allow local spokesmen to speak freely of their concerns. Many of the speeches simply noted the particular economic activities undertaken in these regions, reflecting the attempt of political leaders to learn their briefs.

Stalin's keynote speech to the congress noted that a new imperialist war was already in its second year and that the danger of a new world war loomed. He censured those in the West who sought to turn Germany against the USSR, pushing it to attempt the annexation of Soviet Ukraine. Stalin noted the relative decline of Ukraine as the country's main grain supplier. He stressed the strong 'friendship of nations' in USSR and the strength of 'Soviet patriotism'. The purge of 1937–8, he claimed, had been unavoidable, but there would be no repetition of this mass purge. Errors had occurred. Party membership stood at 1,600,000, that is 270,000 less than in 1934. They had promoted 500,000 young Bolsheviks. The state would not wither away while capitalist encirclement persisted; and he underscored the importance to the socialist state of its 'military, penal and intelligence organs'.[28]

The main reports were Stalin's report for the Central Committee, Molotov's report on the Third Five-Year Plan, Kaganovich's report on the state of industry and Zhdanov's report on changes in the party statutes. The congress saw no real debate on the Third Five-Year Plan. For regional and republican leaders it was an opportunity to draw attention to the importance of their regions, to criticise the performance of other institutions and, to a limited extent, to lodge claims for resources to promote projects in their regions.

RSFSR

A. S. Shcherbakov, the newly appointed first secretary of Moscow city and oblast party committees, drew attention to the phenomenal growth of industrial output of the region since 1932, citing the extraordinary growth in the output of the Stalin automobile works.[29] G. N. Pal'tsev of Moscow oblast criticised NKZem USSR and NKSovkhoz USSR for poorly disseminating the experience of the Stakhanovites.[30] B. N. Chernousov criticised the widespread tendency of party raikoms to substitute themselves (*podmenyat'*) for the soviet raiispolkoms in agricultural campaigns, thereby undermining their responsibility.[31]

A. A. Kuznetsov of Leningrad oblast underlined the huge expansion of the region's industry, and its key role in supplying the Soviet army and navy. He also criticised poor cooperation between industries, the failure of suppliers to provide vital components and highlighted major shortcomings in transportation policy with the problem of wasteful cross-hauls of metal sent between Leningrad and the South,[32] P. S. Popkov of Leningrad, urged measures to develop the region's peat and coal reserves, and to reduce it depency on the Donbass wreckers, it was asserted, had held up the development of local coal reserves.[33]

I. P. Boitsov, of Kalinin oblast, the country's largest flax producer, stressed the need to develop peat extraction for local needs and to supply fuel for Leningrad and Moscow.[34] V. G. Zhaboronkov of Tula oblast stressed the oblast's role as a vital part of the Soviet defence industry and the necessity of developing local coal and iron ore reserves. He urged that the planned new tube-rolling works, which Molotov had suggested should be built in the middle of the country, be built in Tula.[35] P. I. Doronin of Kursk oblast stressed the need to develop the Kursk magnetic anomaly (KMA). The same issue had had been posed at the XVII party congress by E. I. Ryabinin. The project, Doronin argued, had been obstructed by the Pyatakovites in NKTyazhProm.[36] S. P. Ignatov of Kuibyshev oblast highlighted the grandiose Kuibyshev hydro complex on the Volga, which Molotov described as the greatest construction project in the world. Work had commenced in 1938; Ignatov called for general plan of construction to be approved in 1939, with the aim that it will be completed by 1947.[37]

In 1938–9 the central authorities passed resolutions which censured the work in agriculture of a number of oblasts, including Yaroslavskii, Sverdlovsk and Novosibirsk.[38] Regional spokesmen sought to deflect some of the criticism.

V. D. Nikitin of Voronezh oblast stressed the success of agriculture in the oblast.[39] I. A. Vlasov of Saratov krai criticised NKZem USSR and Gosplan USSR for neglecting the cultivation of spring and winter wheat, and assigning too much acreage to oats and barley in the Black Earth provinces. There were corresponding errors in NKZem USSR's allocation of tractors and implements to different raions.[40]

A. S. Chuyanov of Stalingrad krai, home of the giant Stalingrad tractor works and the Krasnyi Oktyabr steel works, urged efforts to speed up the exploitation of the Khoper iron ore reserves to meet the needs of local industry, and to improve its rail links with the Donbass and North Caucasus.[41] The Volga–Don canal, first proposed for the Second Five-Year Plan, was included in the Third Five-Year Plan. Chuyanov, as well as M. D. Bagirov of Azerbaidzhan and B. A. Dvinskii of Rostov welcomed the scheme as an important means to irrigate the Don steppe land, ensuring supplies of food and vegetable to the towns of the regions and to Baku.[42] The Second World War interrupted construction work on the canal, which was completed only in 1952.

Dvinskii of Rostov oblast called for urgent consideration to be given to deciding who were the customers for Rostov coal.[43] P. I. Seleznev of neighbouring Krasnodar oblast recounted the reputation of the Kuban as a centre of White counter-revolution, but noted its economic and social transformation as a result of collectivisation and industrial development.[44]

F. V. Shagimardanov of Bashkiriya ASSR underlined the importance of developing the Izhimbaev and Tyumazin oilfields as part of the 'Second Baku in the East'. He endorsed Molotov's call for efforts to force coal extraction in the region, proposing that by the end of Third Five-Year Plan there should be an output of 4 million tons per annum.[45] He called for the establishment of a People's Commissariat of Local Fuel to promote local developments. He urged greater efforts to develop local reserves of iron ore and manganese to supply the metallurgical industry of Urals.[46] He also proposed the establishment of a meat processing plant in Bashkiria, to reduce the costs of transporting livestock by train to the central regions of the USSR.

N. S. Patolichev of Yaroslavskii oblast focused on developing the work of the giant Yaroslavskii synthetic rubber combine.[47] A. I. Shakhurin, first secretary of Gorky obkom, noted with pride the enormous investment channelled into the giant Molotov motor works, and other new engineering works during the Second and Third Five-Year Plans.[48] V. M. Andrianov of Sverdlovsk oblast focused on the need to develop the region's copper industry and to improve its rail transport.[49] G. A. Borkov of Novosibirsk oblast noted the urgent need to reduce the overloading of the region's rail network that served the Kuzbass coalfield and the Kuznetsk metallurgical combine. It was necessary to modernise the Ob–Enissei canal, which had been built in the tsarist period.[50]

The party representatives of the Soviet Far East voiced their concerns about the defence of the region, the need to strengthen the defence base of the Red Army, strengthen the local economy, encourage settlement and improve rail communications with European Russia.[51]

Ukraine and Belorussia

The Ukrainian representatives at the congress stressed the problems of agriculture in the republic. Khrushchev, the new General Secretary of the Ukrainian Communist Party, stressed the potential for promoting the republic's agriculture, especially of sugar beet cultivation.[52] L. P. Korniets, chairman of Sovnarkom UkSSR, drew attention to the poor organisation of labour in the collective farms, which he blamed in part on NKZem USSR and its failure to ensure an effective system of remuneration.[53] Other Ukrainian spokesmen demanded the expansion of the repair base of the MTS for tractors and combines, and called for the production of spare parts for Chelyabinsk tractors to be organised in Ukraine.[54]

In 1938 and 1939 the Soviet regime faced a mounting crisis of food supply for the urban population. This had serious repercussions with regard to retaining workers in industry. At the beginning of 1939 L. M. Kaganovich, commissar for heavy industry, launched a campaign to attract the wives of miners to work in the coal industry. P. I. Shpilevoi of Stalinsk oblast and M. E. Kvasov of Voroshilovgrad oblast, both stressed the need to improve housing conditions and food supply as a means of creating a stable cadre of workers for the Donbass coalfield.[55]

P. K. Ponomarenko of Belorussia noted only the importance of putting the organisation of the kolkhozy in the republic in order, and the sensitive border position of the republic.[56]

Transcaucasus

The three representatives of Georgia, K. N. Charkvianin, V. M. Bakradze and M. I. Dzashi, were extremely forceful in arguing the interests of the republic. They lauded Beria's role in promoting the republic's development and in leading the struggle to destroy internal enemies. Tribute was paid to Kaganovich's role in overcoming problems in the oil industry. K. N. Charkvianin called for Georgia and the Transcaucasus to become self-sufficient in coal, in order to reduce the expense of long-hauled coal. He boasted of the republic's success in developing viticulture, tea cultivation and the production of citrus fruit.[57]

Bakradze strongly criticised the all-union agencies NKZem, NKPishProm and Tsentrosoyuz for allocating insufficient mineral fertiliser for the republic's needs, and called for measures to develop the republic's own fertiliser industry. He urged additional investment to complete the Black Sea railway, which was to link Georgia and the centre of USSR, the construction of which had started in 1929, so that it was completed during the Third Five-Year Plan. It was necessary to build a motor works in Tiblisi to serve the whole of the Transcaucasus and reduce the burden on the railways in importing cars.[58]

Bagirov, first secretary of the Azerbaidzhan Communist Party, acknowledged the help provided by Kaganovich in resolving problems in the oil industry. He urged further efforts to develop viticulture, citrus fruits and tea cultivation in the republic.[59] G. A. Arutinov of Armenia SSR called on the People's Commissariat of Non-Ferrous Metals to direct serious attention to the reserves of copper and molybdenum in the republic. He criticised 'gigantomania' in NKZem USSR and its preoccupation with large-scale irrigation projects, while neglecting more modest projects that would yield more immediate benefits.[60]

Delegates stressed the close help which they had received from the centre, and from Stalin personally. Charkvianin and Bakradze noted the transformation of Georgia from being a tsarist colony to being a developed economy.[61] Bagirov of Azerbaidzhan Communist Party noted progress in promoting literacy and disseminating party propaganda in the republic.[62]

Central Asia

Kazakhstan SSR was created in 1937, and in terms of territory was the second largest republic in the USSR. N. A. Skvortsov welcomed the rapid industrialisation of the republic, but argued that the targets set in the Third Five-Year Plan for the Karaganda coalfield and the Emba oilfield were too modest. In spite of Central Committee–Sovnarkom decrees authorising projects for exploiting the region's rich lead, copper and iron ore deposits the central economic commissariats had held up the work. Agriculture was held back by the lack of facilities for the repair of tractors and combines in the MTS, and by the low targets set for expanding the livestock herds. Poor communications remained a problem with 120 raions in Kazakhstan still having no telephone link with their oblast centres.[63]

A complaint voiced by Central Asian spokesmen at the XVII party congress in 1934 was the region's overdependence on cotton. At the XVIII party congress regional spokesmen for Kirghiziya, Tadzhikistan and Turkmenistan again stressed the importance of developing the industrial potential of the region, urging greater efforts to exploit its natural resources, reducing its dependence on outside supplies, particularly of coal, developing rail communication, as well as developing irrigation projects. In this the Economic Council, Gosplan, the central industrial and agricultural commissariats were censured for paying insufficient attention to the needs of these republics.[64] The Central Asian representatives trumpeted the unbreakable unity of the Soviet people, the help received from the centre in transforming their republics and the benefits bestowed by Russian culture and language. U. Yusupov for Uzbekistan SSR compared the economic and cultural advances made by the republic to the stagnation in neighbouring states such as Afghanistan, Iran and Turkey.[65]

Common themes

At the XVIII party congress, as at the XVII party congress, the speeches of regional leaders pointed to considerable strains in their relations with the central economic commissariats. In 1939 these tensions were evident in a number of areas. They were evident in the field of agriculture, associated with mounting concern in 1938–9 about the problem of food supply to the main urban areas. The republican and regional leaders sought to deflect the criticisms levelled against them by criticising in turn the failure of NKZem USSR and NKSovkhoz USSR to ensure adequate supplies of artificial fertiliser, or to make proper provision for the repair of tractors, combines and other implements.

The second area of tension concerned the problem of energy supply to meet the growing needs of industry and of the urban centres. In 1938–9 shortages of coal, oil and electricity began to restrict expansion. As a result many republican and regional leaders pressed for the development of their own local coal and peat reserves. The most critical problem was the electricity shortage. Shcherbakov, Moscow party secretary, argued that they needed in 1939 to start building 10–15 medium-sized electricity-generating stations in Moscow city and oblast.[66] Popkov of Leningrad warned that Leningrad by the end of 1942 would suffer a major deficit of electrical power.[67] The Georgian representatives issued a similar warning[68] as did the spokesmen for Ivanovo, Krasnodar, Sverdlovsk, Kharkov and Azerbaidzhan SSR .[69]

A third area of conflict was over the huge house-building programme.[70] Shcherbakov and G. M. Popov of Moscow both strongly condemned the failure of the all-union economic commissariats (Defence Industries and Machine Building) to meet their obligations with regard to house-building in the capital. They proposed that the Moscow Soviet be assigned a greater role in house-building, and that the necessary investment be provided to develop the local building-materials industry.[71] House-building targets were not being met, with the economic commissariats diverting funds and building materials to industrial construction. P. S. Popkov of Leningrad voiced similar complaints and proposed that all house-building in the city be concentrated in the hands of the Leningrad Soviet.[72]

The dispute over housing was part of a long-running dispute between regional authorities and the central economic commissariats, which after 1929 had taken over the running of most republican and regional industries. The tension remained. Dvinskii of Rostov oblast complained of the neglect of local industry, and noted that the People's Commissariat of Local Industry had taken over many enterprises from the oblast administration.[73]

None of these grievances appears to have been redressed. In agriculture I. A. Venediktov, head of NKZem USSR, and T. A. Yurkin, head of NKSovkhoz, retained their posts. In industry a substantial restructuring had taken place prior to the congress in January 1939 with the break-up of the super-industrial commissariat NKTyazhProm into six separate branch industrial commissariats, which were responsible for fuel (coal and oil), ferrous metal, non-ferrous metal, chemicals, electrical power generation and construction materials. This reorganisation was supposed to bring the commissariats closer to the work of the republican and regional authorities.

The purge in the republics and provinces

The congress saw no hint of criticism either of the purges or of the NKVD. Stalin underlined the importance of selecting and promoting new cadres. Zhdanov noted the large-scale training of technical specialists undertaken since the Shakhty affair of 1928. As the society became better educated so it was necessary, he argued, to have better-educated party cadres. There was no longer, he insisted, any rift between the intelligentsia and the Soviet people; the new Soviet intelligentsia was drawn from the people and tempered in the struggle with the 'enemies of the people'. It included a high proportion of young people, women and members of national minorities. The old system of party recruitment, which had discriminated against the intelligentsia, was no longer appropriate. The party should embrace the intelligentsia. This marked a profound shift in the nature and character of the regime as it sought to stabilise itself, based on the support of the new elite, which it had brought to power.

Chernousov of Moscow complained of past restrictions limiting admission into the party, and noted the grave weakness of the party in agriculture. In Moscow oblast of 6,556 kolkhozy only 304 (4.6 per cent) had primary party organisations.[74] In Moscow 50 enterprise had party organisations with over 500 members. He urged that the shop party organisations in such enterprises be given the right to admit members. He reported a substantial rise in the proportion of party secretaries with higher- and middle-level education. The election of large numbers of engineers and technicians to the leadership of factory party organisations ensured more effective control by the party in production.[75]

Charkvianin of Georgia reported that from January 1937 to March 1939 2,600 young workers had been promoted to leading party, soviet and economic posts.[76] Dzhashi reported that in Georgia in 1937–8 4,238 people had been promoted to party, soviet and economic work.[77] The party had strengthened its ideological work. Out of 7,841 candidates who had become members 42.8 per cent were white-collar. Spokesmen from the main republics and regions reported a similar large-scale promotion of young cadres, most with completed middle or higher education, into leading party, soviet and economic posts.[78] There was a revival of the party organisations, with the creation of new primary party organisations and party candidate groups. A high proportion of the promotees in the non-Russian republics were from the native population. Educated people now filled posts in rural and backward regions, which previously had been filled by semi-literate personnel. Several delegates welcomed Zhdanov's call to abandon the policy of discrimination against the intelligentsia in party recruitment.[79]

Zhdanov proposed to dispense with the branch departments (industry–transport, agriculture, trade, culture–enlightenment) of the obkoms and gorkoms, which it was argued duplicated the work of the economic and soviet bodies and distracted the party from its real responsibilities in providing political leadership and controlling cadres. A. A. Kuznetsov and T. F. Shtykov of Leningrad oblast endorsed Zhdanov's proposals, criticising excessive interference by party bodies in the work of enterprise directors.[80] The branch departments were engaged mainly in securing equipment, instruments and metals that were in short supply.[81] However, with the fragmentation of the commissariats and the territorial units the coordinating role performed by the local party bodies became ever more important. In a very brief time, as experience proved, it would be necessary to recreate these bodies.

The new Central Committee

The XVIII party congress served the purpose of partly reasserting the authority of the party after the purges, and it ensured that the constitutional proprieties of the election of a new Central Committee were preserved. The congress elected a new Central Committee of 71 full members and 68 candidates, about one-third of whom were republican and regional representatives. Among the full members the local organisations represented were Moscow (Shcherbakov), Leningrad (Zhdanov, Kuznetsov), RSFSR (A. E. Badaev) and Ukraine (Khrushchev, M. A. Burmistenko, L. P. Korniets). The other republics represented were Azerbaidzhan (M. D. Bagirov), Belorussia (P. K. Ponomarenko), Uzbekistan (U. Yusupov) and Kazakhstan (N. A. Skvortsov). The six economically most important Russian oblasts were also represented: Ivanovo (I. K. Sedin), Gorky (A. I. Shakhurin – who was to go on to a distinguished career as head of the People's Commissariat of the Aviation Industry), Sverdlovsk (V. M. Andrianov), Novosibirsk (G. A. Borkov), Rostov (B. A. Dvinskii) and Voronezh (V. D. Nikitin); plus the two strategically important krai in the Far East: Primorskii (N. M. Pegov) and Khabarovsk (V. A. Donskoi); and the two most important industrial oblasts in Ukraine: Dnepropetrovsk (S. B. Zadionchenko) and Stalinsk (P. M. Lyubavin).

The Politburo, which was elected following the congress, comprised nine full members: Stalin, Molotov, Kaganovich, Voroshilov, Kalinin, Andreev, Mikoyan, Zhdanov, Khrushchev; and two candidates, Beria and N. M. Shvernik. Zhdanov and Khrushchev were elevated from candidate members and Beria and Shvernik were brought in as new candidates. In February 1941 three new candidates were elected N. A. Voznesenskii (Gosplan), Malenkov (secretariat) and Shcherbakov (Moscow party). In 1939 the most important republican and regional leaders still had some access to Stalin in his

Kremlin office, notably Zhdanov (Leningrad), Shcherbakov and V. P. Pronin (Moscow), Khrushchev (Ukraine) Ponomarenko (Belorussia), but these were overshadowed by the vast numbers of meetings held with representatives of the military, the defence industries and the internal security apparatus.

Conclusion

Centre–local relations in the USSR from 1937 onwards underwent a significant change. The Soviet economy was managed essentially as a unified whole. The move towards a unitary state was associated with the growing preoccupation both with internal and external security concerns. However, the fragmentation of regional units, as with the fragmentation of the commissariats, created for the central authorities enormous difficulties in controlling and coordinating the work of these bodies. It was tied to changes in nationalities policy, with the reversal of the policy of favouring the non-Russian peoples in terms of language and cultural policy, the weakening of institutions representing national interests and the extension of the purge to the republics and regions.

In spite of the terror, the fact that most spokesmen were only recently appointed, and the fragmentation of regional bodies, some of the local spokesmen at the XVIII party congress continued to press the claims of their regions, often pressing the very same claims made by their purged predecessors. The role of local leaders in promoting and defending local interests was recognised and accepted by the centre. This was clearly differentiated from what was construed as wrecking, sabotage, or the creation of local fiefdoms. Sometimes the boundary between these two became blurred. Republican and local leaders were expected to navigate a course between these shoals.

The republican and local leaders were purged in 1936–8 not because they were too vigorous in promoting their local interests. They fell victim primarily because they were seen as potentially disloyal, having lost their energy, having become complacent and corrupt. The purge removed the existing layer of leaders, and promoted in its place a new generation of leaders, who were more loyal, better educated and more businesslike, and who were tempered in this struggle with 'enemies of the people'. The terror severely damaged economic performance in 1937–8 and it took time before the new promoted cadres were able to fully master their new responsibilities. Those advanced were drawn mainly from the new Soviet intelligentsia. The system of administrative control developed by the centre over the regions from the early 1930s onwards failed to provide Stalin with the administrative system he sought. In 1937–8 by the promotion of a new generation of administrators he sought to base centre–local relations on new bonds of allegiance and loyalty of a new generation of administrators, supplemented by the fear instilled by police surveillance and terror.

Notes

1. J. Arch Getty and O. V. Naumov, *The Road to Terror: Stalin and the Self-Destruction of the Bolsheviks, 1932–1939* (New Haven, London, 1999), p. 316.
2. *Ibid.*, p. 265 cited speeches by Malenkov, Mekhlis, Beria and Kudriatsev to the February–March 1937 Central Committee plenum in *Voprosy Istorii*, No. 5–6, 1995, p. 10; No. 7, 1995, pp. 19–21; No. 10, 1995, pp. 10–15.
3. *Ibid.*, p. 564.
4. *Ibid.*, pp. 431–2.
5. T. Martin, 'The Origins of Soviet Ethnic Cleansing', *Journal of Modern History*, 70(4), December 1998, pp. 831–61.
6. Oleg Khlevnyuk, 'The Objectives of the Great Terror' in Julian Cooper, Maureen Perrie and E. A. Rees (eds), *Soviet History 1917–53* (Basingstoke, London, 1995), O. V. Khlevnyuk, *Politbyuro: mekhanizmy politicheskoi vlasti v 1930-e gody* (Moscow, 1996); Oleg Hlevnjuk [Khlevnyuk], 'Les mecanismes de la 'grande terreur' des annees 1937–1938 au Turkmemistan', *Cahiers du Monde russe*, January–June 1998, pp. 197–208.
7. O. V. Khlevnyuk *et al.* (eds), *Stalinskoe Politbyuro v 30-e gody: Sbornik dokumentov* (Moscow, 1995), p. 157.
8. *Ibid.*, pp. 157–8. Those promoted included U. D. Isaev (chairman of Sovnarkom Kazakhstan), P. I. Smorodin (first secretary of Stalingrad obkom), M-D, A. Bagirov (first secretary of the Communist Party of Azerbaidzhan), E. K. Pramnek (first secretary of Donetsk obkom), M. E. Mikhailov (first secretary of Voronezh obkom), A. I. Ugarov (second secretary of Leningrad obkom).
9. There are three principal schools of thought regarding the Great Purges: Firstly, those who see it as principally directed from the centre, and as part of the unfolding of the 'totalitarian' logic of Bolshevism, as represented by Robert Conquest, *The Great Terror* (Harmondsworth, 1971); secondly, those who see the terror as a politically directed campaign directed and controlled from the centre, but without subscribing to the totalitarian model of Stalinism, such as Khlevnyuk, *Politbyuro*; thirdly, those who emphasis the importance of local initiative and the weakness of the 'centre', and who fundamentally reject the totalitarian approach, as in J. Arch Getty, *Origins of the Great Purges: The Soviet Communist Party Reconsidered, 1933–1938* (Cambridge, 1985) and Arch Getty and Naumov, *The Road to Terror*.
10. Malenkov's speech to the February–March 1937 Central Committee plenum, *Voprosy Istorii*, No. 10, 1995, p. 7.
11. Getty and Naumov, *The Road to Terror*, p. 265. On the nature of regional cliques, see also James R. Harris, *The Great Urals: Regionalism and the Evolution of the Soviet System* (Ithaca, London, 1996), Chapter. 6 'The Terror'.
12. Getty and Naumov, *The Road to Terror*, p. 267.
13. Getty and Naumov, *The Road to Terror*, pp. 446–51.
14. See E. A. Rees, 'Stalinism: The Primacy of Politics', in John Channon (ed.), *Politics, Society and Stalinism in the USSR* (London, 1998), pp. 35–68.
15. A parallel might be drawn with the Nazi regime. See Ian Kershaw, 'Working towards the Führer: Reflections on the Nature of the Hitler Dictatorship', in Ian Kershaw and Moshe Lewin (eds), *Stalinism and Nazism: Dictatorships in Comparison* (Cambridge, 1997), pp. 88–106.
16. N. S. Khrushchev, *Khrushchev Remembers* (trans. by Strobe Talbot, introduction, and commentary by Edward Crankshaw) (London, 1971), pp. 582–3.
17. *Ibid.*, pp. 578–81.

18. *Ibid.*, p. 81.
19. See Oleg Khlevnyuk, 'Party and NKVD: Power Relationships in the Years of the Great Terror', in Barry McLoughlin and Kevin McDermott (eds), *Stalinist Prophylaxis: Mechanisms and Dynamics of the Great Terror in the Soviet Union, 1937–38* (Basingstoke, 2002). Khlevnyuk cites the cases of L. Gasov, first secretary of Krasnodar kraikom, Valukhin, first secretary of Sverdlovsk obkom, Teleshov, first secretary of Odessa obkom and Goncharov, first secretary of Ordzhonikidze obkom.
20. Silvio Pons, *Stalin e la guerra inevitabile* (Turin, 1995), pp. 134–42.
21. Hélène Carrère d'Encausse, *Stalin: Order Through Terror* (London, 1981).
22. Oleg Khlevnyuk, 'The Objectives of the Great Terror, 1937–38', pp. 158–76; Oleg Khlevnyuk, 'The Reasons for the 'Great Terror': The Foreign Political Aspect', in Silvio Pons and Andrea Romano (eds), *Russia in the Age of Wars 1914–1945* (Milan, 2000), pp. 159–170.
23. Trotsky, who was very critical of the Stalinist system, shared the official Soviet view of the beneficial effects of central direction and planning on the backward regions and republics. See Leon Trotsky, *The Revolution Betrayed* (London, 1967), pp. 170–1.
24. *Tretyi pyatiletnii plan razvitiya narodnogo khozyaistva Soyuza SSR (1938–1942gg)* (Moscow, 1939).
25. E. A. Rees, *Stalinism and Soviet Rail Transport, 1928–41* (Basingstoke, 1995), pp. 196–205.
26. See Oleg Khlevnyuk, 'Party and NKVD: Power Relationships in the Years of the Great Terror', pp. xx.
27. Khrushchev, *Khrushchev Remembers*, pp. 572–3.
28. *XVIII s"ezd. Vsesoyuznoi Kommunisticheskoi Partii (b), 10–21 marta 1939: Stenograficheskii otchet* (Moscow, 1939), pp. 13–32.
29. *Ibid.*, pp. 69–70.
30. *Ibid.*, p. 321.
31. *Ibid.*, p. 558.
32. *Ibid.*, p. 78.
33. *Ibid.*, p. 367.
34. *Ibid.*, pp. 324–5.
35. *Ibid.*, pp. 270–1.
36. *Ibid.*, p. 428.
37. *Ibid.*, pp. 378–9.
38. *Ibid.*, pp. 585–9 (Patolichev), 222–4 (Andrianov), 395–6 (Borkov).
39. *Ibid.*, p. 182.
40. *Ibid.*, pp. 91–2.
41. *Ibid.*, pp. 228–31.
42. *Ibid.*, pp. 82–3, 230, 88.
43. *Ibid.*, p. 88.
44. *Ibid.*, p. 487.
45. *Ibid.*, p. 342.
46. *Ibid.*, p. 344.
47. *Ibid.*, pp. 585–6.
48. *Ibid.*, pp. 152–4.
49. *Ibid.*, pp. 222–4.
50. *Ibid.*, pp. 395–6.

51. *Ibid.*, p. 225 N. M. Pegov (Primorskii krai); p. 141 V. A. Donskoi (Khabarovsk krai), pp. 489–90 K. I. Kachalin (Irkutsk oblast); p. 617 I. V. Murugov (Chita oblast).
52. *Ibid.*, p. 169.
53. *Ibid.*, p. 329.
54. *Ibid.*, p. 469 A. Frolkov (Kharkov oblast); p. 81 S. B. Zadionchenko (Dnepropetrovsk oblast).
55. *Ibid.*, pp. 418, 86–7.
56. *Ibid.*, pp. 121–5.
57. *Ibid.*, pp. 206–8.
58. *Ibid.*, pp. 454–6.
59. *Ibid.*, pp. 82–3.
60. *Ibid.*, pp. 407–8.
61. *Ibid.*, pp. 206–8, 454–5.
62. *Ibid.*, pp. 82–3.
63. *Ibid.*, pp. 102–3.
64. *Ibid.*, pp. 481–4 A. V. Vagov (Kirghiziya); pp. 162–5 D. Z. Protopov (Tadzhik SSR); p. 447 Ya. A. Chubin (Turkmen SSR).
65. *Ibid.*, p. 76.
66. *Ibid.*, p. 71.
67. *Ibid.*, p. 367.
68. *Ibid.*, pp. 206–8, 454–5.
69. *Ibid.*, pp. 85 (I. K. Sedin, Ivanovo oblast); 487 (P. I. Seleznev, Krasnodar krai); 222–4 (Andrianov, Sverdlovsk oblast); 469 (Frolkov, Kharkov oblast); 82–3 (Bagirov, Azerbaidzhan SSR).
70. Some indication of the scale of house-building is provided in the speech by A. E. Badaev (chairman of the presidium of the Supreme Soviet of the RSFSR), *ibid.*, p. 167.
71. *Ibid.*, p. 434.
72. *Ibid.*, p. 370.
73. *Ibid.*, p. 88.
74. *Ibid.*, p. 555.
75. *Ibid.*, p. 556.
76. *Ibid.*, pp. 206–8.
77. *Ibid.*, p. 578.
78. *Ibid.*, pp. 272 (V. G. Zhaboronkov, Tula oblast); 571–2 (T. F. Shtykov, Leningrad gorkom); 581–2 (M. I. Rodionov, Gorky oblast); 364 (V. I. Boitsov, Orlov oblast); 162 (A. M. Alemasov, Tatar ASSR); 567–8 (A. P. Matveev, Belorussia SSR); 238 (M. A. Burmistenko, second secretary of Ukrainian Communist Party); 596 (Z. T. Serduk, Kiev oblast); 553 (P. M. Lyubavin, Stalinsk oblast); 547 (P. F. Cheplakov, Azerbaidzhan SSR); 76 (U. Yusupov, Uzbekistan SSR); 607–10 (M.Yuldashev, Uzbekistan SSR).
79. *Ibid.*, pp. 364 (V. I. Boitsov); pp. 571–2 (T. F. Shtykov); pp. 567–8 (A. P. Matveev).
80. *Ibid.*, pp. 571–2.
81. *Ibid.*, p. 572.

Bibliography

Archives

Arkhiv FSB RF po RK – *Archive of the Federal Security Agency of the Russian Federation in the Republic of Karelia (Arkhiv Federalnaya Sluzhba Bezopasnosti Rossiskoi Federatsii v Respublike Karelii).*

DADO   State Archives of Donets oblast (Derzhavnyi Arkhiv Donet'skoi oblasti).

GARF   State Archives of the Russian Federation (Gosudarstvennyi Arkhiv Rossiskoi Federatsii).

GAOPDF RK   State Archive of Social–Political Movements and Formations of the Republic of Karelia (Gosudarstvennyi Arkhiv Sotsial'no-Politicheskikh Dvizhenii i Formastsii Respubliki Karelii).

GAVO   State archives of Vinnitsa oblast (Gosudarstvennyi Arkhiv Vinnitskoi oblasti).

NA RK   National Archive of the Republic of Kareliya (Natsional'nyi Arkhiv Respubliki Karelii).

RGAE   Russian State Archives of the Economy (Rossiskii Gosudarstvennyi Arkhiv Ekonomiki).

RGASPI   Russian State Archves of Social–Political History (Rossiskii Gosudarstvennyi Arkhiv Sotsial'no-Politicheskoi Istorii) (formerly RTsKhIDNI).

TsDAGO   Central State Archives of Social Organisations of Ukraine (Tsentral'nii derzhavnii arkhiv gromads'kikh ob'ednan' Ukraini).

TsGAMO   Central State Archives of Moscow Oblast (Tsentral'nyi Gosudarstvennyi Arkhiv Moskovskoi oblast).

Periodical publications

Bol'shevik
Cahiers du Monde russe
Europe–Asia Studies
Istoricheskii arkhiv
Izvestiya
Izvestiya TsK KPSS
Partiinoe stroitel'stvo
Pravda
Russian Review
Slavic Review
Sotsialisticheskii Donbass
Soviet Studies
Svobodnaya mysl'
Voprosy istorii

Collections of decrees, resolutions, laws; collections of materials on the economy; officials reports of party congresses, conferences and other officials bodies

Direktivy KPSS i sovetskogo pravitel'stva po khozyaistvennym voprosam, i (Moscow, 1957).
Resheniya partii i pravitel'stva po khozyaistvennym voprosam (Moscow, 1967), tom 2.
Sobranie uzakonenii i rasporyazhenii RSFSR.
Sobranie zakonov i rasporyazhenii SSSR (referred to as *SZ*).
Kommunisticheskaya partiya Sovetskogo Soyuza v rezolyutsiyakh i resheniyakh s"ezdov, konferentsii i plenumov TsK, 9th edn (Moscow, 1984).
Narodnokhozyaistvennyi plan na 1936 god: Tom Vtoroi: Plan Razvitiya Raionov (Moscow, 1936).
Osnovyne ukazaniya k sostavleniyu Vtorogo Pyatiletnego Plana narodnogokhozyaistva SSSR (1933–1937) (Moscow, 1932).
Osnoynye pokazateli vypolneniya narodno-khozyaistvennogo plana po respublikam, kraiyam i oblastyam (Moscow, 1937).
Proekt vtorogo pyatiletnego plana razvitiya narodnogo khozyaistva SSSR, vol. 1. (Moscow, 1934).
[Semnadtsataya] XVII konferentsiya Vsesoyuznoi Kommunisticheskoi partii(b): stenograficheskii otchet (Moscow, 1932).
[Semnadtsatyi] XVII s"ezd Vsesoyuznoi Kommunisticheskoi partii(b): stenograficheskii otchet (Moscow, 1934).
[Shestnadtsatyi] XVI s"ezd Vsesoyuznoi Kommunisticheskoi partii (b): stenograficheskii otchet (Moscow, 1930).
[Vosemnadtsatyi] XVIII s"ezd Vsesoyuznoi Kommunisticheskoi partii (b): stenograficheskii otchet (Moscow, 1939).
XVIII s"ezd Vsesoyuznoi Kommunisticheskoi Partii (b), 10–21 marta 1939: Stenograficheskii otchet (Moscow, 1939), pp. 13–14.
IV Moskovskaya oblastnaya i III gorodskaya konferentsii Vsesoyuznoi Kommunisticheskoi Partii (b), 16–24 yanvarya 1934g; Stenograficheskii otchet (Moscow, 1934).
Sotsialisticheskoe stroitel'stvo SSSR: statisticheskii ezhegodnik (Moscow, 1935).
Upravlenie narodnym khozyaistvom SSSR 1917–1940gg. Sbornik dokumentov (Moscow, 1968).
Vtoroi pyatiletnii plan razvitiya narodnogo khozaistva SSSR (1933–1937gg), vol. 1 and vol. 2 Plan razvitiya raionov (Moscow, 1934).
Tretii pyatiletnii plan razvitiya narodnogo khozyaistva Soyuza SSR (1938–1942) (Moscow, 1939).

Books and articles in Russian and Ukrainian

Bol'shaya Sovetskaya Entsiklopaediya.
Chuev, F., *Sto sorok besed s Molotovym* (Moscow, 1991).
Chuev, F., *Tak govoril Kaganovich* (Moscow, 1992).
Ekonomicheskaya zhizn' SSSR: khronika sobytii i faktov, 1917–1959, ed. S. G. Strumilin (1961).
Golod 1932–1933 rokiv na Ukaini: achima istorikiv, movoyu dokumentjv (Kiiv, 1990).
Golodomor 1932–33 rr Ukraini: prichini i naslidki. Mizhnarodna naukova konferentsiya (Kiiv, 1993).
Gorodetskii, E. N. *(et al.) Stroitel'stvo sovetskogo gosudarstva* (Moscow, 1972).
Ivnitskii, N. A., *Kollektivizatsiya i raskulachivanie (nachalo 30-x godov)* (Moscow, 1994).

Khavin, A., *Sotsialisticheskaya industrializatsiya natsional'nykh respublik i oblastei* (Moscow, 1933).

Khlevnyuk, O. V., *1937-i: Stalin, NKVD i sovetskoe obshchestvo* (Moscow, 1992).

Khlevnyuk, O. V. *Stalin i Ordzhonikidze: Konflikty v Politbyuro v 30-e gody* (Moscow, 1993).

Khlevnyuk, O. V., *Politbyuro: Mekhanizmy politicheskoi vlasti v 1930-e gody* (Moscow, 1996).

Khlevnyuk, O. V., Kvashonkin, A. V., Kosheleva, L. P. and Rogovaya, L. A. (eds), *Stalinskoe Politbyuro v 30-e gody* (Moscow, 1995).

Khlevnyuk, O. V., Davies, R. W., Kosheleva, L. P., Rees, E. A. and Rogovaya, L. A. (eds), *Stalin i Kaganovich: Perepiska. 1931–1936gg.* (Moscow, 2001).

Kosheleva, L., Lelchuk, V., Naumov, V., Naumov, O., Rogovaya, L. and Khlevnyuk, O. (eds), *Pis'ma I. V. Stalina V. M. Molotovu 1925–1936gg: Sbornik dokumentov* (Moscow, 1995).

Krzhizhanovskii, G. M. (ed.), *Voprosy ekonomicheskogo raionirovaniya SSSR: Sbornik materialov i statei (1917–1929gg.)* (Moscow, 1957).

Kuz'min, V. I., *V bor'be za sotsialisticheskuyu rekonstruktsiyu, 1926–1937: ekonomicheskaya politika Sovetskogo gosudarstva* (Moscow, 1976).

Kvashonkin, A. V., Khlevnyuk, O. V., Kosheleva, L. P. and Rogovaya, L. A. (eds), *Bol'shevistskoe rukovodstvo. Perepiska. 1912–1927* (Moscow, 1996).

Kvashonkin, A. V., Kosheleva, L. P., Rogovaya, L. A. and Khlevnyuk, O. V. (eds), *Bol'shevistskoe rukovodstvo. Perepiska. 1928–1941* (Moscow, 1999).

Livshin, A. Ya., Orlov, I. B. (eds), *Pis'ma vo vlast'. 1917–1927* (Moscow, 1998).

Oskolkov, E. N., *Golod 1932–1933gg v zernovykh raionakh Severo-Kavkazskogo kraya* (Rostov on Don, 1991).

Stalin, I. V., *Sochineniya, v, vii, xi, xii, xiii* (Moscow, 1954–1956)

Vasil'ev, Valerii and Viola, Lynne, *Kollektivizatsiya i krest'yanskoe soprotivlenie na Ukraine (noyabr' 1929-mart 1930gg)* (Vinnitsa, 1997).

Venediktov, A. V. *Organizatsiya gosudarstvennoi promyshlennosti v SSSR, tom 2* (Moscow, 1961).

Vihavainen, Timo and Takala, Irina (eds), *V sem'e edinoi: natsional'naya politika partii bol'shevikov i ee osushchestvlenie na Severo-Zapade Rossii v 1920–1950e gody* (Petrozavodsk, 1998).

Yakubovskaya, S. I., *Razvitie SSSR kak soyuznogo gosudarstva 1922–1936gg* (Moscow, 1972).

Books and articles in English

Bahry, Donna, *Outside Moscow: Power, Politics and Budgetary Policy in the Soviet Republics* (New York, 1987).

Breslauer, George W., 'Regional Party Leaders: Demand Articulation and the Nature of Centre-Periphery Relations in the USSR', *Slavic Review*, 4, 1986, pp. 650–72.

Brower, Daniel R., 'The Smolensk Scandal and the End of NEP', *Slavic Review*, 4, 1986, pp. 689–706.

Carr, E. H., *The Bolshevik Revolution, II* (London, 1966).

Carr, E. H., *Socialism in One Country, 1924–1926, I* (London, 1958).

Carr, E. H. and Davies, R. W. *Foundations of a Planned Economy, 1926–1929, I* (London, 1969).

Carr, E. H., *Foundations of a Planned Economy 1926–29, II* (London, 1971).

Carrère d'Encausse, Hélène, *Stalin: Order Through Terror* (London, 1981).

Carrère d'Encausse, Hélène, *The Great Challenge: Nationalities and the Bolshevik State 1917–1930* (New York, London, 1992).

Channon, John (ed.), *Politics, Society and Stalinism in the USSR* (London, 1998).

Chase, William, *Workers, Society and the Soviet State: Labour and Life in Moscow 1918–1929* (Urbana, 1987).

Clark, M. Gardner, *The Economics of Soviet Steel* (Cambridge, Mass., 1956).

Cohen, Stephen F., *Bukharin and the Bolshevik Revolution: A Political Biography, 1888–1938.* (Oxford, 1975).

Colton, Timothy J., *Moscow: Governing the Socialist Metropolis* (Cambridge, Mass., 1995).

Conquest, R., *Soviet Nationalities Policy in Practice* (London, 1967).

Conquest, R., *The Great Terror* (Harmondsworth, 1971).

Conquest, R., *Inside Stalin's Secret Police: NKVD Politics 1936–39* (Basingstoke, London, 1986).

Conquest, R., *The Harvest of Sorrow* (London, 1986).

Conquest, R., *Stalin, Breaker of Nations* (London, 1993).

Cooper, Julian, Perrie, Maureen and Rees, E. A. (eds), *Soviet History 1917–1953: Essays in Honour of R. W. Davies* (Basingstoke, London, New York 1995).

Daniels, Robert V., 'The Secretariat and the Local Organisations of the Russian Communist Party, 1921–23', *American Slavic and East European Review*, 3 (1957).

Davies, R. W., *The Soviet Budgetary System* (Cambridge, 1958).

Davies, R. W., 'The Decentralisation of Industry: Some Notes on the Background', *Soviet Studies*, 9(4), 1958, pp. 353–67.

Davies, R. W., 'A Note on Defence Aspects of the Ural–Kuznetsk Combine', *Soviet Studies*, 26(2), 1974, pp. 272–3.

Davies, R. W., 'The Syrtsov–Lominadze Affair', *Soviet Studies*, 33, 1981, pp. 29–50.

Davies, R. W., *The Industrialisation of Soviet Russia 1: The Socialist Offensive: The Collectivisation of Soviet Agriculture, 1929–1930* (London, 1980).

Davies, R. W., *The Industrialisation of Soviet Russia 2: The Soviet Collective Farm, 1929–1930* (Basingstoke, London, 1980).

Davies, R. W., *The Industrialisation of Soviet Russia 3: The Soviet Economy in Turmoil, 1929–1930* (London, 1989).

Davies, R. W., *The Industrialisation of Soviet Russia 4: Crisis and Progress in the Soviet Economy, 1931–1933* (London, 1996).

Davies, R. W., *Soviet History in the Gorbachev Revolution* (Basingstoke, London, 1989).

Davies, R. W., *Soviet History in the Yeltsin Era* (Basingstoke, London, 1997).

Davies, R. W., Harrison, M. and Wheatcroft, S. G. (eds), *The Economic Transformation of the Soviet Union, 1913–1945* (Cambridge, 1994).

Davies, R. W., Rees, E. A., Khlevnyuk, O. V., Kosheleva, L. P. and Rogovaya, L. A. (eds), *The Stalin–Kaganovich Letters* (New Haven, 2003).

Deutscher, I., *Stalin: A Political Biography* (London, 1966).

Dobb, M., *Soviet Economic Development Since 1917* (London, 1966).

Fainsod, M., *Smolensk under Soviet Rule* (Cambridge, Mass., 1958).

Fainsod, M., *How Russia is Ruled* (Cambridge, Mass., 1st edn 1953, 2nd edn 1963).

Fitzpatrick, Sheila (ed.) *Cultural Revolution in Russia, 1928–1931* (Bloomington, London, 1978).

Fitzpatrick, Sheila, *The Cultural Front. Power and Culture in Revolutionary Russia* (Ithaca, 1992).

Fitzpatrick, Sheila, *Stalin's Peasants: Resistance and Survival in the Russian Village after Collectivization* (New York, 1994).

Fitzpatrick, Sheila, *Everyday Stalinism* (New York, Oxford, 1999).

Fitzpatrick, Sheila (ed.), *Stalinism: New Directions* (London, 2000).

Flora, Peter, Kuhnle, Stein and Urwin, Derek (eds), *State Formation, Nation Building and Mass Politics in Europe* (Oxford, 1995).

Getty, J, Arch, *Origins of the Great Purges: The Soviet Communist Party Reconsidered, 1933–1938* (Cambridge, 1985).

Getty, J. Arch, and Manning, R. (eds), *Stalinist Terror* (Cambridge, 1993).

Getty, J. Arch, and Naumov, O. V., *The Road to Terror: Stalin and the Self-Destruction of the Bolsheviks, 1932–1939* (New Haven, London, 1999).

Gill, Graeme, *The Origins of the Stalinist Political System* (Cambridge, 1990).

Gregory, Paul, *Restructuring the Soviet Economic Bureaucracy* (Cambridge, 1990).

Grin'ko, G. T., *The Five-Year Plan of the Soviet Union: A Political Interpretation* (London, 1930).

Harris, James R., *The Great Urals: Regionalism and the Evolution of the Soviet System* (Ithaca, 1999).

Haslam, J., *The Soviet Union and the Threat from the East* (Basingstoke, London, New York, 1992).

Hill, Ronald J., *Soviet Political Elites: The Case of Tiraspol* (London, 1977).

Hoffman, David, *Moscow: Peasant Metropolis* (Ithaca, London, 1994).

Hosking, Geoffrey and Service, Robert, (eds), *Russian Nationalism, Past and Present* (London, 1997).

Hough, Jerry F., *The Soviet Prefects: The Local Party Organs in Industrial Decision-Making* (Cambridge, Mass., 1969).

Hughes, James, 'The Irkutsk Affair: Stalin, Siberian Politics and the End of NEP', *Soviet Studies*, 41(2), 1989, pp. 228–53.

Hughes, James, *Stalin, Siberia and the Crisis of the New Economic Policy* (Cambridge, 1991).

Hughes, James, *Stalinism in a Russian Province: Collectivisation and Dekulakisation in Siberia* (Basingstoke, London, 1996).

Hughes, James, 'Patrimonialism and the Stalinist System: The Case of S. I. Syrtsov', *Europe–Asia Studies*, 48(4), 1996, pp. 551–68.

Jasny, N., *Soviet Industrialization, 1928–1952* (Chicago, 1961).

Kershaw, Ian, and Lewin, Moshe (eds), *Stalinism and Nazism: Dictatorships in Comparison* (Cambridge, 1997).

Khlevnyuk, O. V., *In Stalin's Shadow. The Career of 'Sergo' Ordzhonikidze* (New York, London, 1995).

Khrushchev, N. S., *Khrushchev Remembers* (trans by Strobe Talbot, Introduction and Commentary by Edward Crankshaw) (London, 1971).

Knight, Amy, *Beria: Stalin's First Lieutenant* (Princeton, 1993).

Kostiuk, H., *Stalinist Rule in the Ukraine: A Study of the Decade of Mass Terror (1929–39)* (London, 1960).

Kotkin, Stephen, *Magnetic Mountain: Stalinism as a Civilization* (Berkeley, 1995).

Kuromiya, H., *Stalinist Industrial Revolution: Politics and Workers 1928–1932* (Cambridge, 1988).

Kuromiya, H., *Freedom and Terror in the Donbas: A Ukrainian–Russian Borderland, 1870s–1990s* (Cambridge, 1998).

Lewin, M., *Russian Peasants and Soviet Power* (London, 1968).

Lewin, M., *The Making of the Soviet System* (London, 1985).

Lih, Lars T., Naumov, O. V. and Khlevniuk, O. V. (eds), *Stalin's Letters to Molotov* (New Haven, 1995).

Mace, James E., *Communism and the Dilemmas of National Liberation. National Communism in Soviet Ukraine* (Cambridge, Mass., 1983).

Mace, James E., *Famine in the Soviet Ukraine 1932–33* (Cambridge, Mass., 1986).

Manning, Roberta, 'Government and the Soviet Countryside in the Stalinist 1930s: The Case of Belyi Raion in 1937', *Carl Beck Papers in Soviet and East European Studies*, No. 301 (Pittsburgh, 1984).

Martin, Terry, *The Affirmative Action Empire: Nations and Nationalism in the Soviet Union , 1923–1939* (Ithaca, London, 2001).

Mawdsley, Evan and White, Stephen, *The Soviet Elite from Lenin to Gorbachev: The Central Committee and its Members* (Oxford, 2000).

McAuley, Mary, *Bread and Justice: State and Society in Revolutionary Petrograd 1917–22* (London, 1991).

McLoughlin, Barry and McDermott, Kevin (eds), *Stalinist Prophylaxis: Mechanisms and Dynamics of the Great Terror in the Soviet Union, 1937–38* (Basingstoke, 2002).

Medvedev, R. *On Stalin and Stalinism* (Oxford, 1979).

Medvedev, R., *All Stalin's Men* (Oxford, 1983).

Medvedev, R., *Let History Judge* (New York, 1989).

Merridale, Catherine, *Moscow Politics and the Rise of Stalin: The Communist Party in the Capital, 1925–1932* (Basingstoke, London, 1990).

Nelson, Daniel N., 'Dilemmas of Local Politics in Communist States', *Journal of Politics* 41, 1979, pp. 23–54.

Pipes, Richard, *The Formation of the Soviet Union: Communism and Nationalism , 1917–1923* (Cambridge, Mass., 1964).

Raleigh, Donald J., *Revolution on the Volga: 1917 in Saratov* (Ithaca, 1986).

Rassweiler, Anne D. and Dickason, Anne D., *The Generation of Power: The History of Dneprostroi* (New York, 1988).

Rees, E. A., *State Control in Soviet Russia: The Rise and the Fall of the Workers' and Peasants' Inspectorate* (London, New York, 1984).

Rees, E. A., *Stalinism and Soviet Rail Transport, 1928–1941* (Basingstoke, London, New York, 1995).

Rees, E. A. (ed.), *Decision-Making in the Stalinist Command Economy, 1932–1937* (Basingstoke, London, New York, 1997).

Rigby, T. H., *Communist Party Membership in the USSR, 1917–1967* (Princeton, 1968).

Rigby, T. H., 'Early Provincial Cliques and the Rise of Stalin', *Soviet Studies*, 1, 1981, pp. 3–28.

Rigby, T. H., *Political Elites in the USSR: Central Leaders and Local Cadres from Lenin to Gorbachev* (Aldershot, 1990).

Rigby, T. H. and Harasymiw, Bohdan, *Leadership Selection and Patron-Client Relations in the USSR and Yugoslavia* (London, 1983).

Rittersporn, Gabor Tamas, *Stalinist Simplifications and Soviet Complications: Social Tensions and Political Conflicts in the USSR, 1935–1953* (Chur, 1991).

Rokkan, Stein, *Building States and Nations* (Beverly Hills, 1973).

Rokkan, Stein, *Economy, Territory, Identity: Politics of West European Peripheries* (London, 1983).

Rokkan, Stein, *Centre–Periphery Structures in Europe* (Frankfurt on Main, 1987).

Rosenberg, William G. and Siegelbaum, Lewis H. (eds), *The Social Dimension of Soviet Industrialization* (Bloomington, 1993).

Rossman, Jeffrey J., 'The Teikovo Cotton Workers Strike of April 1932: Class, Gender and Identity Politics in Stalin's Russia', *The Russian Review*, 56, January 1997, pp. 44–69.

Sakwa, Richard, *Soviet Communists in Power: A Study of Moscow During the Civil War, 1918–21* (London, 1988).

Schwartz, H., *Russia's Soviet Economy* (New York, 1954).

Shearer, David R., *Industry, State and Society in Stalin's Russia, 1926–1934* (Ithaca, London, 1996).

Shimotomai, N., 'A Note on the Kuban Affair (1932–1933): The Crisis of Kolkhoz Agriculture in the North Caucasus', *Acta Slavica Iaponica*, I, 1983, p. 46.

Shimotomai, N., *Moscow under Stalinist Rule, 1931–34* (Basingstoke, London, 1991).

Smith, Jeremy, *The Bolsheviks and the National Question, 1917–1923* (London, 1999).

Soviet Government Officials, 1922–1941: A Handlist, eds, R. W. Davies, M. Ilič, H. J. Jenkins, C. Merridale and S. G. Wheatcroft (Birmingham, 1989).

Subtelny, Orest, *Ukraine: A History* (Toronto, 1994).

Swianiewicz, S., *Forced Labour and Economic Development: An Enquiry into the Experience of Soviet Industrialization* (London, 1965).

The Second Five-Year Plan for the Development of the National Economy of the USSR (1933–37) (Moscow, 1935).

Thorniley, D., *The Rise and the Fall of the Soviet Rural Communist Party, 1927–39* (Basingstoke, 1988).

Thurston, Robert W., *Life and Terror in Stalin's Russia 1934–1941* (New Haven, London, 1996).

Viola, Lynne, *Peasant Rebels under Stalin. Collectivisation and the Culture of Peasant Resistance* (New York, 1996).

Volkogonov, D., *Stalin: Triumph and Tragedy* (New York, 1988).

Watson, D. H., *Molotov and Soviet Government: Sovnarkom 1930–1941* (Basingstoke, 1996).

Zaleski, E., *Planning for Economic Growth in the Soviet Union, 1918–1932* (Chapel Hill, 1971).

Zaleski, E., *Stalinist Planning for Economic Growth, 1933–1952* (London, 1980).

Books in other languages

Courtois, S., *et al.*, *Le livre noir du communisme: Crimes, terreur, repression* (Paris, 1997).

Pons, Silvio, *Stalin e la guerra inevitabile* (Turin, 1995).

Name Index

Abakumov, Y. T.   104
Abdarakhmanov   84
Abolin, K. K.   139
Al'bert, A. K.   142
Alekseev, M. A.   176
Almazov, Z. A.   125
Amosov, M. K.   78, 81
Andreev, A. A.   15, 39, 52, 63 n47, 82, 90 n103, 136, 170, 174, 192, 207
Andrianov, V. M.   202, 207
Antonov-Ovsenko, A. V.   47
Artyunyants   108
Arutinov, G. A.   204

Badaev, A. E.   69, 207
Bagirov, M. D.   202, 204, 207
Baichurin, G. G.   74
Bakradze, V. M.   203, 204
Balitskii, V. A.   23, 43, 76, 171
Bauman, K. Ya.   15, 16, 39, 40, 78, 79, 81, 82, 84, 85, 86, 93, 95, 101
Begailo, R.   186
Bergavinov, S. A.   45
Beria, L. P.   40, 45, 54, 62 n12, 66, 77, 82, 84, 86, 88, 194, 199, 203, 207
Berman, M. D.   107, 108
Berztys, Ya. K.   128–9
Blyukher, V. K.   74
Boitsov, I. P.   201
Bondarev   184
Borkov, G. A.   202, 207
Borshch   184
Broido, G. I.   47
Bukharin, N. I.   65
Bulatov, D. A.   50–1
Bulganin, N. A.   69, 94, 103, 104, 105, 106, 107, 109
Burmistenko, M. A.   207
Burov   186
Bushuev, P. I.   135, 141
Bykin, Ya. B.   75, 85, 193–4

Carrère d'Encausse, Hélène   198
Charkvianin, K. N.   203, 204, 206

Chernousov, B. N.   201, 206
Chernov, M. A.   30, 31, 34 n33, 82, 100
Chernyavskii, V. I.   35 n54, 41, 176, 177, 178–9, 180, 181, 182, 183, 184–5, 186, 187
Chubar', V. Ya.   20, 21, 22, 23, 25, 43, 48, 75, 76, 81, 82, 84, 86, 90 n103, 138, 176, 182, 194
Chudov, M. C.   86, 139
Chuyanov, A. S.   202
Cohen, Stephen   38
Colton, Timothy   94

Daniels, R. V.   13
Danilov, I. A.   123
Demchenko, M.   184
Demchenko, N. N.   35 n54, 48, 193
Deniskevich   192
Deutscher, I.   13
Dimitrov, G.   158
Donskoi, V. A.   207
Doronin, P. I.   201
Drok   181
Dvinskii, B. A.   202, 205, 207
Dzashi, M. I.   203, 206

Eikhe, R. I.   16, 22, 34 n33, 35 n54, 39, 40, 47, 50, 51, 53, 58, 73, 83, 86, 194, 197
Eismont, N. B.   24, 25, 65
Evdokimov, E. G.   35 n54, 60, 74, 86, 88
Ezhov, N. I.   32, 50, 60, 111, 136, 139, 191, 192, 194, 196

Fainsod, Merle   5
Firin, S. G.   106
Fitzpatrick, Sheila   60
Furer, F. Ya.   77

Gaister, A. I.   91 n103
Gamarnik, Ya.   41, 73
Gasov, L.   210 n19
Getty, J. Arch.   6, 30, 157, 160, 194–5
Gikalo, N. F.   35 n54, 48, 66, 75, 84, 194

Ginsburg, Moisei   101
Goloded, N. M.   35 n54, 48, 75, 82, 84, 85, 90 n103
Goloshchekin, F. I.   34 n33, 45, 78
Goncharov   210 n19
Gorbachev, M. S.   1
Goryanoi, S.   184, 186
Gramsci, Antonio   152
Grin'ko, G. F.   16, 17, 18, 23, 181, 193
Gryadinskii, F. P.   34 n33, 35 n54, 53, 73, 80, 81, 82, 91 n103, 193
Gylling, Edvard   117, 118, 120, 123, 126, 130, 133, 135, 138, 139, 143

Hitler, A.   24, 155
Hough, J. F.   5, 54
Hughes, James   14–15
Hughes, John   150

Ignatov, S. P.   201
Ikramov, A. I.   79, 85, 86, 193
Irklis, P.   135, 139, 141
Isaev, U. D.   35 n54, 79, 85, 91 n103
Ivanchenko, Ya. P.   72
Ivanov, N. I.   148 n95
Ivanov, V. I.   35 n54, 70, 86, 194
Ivanov   125
Ivanov   21

Kabakov, I. D.   19, 32, 35 n54, 39, 59, 72, 82, 86, 91 n103, 197
Kaganovich, L. M.   11, 12, 15, 20, 21, 22, 23, 24, 25, 30, 31, 41, 43, 44, 45, 48, 53, 54, 69, 70, 71, 74, 75, 77, 78, 85, 86, 87, 90 n103, 93, 94, 95, 96, 97, 98, 99, 100, 101, 102, 103, 104, 105, 106, 107, 108, 109, 110, 111, 160, 169, 175, 176, 177, 178, 179, 180, 181, 183, 192, 200, 203, 204, 207
Kalinin, M. I.   90 n103, 103, 131, 134, 143, 207
Kalmanovich, M. I.   82
Kalygina, A. S.   193
Kamenev, L. B.   14, 15, 57, 65, 93, 101, 191, 196
Kaminskii, G. N.   69, 98, 100, 107, 109
Karpov, I. N.   52
Kartvelishvili, L. I.   *see* Lavrent'ev, L. I.

Khataevich, M. M.   16, 22, 31, 44, 45–6, 55, 60, 76, 80, 83, 86, 178, 181, 186, 193
Khlevnyuk, O.   196, 198
Khodzhaev, F.   79, 82, 85
Khodzhaev   84–5
Khrushchev, N. S.   1, 47, 60, 62 n12, 69, 86, 94, 100–1, 103, 104, 105, 106, 107, 110, 192, 197, 199, 203, 207, 208
Khvylei   185–6
Kim   83
Kirov, S. M.   14, 15, 40, 46–7, 65, 70, 80, 82, 86, 90 n103, 130, 135, 159, 183
Kisis   45–6
Kodatskii, I. F.   70, 80, 86
Kogan, L. I.   106, 107, 108
Kolotilov, N. N.   39, 71
Koltypin   179
Korniets, L. P.   203, 207
Kosior, S. V.   14, 15, 20, 22, 23, 25, 35 n54, 43, 47, 48, 55, 75, 76, 81, 86, 90 n103, 170, 172, 174, 178, 179, 180, 181, 182, 183, 184, 186, 194
Kovalev   48
Kozlov, I. I.   73
Kozlov   45
Krasin, German   101
Krinitskii, A. I.   49–50, 58, 193
Krupskaya, N. K.   98
Krzhizhanovskii, G. M.   19
Kudryavtsev, S. A.   48
Kuibyshev, V. V.   19, 26, 27, 29, 34 n33, 44, 67, 68, 69, 70, 72, 73, 74, 75, 76, 79, 81, 82, 85, 90 n103, 106, 109
Kuznetsov, A. A.   201, 207
Kvasov, M. E.   203

Ladovskii, N. A.   101
Larin, V. F.   74
Larin, Yu.   12, 102
Lavrent'ev, L. I.   (Kartvelishvili, L. I.)   34 n33, 35 n54, 40, 57, 62 n12, 83, 86
Lebed', D. Z.   139, 193
Le Corbusier   101
Lenin, V. I.   11, 13, 38, 93, 104, 117
Leonov, F. G.   40–1, 45
Lepa, A. K.   54, 59, 194
Lerman   176, 183, 186
Levinson   176

Likhachev, I. A.   108
Lobov, S. S.   122
Lobov   142
Lominadze, V. V.   25
Lord Simon   107
Lysenko, P.   160
Lyubavin, P. M.   207
Lyubchenko, N.   185
Lyubchenko, P. P.   35 n54, 176, 177,
    181, 184, 185, 186, 187, 193
Lyubimov, I. E.   90 n103

Makarov, I. G.   77
Maksum   85
Malenkov, G. M.   52, 59, 94, 192, 207
Marchernko   169
Marnevich   181
May, Ernst   101
Mazurenko, Yu.   185
Medvedev, R.   46–7, 100, 103
Mekhlis, L. Z.   50, 59
Melnikov, Konstantin   101
Mezhlauk, V. I.   90 n103, 138, 139
Mikhailov, M. E.   194
Mikhailov   107
Mikoyan, A. I.   31, 46, 58, 181
Mironov, L. G.   62 n46
Mirzoyan, L. I.   35 n54, 45, 55, 59,
    78, 81, 86, 192, 207
Molotov, V. M.   22, 23, 26, 27, 39,
    40, 41, 43, 44, 48, 49, 53, 55, 56,
    67, 68, 77, 79, 80, 83, 85, 87,
    90 n103, 93, 94, 103, 109, 126,
    138, 139, 158, 161, 173, 174,
    175–6, 200, 201, 202, 207
Musabekov, G.   77, 84, 85, 91 n103

Naumov, Oleg   6, 194, 195
Nikitin, V. D.   202, 207
Nikolaeva, N. I.   86
Nosov, I. P.   51, 71, 86, 193

Orakhelashvilli, M. D.   40, 45, 46
Ordzhonikidze, G. K.   40, 46, 48, 53,
    55, 56, 62 n12, 77, 85, 90 n103,
    94, 96, 97, 138, 171–2

Pakhomov, N. I.   79–80, 82, 91 n103
Pal'tsev, G. N.   201
Papernyi, L.   178, 179

Patolichev, N. S.   202
Pegov, N. M.   207
Peters, Ya. K.   95, 107
Petlura, Simon   23, 168
Petrovskii, G. I.   20, 35 n54, 45,
    76, 86, 178
Pilipenko   171
Polonskii, V. I.   40
Ponomarenko, P. K.   203, 207, 208
Pons, Silvio   198
Popkov, P. S.   201, 205
Popov, G. M.   205
Postyshev, P. P.   15, 25, 34 n33,
    35 n54, 41, 43, 44, 48, 53, 55, 57,
    58, 60, 71, 75–6, 84, 86, 174, 178,
    179, 180, 181, 184, 185, 191, 194
Pramnek, E. K.   35 n54, 59, 80
Prokof'ev, G. E.   62 n46
Pronin, V. P.   208
Ptukha, V. V.   35 n54, 44, 47, 71,
    81, 194
Pyatakov, Yu. L.   71, 90 n103

Rakhimbaev, A. R.   91 n103
Razumov, M. O.   35 n54, 55, 58,
    73, 81, 86
Rechitskii   84
Redens, S. F.   22, 23
Rigby, T. H.   13
Rogozhin, G. D.   141, 142
Rotert   104
Rovio, K.   138, 139
Rudzutak, Ya. E.   91 n103
Rumyantsev, I. P.   53, 59, 71, 81
Ryabinin, E. I.   72, 91 n103, 201
Rykov, A. I.   74
Ryndin, K. V.   31, 35 n54, 59, 72,
    86, 94, 107, 194
Ryutin, M. N.   25, 65, 95

Sabsovich, L. M.   101, 102
Sarkis (Sarkisov), S. A.   32, 35 n54,
    76, 77, 89 n51, 193
Sedin, I. K.   207
Seleznev, P. I.   202
Semenov, B. A.   57, 178, 193
Shadunts, S. K.   57
Shafranskii   50
Shagimardanov, F. V.   202
Shakhurin, A. I.   202, 207

Sharangovich, V. F.   192
Shcherbakov, A. S.   110, 201, 205,
   207, 208
Sheboldaev, B. P.   16, 22, 23, 35 n54,
   47, 54, 55, 57, 58, 74, 83, 86, 191
Shelemen'tev   184
Shils, Edward   144
Shkiryatov, M. F.   23, 41, 51
Shlikhter, A. G.   76, 84
Shpilevoi, P. I.   203
Shreider, M. P.   51
Shtykov, T. F.   207
Shubrikov, V. P.   34 n33, 35 n54, 44,
   57, 58, 71, 80, 81, 193
Shvernik, N. M.   15, 19, 39, 77,
   91 n103, 207
Skalyga   181
Skrypnik, M.   20, 22, 83, 84
Skvortsov, N. A.   204, 207
Smirnov, A. P.   24, 25, 65
Smirnov, G. I.   122
Stakhanov, A.   152–3
Stalin, I. V.   1, 10, 11, 12, 13, 14, 15,
   16, 19, 22, 23, 24, 25, 30, 31, 32,
   35 n54, 37, 38, 39, 40, 41, 42, 43, 44,
   45, 46, 47, 48, 49, 51, 52, 54, 55,
   57, 58, 59, 60, 61, 65, 67, 69, 70,
   72, 74, 75, 76, 77, 78, 79, 80, 81,
   82, 83, 84, 85, 87, 90 n103, 93, 94,
   95, 97, 98, 100, 101, 102, 103, 104,
   105, 106, 107, 110, 111, 138, 151,
   152, 153, 154, 155, 156, 157, 158,
   159, 160, 161, 162, 170, 171, 172,
   174, 175, 177, 178, 179, 180, 181,
   182, 184, 185, 186, 187, 188, 191,
   192, 193, 194, 195, 196–7, 198,
   199, 200, 204, 206, 207, 208
Starobin, I.   182–3, 185, 186
Stroganov, V. A.   44, 45
Struppe, P. I.   70
Sukhomlin, K. V.   82, 177
Sulimov, D. E.   15, 19, 69, 79, 86,
   91 n103
Syrtsov, S. I.   15, 25, 39

Teleshov   210 n19
Terekhov, R. Ya.   24, 89 n51
Tolmachev, G. G.   24, 25, 65
Travkin, P. N.   136, 141, 142
Trilisser, M. A.   180
Trilisskii, A. L.   176, 177, 180, 181,
   182, 186, 187
Trotsky, L. D.   93, 210 n23
Tukhachevskii, M. N.   161, 192, 196
Tyuvaev, G. D.   122, 123

Ugarov, A. I.   110
Uglanov, N. A.   13, 14, 15, 93, 95, 101

Vaganyan, V.   12
Vaionov   58
Valukhin   210 n19
Vareikis, I. M.   15, 34 n33, 46, 48,
   57, 71, 72, 81, 86, 193
Veger, E. I.   35 n54, 51, 58, 178
Venediktov, I. A.   205
Vlasov, I. A.   202
Voroshilov, K. E.   48, 71, 81, 90 n103,
   103, 138, 207
Voznesenskii, N. A.   207
Vyshinskii, A. Ya.   155, 157

Yagoda, G. G.   63 n46, 156
Yakir, I. Ye.   187
Yakovlev, A. I.   49–50
Yakovlev, Ya. A.   20, 21, 71, 76,
   81, 82, 90 n103
Yaroslavskii, E. M.   73
Yurkin, T. A.   82, 91 n103, 205
Yusupov, U.   204, 207

Zadionchenko, S. B.   207
Zelenskii, I. A.   15
Zhabronokov, V. G.   201
Zhdanov, A. A.   15, 50, 71, 82, 86, 135,
   138, 192, 201, 206, 207, 208
Zhuk, S. Ya.   106
Zimin, N. N.   40–1
Zinoviev, G. E.   12, 14, 15, 57, 191, 196

Subject Index

Academy of Sciences   27, 84, 103
Agriculture   98–101, 167–88
  cotton cultivation   19, 77–9, 81, 84,
    85, 87, 204
  grain production/procurement   16,
    21–4, 26, 31, 42–4, 53, 74–6,
    168–70, 173–9, 181, 183–5
  sugar beet production   167, 175,
    181–2, 184–5
All-Union Agricultural Academy   84
Archangel oblast   199
Architectural Planning Commission
  (Moscow)   103
Armenia SSR   204
Association for the Liberation of Ukraine
  (SVU)   12, 173
ASSR   198
Azerbaidzhan SSR   40, 58, 202, 205, 207
Azov-Black Sea krai   47, 74
Azov-Black Sea kraikom   31, 54, 55,
    57, 86, 191

Baikal-Amur railway   86
Baku   15, 77, 202
Baltic White Sea Canal (BBVP)   70, 106,
    119, 123, 129, 132, 134, 143, 144
Baltic White Sea Combine (BBK)   123–9,
    131–3, 140, 142, 144
Bashkiriya ASSR   28, 31, 68, 74–5, 85,
    192, 193, 202
Belorussia SSR (BSSR)   23, 25, 27–8, 57,
    66, 75, 82, 83, 87, 157, 158, 199,
    203, 207
Bol'shevik   46
Border security   88, 119, 137, 139–40,
    160, 167, 171, 175, 180, 182, 183, 184
Borot'bists   176, 181, 182, 185, 186, 193
Budget (State)   20, 118, 139

Cadres   41, 148 n95, 152, 153, 154, 156,
    172, 173, 175, 178, 186, 194–5, 196,
    206, 208
Central Asia   11, 12, 16, 17, 19, 25, 27,
    28, 68, 78–9, 81, 86, 87, 204–5

Central Asian Bureau   39, 78, 81, 82, 84
Central Asian Economic Council   17
Central Black Earth (CBE) obkom   15,
    46, 66, 71–2, 81, 86, 193
Central Black Earth (CBE) oblast   22, 28,
    47, 71–2, 79
Central Control Commission
  (TsKK)   14, 41, 46, 180
  TsKK-NKRKI   29, 30, 83, 85
Central Volga krai   16, 22, 28, 30, 47, 170
Central Volga kraikom   44, 66, 71, 76,
    80, 81, 193
Cheka   9, 77
Chelyabinsk obkom   72, 86, 194
Chelyabinsk oblast   31, 47, 59, 192
Chelyabinsk rabochii   59
Chelyabinsk tractor works   68, 72
Chernigov oblast   175, 183
Chitinskaya oblast   199
Civil war   9, 17, 151, 167–8
Collectivisation of agriculture   16, 20,
    25, 81, 170, 171, 172, 173, 174
Commission of Party Control (KPK)   30,
    32, 49, 50, 51, 85, 135, 141, 195
Commission of Soviet Control
  (KSK)   30, 32, 49, 85
Committee for Agricultural
  Procurements (KomZag)   29, 30,
    32, 44, 100, 184
Communist Academy   128
Communist Party of Azerbaidzhan   204
Communist Party of Belorussia   48, 75,
    84, 192, 194
Communist Party of Georgia   206
Communist Party of the Soviet Union
  (CPSU)   199–200
  Central Committee   19, 21, 22, 23,
    30, 37, 38, 39, 41, 43, 44, 45, 47,
    48, 49, 50, 51, 52, 53, 55, 58, 69,
    70, 71, 72, 73, 75, 76, 77, 78, 79,
    81, 84, 86, 93, 95, 97, 99, 101, 102,
    103, 105, 107, 139, 168, 169, 171,
    172, 176, 180, 181, 183, 184, 186,
    191,194, 196, 199, 200, 207

Communist Party of the Soviet Union
  (CPSU) – *Continued*
  Central Committee (members) 13,
    25, 37, 38, 69, 70, 71, 72, 75, 77,
    78, 79, 86, 176, 193, 207
  Central Committee plenums 24
    1929 Nov 170
    1930 Dec 173
    1931 June 69, 102, 104, 105
    1933 Jan 24, 178
    1934 Nov 29, 48
    1936 Dec 196
    1937 Feb–Mar 9, 37, 58, 60,
      192, 196
    1937 Oct 193
  Joint CC-CCC plenums
    1928 April 169
    1932 Nov 23
    1933 Jan 23–4, 81, 88
  CPSU Central Committee sectors 55
    agriculture 24, 82, 178, 180
    transport 82, 106
  CPSU congresses
    XII 10
    XV 16
    XVI 12, 19, 72, 76, 95
    XVII 14, 27, 30, 46, 47, 48, 65–91,
      132, 182, 188, 199, 200, 201, 204
    XVII 61, 199–208
    XX 60, 197, 199–200
  Politburo 24, 26, 31, 32, 38, 41, 43,
    44, 45, 48, 50, 51, 55, 56, 58, 59,
    61, 69, 71, 73, 74, 78, 83, 93, 97,
    98, 99, 101, 102, 103, 104, 105,
    106, 107, 110, 139, 152, 157,
    158, 171, 173, 174, 175, 178,
    180, 182, 184, 185, 187, 192, 194
  Politburo (members) 14, 15, 20,
    25, 39, 70, 75, 86, 93, 94, 106,
    194, 207
  Politburo-Presidium TsKK 47, 57
  Secretariat 14, 15, 23, 24, 25, 39, 55,
    75, 94, 106
  Orgburo 14, 15, 24, 25, 55, 94, 106
  Orgraspred 14, 15, 94
  ORPO 30, 32, 48, 50, 52, 59, 86, 199
Communist Party of Tadzhikistan 47, 57
Communist Party of Ukraine (CPUk)
  15, 21, 23, 43, 44, 53, 57, 75, 94,
  110, 169, 170, 176, 181, 185, 203, 207

Central Committee 22, 84, 159, 168,
  169, 170, 171, 173, 174, 176, 177,
  179, 180, 182, 183, 185, 186
Politburo 11, 20, 21, 76, 157, 159,
  171, 173, 174, 175, 176, 177,
  178, 179–80, 181, 186, 187
Party Congress
  XII 181–2
  XIII 186
Party Conference
  III 22, 175
Communist Party of Uzbekistan 70,
  79, 193
Constitution of USSR 7
Control Commission (KK) 41, 95, 107
Counter-revolution 154, 155, 156, 180,
  185–6
Counter-revolutionary groups 98, 142,
  159, 177, 180
Crimean ASSR 28, 57, 178

Defence 27, 28, 138
'Dekulakisation' 171
Dnepropetrovsk obkom 31, 44, 45,
  57, 60, 66, 76, 80, 83, 86, 176,
  178, 193, 200, 207
Dnepropetrovsk oblast 43, 55, 154,
  160, 175,
Dneprostroi 12
Donbass coalfield 12, 17, 29, 32, 58,
  77, 79, 149–62, 192, 202, 203
Donetsk 168
Donetsk obkom 32, 66, 76, 77, 193
Donetsk oblast 154, 160, 175
Donnarpit 156

East Siberia krai 28, 47, 73, 97
East Siberia kraikom 40–1, 45, 55,
  66, 73, 81, 86
Emba oilfield 78, 79, 80, 204
'Enemies of the people' 153, 154,
  156–9, 186, 208

Famine 21–4, 42, 53, 83, 100, 104, 153–5,
  157, 168, 174, 175, 178, 180, 183, 192
Far Eastern krai 28, 68, 73, 199, 202–3
Far Eastern kraikom 45, 47, 57, 66, 73,
  83, 86, 193, 194
Federalism 10, 20
Finland 117, 118, 137

Five Year Plan, First 4, 12, 26, 27, 29, 32, 38, 42, 68, 71, 73, 96, 97, 110, 118, 120, 124, 153, 159, 186
Five Year Plan, Second 4, 16–18, 19, 20, 26–7, 28–9, 42, 49, 54, 66, 67, 68, 69, 74, 76, 77, 79, 81, 85, 86, 94, 96, 97, 98, 105, 107, 108, 109, 110, 111, 119, 126, 127, 129, 130, 131, 132, 133, 134, 143, 144, 149, 152, 159, 181, 182, 184, 185, 186, 187, 202
Five Year Plan, Third 104, 128, 200, 201, 202, 203, 204
France 158

Georgia SSR 11, 203, 204, 205
Germany 12, 24, 67, 107, 137, 142, 158, 159, 161, 200
Gidroelektropoekt 125
'Gigantomania' 68, 204
Glavenergo 126, 131
Glavgidroenergo 128
Glavsevles 137
Glavzapbumprom 136
Goelro 16, 18, 97
Gorkoms 14, 48, 192
Gorky krai 15, 28, 47, 59, 71, 79, 200
Gorky kraikom 31, 59, 66, 71, 80, 82, 202, 207
Gosplan Karelia (Karplan) 119, 120, 121, 122, 123, 124, 125, 133
Gosplan RSFSR 122, 123
Gosplan USSR 16, 19, 26, 27, 29, 30, 55, 68, 69, 73, 74, 79, 82, 87, 97, 103, 104, 106, 108, 109, 111, 118, 122, 123, 127, 128, 132, 133, 134, 138, 139, 140, 198, 202, 204, 207
GPU Ukraine 43, 76, 154, 156, 158, 160, 168, 174, 178,
GPU USSR 14, 73, 88, 156, 187
GPU Vinnitsa 180
Great Northern Sea Route 127
Great Terror, 'Ezhovshchina' 56–61, 141–3, 149, 157–61

Housing 80, 102, 205

Industrial combines and works 80, 83, 96, 98
Industrial Party trial 153

Industry
Coal 60, 79, 97, 149–51, 203
Electrical power 97, 100, 205
Oil 75, 77, 202
Textile 96, 97
Timber 117–45
Internal Passport system 26, 136, 137, 161
Irkutsk obkom 199
Irkutsk oblast 110
Ivanovo obkom 39, 48, 51, 66, 71, 86
Ivanovo oblast 28, 47, 71, 99, 192, 200, 205
Izhimbaev oilfield 75, 202

Japan 24, 67, 73, 107, 158

Kalinin 98
Kalinin obkom 194
Kalinin oblast 200, 201
Kalmyk obkom 52
Kaluga oblast 110
Kamenetsk-Podolsk okrug/oblast 175, 199
Kandalaksha GES 120, 123, 126, 129, 133, 138
Karaganda coalfield 68, 79, 204
Karelian ASSR 12, 28, 116–45
Karelian Labour Commune (KTK) 117–18
Karelian obkom 136, 138, 142
Karelles 118, 136, 137, 142
Kazakhstan ASSR 22, 24, 28, 45, 58, 59, 66, 68, 78, 79, 81
Kazakhstan SSR 204, 207
Kazan 54
Kemerovo 196
Khabarovsk krai 199
Khabarovsk kraikom 207
Kharkov gorkom 24, 75, 158, 160, 176
Kharkov oblast 23, 25, 45, 48, 57, 66, 86, 104, 175, 177, 178, 183, 193, 200, 205
Khorezm 79, 82, 86
Kiev 55
Kiev oblast 43, 57, 91, 158, 160, 175, 177, 183, 186, 193, 200
Kirgiziya SSR 57
Kirov krai 47
Kirovograd oblast 199

Kolkhoztsentr 29
Kolkhozy 100, 154, 174, 178
Kommunist 177
Komsomol 122
Kondopoga Paper Mill 119, 120, 131, 136, 140–1, 142
Kraikom 14, 31, 37, 41, 83, 86, 198
Krasnaya Kareliya 142
Krasnodar obkom 210 n19
Krasnodar oblast 54, 192, 199, 200, 202, 205
Krasnoyarsk krai 47
Krasnyi Oktyabr works 202
Kuban 74, 202
Kuibyshev obkom 57, 193, 194
Kuibyshev oblast 192, 201
Kursk Magnetic Anomaly (KMA) 68, 73, 79, 202
Kursk obkom 31, 57
Kursk oblast 47, 192, 201
Kuzbass coalfield 68, 73, 79, 202
Kuznestk metallurgical combine 68, 202

Leningrad obkom 27–8, 129, 130, 135, 136
Leningrad oblast 13, 14, 15, 17, 18, 19, 27–8, 40, 66, 70, 82, 86, 87, 92, 103, 107, 110, 118, 122, 126, 127–8, 129, 158, 192, 200, 201, 205, 207, 208
Leningrad Soviet 80, 205
lespromkhoz(y) 124, 136, 137, 142
Lipetsk 72
Local leaders
  cliques 42, 58, 94, 95, 142, 177, 192, 195
  cults 59, 108, 141, 176–7, 192, 195
Location policy 16–18, 26–8, 67–9
  charges of 'colonialism' 84, 85, 135
Lower Volga krai 16, 23, 24, 28, 30, 31, 47, 66, 170
Lower Volga kraikom 43–4, 71
Lugansk 171

Magnitogorsk 68, 72
Makeevka 156
Managers/directors (industry) 80, 108, 135–6, 153, 156, 207
Mariinskii lock system 70, 86, 119
Molotov Motor Works 71, 202

Moscow 16, 17, 19, 27, 66, 69–70, 92–112, 200, 201, 205, 206, 207, 208
Moscow gorkom 13, 14, 40, 69, 94, 103, 106, 107, 110
Moscow obkom 15, 94, 100, 107, 110
Moscow party conference 100, 107–8
Moscow Metro (Metrostroi) 68, 102, 104–5
Moscow Soviet 69, 93, 100, 102, 103, 104, 105, 106, 205
Moscow-Donbass railway 68, 97–8
Moscow-Volga canal (Moskanalstroi) 68, 102, 104, 105–7, 108
MTS 24, 29, 45–6, 83, 100, 101, 140, 178–9, 185, 187, 203
Murmansk 70, 124, 129, 144
Murmansk oblast 133

NEP 1, 9, 13, 119, 168
NKFin 20, 29, 139, 181, 193
NKInDel Uk 84
NKLegProm 74, 193
NKLes 131, 133, 136, 137, 139, 142, 143, 194
NKOboron 131
NKOboronProm 203
NKPishProm 101, 181, 203
NKPros Bel. 84
NKPros RSFSR 47
NKPros Uk 84
NKPS 32, 73, 75, 76, 77, 82, 97, 98, 110, 111, 125
NKRKI *see* Central Control Commission-NKRKI
NKSovkhoz 27–30, 32, 81, 82, 182, 193, 201, 205
NKSvyaz 74
NKTorg 29
NKTyazhProm 27, 28, 29, 32, 53, 55, 72–80, 82, 87, 94, 96, 106, 111, 125, 126, 128, 131, 138, 201, 206
NKVD Donbass 159, 160
NKVD Karelia 135, 136, 137, 141, 142
NKVD Leningrad (UNKVD) 135, 136
NKVD Uk 185
NKVD USSR 30, 49, 106, 119, 124, 125, 127, 128, 136, 138, 141, 142, 187, 191, 192, 193, 194, 195, 196, 197, 199, 206
  Gulag 107, 126, 127, 131, 144, 145, 160

NKVD Vinnitsa 186
NKVMDel 96
NKVodTrans 74, 76, 77, 82, 106
NKYust USSR 30
NKZem Belorussia 84
NKZem Karelia 140
NKZem UkSSR 176, 180, 181
NKZem USSR 20, 21, 27–30, 32, 48,
   49, 71, 76, 77, 81, 82, 84, 178,
   181–3, 193, 201–5
National minorities – deportation 159,
   183
Nationalism 160, 182
Nationalities policy 10, 11–12, 25,
   83–5, 87, 135, 111, 117, 143
Nezamozhiki 168
Nikolaev oblast 199
North Caucasus krai 16, 17, 23, 24,
   28, 31, 44, 47, 66, 74, 154, 179
North Caucasus kraikom 15, 16, 22,
   23, 60, 66, 74, 86
Northern krai 28, 194
Northern kraikom 57, 66, 70, 86
Novocherkassk 74
Novosibirsk obkom 207
Novosibirsk oblast 50, 199, 201, 202, 207
Novotula combine 68, 96, 109

Obkom 14, 24, 31, 37, 41, 46, 61, 85,
   192, 207
Oblast 175, 198, 199
Obsko-Irtush oblast 47, 72
Odessa 171, 174, 176
Odessa obkom 45, 51, 66, 178
Odessa oblast 175
OGPU North Caucasus 74
OGPU UkSSR 22, 23, 43
OGPU USSR 43, 83, 98, 99, 106, 123,
   124, 125, 127, 137
OGPU Vinnitsa 177
Omsk oblast 47
Order of Lenin 52, 101, 108, 184
Ordzhonikidze obkom 210 n19
Orenburg oblast 47, 192
Orlov oblast 199
Orsk 80

Palace of Soviets 103–4
Party purge 23, 25, 30, 73, 107, 154,
   160, 178, 179, 200

Peasantry
   deportation/resettlement 23, 74, 154,
      174, 175, 179, 180, 183
   resistance 42, 75, 168, 171, 172, 173
Penza oblast 199
People's Commissariat of Aviation
   Industry 207
People's Commissariat of Local
   Industry 205
People's Commissariat of Machine
   Building 205
People's Commissariat of Non-Ferrous
   Metals 204
Perm oblast 199
'Petluraists' 23, 177, 179
Petrozavodsk 130, 137, 144
politotdel(y) 24, 29, 32, 45–6, 48, 49,
   83, 100, 178–9, 182–3, 187
Poltava oblast 199
Pravda 50, 51, 59, 186
Primorskii krai 199
Primorskii kraikom 207
Procuracy USSR 21, 30, 83, 193

Raikom 22, 24, 43, 48, 83, 86, 172, 173,
   174, 175, 178, 179, 185, 192
Raions 107, 175, 204
Red Army 9, 73, 74, 88, 107, 138, 167,
   168, 178, 203
Regional representatives (tolkachi) 53,
   56, 123, 130, 132, 133
Romania 167, 180
Rostov on Don 17, 23, 74
Rostov oblast 192, 200, 202, 205, 207
RSFSR 20, 27, 28, 66, 69, 86, 122, 130,
   198, 199, 201, 207
Ryazan oblast 110, 199

Saratov krai 23, 47, 192, 202
Saratov kraikom 31, 49–50, 193
Scandinavia 118
Segezha combine 127–8, 144
Sel'khozsnab 71
Shakhty trial 13, 17, 58, 74, 151–3, 206
Siberian kraikom 15
Smolensk oblast 192, 199
Smolensk 'scandal' 13
Sotsialisticheskii Donbass 156
Sovkhozy 24, 29, 45–6, 100, 178–9
Sovnarkom Belorussia 48, 75, 84

Sovnarkom Karelia   119, 121, 124, 125, 126, 128, 130, 135
Sovnarkom Kirghiziya   84
Sovnarkom RSFSR   15, 19, 39, 56, 69, 79, 93, 123, 193
Sovnarkom Tadzhikistan   85
Sovnarkom Transcaucasus   77, 84
Sovnarkom UkSSR   20, 21, 23, 43, 75, 76, 177, 185, 193, 194, 203
Sovnarkom USSR   26, 29, 46, 49, 53, 54, 55, 56, 78, 85, 92, 99, 100, 103, 106, 121, 124, 128, 139, 184
Sovnarkom Uzbekistan   79
Sovnarkom-CC decrees   103, 104, 106, 130, 177, 180, 204
Specialists   151–4, 156
Stalin Motor Works (ZIS)   68, 96, 108
Stalingrad krai   47, 57, 202
Stalingrad kraikom   31, 71, 81, 193, 194, 200
Stalingrad tractor works   202
Stalino   150, 156, 161
Stalinsk obkom   110, 207
Stalinsk oblast   200, 203
Stakhanovite movement   32, 33, 157, 184, 185, 201
STO   26, 29, 106, 120
Sumskaya oblast   199
Sunastroi dam project   131, 136, 139, 140, 141, 142
Supreme Soviet USSR   111
   Economic Council   204
Sverdlovsk obkom   31, 59, 66, 86, 197, 200, 207
Sverdlovsk oblast   192, 205
Svir GES   70, 119, 126, 129

Tadzhikistan SSR   17
Taganrog   55
Tambov oblast   199
Tashkent   79
Tatar ASSR   28, 54, 74, 192, 194
Taxation   20
Terror (*Terakty*)   98, 175, 177
Tiblisi   203
Traktortsentr   29, 84
Transbaikal   73, 81
Transcaucasian Federation   17, 25, 27, 48, 77, 82, 84, 86, 203–4
   Kraikom   40, 45, 54

Trans-Volga region   28, 67, 81
Tsentrosoyuz   21, 109, 203
TsIK Karelia   120
TsIK Kirghiziya   85
TsIK UkSSR   76
TsIK USSR   46, 105
TsSU   26
TsUNKhU   26
Tula oblast   110, 199, 201
Turkestan   11
Turkmenistan SSR   17
Turksib line   82
Tver oblast   110
Tyumazin oilfield   202

Ukraine SSR (UkSSR)   11, 12, 13, 14, 16–25, 27, 28, 29, 31, 39, 43, 44, 66, 69, 75–7, 81, 109, 192, 199, 200, 203
'Ukrainisation'   11–12, 177
UNKhU   125
Urals krai   13, 16, 19, 22, 27–8, 47, 58, 68, 69, 72, 109
Urals kraikom   15, 19, 39, 45, 66, 72
Urals-Kuznetsk combine (UKK)   19, 28, 68, 69, 72, 73, 127
USLON   124
USSR   9, 10, 12, 27, 28, 29
Uzbekistan SSR   17, 85, 199, 204, 207

Vesenkha USSR   19, 20, 29, 32, 79
Vinnitsa obkom   44, 176, 177, 179, 180, 182, 184, 186
Vinnitsa oblast   66, 167–90
Volga-Don canal   86, 202
Volga hydro complex   201
Vologda oblast   199
Voronezh obkom   31, 48, 193, 194, 200, 207
Voronezh oblast   47, 192, 202
Voroshilovgrad oblast   199, 200, 203
VTsIK   117, 122, 125
VTsSPS   39
VUKTsIK   169

War Communism   169
West Siberia krai   19, 22, 27–8, 47, 72, 73, 80, 81, 82, 85
West Siberia kraikom   16, 39, 40, 47, 50–1, 53, 66, 73, 86, 193, 194

Western obkom   53, 59, 66, 71
Western oblast   28, 79

Yakutia ASSR   28
Yaroslavlskii oblast   47, 58, 192, 200, 201, 202

Zaporozhe oblast   199
Zhelles   124, 125
Zhitomir oblast   199
Zinoviev-Kamenev trial   57, 191, 196
ZSFSR *see* Transcaucasus   28